NATIONAL
PARKS *of*
AMERICA

Contents

NORTH DAKOTA
BISMARCK

SOUTH DAKOTA
PIERRE

MINNESOTA

WISCONSIN
ST. PAUL
MADISON

NEBRASKA
LINCOLN

IOWA
DES MOINES

KANSAS
TOPEKA

MISSOURI
JEFFERSON CITY

OKLAHOMA
OKLAHOMA CITY

ARKANSAS
LITTLE ROCK

TEXAS
AUSTIN

MISSISSIPPI
JACKSON

LOUISIANA
BATON ROUGE
New Orleans

Gulf of
Mexico

AGO PAGO
AMERICAN
SAMOA
cific Ocean

CANADA

Lake
Superior

MICHIGAN
LANSING

Lake
Michigan

Lake
Huron

Lake
Ontario

Lake Erie

ILLINOIS
SPRINGFIELD

INDIANA
INDIANAPOLIS

OHIO
COLUMBUS

Ohio River

KENTUCKY
FRANKFORT

TENNESSEE
NASHVILLE

Tennessee River

ALABAMA
MONTGOMERY

GEORGIA
ATLANTA

Mississippi River

Missouri River

MADISON

PENNSYLVANIA
HARRISBURG

NEW YORK

VERMONT
NEW HAMPSHIRE
MAINE

MASSACHUSETTS
CONNECTICUT
RHODE ISLAND

NEW JERSEY
New York

Atlantic
Ocean

WEST
VIRGINIA
CHARLESTON

MARYLAND
WASHINGTON, DC

VIRGINIA
RICHMOND

NORTH
CAROLINA
RALEIGH

SOUTH
CAROLINA
COLUMBIA

FLORIDA
Orlando

TALLAHASSEE

Miami

St Thomas
CHARLOTTE
AMALIE

St John

US VIRGIN
ISLANDS

Caribbean
Sea

Christiansted
St Croix

1	Acadia
2	American Samoa
3	Arches
4	Badlands
5	Big Bend
6	Biscayne
7	Black Canyon of the Gunnison
8	Bryce Canyon
9	Canyonlands
10	Capitol Reef
11	Carlsbad Caverns
12	Channel Islands
13	Congaree
14	Crater Lake
15	Cuyahoga Valley
16	Death Valley
17	Denali
18	Dry Tortugas
19	Everglades
20	Gates of the Arctic
21	Gateway Arch
22	Glacier
23	Glacier Bay
24	Grand Canyon
25	Grand Teton
26	Great Basin
27	Great Sand Dunes
28	Great Smoky Mountains
29	Guadalupe Mountains
30	Haleakalā
31	Hawaii Volcanoes
32	Hot Springs
33	Indiana Dunes
34	Isle Royale
35	Joshua Tree
36	Katmai
37	Kenai Fjords
38	Kings Canyon
39	Kobuk Valley
40	Lake Clark
41	Lassen Volcanic
42	Mammoth Cave
43	Mesa Verde
44	Mount Rainier
45	North Cascades
46	Olympic
47	Petrified Forest
48	Pinnacles
49	Redwood
50	Rocky Mountain
51	Saguaro
52	Sequoia
53	Shenandoah
54	Theodore Roosevelt
55	Virgin Islands
56	Voyageurs
57	White Sands
58	Wind Cave
59	Wrangell–St. Elias
60	Yellowstone
61	Yosemite
62	Zion

Introduction

I got lucky the first time that I visited an American national park. I was in Utah and with a few days free before my flight out of the state, and a pair of hiking boots in my luggage, I headed for the closest national park, not knowing what I'd find. That park was Bryce Canyon (see p46). It was October and there had already been some flurries of snow. When I arrived at a viewpoint overlooking a vast bowl – that I later discovered was called 'Silent City' – snow remained in the sun's shadow, highlighting every ridge and feature. But glowing red, yellow and orange under the blue sky were row upon row of Bryce Canyon's extraordinary hoodoos, narrow spires of rock formed as fins created by water erode into columns. It was an epiphany.

America's national parks are full of such marvels: the world's largest trees in Sequoia; its most spectacular geothermal site in Yellowstone; the grandest canyon. It's around these world-famous places that the story of the National Park Service is woven. President Woodrow Wilson created the National Park Service (NPS) on August 25, 1916, but the drive to protect some of America's most remarkable wild spaces, to be 'used and preserved for the benefit of mankind', began in the 1860s.

Perhaps the movement's most eloquent advocate was Scottish-born writer John Muir. He had worked in the Yosemite Valley in the 1860s and later, in 1903, camped there under the stars with President Theodore Roosevelt, who created five national parks during his administration. 'Thousands of tired, nerve-shaken, over-civilized people,' Muir wrote in *Our National Parks*, 'are beginning to find out that going to the mountains is going home; that wildness is a necessity...'

This book is intended to be a practical introduction to each of America's 62 national parks, distilled by Lonely Planet's expert authors. We highlight the best activities and trails, explain how to get there and where to stay, show you the wildlife to watch out for, and suggest ideal itineraries. Whether you're lucky enough to have a national park on your doorstep or need to travel further, we hope that the following pages inspire you to explore what Stephen Mather, the first director of the NPS, described as America's 'national properties.'

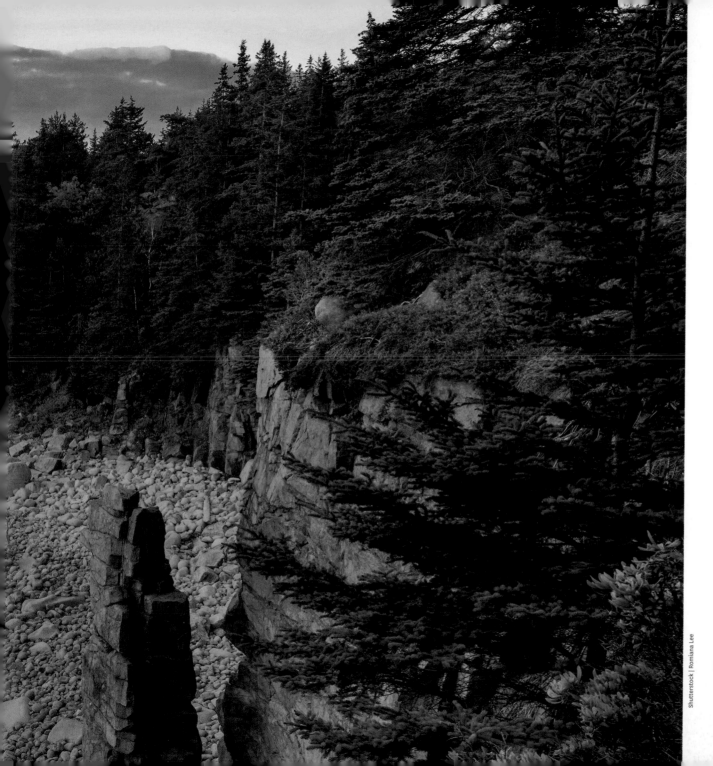

01

ME

Acadia National Park

See New England at its most glorious from the seaside cliffs of Acadia, at the easternmost tip of the United States.

You're sitting on a smooth granite outcropping, the dark ocean pounding some 1530ft (466m) below. Finally, you see it: a blood-red finger of sunlight piercing the horizon. Slowly, the dark clouds go rosy pink, the ocean becoming an ever-lightening purple. This is sunrise on Cadillac Mountain in Acadia National Park, the first place the sun shows its face in the United States.

Much like New England itself, Acadia pings between utterly civilized and utterly wild. There's high tea on the lawn and there's harsh, crashing gray surf along rocky beaches. There are horse-drawn carriage rides and hikes through leg-slashing thorn bushes. There's lobster ravioli in thyme butter at the elegant bistros of Bar Harbor and there's roasting hot dogs over an open fire at the park's primitive campgrounds.

Painters and other artists 'discovered' the Acadia area in the mid-1800s, spending summers boarding with local fishermen and painting the stunning scenery. These 'rusticators' grew in number so quickly there were soon several dozen hotels catering to their needs. By the 1890s, Gilded Era captains of industry were arriving to summer in enormous 'cottages' on the island. But the Great Depression, WWII and, finally, a huge wildfire in 1947 destroyed this lavish lifestyle, along with most of the cottages.

In the early 1900s, George Dorr, heir to a New England textile fortune, began working to preserve the area from the onslaught of tourism and industry. The land that he and others donated to the federal government became Lafayette National Park in 1919, the first national park east of the Mississippi; its

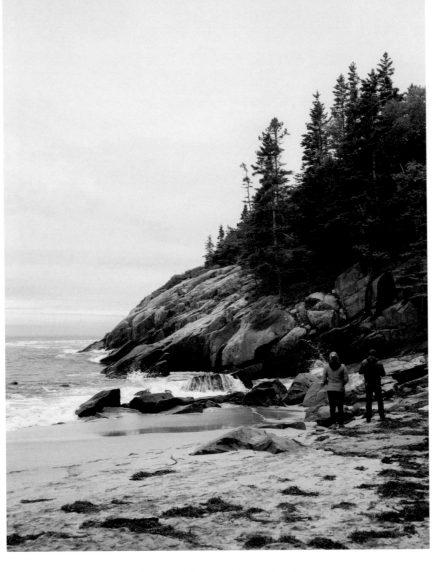

name was changed to Acadia in 1929. Today, Acadia and the nearby town of Bar Harbor still attract moneyed Eastern elites who sail, hold charity balls and dine in the area's many fine restaurants. But like all national parks, Acadia is a democratic place, welcoming everyone.

⬆ There are lots of beaches to explore in Acadia National Park.
➡ Try cross-country skiing in winter. Previous page: dawn lights the Acadia coast.

Rush Jagoe; Getty Images | Patryce Bak

Toolbox

When to go
The park gets the usual July/August rush, but it's just as pretty (if a bit colder) in May, June and September. In October, when the leaves burst into flaming reds and golds, it's heavenly.

Getting there
Acadia is on Maine's coast, near the town of Bar Harbor. Most of the park is on Mt Desert Island. The nearest airport is in Bangor, about an hour's drive away; week-long passes are $30.

Events
In June and July, the Bar Harbor Music Festival draws classical and jazz musicians. September sees the Acadia Night Sky Festival celebrate all things celestial.

Accessibility
Blackwoods and Seawall Campground offer accessible sites. Echo Lake has accessible changing rooms and paths. The Wild Gardens of Acadia's paths and the Jesup Path are wheelchair accessible.

Park in numbers
74 Area covered (sq miles)
1530 Highest point: Cadillac Mountain (ft)
40 Miles of shoreline

→ Hold onto the handrails if you hike the steep and exposed Precipice Trail.

Stay here...

Blackwoods Campground
This massive NPS campground has 306 tent sites set in shady forest. Roll out of your tent and onto the trail to Cadillac Mountain and other popular hikes. In summer, facilities such as a store and showers are available; in winter it's primitive all the way. The shuttle stops outside.

Bar Harbor Campground
This ultra-popular waterfront campground has been family run for half a century. It's open from Memorial Day to Columbus Day, with tent and RV sites, hot showers, a heated pool, and a playground, all a five-minute drive from the park. No advance reservations, no credit cards.

Saltair Inn
Built in 1887 as a summer 'cottage' for a New York businessman and his wife, this Victorian mansion is now a charming B&B. Guests watch the light play over Frenchman Bay from the deck. Owners earn kudos for their advice about local sights and activities.

Do this!

Mountain summiting
The gem in Acadia's crown, Cadillac Mountain rises 1530ft (466m) above the crashing surf. The highest point on the North Atlantic seaboard, it's the first place to see the sun rise in America for much of the year. You can hike Cadillac but the easiest way to get here is to drive the 3.5-mile (5.6km) road to the top. Come at dawn bundled in your wooliest sweater to watch light break over Frenchman Bay.

Cycling
Acadia has some 45 miles (72km) of carriage roads, built by philanthropist John D Rockefeller Jr, who wanted to be able to get into the park without using a car. The hand-hewn stone roads and bridges are made of locally quarried granite – and are extremely photogenic and perfect for cycling.

Having high tea
In summer everyone flocks to the rolling green lawns of Jordan Pond House to sit in wooden chairs, sip tea and munch warm popovers with jam. It's one of the park's most charming traditions, dating back to the 1890s. After filling your belly, head down the hill to stroll around the pond itself. This is a particularly family-friendly walk, with wood and gravel paths circling the clear water.

What to spot...

Encompassing roiling ocean, rocky beaches, dense forests, boggy marshes and granite peaks, Acadia has a dramatic diversity of flora and fauna. While you won't see many large mammals here, there's a wealth of amphibians, reptiles, birds and smaller mammals. Bar Harbor is a jumping-off point for whale-watching tours, while colorful starfish, crustaceans and sponges can be found on Acadia's shoreline. Much of the park is blanketed in spruce-fir forest; unique scrub oak and pitch pine woodlands can be found as well.

SPOTTED SALAMANDER
These inky black amphibians with mustard-yellow spots typically burrow under moist leaves on the forest floor. In early spring, they head to ponds to breed.

PEREGRINE FALCON Acadia has been integral in boosting the population of these magnificent, light-brown birds of prey, who nest in the park in spring.

RACCOON Recognizable by their distinctive black 'eye masks,' these medium-sized mammals are considered pests in most of the US for their garbage-eating habits. (Store your trash properly when camping.)

Getty Images | Chris Bennett

Hike this...

01 Cadillac Mountain South Ridge Trail
The park's longest hike, this 7.4-mile (11.9km) round-trip climb gives killer views over the crashing gray Atlantic on the way to the top of the park's highest peak.

02 Ocean Path
Explore tide pools along this 4-mile (6.4km) round-trip walk, which runs from Sand Beach to Otter Cliffs, passing the roaring Thunder Hole along the way.

03 Precipice Trail
Ascend ladders and cling to metal rungs as you traverse a sheer granite slope high above Frenchman Bay. This 3.2-mile (5.1km) loop is not for kids or those with fear of heights.

⬆ Winter brings storms to the coast and snow and ice to inland areas for activities such as ice-climbing.

Itineraries

Be the first person in America to watch the sun rise, hike along pink granite cliffs or eat buttery lobster by the Atlantic. Whale spotting? That too.

➡ Fishing is a popular pastime along the Maine coast.

01

A day

Get the best of the park in the least amount of time by hitting the major sights on Park Loop Rd, a 27-mile (43.5km) scenic drive around the east side of the park. The roads starts at the Hulls Cove Visitor Center (stop for a map), then ascends Paradise Hill for dramatic views over Frenchman Bay, with Bar Harbor glimmering in the distance. Continue on to Sand Beach, the island's only proper sandy beach. (We must warn you, however, that the gray ocean water rarely rises above 55°F (13°C) – even in mid-summer – so unless you're a polar bear you'll probably just want to dip your toes.) A mile (1.6km) south is one of Acadia's icons, Thunder Hole. When large swells hit this small, underground cave in just the right way, it produces a terrifying roar. Take in the 100ft-high (30.5m) Otter Cliffs before heading for tea and popovers at Jordan Pond House (summer only). Cap off the day with a drive up Cadillac Mountain to watch the late afternoon sun play on the waters more than 1500ft (457m) below.

02

Two days

On your first day, hit Park Loop Rd. At Sand Beach, walk the 4-mile (6.4km) round-trip Ocean Path to Otter Cliffs, taking time to explore the short spur trails leading along the pink granite cliffs to tide pools full of quirky sea creatures. If the tide's coming in the right way (ask at the visitor center), stop at Thunder Hole. Otherwise continue on to Jordan Pond House for lunch. Though famous for its afternoon tea, it also serves New England–inflected mains, such as lobster quiche and seafood chowder. Digest lunch with a stroll around Jordan Pond, whose picture-pretty waters seem like they could be home to fairies or other mystical creatures. Head back to Bar Harbor for an evening of exploring the town's boutiques and cafes. The next morning, get up in the pre-dawn darkness and drive up Cadillac Mountain to be among the first people in America to see the sun rise. Then head to the park's west side to spend the day paddling the waters of Long Pond, with dozens of hidden coves perfect for exploring.

03

Five days

On day one, do Park Loop Rd as per the one-day itinerary, bringing a picnic lunch to eat at Sand Beach. On day two, hike the Cadillac Mountain South Ridge Trail, which traverses rocky outcrops and cool maritime forest to finish with jaw-dropping views over the gray Atlantic. On clear days you can imagine seeing straight to Ireland. Reward yourself with a red lobster drenched in butter at the Trenton Bridge Lobster Pound on the causeway. On day three, explore the park's 45 miles (72km) of stone carriage roads by bike. The 8.3-mile (13.4km) Jordan Pond–Bubble Pond loop is popular for its shady forest and pond views; end at stately Jordan Pond House for afternoon tea and popovers. On day four, drive an hour to the Schoodic Peninsula, Acadia's wilder side. The six-mile (10km) park loop takes you past rock formations, lighthouse views and coastal forests. Reserve in advance to camp at the NPS site here. Spend your last day on a guided sea kayak tour from Bar Harbor: you may spot humpback, finback or minke whales.

02

AS

American Samoa National Park

America's only south-of-the-equator national park occupies an island cluster offering beautiful beaches, remote reefs, magical mountains and extraordinary cultural encounters.

S cattered across three volcanic islands and two coral atolls in the deep blue immensity of the Pacific Ocean, 2600 miles (4184km) southwest of Hawaii, American Samoa hosts the USA's southernmost national park. It features unique wildlife, towering topography and reef-fringed beaches. Immerse yourself in the 3000-year-old traditions of Polynesia's oldest surviving culture, discover 950 species of fish while exploring 450 aquatic acres (1.8 sq km) of coral reef and trek through cloud forests to volcanic peaks.

Samoan history isn't recorded in written form – instead, beliefs, traditions and creation myths are kept alive through storytelling. The account of how a US national park came to be created in this far-flung land is an intriguing addition to the canon. It began with a 19th-century squabble between the US and Germany. Both nations used Samoa as a whaling base; the deepwater harbor of Pago Pago was perfect for refuelling their steam-driven ships. In 1889, an altercation threatened to flare into all-out warfare, until nature intervened and a typhoon sank all six battleships. Subsequently, the two powers agreed to split the islands between them.

A century later, US Congress authorized the creation of the country's 50th national park on the islands. Samoa means 'sacred earth,' and it wasn't until 1993 that the Samoan chiefs, guardians of the islands for three millennia, agreed to sign a 50-year lease allowing the National Park Service (NPS) to manage an area of rainforest, coast and coral reef on the three islands of Tutuila, Ofu, and Ta'ū. In 2002, the park was expanded to include Olosega, connected to Ofu by a bridge. Samoans retain a role as custodians, with villages offering visitor facilities in a traditional setting, adding a cultural layer to an unique experience.

Toolbox

When to go
Located 14° south of the equator, the park has a tropical climate and is warm and wet year-round. June to September, the dry season, is the most comfortable time to go.

Getting there
Fly to the main island of Tutuila from Honolulu, Hawaii (6 hours). Take a Samoa Airways flight from Tutuila to Ta'ū (4 times per week) or Ofu (two times a week).

Events
August and September are whale-watching months. October is carnival season. The last week of the month brings the Moso'oi Festival, which features boat racing

Accessibility
The park is rugged and trails unpaved. One overlook, at Lower Sauma Ridge, is wheelchair-accessible, with assistance.

Park in numbers

21.1 Area in sq miles (about one third is underwater)
3170 Height in ft of Mt Lata (Ta'ū Island)
3000 Years that the Samoan culture has existed on the islands

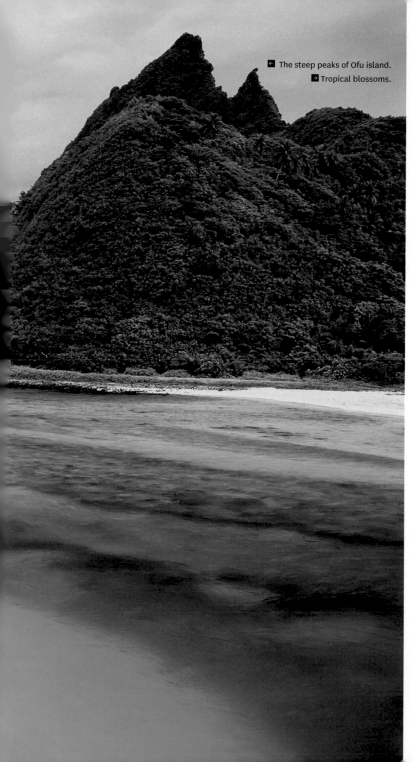

◄ The steep peaks of Ofu island.
► Tropical blossoms.

Stay here...

🏠 Tisa's Barefoot Bar
Camping isn't permitted anywhere in the park, but accommodations are available on all of the islands except Olosega. There are standard hotels in central Pago Pago, but a more memorable option is to stay in a beach-facing *fale* (Samoan house), such as those available at Tisa's Barefoot Bar on Tutuila.

🏠 Village homestay
Make the most of your visit and stay with a local family to learn about Samoan culture and homelife. The park facilitates homestays in several villages, including Fagasa and Vatia on Tutuila and Fitiuta on Ta'ū. Check with the park office in Pago Pago or use the email form on the NPS website.

🏠 Vaoto Lodge
Family-owned and -run lodges, such as Vaoto Lodge on Ofu Island, also offer accommodations with a distinct Polynesian flavor; the communal meals are often cooked around the barbecue pit and served 'family style' around a large table, while its position, a short stroll from a beautiful beach, can't be beat.

Do this!

🤿 Snorkeling
About a third of this 21.1 sq mile park is covered by coral reef and ocean, home to thousands of fish and 250 kinds of coral – the snorkeling and diving are world-class. Ultra-remote Ofu Beach is particularly special. Bring your own good-quality mask and snorkel. For cultural reasons, avoid revealing swimwear.

🏈 Connecting with locals
There are many opportunities for meeting the friendly locals, from taking public buses to watching village dances and sports. Rugby is very popular, but Samoa's favorite game is *kirikiti*, a local version of cricket. Look out for longboat racing too. Ask permission before taking photos or accessing local lands. Observe quiet on Sundays and during evening village prayers.

🪧 Guided touring
Tours are available, including around the marine sanctuary, to millennia-old archaeological sites or through the park's forests, where a local expert explains how native plants were used in traditional medicines.

Hike this...

01 Mt Alava Trail
Trek the 7-mile (11.3km) round-trip through plantations and tropical rainforests to the top of Tutuila. Enjoy stunning vistas across the island, looking out for bats and birds en route.

02 Si'u Point Trail
Walk through the coastal forest of Ta'ū, past the sacred site of Saua (considered the birthplace of the Polynesian people) to the southeastern tip of the island; it's a 5.7 mile (9.2km) round-trip.

03 Tuafanua Trail
Ascend this 2.2-mile (3.5 km) track from Vatia Village, gripping ropes where it gets steep. Your reward is a secluded rocky beach (dangerous currents: don't swim). Closed Sunday.

What to spot...

Thanks to their lonely location, these remote islands are cloaked in endemic vegetation. Native mammals are scarce, and most birdlife is migratory. Tree life, particularly on Tutuila and Ta'ū, is rich, with all five distinct rainforest communities present – lowland, montane, coast, ridge, and cloud (the only place on US territory where this happens). Sea life here is exceptionally diverse, with hundreds of species of fish, plus whales and turtles.

SAMOA FLYING FOX These bats, American Samoa's only native mammals, play a crucial role in pollinating the islands' plants. They're featured on Samoa's 2020 'America the Beautiful' quarter coin.

ORNATE BUTTERFLYFISH An intricately colored but fragile species of tropical fish, which occurs only in coral-rich areas – commonly encountered in lagoons and on reefs around American Samoa.

ANTLER CORAL This stony coral, part of the park's sub-aquatic decor, owes its colors to millions of single-celled marine plants, called zooxanthellae, that live embedded in its flesh.

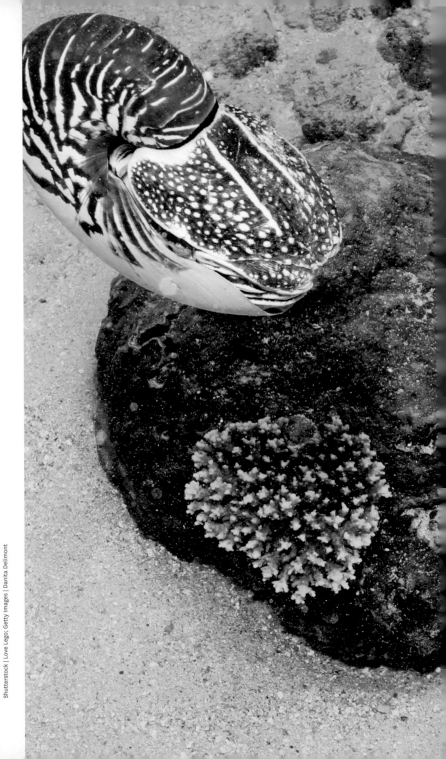

Itineraries

Laze under coconut palm trees, snorkel in a coral paradise or hike some of the highest sea cliffs in the world, your only dilemma is: which island?

 A nautilus propels itself through the National Marine Sanctuary of American Samoa.
→ Ta'ū Island's harbor.

01

A long weekend

Few come all this way for a quick jaunt, but if your time is limited plunge right into the Tutuila parkland around Pago Pago. Take in the coastline from the rocky beach at the end of the super-short Pola Island Trail; check out the ancient earthworks at Lower Sauma Ridge, keeping your eyes open for sea birds; wind your way between ancient volcano craters on the shoreline; and gawk at the WWII-era gun emplacements that once protected the territory from Japanese attacks.

If you can only do one big hike, make it the climb up Mt Alava for the panoramic views – if you're feeling wild, try the mountain's 'adventure trail,' which involves stairs so steep you need to hold a rope. Afterwards, enjoy some R&R in Pago Pago, American Samoa's biggest settlement, surrounding a legendary deepwater harbor that once brought in whalers and merchants from all corners of the globe. Gorge on coconut and mango, nibble breadfruit fries, or find a *fiafia* (suckling pig feast).

02

Five days

Leave the main island behind aboard the twin-prop light aircraft bound for Ta'ū, 70 miles (113km) west of Tutuila, before touching down in the village of Fitiuta, arrival point for American Samoa's Manu'a island group – Ofu, Olosega and Ta'ū. While the pace of life here is somnambulant, the scenery is anything but, with cloud-piercing peaks forming a serrated skyline and some of the highest sea cliffs in the world erupting right out of the ocean.

Ta'ū is home to American Samoa's highest peak, the 3170ft (966m) Lata Mountain, as well as the culturally significant site of Saua, popularly believed to be the birthplace of the Polynesian people. From the airport, you can find yourself in the national park within 30 minutes' walk, but there's no rush. With accommodations available on the island you can split your time between bumming on the beautiful beaches with a book and exploring the cloud forests skirting the volcanic cones that form the roof of the island.

03

A week or more

Going the extra distance to the remote island of Ofu is an experience reserved for true explorers. To reach the sensational shores of this little paradisiacal Pacific Ocean isle, take a small plane from Pago Pago or hire a local fishing boat from Ta'ū.

This isn't a place for clockwatchers or those on a tight schedule – time is an abstract concept in American Samoa at the best of times. And once you do arrive, worries about how you might get back will likely evaporate, since you won't want to leave.

Ofu is all about the ocean.

Here, coconut palm–framed beaches lead snorkelers out into a warm aquatic universe, where thousands of fish scoot around cathedrals of coral in a kaleidoscope of color and activity.

You'll spend nights in a seaside *fale*, being lulled to sleep by the lapping of the water on the sand. And when you've had enough of idyllic indolence, there is plenty of walking to do, along ridgelines up in the hills and even across a bridge to the rainforest-cloaked neighboring island of Olosega.

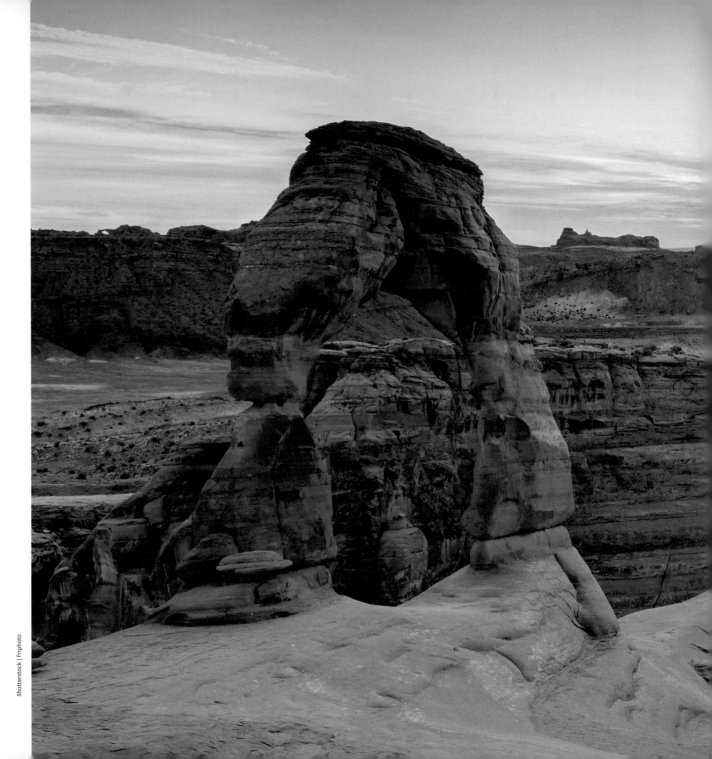

03

UT

Arches
National
Park

This labyrinth of sandstone arches, rock mazes and sun-bleached desert provides an enchanting and exhilarating entrance into Utah's wide-open spaces.

Red rock formations rise from the desert floor in strange clusters, holding your gaze as their colors and shapes transform on your approach. But it's the up-close views of the sandstone monoliths that will surprise you most, as you realize just how fragile it all is. Erosion is a process that continues before your eyes. Balanced Rock teeters on its stem. And Landscape Arch? This golden span looks hardly more solid than a whisper. There are now more than 2000 arches in this high-desert park.

About 65 million years ago, dry seabeds covered the sandstone here. Geological forces squeezed the rock into folds, which eventually fractured. After a massive uplift punched the region skyward, the sandstone expanded and cracked all over again. Erosion revealed the sandstone to the elements, and water sculpted the fantastical shapes travelers see today. Rock formations in the park highlight the stages of this geologic progression. The Fiery Furnace and its fins emerged when ice fractured immense blocks of sandstone; arches formed when rocks broke away from the fins. Waterways carved the lofty bridges. And the hoodoos? Eroding fins left these skinny pinnacles in their wake. An 18-mile (29km) road rolls straight through the park, providing easy access to geological highlights and adventures both big and small in this wonderland of rocks.

But 10,000 years ago hunter-gatherers roamed the region. Ancestral Puebloans followed, living in villages and cultivating crops across the Four Corners region, where Arizona, New Mexico, Colorado, and Utah collide. Ute and Paiute tribes arrived next, followed by European explorers, trappers and Mormon settlers. The most famous inhabitant was perhaps author Edward Abbey, a park ranger at Arches National Monument in the

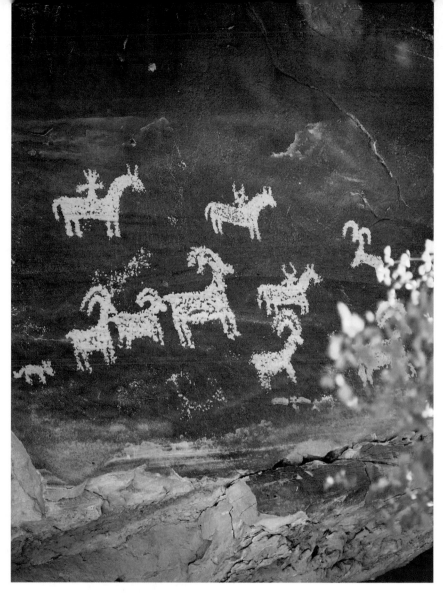

1950s. His classic book *Desert Solitaire: A Season in the Wilderness* criticized industrial tourism while encouraging conservation. He urged visitors to ditch their cars and explore the sandstone wilderness with intensity – an intensity that should cause you, he said, to bleed (a few blisters should suffice).

◀ Double Arch at sunset.
▲ Petroglyphs drawn by Ute tribespeople on the sandstone.
Previous page: Delicate Arch at sunrise.

Shutterstock | Checubus; Wirestock Images

Toolbox

When to go
The park is most inviting in April and May and from mid-September through October. Summer temperatures are typically in the 90s F (30s C), but regularly top 100°F (38°C). Traffic is thick March through October, with crowds on weekends and holidays.

Getting there
Arches is located in southeastern Utah. The park entrance is 27 miles (43.5km) south of I-70. Salt Lake City, Utah, is 236 miles (380km) northwest; Grand Junction, Colorado, is 110 miles (177km) northeast. Moab is a popular base.

Events
The open-air Moab Music Festival is in September.

Accessibility
The Devil's Garden Campground has accessible campsites. Ranger-led talks and hands-on exhibits at the visitor center provide overviews for people with limited seeing or hearing.

Park in numbers
120 Area in sq miles
8–10 Annual rainfall (in)
3577 Weight of Balanced Rock (lbs)

Stay here...

Devils Garden Campground
What exactly does the Devil grow? In this striking garden, located 18 miles (29km) north of the park entrance, tents and RVs sprout beside prickly pear cacti, yucca and stands of juniper and piñon pines. Massive crimson fins double as the garden wall.

Cali Cochitta
An oasis of cozy style in the heart of Moab, this lovely B&B will relax you in a heartbeat with hammocks, porch chairs and a backyard hot tub. The smartly decorated rooms are tucked inside brick cottages that surround a well-manicured yard. The communal outdoor breakfast table is made for sharing tall tales from yesterday's hike.

Sunflower Hill Inn
A tempting oasis cut from the desert landscape, this welcoming inn has gardens, a swimming pool, and walking access to all of Moab's best eateries. The rooms are set across a series of historic cottages, some come with private balconies and jetted hot tubs.

Do this!

Hiking
This is one of America's premier desert landscapes. The three-hour ranger-led Fiery Furnace Hike takes you through a maze of red rocks in the heart of the park. A backcountry permit is required. Check the park's website or inquire at the visitor center for more information. Anywhere in the park, you'll scramble over boulders, squeeze through narrows and navigate ledges, with geologic wonders around every bend.

Photographing
Morning and sunset are the best times to shoot in red rock country, with the warmest blues at sunset. While Delicate Arch makes it to the top of most shot lists, look around for massive landscapes, wild canyon shots and close ups of the remarkable flora and fauna that bring this park to life.

White-water rafting
Whomp! Splash! Oww! Ah yes, the poetic sounds of a paddle fight on the Colorado River, which tracks the southern border of the park. Wildlife viewing is a highlight on the stretch between Dewey Campground and Hittle Bottom, northeast of the park. Class I and II water closer to Moab keeps the ride lively and family-friendly.

▶ Utah's iconic rock formations are the result of millions of years of erosion.

What to spot...

Arches National Park sweeps across the high desert, where the climate is marked by very hot summers, cold winters and sparse rainfall. Habitats include mixed grasslands, dry washes and riparian areas, with lots of slickrock in between. Larger mammals like foxes and bobcats, as well as most rodents, are nocturnal, saving their hunting and scavenging for cooler nights. As for amphibians, calls from a chorus of male toads may fill a canyon after a spring or summer rainstorm.

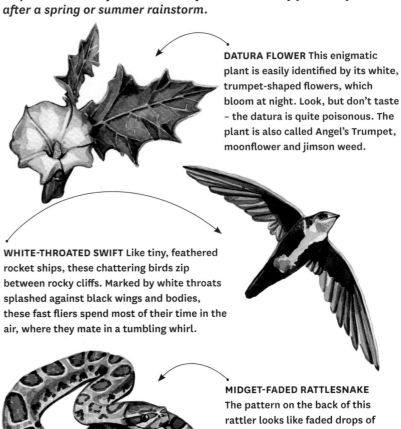

DATURA FLOWER This enigmatic plant is easily identified by its white, trumpet-shaped flowers, which bloom at night. Look, but don't taste – the datura is quite poisonous. The plant is also called Angel's Trumpet, moonflower and jimson weed.

WHITE-THROATED SWIFT Like tiny, feathered rocket ships, these chattering birds zip between rocky cliffs. Marked by white throats splashed against black wings and bodies, these fast fliers spend most of their time in the air, where they mate in a tumbling whirl.

MIDGET-FADED RATTLESNAKE The pattern on the back of this rattler looks like faded drops of blood. It's known for its highly toxic venom – fortunately, it keeps a low daytime profile.

Hike this...

01 Delicate Arch
Hustle up the slickrock, navigate a ledge, then unpack your fancy camera for the park's marquee attraction: a freestanding arch gracefully framing the La Sal Mountains. The hike is 3 miles (4.8km) round-trip.

02 Devils Garden Trail
This 7.2-mile (11.6km) round-trip hike passes eight arches; it's a 1.6-mile (2.6km) round-trip from the trailhead to Landscape Arch. Stretching more than 290ft (88.4m), it's the largest natural rock arch in the world.

03 Courthouse Wash
Sign up for a backcountry permit to dusty-bottom your way to this designated backcountry camping site on a two-day adventure over rock, brush and rugged desert terrain.

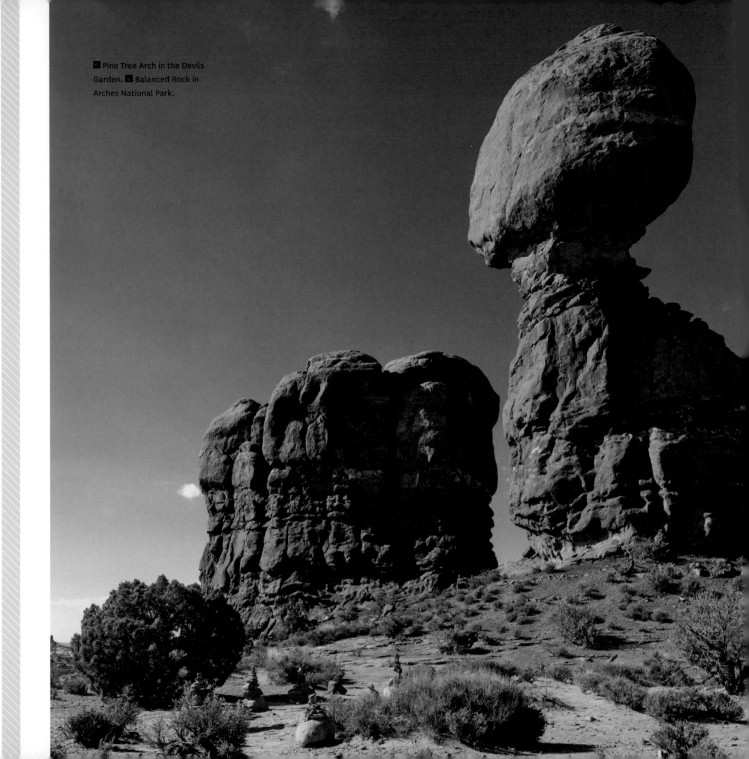

Pine Tree Arch in the Devils Garden. Balanced Rock in Arches National Park.

Itineraries

Watch the sun set stone arches and fins aglow as you hike these sandstone formations. Or take to two knobbly wheels to see this widescreen landscape by mountain bike.

 Mountain bike trails around Moab, like Hymasa Trail here, flow over grippy slickrock.

01

A half-day

Courthouse Towers and Balanced Rock are red rock showoffs, begging for attention on your morning drive to the Wolfe Ranch parking area. From here it's a 1.5-mile (2.4km) hike with a slickrock climb and a final spin on a wall-hugging ledge. Your reward? A highly photogenic view of Delicate Arch – an already familiar sight if you've seen the Utah license plate. The colors of the arch change hypnotically as the sun climbs. Check out petroglyphs carved into the rocks near the footbridge on your return hike, then continue to Wolfe Ranch, a well-preserved pioneer cabin built in the early 1900s.

Next up? Five magnificent arches on a 1-mile (1.6km) loop. North Window opens onto canyon views, followed by South Window and the castle-like Turret Arch. Across the way, a short walk ends at the joined Double Arches. For lunch, unpack your cooler at the picnic area across from Balanced Rock.

02

A day

Parking at Arches can be challenging, so start early. Buy picnic sandwiches at Sweet Cravings Bakery + Bistro in Moab, then stop at the park visitor center to collect permits for a ranger-led hiking tour of the Fiery Furnace. The half-day adventure twists and turns through wondrous sandstone formations. These have been carved by natural forces for thousands of years and they are fragile. Worked up an appetite? Drive north to Devils Garden for a picnic near a grove of colorful fins and arches.

From here, hikers can drive to the short trails at Window Rock and Balanced Rock, close to the road.

If education is your jam, join a ranger walk or drive to the Wolfe Ranch parking area to view Native American petroglyphs and an early-1900s cabin. End the day with a late-afternoon hike to Delicate Arch. You won't be alone as the sun drops, but crowds don't detract from the fragile beauty of this iconic arch. Stay past sunset for an hour or two for some of the USA's best stargazing.

03

Two days

Grab a burrito and coffee at Love Muffin in Moab, then drive north to the park's visitor center to check the daily program schedule. From here, it's a Technicolor trip on the 18-mile (29km) scenic road to Devils Garden Campground, where you'll pitch your tent and revel in the wonderful night skies. Follow the Devils Garden Trail to soaring Landscape Arch, the largest natural arch in the world; if you hike to the end of the trail, you'll pass seven more. In the afternoon, walk to Window Rock, then stroll around the base of Balanced Rock, a formation that defines the word 'precarious.' Join a ranger talk, then hike to Delicate Arch for sunset. Hungry? Savor smoked elk at the Desert Bistro, followed by local brews at Moab Brewery. In the morning, try to land a Fiery Furnace permit. In the afternoon, splash down the Colorado River on a raft or cycle the family-friendly Bar M Loop. Moab is mountain bike central; ask at the bike rental shop about rides like the Whole Enchilada and Slickrock. Celebrate the day with a burger at Milt's, a Moab favorite.

04

SD

Badlands National Park

People tend to go rather quiet when they first approach the Badlands. The otherworldly landscape defies clever commentary or summing-up.

rench trappers called it 'bad lands to travel across'; before them, the Lakota held much the same opinion. It's eerie, this rocky desert moonscape, with its weird, crinkly shapes and seeming absence of vegetation. But the longer you stay, the more you see.

For starters, these seemingly barren rocks are actually full of life – and the evidence of life. The Badlands hold one of the most plentiful concentrations of fossils in the world. The study of fossils here has thrived since 1846, when paleontologist Dr Hiram Prout dug up and described a titanothere mandible (the jawbone of an extinct hoofed mammal related to horses and rhinos).

The other thing you might begin to notice is that the Badlands aren't finished. The rocky formations consist of distinct layers. These are the result of the accumulation of different kinds of sediment over different periods. Some of it is volcanic; some is mud left over from the floors of long-vanished rivers and seas. It took ages – literally – to build the landscape you see here, but for the past 500,000 years or so erosion has been un-building it: the Badlands erode at a rate of about an inch a year.

In addition to the secrets held within the Badlands themselves, the park also encompasses two kinds of prairie grasslands in the surrounding area. These are teeming with activity – animal, vegetable and meteorological. A huge variety of birds and other wildlife can be seen here, including about 400 plant species, from shrubs and flowers to, unsurprisingly, grass. Often, though, the main attraction is the weather: sudden, violent rain and hailstorms all through spring and summer, blizzards in winter, and extreme temperature variations mean visitors should be prepared for atmospheric drama.

Toolbox

When to go

Summers are hot, with frequent sudden hail or rainstorms; June sees the most rain. Winters are snowbound and cold. And shoulder season weather is unpredictable: take your pick. The park and the Ben Reifel Visitor Center are open year-round. The visitor center at the south entrance is open in summer only.

Getting there

The Badlands are located in southwestern South Dakota, 75 miles (121km) east of Rapid City. There's no public transportation to the park so bring a car.

Events

The annual astronomy festival is held in July.

Accessibility

Visitor centers, scenic overlooks and wayside exhibits are accessible, as is Cedar Pass campground. The Fossil Exhibit and Window Trails have boardwalks and the first section of the Door and Cliff Shelf Trails are also accessible.

Park in numbers

381 Area in sq miles
1 Annual erosion rate (in)
3247 Highest point (ft)

Stay here...

Cedar Pass Lodge

There's been a lodge here since 1928, when local businessman Ben Millard and his sister, Clara, opened a service camp for trend-setting tourists. Times have changed but the rustic charm lives on in cabins that resemble the originals, albeit made from sustainably sourced wood and with other eco-friendly details. Open mid-April to mid-October.

Badlands Inn

A 15-minute drive from the park entrance, this working cattle ranch has comfortable modern rooms in an unrivaled setting. You can feed the chickens, collect the eggs, and visit the cows, donkeys and other barnyard residents, or simply enjoy the sunsets from the back porch. You can also stay in an original 1880 homestead cabin for a taste of old-time prairie life.

Sage Creek Campground

Bypass the popular Cedar Pass Campground and seek out this primitive area, where camping is free. The 22 sites are first-come, first-served, and it's so remote that wildlife often strolls through. Located off the unpaved Sage Creek Rim Rd, access may be restricted in severe weather.

Do this!

Scenic driving

The scenic, 39-mile (63km) Badlands Loop Rd (Hwy 240) roams a winding, U-shaped path between the towns of Cactus Flat and Wall and it's easily worth taking the time to drive. From it you can see most of the park's characteristic features, especially if you stop at the various information points and scenic overlooks and walking trails.

Learning

 The working paleontology lab (open mid-June to mid-September in the Ben Reifel Visitor Center) allows visitors of all ages to learn more about the importance of the fossil studies that go on in the park.

Stargazing

Big open skies and the lack of light pollution means you can get an unparalleled look at the stars from the Cedar Pass Campground area, either with the naked eye or through telescopes staffed by rangers, who will point out interesting features. Seeing the Milky Way Galaxy with this level of clarity is an unforgettable experience.

◄ Eroded rock formations in Badlands National Park.
▶ Notch Trail ladder.

Hike this...

01 Castle Trail

The park's longest trail – 10.5 miles (17km) round-trip – passes striking Badlands formations, including rugged gullies, twisted spires and intricately carved buttes, along with open prairie.

02 Notch Trail

Starting from the Door and Window parking area, this 1.5-mile (2.4km) round-trip trail includes scaling a ladder up to a high ledge with dizzying views over the White River Valley.

03 Sage Creek

Backcountry hikes in the Badlands require no permits; inquire at the visitor center first for detailed info and topographical maps. A two-day hike along Sage Creek provides a taste.

What to spot...

The Badlands, as well as the grassland areas that surround them, are home to a huge variety of plants and wildlife. Hundreds of kinds of birds inhabit the area, along with grasses and wildflowers, hardy shrubs, butterflies, snakes and lizards, and a wide variety of mammals, from prairie dogs to bison. Wildlife photographers can have a field day here, capturing these creatures against the glamorous backdrop of the rock formations and wide-open sky.

BISON These 2000lb (907kg) creatures are often spotted in the western part of the North Unit, along Sage Creek Rim Rd.

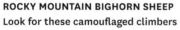

ROCKY MOUNTAIN BIGHORN SHEEP Look for these camouflaged climbers near the Pinnacles or Cedar Pass. The impressive horns and sturdy skulls of bighorn males are built to withstand the impact of annual pre-mating-season headbutt battles for dominance.

TURKEY VULTURE With the face of a puppet-movie villain, this large bird, also called a buzzard, has an unusually well developed sense of smell for sniffing out fresh carrion.

Itineraries

Loop the Loop Rd for iconic photo pitstops, camp under the stars, or just hike this park's backcountry for middle-of-nowhere solitude.

◀ Bighorn sheep battle.
⬆ The eerie landscape of the Badlands National Park.

01
A day

The Badlands Loop Rd (Hwy 240) is a beautiful drive of 39 miles (63km) in a rough 'U' shape south of I-90. If you're traveling east to west, you'll enter the park at the Northeast Entrance Station. Be sure to stop and look around at the Big Badlands Overlook inside the entrance; in fact, plan on stopping as often as you like at the many overlooks and information points along the drive. After 2.5 miles, you'll arrive at the Window Trailhead, where you can take a short stroll to a fabulous lookout over the eroded canyon. Next pull over at the Fossil Exhibit trailhead – hop out here and take the short, easy walk along the boardwalk path, which is lined with displays about fossil collecting and the history of paleontology in the area. Continue along the Loop Rd, but stop again at the Window Trail parking lot to snap a photo against the iconic background. Don't miss a stop at Yellow Mounds Overlook and the Pinnacles Overlook as well, before leaving the park and returning to I-90 at the town of Wall. This little place is a good spot for refreshments.

02
A weekend

Enter at the Northeast Entrance Station and follow the Loop Rd to the Notch trailhead and hike the 1.5 miles (2.4km) round-trip to a point overlooking the river valley. Back on the road, pause at the Ben Reifel Visitor Center for a schedule of the evening's events. Set up camp at the Cedar Pass Campground or check into an eco-friendly cabin at the Cedar Pass Lodge before dinner. Finish up in time for the ranger-led Night Sky presentation, after which you can stargaze solo. Next day, get an early start (with plenty of water) and make the 10.5 mile round-trip hike on the Castle Trail. Afterwards, check out the nearby fossil laboratory in the visitor center. Having restocked your supplies – especially water – continue along the loop road. After the Pinnacles Overlook, you'll come to the turnoff for the gravel Sage Creek Rim Rd (a good place to break out a fat-tire bike). Keep an eye out for bison and pronghorn as you follow this road to the Sage Creek Campground, a good base for backcountry hikes.

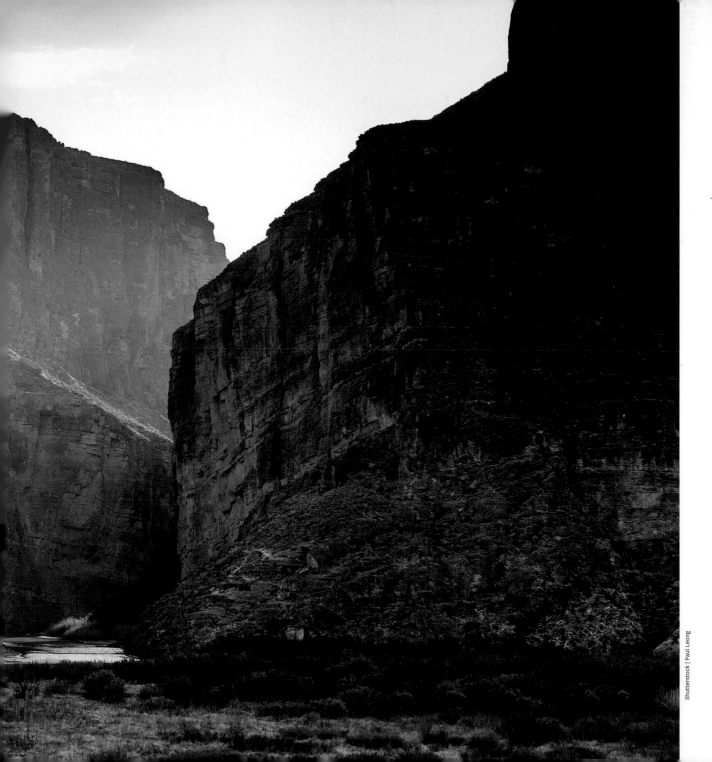

05

TX

Big Bend National Park

A vast and sunbaked wilderness, Big Bend has long captivated those who make the journey to this remote corner of Texas.

In the heart of the Chihuahuan Desert, where summer temperatures often surpass 100°F (38°C), Big Bend may appear at first glance like a barren wasteland. But, in fact, amid its steep-walled canyons, fertile river corridor, desert scrubland and forested ridges, you'll find varied microclimates that support abundant wildlife – including more recorded bird species than any other national park in America.

The area has a complicated geological history, with a mix of 500-million-year-old rocks and sand dunes still being shaped by today's desert winds. Walking this parched landscape, it's difficult to imagine that Big Bend once lay beneath an ancient tropical sea, which later evaporated and disappeared beneath clay and limestone sediments. Deposits found here reveal an incredible record of life from this time. Among the fossilized treasures is the skull of a three-horned chasmosaurus, a 50ft-long (15m) crocodile and a flying reptile with a wingspan of 36ft (11m).

Home to a long stretch of the Rio Grande, a life-giving river system in these inhospitable lands, Big Bend has a deep connection to human history in the region. Artifacts from Paleo-Indians that lived in the region date back 10,000 years. Later groups include the Chiso, followed by Comanche, who led raiding parties into the interior of Mexico. The Spanish also had a presence here, with explorers crossing the Rio Grande in search of gold and silver. Following the Mexican-American War, Big Bend saw a succession of ranchers, miners, revolutionaries, outlaws and intrepid homesteaders.

The creation of the national park is largely credited to Everett Townsend, a Texan-born

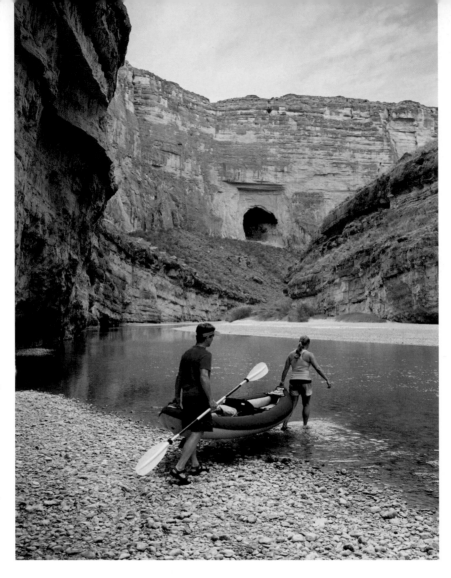

deputy marshal who first ventured into the Chisos Mountains while tracking a pack of stolen mules back in 1894. Inspired by the natural beauty around him, Townsend vowed to preserve this landscape, a promise he later fulfilled while serving on the state legislature. Big Bend officially became a national park in 1944, and Townsend – then in his 70s – became its first commissioner. He is remembered today as 'the father of Big Bend National Park.'

⬆ Kayaking on the Rio Grande in Big Bend National Park.
➡ Epic Texan landscapes. Previous page: Santa Elena Canyon.

Toolbox
When to go
The most pleasant time to visit is from October to April. In the summer, temperatures regularly soar above 100°F (38°C) – even reaching 110°F (43°C) – making long hikes unbearable.

Getting there
Set in the southwestern corner of Texas, the closest airports are in Midland, 195 miles (314km) north (a three-hour drive); and El Paso, 290 miles (467km) northwest. Rental cars are available at either airport.

Events
The spring migration (March to early May) offers stellar bird watching. The last two weeks in April are best.

Accessibility
Three nature trails are accessible, as are the visitor centers and several picnic areas. Two campgrounds have an accessible site and some outfitters, like Desert Sports, offer accessible tours.

Park in numbers
1252 Area in sq miles
1200 Number of plant species
7832 Highest point (ft)

Stay here...

🏠 **Chisos Mountain Lodge**
Aside from camping, this is the only in-park accommodations. It offers a range of options for all budgets, all with scenic views and a location a few steps from hiking trails in the Chisos Mountains. Book ahead for one of the five Roosevelt Cottages, with stone floors, wood-beamed ceilings and porches with views of the mountains. A few rooms are accessible for people with disabilities.

⛺ **Chisos Basin Campground**
Surrounded by mountains, this campground earns rave reviews for its location. It's great for sunsets and the nightly spectacle of stargazing, and it's a short walk to the trailheads and a restaurant. Back in the 1930s, this site was used as barracks for the Civilian Conservation Corps, the young men who blazed trails and built access roads and park lodging.

🏠 **Ten Bits Ranch**
In a secluded setting about 25-minutes' drive north of the park's western entrance, Ten Bits provides full immersion in the mountain-studded Chihuahuan desert. The 100% sustainable property has adobe and wood cabins decked out like old 'Wild West' buildings.

Do this!

〰️ **Rafting**
You can go for a scenic paddle along the Rio Grande, taking in the dramatic beauty of Santa Elena Canyon and Big Bend's cliffs. Recent rainfall sets conditions, which range from class I to IV. Outfitters located in nearby Terlingua provide guided trips.

✨ **Stargazing**
Far from city lights, this remote park is an outstanding site for taking in the night sky. You'll be able to see over 2000 stars on a clear night. It's well worth camping a few nights here – or else just gazing up at the sky while soaking in the hot springs.

🔭 **Birdwatching**
One of the great birding hot spots in North America, Big Bend has over 450 documented avian species, and you'll find unique ones (like the rare Colima warbler) among the park's diverse habitats. The Rio Grande Village offers some of the best year-round birdwatching; you can see herons, ducks, kingfishers, white-tailed doves, vermilion flycatchers and Cooper's hawks.

◧ Balanced Rock on the Grapevine Hills trail in Big Bend National Park.

What to spot...

At first glance, Big Bend seems like a barren and unforgiving desert landscape. But delve deeper and you'll encounter a wondrous variety of plant and animal life. In fact, among its three different habitats – desert badlands, river valley and forested mountains – Big Bend harbors over 1200 plant species and more species of birds, bats and cacti than any other park in America.

TEXAS BROWN TARANTULA
Covered in hair and nearly as large as a mouse, the Texas brown tarantula looks frightening, but is actually quite docile and not dangerous to humans. These spiders live in burrows, in front of which they place lines of webbing to detect passing prey.

GIANT SWALLOWTAIL BUTTERFLY
Found throughout the southern and eastern United States, the yellow and dark brown giant swallowtail is the largest butterfly species in North America, with a wingspan of 3.9–6.3in (10–16cm).

COYOTE One of 75 mammal species in Big Bend, coyotes have gray or reddish gray fur, stand 2ft (61cm) high at the shoulder and weigh 30–70lbs (14–32kg). They mate for life and have a home range of 40 to 100 miles (64 to 160km).

Hike this...

01 Window Trail

Not to be confused with the shorter Window View, this 5.6-mile (9km) round-trip hike descends 800ft (note the tough return climb) through a canyon to a chisel-peaked desert vista.

02 Lost Mine Trail

This moderate 4.8-mile (7.7km) round-trip hike is an excellent introduction to the natural riches of the Chisos Mountains. You'll pass through forests of pine, juniper and oak before reaching a ridge with views out to the Sierra del Carmen in Mexico.

03 Emory Peak

Emory Peak, a strenuous 10.5-mile (17km) round-trip hike winds up to Big Bend's highest point – offering spectacular views over the desert landscape from its summit in the Chisos Mountains.

Itineraries

Hike up Emory Peak for the best Big Bend views, raft down the Rio Grande, cross the border to Mexico or just watch wildlife under the starry sky.

◄ Look out over the Chisos Mountains from several Big Bend hiking trails.
➡ Canoeing in Santa Elena Canyon on the Rio Grande; the river is a national border.

01
A weekend

On a weekend visit, hike up into the Chisos Mountains on the first day: the 10.5-mile (17km) round-trip ascent up Emory Peak offers some of the finest views in Big Bend. You'll pass through valleys of wildflowers, taking in cactus blooms with Mexican jays flittering overhead. The views get more inspiring the higher you go. Keep an eye out for white-tailed deer that graze near the trail. Treat yourself to a first-rate meal at the Chisos Mountain Lodge.

On day two, take the 30-mile (48km) Ross Maxwell Scenic Drive. You can make a day of it, looking for desert wildlife at the Sam Nail Ranch, taking in views over the desert floor at the Sotol Vista Overlook, then pulling off on a side road to the colorful cliffs of Burro Mesa. Wander through the Castolon Historic District to find remnants of an early 20th-century cavalry camp, and learn how rural families lived a century ago at the Magdalena House. End the day at 1500ft (457m) Santa Elena Canyon. The 1.7-mile (2.7km) trail follows the river along one of the park's most picturesque chasms.

02
Four days

After doing an all-day hike and a scenic drive on days one and two, spend your third day rafting down the Rio Grande. For a leisurely paddle, head to the Hot Springs Canyon, where you'll have superb views of the Sierra del Carmen in Mexico. Later, rest those weary arms on a soak in the Historic Hot Springs, which you'll reach on an easy half-mile trail, passing Native American pictographs along the way. That evening, stay up to watch Big Bend's dark skies fill with stars. The park has the least light pollution of any national park in the lower 48 states. Today, park managers are trying to keep it that way by reducing unnecessary lighting in the park.

On the fourth day, head to the Rio Grande Village, where wildlife-watching opportunities abound, especially for avian species in this birding hot spot. At dusk, head west to the Chisos Basin and make the short hike along the Window View Trail, one of the best places in Big Bend to watch the sun set.

03
A week

Do the four-day itinerary, then spend a fifth day exploring the tiny Mexican village of Boquillas – the border at this laid-back crossing reopened in recent years. A boatman will row you across the river; from there you can take a truck or donkey, or walk the 1 mile (1.6km) to Boquillas. Once there, snack in a local eatery before returning in the afternoon. (Don't forget your passport!)

On day six, explore the old ghost town of Terlingua, just outside the park. You can visit ruins and a cemetery, then dine at the Starlight Theatre, a former roofless cinema turned Western-themed restaurant. On your last day in Big Bend hike the Lost Mine Trail, a 4.8-mile (7.7km) trail that offers grand views from a promontory overlooking Juniper Canyon.

If time allows, squeeze in a scenic drive outside the park. Drive west of Terlingua to Lajitas on one of Texas' most spectacular highways. With the Rio Grande (and a barren stretch of Mexico) on your left and looming mountains to your right, desolate, winding Rte 170 offers astounding scenery at every rise.

06

FL

Biscayne National Park

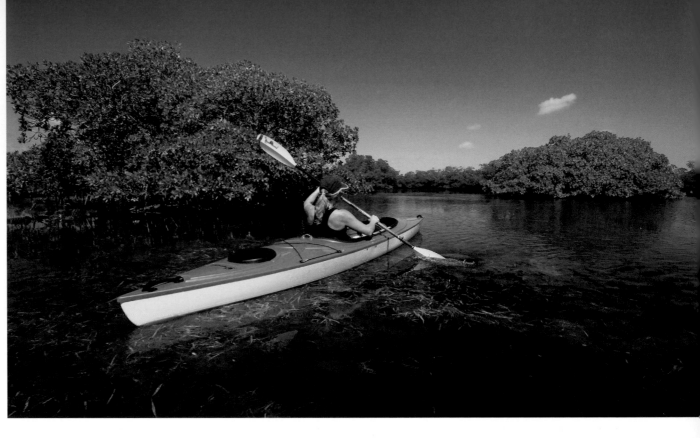

Haunted by shipwrecks, populated by turtles and manatees – Biscayne is an ex-pirate's paradise rescued from the claws of developers to become the Atlantis of America's parks.

East of the Everglades, just off Miami, lies a drowned dreamland that nurtured human life 10,000 years ago – and has since hosted indigenous tribes, Spanish conquistadors, plundering privateers and partying presidents. Biscayne thrills modern adventurers who camp on the keys, kayak around atolls and snorkel in a seascape that comprises 95% of the national park, home to a vast coral reef with over 600 species of fish.

But it could have been very different. Wandering Spaniard Juan Ponce de León 'discovered' Florida in 1513, delivering disease and destruction to the Tequesta people; subsequently, several Spanish ships, some laden with treasure, came to grief on

the reef here. Later, Elliott Key was home to Black Caesar, an 18th-century African pirate. Biscayne continued to see eyebrow-raising activity well into the 20th century. During Prohibition the raised-shacks community of Stiltsville hosted drinking and gambling shindigs, and the CIA used the area as a training ground for Cuban exiles ahead of the Bay of Pigs invasion.

Israel Jones, one of America's first black millionaires, made a fortune from growing pineapples and limes here. His sons offered guided fishing tours; their clients included John F Kennedy, Lyndon Johnson, Richard Nixon and – crucially – vacuum-cleaner magnate Herbert W Hoover Jr and his family.

As Florida flourished, developers

announced plans to dredge the bay and gouge a 40ft (12m) channel through the reef to create a new city and port. People protested, calling for the area to be protected, and they gained support from the *Miami Herald* and Hoover himself, who flew legislators down to see the area he'd loved as a child.

As momentum for the park grew, landowners attempted to despoil the area by bulldozing a strip across Elliott Key, ostensibly to build a road. It became known as 'Spite Highway' since it led nowhere. In 1968, congress approved the creation of Biscayne National Monument, which became a national park in 1980. Today, Spite Highway has greened over to become a hiking trail.

Toolbox

When to go

The park is open year-round, but camping is more comfortable during the winter, when mosquitoes and no-see-ums (little biting flies) are less of a nuisance. But the snorkeling is better during summer and fall.

Getting there

The park is accessed via the Dante Fascell Visitor Center at Convoy Point, 7 miles (11km) east of the city of Homestead (an hour's drive from South Beach), where there's a museum, and boat launching facilities.

Events

Rangers offer lighthouse tours, Stiltsville trips and special talks on weekends (December to April).

Accessibility

Dante Fascell Visitor Center at Convoy Point is accessible. Boca Chita Key has sidewalks around the harbor but the rest of the island consists of grass cover and rocky ground.

Park in numbers

270.3 Area in sq miles
44 Number of documented wrecks in the park
10,000 Years that humans have been active here

Stay here...

This is a place for explorers, not the pampered. There are no hotels, motels, lodges or cabins within park boundaries – it's camp or go home. (The nearest accommodations to the park's entrance are in Homestead or Florida City.) Camping can be uncomfortable during summer, when mosquitoes and no-see-ums are a problem. Campers should be self-sufficient, packing in all food and water. You'll also need a boat.

Boca Chita Key Campsite
A waterside site on the park's most visited island, next to the harbor and opposite the Pavilion. There's a grassy area, picnic tables and toilets, but no shower.

Elliott Key Campsite
There are waterside and forested camping areas here, plus a seasonally staffed ranger station, picnic tables and grills. You'll also find toilets and even a cold-water shower.

Hoosville Hostel
A 10-mile drive west of the park is a much-loved traveler haunt, with inviting rooms and a lush backyard that's perfect for unwinding after the day's adventures.

Do this!

Snorkeling & diving
Biscayne is 95% underwater and the only way to really explore it is by donning snorkel, mask and fins (and a scuba tank if you're dive-qualified). Besides the astonishing variety of fish, sea turtles and manatees, there are 44 wrecks to discover – including one, the *Mandalay*, in shallow water. Snorkeling is possible from the shore in places, but the reef proper is further out and you'll need to arrange a boat.

Canoeing & kayaking
A paddle-powered adventure around Biscayne's islands is an excellent experience. Explore shallow channels, creeks and lagoons that are off-limits for larger craft, and spot turtles, dolphins and manatees as you glide across turquoise water. Guided trips can be arranged, but confident paddlers can reach the park independently.

Fishing
Responsible fishing is permitted within Biscayne, and the park offers a free Fisheries Awareness Class so you can be sure you're using sustainable practices.

◄ Kayaking in the mangroves of Biscayne Bay in the park.
► The Great Land Crab is a slow-moving critter.

Explore this...

01 Spite Trail
The park's only hiking trail has a great backstory. In the 1960s, when the fight between developers and conservationists got nasty, an ugly gash was bulldozed right across Elliott Key. Originally nicknamed Spite Highway, this scar has healed into a beautiful trail, tunnelling through 6 miles (10km) of tropical hardwood forest.

02 Maritime Heritage Trail
Submerged hikers (divers) can follow this unique underwater archaeological trail – complete with informative site cards – which links a series of shipwrecks, including the *Arratoon Apcar* (sank 1878), *Erl King* (1891), *Alicia* (1905), *Lugano* (1913) and *Mandalay* (1966).

What to spot...

Biscayne boasts four different ecosystems – mangrove swamp, lagoon, island key and offshore-reef habitats – and its biodiversity is extraordinary. More than 50 kinds of crustacean, hundreds of species of fish and 28 types of mammal live here. Among the more interesting locals are American crocodiles, giant blue land crabs, rattlesnakes and Caribbean reef octopuses. A couple of ecozones crash into each other in South Florida too, attracting some species of birds that aren't seen anywhere else in the country.

SPINY LOBSTER Like 'true' lobsters but minus the claws. When threatened, these Biscayne buskers make a screeching noise by rubbing a 'plectrum' on their antennae against their exoskeleton.

FLORIDA MANATEE
These eccentric-looking animals – related to elephants and likely the inspiration for mermaid myths – are star residents. During their evolutionary journey they lost rear legs but kept front fingernails (handy for eating shellfish).

YELLOW-CROWNED NIGHT HERON
Sometimes known as the American night heron or squawk, this small heron is a nocturnal stealth hunter, terrorizing amphibians along the water's edge. They were once eaten in Cajun cuisine.

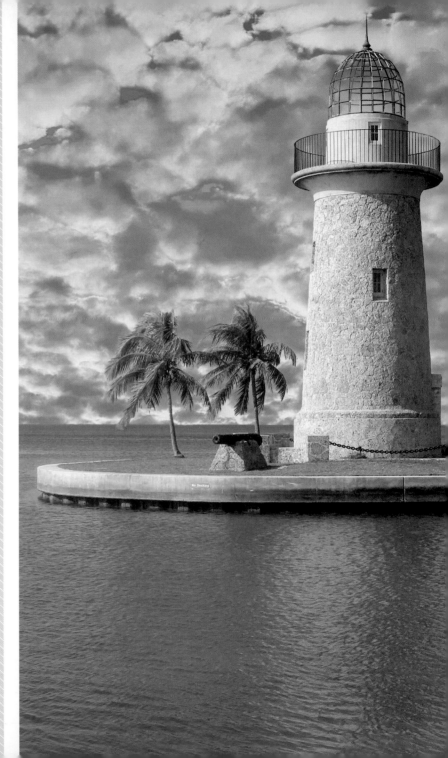

Itineraries

Anchors away, whether you day-trip on a glass-bottomed boat, rent a canoe or plan a significant kayak journey, the diving and snorkeling are excellent here.

◀ Boca Chita Key lighthouse in Biscayne National Park.
▶ The Least Tern is North America's smallest tern.

01

A half-day

Biscayne is unique within the NPS system since you need to board a boat in order to see any of the park – making some degree of organization and planning required for any trip here. But people who are simply passing by (or committed landlubbers) can still get a taste of Biscayne by exploring the Dante Fascell Visitor Center at the entrance to the park. Found 50 miles (80km) south of Miami, and 9 miles (14.5km) east of Homestead, the museum uses multimedia magic to transport you through the four ecosystems of the park without getting a drop of water on you. Several educational films are screened, explaining the biodiversity that exists beneath the waves, and both big and little kids can enjoy the touch-and-play display of bones, feathers, sponges, corals and other items from the park. You can also walk the short Jetty Trail and enjoy a picnic overlooking the water leading out to the park. Let's be honest – this dry run is only going to whet your appetite for a proper exploration, so get planning.

02

A day

If you're dying to dive into Biscayne to see what all the fuss is about there are plenty of options. The non-profit Biscayne National Park Institute offers a range of eco-friendly adventures, including sailing trips, island visits, and sunset cruises. A highlight is the four-hour snorkeling tour, with two stops at either a coral reef, a wreck site or a mangrove (depending on the weather). Besides an abundance of colorful corals and tropical fish, you may be lucky enough to meet a manatee or spot a dolphin. Seeking a more immersive experience? Take a three-hour snorkeling tour (which will get you about 90 minutes in the water) for face-to-face encounters with the finned community of the keys. Canoes can be rented by the hour, and guided half- and full-day canoe and kayak trips can be arranged in winter (late November to April). Qualified divers can arrange trips with operators like Tropic Scuba. If you're flush with cash and want a boutique boat experience, charter a private vessel.

03

Five days

Paddling away from the visitor center, it feels as though you're embarking on the ultimate aquatic adventure. The kayak is sitting deeper in the water than normal, but you've got several days' food on board and a tent in the sealed storage compartment. First stop is the campground at the north of the park, Boca Chita Key, to bag a good pitch and stash your gear. There are two camping sites in the park – here and at Elliott Key – and you'll aim for two nights in each.

You plan to spend a couple of days paddling around, exploring such parts of the park as Jones Lagoon (a good spot to see sharks, rays and upside-down jellyfish), Hurricane Creek (where there's excellent snorkeling among the mangroves), and the shallow lagoons and channels south of Caesar Creek – named after a pirate who once had a base here. One day you'll dedicate to hiking the length of the Spite Highway across Elliott Key, but the thing you're most looking forward to is snorkeling the Maritime Heritage Trail.

07

CO

Black Canyon of the Gunnison National Park

Deeper than the Grand Canyon, the yawning, dark chasm of the Black Canyon of the Gunnison is nature stripped to its most elemental.

This craggy canyon has been two million years in the making. The Gunnison River carved a vertical wilderness with fast-moving water, carrying rock and debris. 'Narrow' is an understatement – only direct overhead light filters down to the canyon floor. A peek over the edge inspires trembling awe, and probably some vertigo. No other canyon in America competes with the sheer and dizzying depths of this 2000ft (610m) chasm.

Experts feed on the challenge of scaling these walls and kayaking the river's Class V whitewater. They grab these extreme photo ops so you don't have to. Most visitors will be more than content to browse the scenic vistas, hike the steep canyon or horseback ride along the rim. Fly-fishers should pack their waders: the clear jade waters of the Gunnison River offers some of the best fishing in Colorado and even the US. It has been designated as Gold Medal Water and Wild Trout Water, an exclusive status few rivers can boast.

Historically, this massive canyon has presented a formidable barrier. Utes settled the rim, but there's no evidence of human habitation within the chasm itself. Surveyor John W Gunnison sought a railroad crossing here, but he was massacred in Utah after bypassing the canyon in 1853. In 1901, two lucky adventurers floated through the canyon on rubber mattresses, traveling 33 hard-won miles (53km) in nine days.

Park status came only in 1999. Today, in addition to being one of the smallest US National Parks, the Black Canyon of the Gunnison happens to be the least-visited of the four that are in Colorado. Maybe that is because it is far from the interstate and major cities. But it does occupy Colorado's sweet spot, a region that has become infamous for its powder skiing and mountain biking.

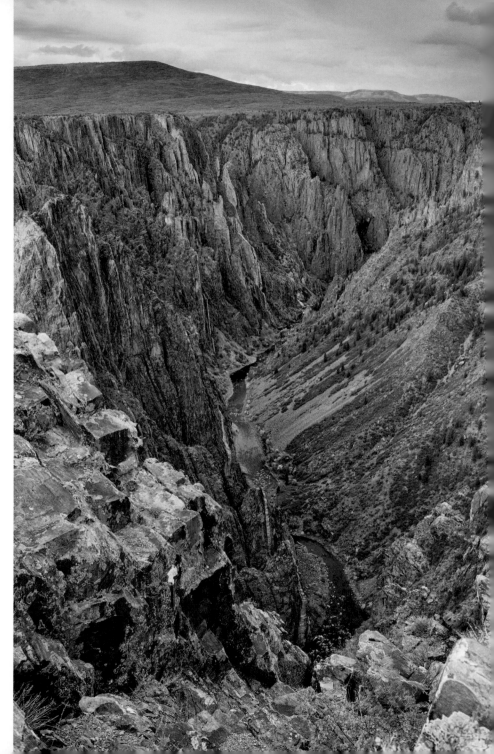

Toolbox

When to go
All park roads are open from mid-April to mid-November. In wintertime the park is covered in snow and the South Rim Rd opens to cross-country skiing and snowshoeing. Fly-fishing is best during the spring hatch and early fall.

Getting there
The park is 262 miles (422km) from Denver International Airport. The closest accommodations and services are in Montrose and Gunnison. A bit further afield, the winter and summer resort of Crested Butte has ample visitor services.

Events
In late June at the south rim, the Black Canyon Astronomy Festival offers stargazing with expert guidance.

Accessibility
There is access for those with impaired mobility at the South Rim Visitor Center and Campground and various scenic overlooks.

Park in numbers

47 Area in sq miles
8775 Highest point (ft)
14°F/88°F Average low/high temperature (-10–31°C)

Stay here...

East Portal Campground
For water access, camp at the riverside East Portal in the adjacent Curecanti National Recreation Area. First come, first served, it's shaded by lovely box elders, a bonus in the summertime heat. Be sure to keep your provisions well protected from curious black bears.

Wanderlust Hostel
In charming Gunnison, this friendly hostel offers a sustainable stay complete with loaner bicycles, communal kitchen, a garden with pickable berries and first-rate adventure advice. Guests can choose from dorm beds or private rooms decked out in whimsical decor. It's located in a tranquil residential neighborhood with riverside trail access.

Ruby of Crested Butte
Ski town Crested Butte is a hub of outdoor fun all year round; plus, there's something to be said for its incongruent fine-dining-and-cowboy style. The pampering continues if you bed down at the Ruby. It's thoughtfully outfitted, down to the bowls of jellybeans and pet beds.

Do this!

Fly-fishing
Come for the spring hatch and snag a few of the plentiful stock of rainbow trout in these Gold-Medal waters. Strict regulations are enforced to maintain this status. A Colorado fishing license is required and bait fishing is not allowed – only lures and flies. River access points may require permits.

Scenery-gazing
Colorado's highest cliff face is the 2300ft-high (701m), marble-striped Painted Wall. You might spot climbers ascending one of its vertiginous climbs, though some routes face seasonal closures to protect nesting raptors – it is a national park, after all. Also stop at Chasm View, which is nearly as wide as it is high.

Horseback riding
Coloradans love a good bluff: match them by not blinking first. So when you find out that the only horse trail at the park is called Deadhorse Trail, well, we say saddle up. The park's only route for horses, the 5-mile (8km) trail travels moderate terrain to the spectacular North Rim.

◀ The Black Canyon itself.
▶ Wild Utah juniper flourishes beside trails in the national park.

Hike this...

O1 Rim Rock Nature Trail
This easy 1-mile (1.6km) walk to the canyon rim is lined with sagebrush, Gambel oaks and Utah juniper.

O2 Oak Flat Loop
This strenuous 2-mile (3.2km) round-trip takes you exploring below the rim. Gaping canyon views will reward the brief but prodigious effort.

O3 S.O.B. Draw
Hiking the North Rim Inner Canyon is no picnic, hence its name. Reserved for experienced hikers, the steepest trails feature chutes and handrails. This one drops a steep 2 miles (3.2km) in two hours – but then the solitude's all yours.

What to spot...

High on the Colorado Plateau, the Black Canyon of the Gunnison is home to a unique vertical wilderness composed of diverse elements. On the plateau, pygmy forest and oak flats once provided edible pine nuts and firewood to early inhabitants. Precipitous cliffs provide shelter for bighorn sheep and raptors. On the canyon floor, trophy trout, beavers and chokecherry thrive in river and wetlands. Bring the binoculars – birdwatching here is excellent, especially in spring and early summer.

MULE DEER Named for their long ears, these elegant deer are ubiquitous in the park. Look for their spotted fawns early in summer.

GREAT HORNED OWL With a 5ft (1.5m) wingspan, this is the Americas' largest native owl. It hunts over the canyon rim in sweeping night patrols.

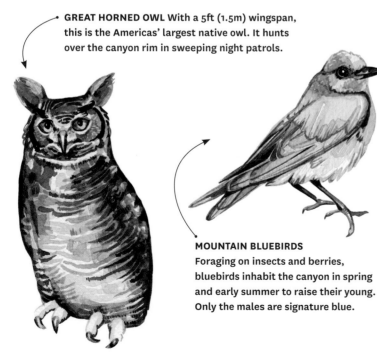

MOUNTAIN BLUEBIRDS
Foraging on insects and berries, bluebirds inhabit the canyon in spring and early summer to raise their young. Only the males are signature blue.

44

Itineraries

One of the smallest parks but challenges abound: rollercoaster drives, steep hikes and wild camping for the adventurous.

◀ Cast for trout in the Gunnison River; rainbows are catch-and-release only.

▲ A local coyote; looking out over the canyon.

01

A day

In the US West the landscapes come oversized and unwieldy. Not so with Black Canyon of the Gunnison National Park, a compact treasure by local standards. A visit to this haunting chasm offers appreciation for the visual diversity of Colorado.

Take the scenic drive along the paved South Rim route, stopping at the Visitor Center for the exhibits on resident wildlife. A little preparation is conducive to potential sightings, best at dawn or dusk.

The South Rim has a dozen scenic overlooks. Black Canyon's metamorphic rock was likely volcanic debris built up on the floor of an ancient sea billions of years ago. It's worth examining the canyon from all angles, since the steep, south-facing wall contrasts with the more eroded north wall, thick with vegetation.

Stroll the 0.8-mile (1.2km) Cedar Point Nature Trail which leads to a river overlook with a 2000-ft (610m) drop. Stop to admire the Painted Wall, the state's tallest cliff, and rock islands that spike from the canyon floor.

02

A weekend

Follow the day-trip itinerary for the first day of your visit. Set up camp at the riverside East Portal Campground. It's accessed via a rollercoaster drive to the canyon floor, where the howls of coyotes punctuate summer nights.

Day two is for adventure. Plan your trip in advance and you will have a shot at the park's most coveted permit: to hike Red Rock Canyon to the Gunnison River. The most gradual descent to the canyon floor at 3.4 miles (5.5km) one-way, it boasts fly-fishing and wild-camping. A lottery system held in early spring issues permits for this partially private route. Come prepared. The stream crossings require careful navigation and poison ivy lines the way.

Another option is to tour the North Rim by car via gravel road. Views from the North Rim are the most vertical and most impressive. Make a brief stop to hike the short Chasm View Trail. Arrange to go horseback riding on Deadhorse Trail or take on the challenging S.O.B. Draw and hike to the canyon floor.

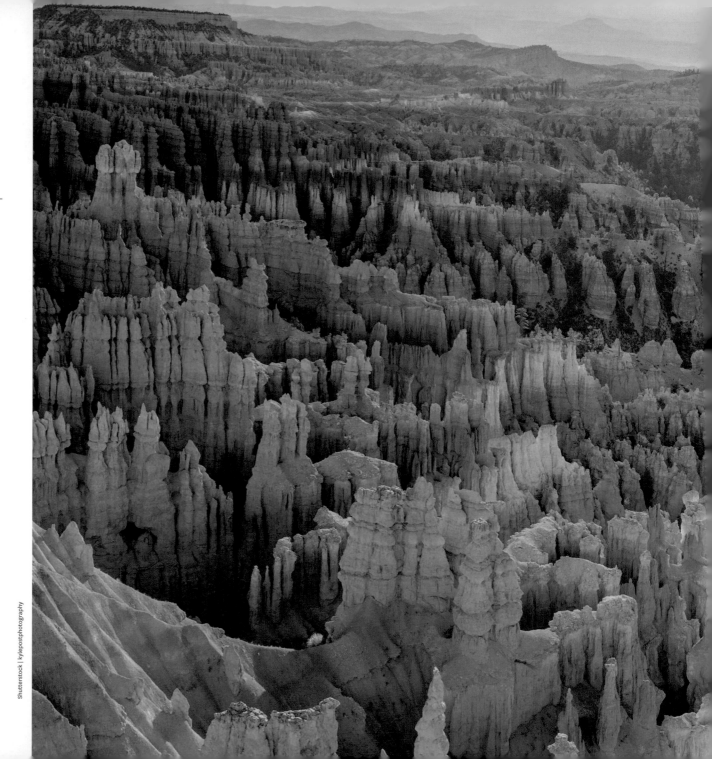

08

UT

Bryce Canyon National Park

Salvador Dalí would have felt right at home wandering this utterly surreal collection of rock spires, slot canyons, arches and castle-like mesas.

Shutterstock | kylepostphotography

The landscape of Bryce stirs your imagination – hoodoos (tall, thin towers of rock) become totem poles carved with strange faces, mesas turn into ships sailing on pink seas, cliff walls look like pulled taffy, buttes become ancient fortresses. The wonderful bizarreness goes beyond the geological formations. Bryce is home to living trees that were saplings around the fall of the Roman Empire. It shelters the delicate, fuchsia Bryce Canyon Paintbrush, a wildflower so rare it was only discovered in 1965. Bryce's skies are so clear you can see all the way to the Andromeda Galaxy, 2.2 million light years away. This is a place of magical extremes, among the finest and strangest sights the world has to offer.

Despite its name, Bryce is technically not a canyon, but a series of natural amphitheaters carved into Utah's Paunsaugunt Plateau, the largest of which is 12-mile (19.3km) Bryce Amphitheater. Limestone was carved by frost and rainwater into whimsical and extravagant shapes, turning the park into the top step of what's known as the Grand Staircase, the enormous geological terrace that includes the Grand Canyon.

Paleo-Indians hunted large mammals in Bryce during the last Ice Age. Later, the Ancestral Puebloans hunted its meadows, and Paiutes gathered pine nuts in the piñon groves. In the 1870s, Mormon settlers Ebenezer and Mary Bryce began cattle-ranching in what's now the park; when visitors marveled at the canyon's beauty, Ebenezer Bryce reportedly told them, 'It's a helluva place to lose a cow.' The canyon became locally known as 'Bryce's,' and the name eventually stuck.

Railroad companies began pushing

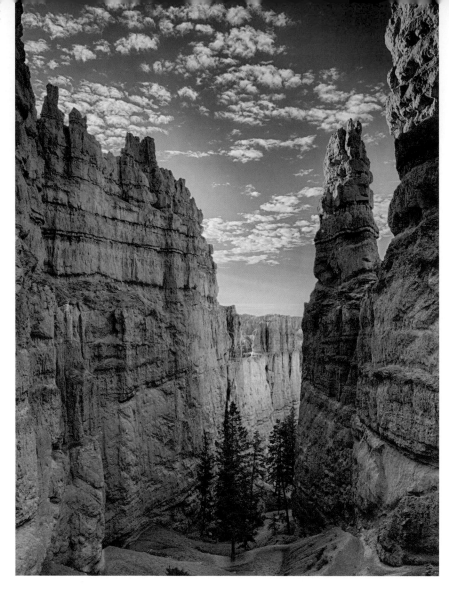

southern Utah as a destination in the early 1900s: 'Colorful – colossal – sublime,' reads a Union Pacific ad for Bryce from 1927. The park was established in 1928 and expanded in the 1930s. Today, it's one of the smaller national parks, often visited in conjunction with nearby Zion.

⬆ The Navajo Loop Trail. Previous page: Bryce Canyon's iconic hoodoos.

Toolbox

When to go
Summer is crowded, so spring and fall are good picks (though they can be chilly at this elevation). In winter, the park turns into an icicle-hung snowy wonderland, but many services are closed.

Getting there
Bryce Canyon is in southwestern Utah. The nearest airports are Salt Lake City and Las Vegas, both about 270 miles (434.5km) away. Closer small airports are in Cedar City and St George, Utah. There's a park shuttle, but you'll need a car to get here.

Events
June's astronomy festival and July's geology festival have ranger-led activities. The week before Christmas is the annual bird count.

Accessibility
Most viewpoints are wheelchair-accessible, as is a 0.5-mile section of the Rim Trail.

Park in numbers

56 Area in sq miles
9105 Highest point: Rainbow Point (ft)
200 Number of Utah prairie dogs in the park

Stay here...

🏠 **Bryce Canyon Lodge**
Built during the 1920s' railroad boom, this is Western 'parkitecture' at its finest, all stone and log and dark-green roof shingles. Guests cozy up to the big stone fireplace in the timbered lobby, relax in hickory rockers on the porch or dine on bison burgers. Accommodations range from small studios and hotel rooms (some accessible) to cabins with fireplaces.

🏕️ **North Campground**
This enormous year-round campground has sites set within stands of shady pines. There's a full complement of amenities – showers, camp store, laundry, etc. Walk up a short hill for views across the canyon; at night, there's plenty of space for gazing at the shimmering Milky Way. It's first-come, first-served. Some of the sites are accessible to people with limited mobility.

🏠 **Ruby's Inn**
A mile (1.6km) north of the park entrance, this sprawling complex has been serving guests for a century. In addition to 400 motel rooms and a campground, there's a grocery store, two gas stations, a post office, laundry facilities, restaurants, and a pool. The Best Western–run facility can arrange any kind of tour you desire – ATV, horseback, plane, walking or sleigh.

Do this!

🔵 **Horseback riding**
Trot along like an 18th-century explorer on the 5.5-mile (8.9km) Peek-a-Boo Loop trail, which takes riders through stunningly varied terrain. Gawp at the Wall of Windows, a series of arches and hoodoos looking like the fortress wall of some ancient desert kingdom. Canyon Trail Rides offers both horses and mules for riding (weight limit 220lbs/100kg).

📷 **Photographing**
The park's most famous viewpoint, Bryce Point offers boggling views across the Silent City, a forest of hoodoos like Martian skyscrapers. The point is a fenced-off outlook jutting over the canyon floor 1000ft (305m) below. In late afternoon, the sinking sun turns the hoodoos a deeper and more alien orange, and shadows play along their craggy edges.

✨ **Stargazing**
Bryce's remoteness makes its night skies as dark as black velvet. You can see an average of 7500 stars here, compared with a mere 2500 in most parts of America. In high season, rangers lead multimedia night-sky programs, followed by stargazing with telescopes. In summer there's a four-day astronomy event: you've never seen the Milky Way so luminous or Venus as radiant as you will here.

What to spot...

Though Bryce's arid spires and crevices may seem inhospitable, the park is home to a variety of plants and animals perfectly adapted to the habitat. Prairie dogs guard their nests in the meadows on the north side of the park, golden-mantled ground squirrels scurry around the base of piñon trees, mountain lions prowl the snowy backcountry in winter, short-horned lizards blend in with trailside pebbles and Clark's nutcrackers perch in juniper trees.

BLACK-CHINNED HUMMINGBIRD These thumb-sized birds breed in the West before heading to winter in Mexico. Spot them by their metallic green backs; only males have black heads.

PONDEROSA PINE Towering ponderosa pine trees dominate the West. Recognize them by their large scales of bark and bright-green needles. You'll find them throughout the park.

BRISTLECONE PINE These gnarled trees are among the oldest living things on earth – the oldest bristlecone is going on 5000 years old! Spot them on Fairyland Loop and Bristlecone Loop.

Hike this...

O1 Bristlecone Loop Trail
See the ancient, weathered bristlecone pine trees along this easy, 1-mile (1.6km) loop, which also takes in hoodoos and long vistas across the canyon.

O2 Fairyland Loop
Loose the crowds with this strenuous 8-mile (13km) rim and canyon hike, passing Chinese Wall, Tower Bridge, and skyscraping hoodoos.

O3 Under-the-Rim Trail
The park's longest trail stretches 23 miles (37km) along creeks and lush runoff oases and past natural arches and painted cliffs. Permits are required for the eight backcountry campsites.

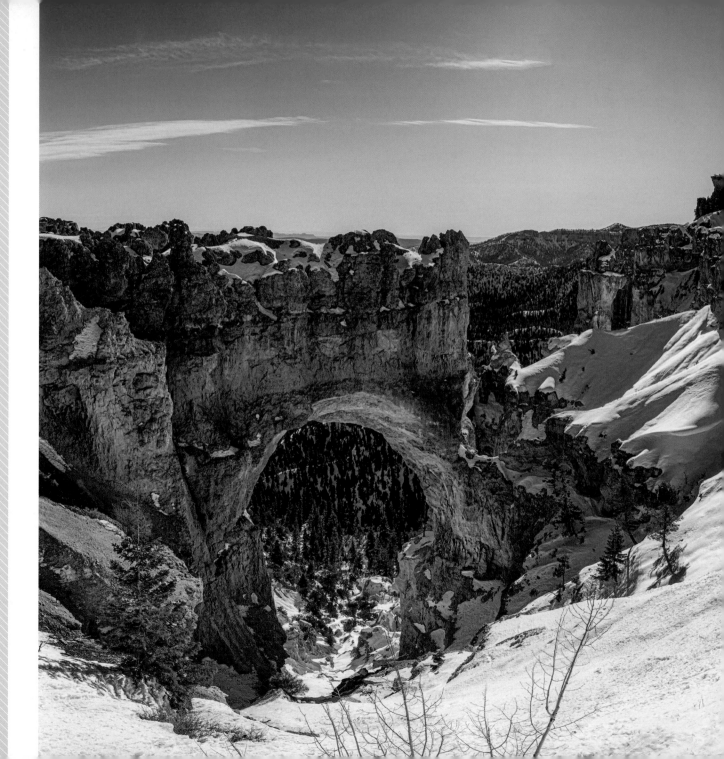

Itineraries

See why Bryce Canyon Scenic Drive got its name, catch some unbelievable sunrises, then hit the rodeo and gorge on buffalo steak.

 A bristlecone pine tree; Natural Bridge is one of several rock arches in Bryce Canyon.
 Hiking the Queen's Garden Trail.

01

A day

Get the most bang for your buck in a short time by driving Bryce Canyon Scenic Drive. This 17-mile (27.4km) road starts at the visitor center and winds south along the rim as far as Rainbow Point. At the very beginning you'll hit three of the park's most iconic viewpoints in quick succession: Sunset Point, Sunrise Point and Inspiration Point. All offer mind-blowing views onto psychedelically shaped hoodoos and mesas glowing red and gold in the sunlight. A little further down, Bryce Point is a don't-miss, with primo views across Silent City.

At Swamp Canyon, take a stroll through the towering pines for close-up views of the canyon's pink walls. Have lunch at the picnic area a few miles further on. Sandwiches taste that much better when eaten gazing over the yellow-and-white layer cake of Noon Canyon Butte. Don't miss the arch at Natural Bridge, which has been defying gravity for millennia. Take in the sunset over Rainbow Point, watching the color slowly drain from the mesas as the sun goes down in a ball of flame.

02

Two days

Begin day one at Fairyland Point; its slightly isolated location makes it quieter than nearby Sunset and Sunrise points. With your backpack loaded with food and water, descend down the 8-mile (13km) Fairyland Loop Trail, which circles the vastness of Boat Mesa, passing primeval bristlecone pines and wandering beneath the shadows of hoodoos that look like something out of a surrealist painting. Keep your eyes open for short-horned lizards and (very occasionally) rattlesnakes.

When you drag yourself, exhausted, back to the rim, treat yourself to a dinner of Wasatch Range buffalo steak or elk chili at the dining room in Bryce Canyon Lodge. On day two, wake early to see the sunrise turn the canyon pink and yellow. Bryce Point is a choice spot for this purpose. Head south on the Bryce Canyon Scenic Drive, hitting the major viewpoints and pausing for a picnic lunch overlooking the mesa. Near the end of the road, take time for a hike along 1-mile (1.6km) Bristlecone Loop Trail.

03

Four days

On day one, get your bearings with a drive down Bryce Canyon Scenic Drive, stopping to gawk (and maybe take a selfie) at the world-class viewpoints. On day two, warm up your legs with a moderate hike along the Navajo Loop and Queen's Garden trails. You'll see Thor's Hammer, traverse the claustrophobic slot that is Wall Street and gaze over Silent City. On day three, book a horseback ride down the Peek-a-Boo Loop Trail. The steep drop-offs to the canyon's distant dusty floor add a touch of thrill to this varied ride. Highlights include the otherworldly Fairy Castle and the mammoth Cathedral. Wake up early on day four for sunrise over Bryce Point, then cool off with a short walk to Mossy Cave, near the park's north end. In the winter, the cave is fringed with icicles like tinsel on a Christmas tree. If it's summer, treat yourself to a night at the rodeo, just outside the park at Ruby's Inn (Wednesday through Saturday only), along with a plate of ribeye at Ebenezer's Barn and Grill.

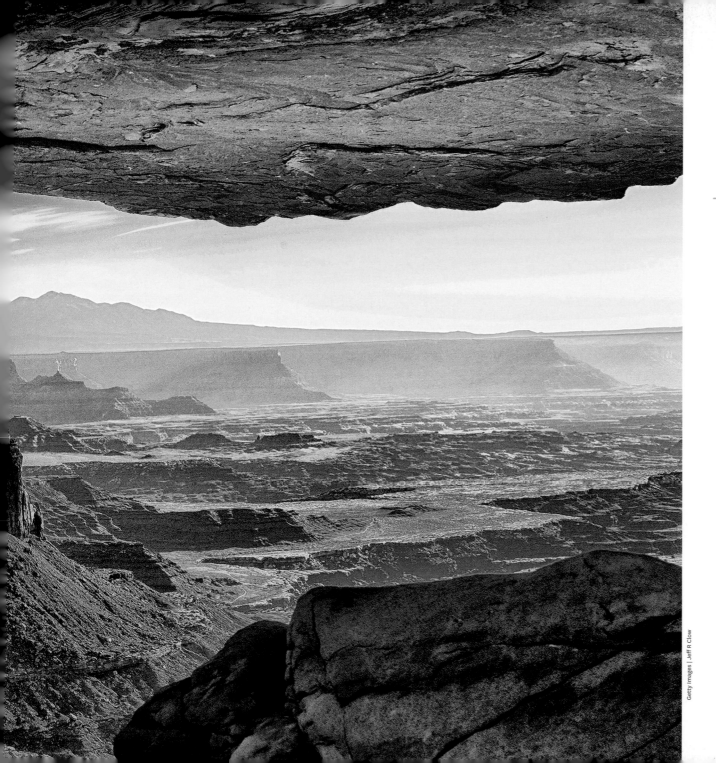

09

UT

Canyon- lands National Park

Mighty rivers carved this high desert plateau into an adventure-ready patchwork of soaring mesas, crumbling pinnacles, graceful arches and impenetrable red rock canyons.

Canyonlands makes you wonder about your place in the universe. With sheer cliffs dropping more than a thousand feet, rugged mesas stretching into the horizon and a vast night sky sharing clear views of the Milky Way, it's easy to feel unmoored. Which might explain the allure of Mesa Arch, a gold-and-crimson span stretching delicately across the rim of the park's central mesa. By directing your gaze and framing a handful of distant sandstone formations, Mesa Arch renders the landscape accessible, less terrifying. You feel as if you're admiring a landscape portrait in Mother's Nature's living room. Mesa Arch is especially beautiful at sunrise, when the fiery sun sets the rocks aglow.

The Colorado and the Green Rivers merge in the northern section of the park, forming a 'Y' that divides Canyonlands into three distinct districts. In the center is the Island in the Sky District, which sprawls across a flat-topped mesa with sweeping views over the Needles and the Maze. Island in the Sky sees the most visitors, luring travelers with unique geologic formations and overlooks perched atop sheer walls. The Needles District is a storybook wonderland of orange-and-white sandstone pinnacles. The Maze, packed tight with labyrinthine canyons and bad roads, is the most remote and inaccessible of the districts. Hiking, canyoneering and other terrestrial adventures are huge here. Or take to the rivers for multi-day adventures to see the canyons in a whole new light.

The park lies within the Colorado Plateau, a 130,000-sq-mile (336,698 sq km) tableland of layered sedimentary rocks that began forming hundreds of millions of years ago. Ten million years ago geologic

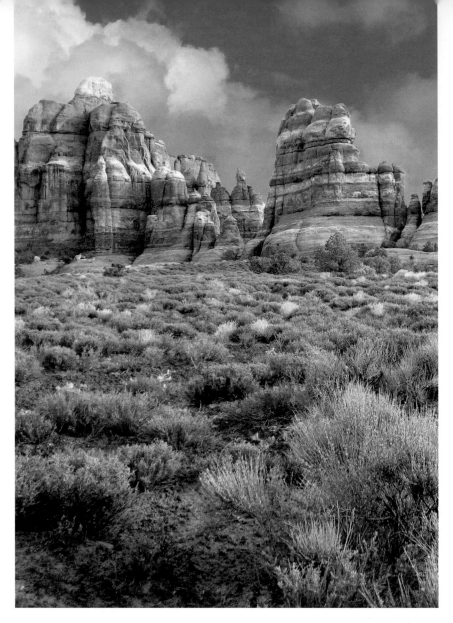

forces pushed this tableland skyward; water carved the spires, arches and bridges. A high desert park, Canyonlands experiences very cold winters and hot summers, and sees less than 10in (25cm) of rain per year.

The park earned an International Dark Skies Park designation in 2015, meaning it's one of the best places in the world to stargaze, with minimal light pollution and vividly clear views of the cosmos.

Shutterstock | Elena Arrigo

Toolbox

When to go
For ideal temperatures, visit in April, May or from mid-September through October. Expect daytime highs from 60°F (16°C) to 80°F (27°C). The temperature drops 30°F (17°C) at night. Summer highs top 100°F (38°C).

Getting there
The park's three sections, are not connected by roads within the park. Island in the Sky is 30 miles (48km) from Moab. The Needles is 75 miles (121km) south of Moab. Dirt roads link Hwy 24 and the Maze, a 3½-hour drive from Moab.

Events
National Public Lands Day, the fourth Saturday in September, is a day to give back, volunteer or just enjoy free park access.

Accessibility
The Island in the Sky District is the most accessible of the park's districts, with paved trails. River trips are a good way of accessing wilderness.

Park in numbers

527 Area in sq miles
7120 Highest point: Cathedral Point (ft)
350 Number of bighorn sheep in the park

Stay here...

 Willow Flat
Ah, sweet solitude. There are only 12 campsites at this lonely campground, which sits atop the Island in the Sky mesa. Well-situated, it's a short distance from the Green River Overlook, Aztec Butte and Mesa Arch.

Squaw Flat
How would you like to pitch your tent beside toadstool red rocks in a campsite at the end of the map? This 26-site campground in the Needles District feels a thousand miles from the modern world, but camping here allows you to sleep-in before hitting nearby trails. (Those hikers staying in Moab? They've got a 90-minute drive to get here.)

Under Canvas Moab
Live the dream of a Victorian explorer in this deluxe glamping spot, a short drive from the Island in the Sky District. Beneath canvas tents you will find all the appointments of a five-star hotel, including king-sized beds – and yes, running water and a shower.

Do this!

Mountain biking
Ready to grunt, sweat and kick up some red dust? Built by uranium prospectors, the 100-mile (160km) dirt-road White Rim Trail loops around the base of Island in the Sky mesa. Steep, exposed switchbacks, dropping from the mesa top to the canyon floor, start the fun. The ride takes about three days; campsites dot the trail. Back-country permits are required: check the park website or visitor center.

Stargazing
Viewing the silky Milky Way from the top of the Island in the Sky district is breathtaking. In the spring and fall, rangers from Canyonlands and nearby Dead Horse Point State Park lead star talks, which are followed by stargazing and telescope-viewing. Canyonlands is an International Dark Skies Park.

Rafting
Class III-V rapids keep the ride wild in Cataract Canyon, just south of the confluence of the Colorado and Green rivers. Local outfitters offer multiday trips. You can also take on your own adventures in a canoe through Labyrinth and Stillwater Canyons on the Green River.

◀ Rock needles in Canyonlands National Park. Previous page: Mesa Arch at sunrise.

What to spot...

In this scrubby high desert, mammals, amphibians and reptiles have adapted to temperature extremes and the unforgiving landscape. Who survives? The quickest, the wariest, the nocturnal foragers and those that are masters of camouflage. Eleven species of cactus grow in the park, including the prickly pear. Cottonwood trees and willows thrive near rivers and streams (which are a birder's delight). Look for wildflower blooms in April and May and again in early fall after summer monsoons.

MOUNTAIN LION
These wide-ranging hunters prey on mule deer and other small mammals, which keeps populations in check. Quiet and elusive, mountain lions are rarely spotted by visitors.

KANGAROO RAT The kangaroo rat doesn't need to drink water – ever! That's right, this desert wunderkind gets all the water it needs from gnawing on plants. Expert long jumpers, these athletic rodents can jump up to 9ft (2.7m) in just one hop!

UTAH JUNIPER This stubborn desert tree seems to thrive on conditions that would destroy other plants. Extreme temps? High winds? No water? No problem. Often seen growing from barren rock outcrops, it's supported by a sprawling root system persistent in its search for water.

Hike this...

01 Mesa Arch & Grand View Point
Short trails lead to big views atop the Island in the Sky mesa. Mesa Arch Trail ends with inspiration; Grand View Trail ends with an exclamation – and a step back from the rim. Mesa Arch Trail is a 0.5-mile (0.8km) round-trip; Grand View Trail is 2 miles (3.2km).

02 Chesler Park/Joint Trail
Striped pinnacles, desert grasslands and slot canyons impress on this 11-mile (17.7km) loop in the Needles District.

03 The Maze
Accessed by 4WD, The Maze is for experienced backcountry enthusiasts only. On multiday treks – you'll need a permit – you will find solitude, exposure, lost rock art and incredible canyoneering.

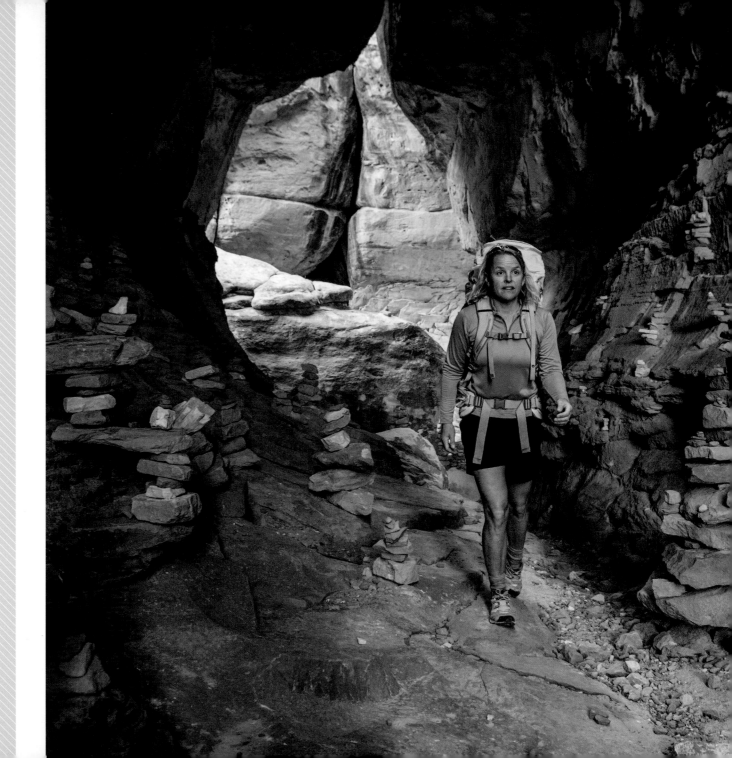

Itineraries

It's all epic roadtrips in this Thelma & Louise *setting. But mountain-biking, whitewater rafting and hiking fans won't be disappointed either.*

◄ Mesa Arch viewpoint; hiking in the Needles District of Canyonlands National Park.
➡ Driving the Island of the Sky route.

01
A day

Got your camera? Water and lunch? And your hat? Then you're ready for the Island in the Sky District, which sits atop a mesa. On your way, detour to Dead Horse Point State Park. From its 2000ft-high (610m) perch you'll enjoy sweeping views of the Colorado River and the Canyonlands. Remember the movie *Thelma & Louise*? This is where the duo soared over the abyss.

At the Island in the Sky Visitor Center, check the daily schedule for ranger-led programs and hikes. Next up is a cruise on the scenic

road, which is dotted with mesa-rim overlooks, short trails to big views and plenty of odd-shaped rocks. For the biggest wows, drive 12 miles (19.3km) to Grand View Point. The expansive views of the park from the overlook are stunning, but stunning jumps to epic at the end of the 1-mile hike (1.6km) to the point, which serves up a glimpse of a sheer drop down the mesa wall.

Savor your picnic at the Grand View Overlook, then head to a ranger talk. Feeling spry? Then hike 0.5 miles (0.8km) to the viewpoint at

Upheaval Dome, a circular depression that may have been created by a meteor strike 60 million years ago. Stop by the Green River Overlook, and then it's time for the end-of-day showstopper: Mesa Arch. This slender arch stretches across the rim of the mesa, framing Washerwoman Arch, Monster Tower and the La Sal Mountains. Mesa Arch is also popular at sunrise, when the span glows fiery red as the sun rises behind it. At the end of the day, burgers and microbrews beckon at Moab Brewery.

02
Two days

For sunrise views, secure a campsite at Squaw Flat Campground in the Needles District. Juniper trees and red rock cliffs provide shade for many sites on side A of the ground. After breakfast, stop by the Needles Visitor Center to watch the short movie *Wilderness of Rock*. Then explore the family-friendly sites and trails along the scenic road. The 0.6-mile (1km) Cave Spring Loop climbs ladders and traverses slickrock on the way to an abandoned cowboy camp. (Don't miss the handprint pictographs in the last cave!)

Other sights along the road include petroglyphs, arches and an Ancestral Puebloan granary. The Pothole Trail passes water-filled basins. This is a nice trail for watching the sunset. Hard-core hikers may prefer spending the day on the Chesler Park/Joint Trail, which loops through grasslands and canyons. On day two, head north to Dead Horse Point State Park and the Island in the Sky District, stopping in Moab to pick up a picnic lunch. Allow time for afternoon scrambles to Aztec Butte and Whale Rock.

03
Six days

Ease into your red rock neighborhood with a one-day jaunt across Island in the Sky mesa, taking a detour to Dead Horse Point State Park. Spend your second day among spires and canyons in the Needles. The last few days? Choose your own adventure. Take a four-day bike ride and camping trip on the 100-mile (160km) White Rim Trail around the base of Island in the Sky District – or if white water is your passion, join a multiday guided trip through Cataract Canyon, where the Green and Colorado rivers collide.

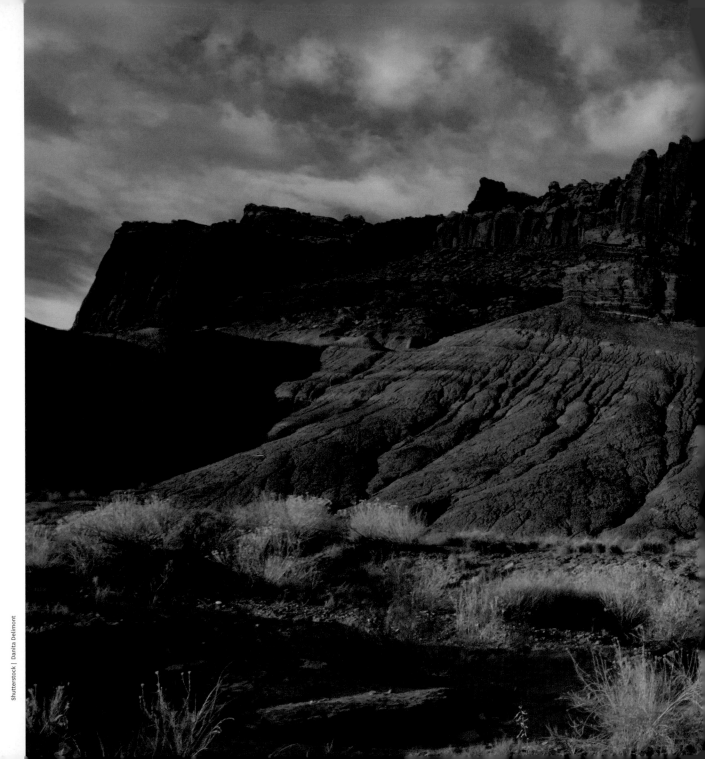

10

UT

Capitol Reef National Park

Once called the Land of the Sleeping Rainbow by Native Americans, this is canyon country at its dazzling best.

Shutterstock | Danita Delimont

It hardly matters that you've never heard of it. Among Utah's many visual riches, this one, large but low-key, has many facets. A wonderland of improbable formations, Capitol Reef is made up of red arches, stone domes, cathedral monoliths and terracotta canyons. It's a geography so convoluted that Butch Cassidy once used it as a hideout.

Visitors explore its serpentine paths, raise dust on its rugged 4WD roads and admire its thousand-year-old rock art. The park has 150 miles (240km) of hiking trails, with the longest and most established routes in the northern and southern sectors. At Gooseneck overlook, gaze out over the Sulphur Creek twisting its way through red rock. Road tours showcase breathtaking scenery on rough roads. Though the pioneers rode them in wagons, you will be much better off with a high-clearance 4WD.

It is all part of the Waterpocket Fold, a 100-mile-long (160km) buckle in the earth's crust that served as a barrier for explorers' westward migration like a reef blocks a ship's passage. The rest of the name comes from the park's white domes, thought to resemble the US Capitol building. At Capitol Reef's heart grow the abundant orchards of Fruita, a Mormon settlement dating back to the 1870s.

Before them, the Fremont people occupied the fertile floodplain of the Fremont River, growing grains, squash and lentils until the 13th century, when their settlements were abandoned. Some of their granaries and intriguing petroglyph panels remain for visitors to peruse.

Yet history runs even deeper here. Scientists have discovered that this area is

part of the oldest megatracksite in North America, with trace fossils from sharks and reptiles that roamed the earth even before the dinosaurs. Capitol Reef has always been a land of transformation – and thus, enchantment – an ancient seabed that is now a majestic desert.

◨ Summer blooms in Capitol Reef National Park. Previous page: cottonwood trees in fall colors along Fremont River.

Toolbox

When to go
Most travelers prefer to visit in spring or fall, as summers bring intense heat and monsoon thunderstorms. Visit between June and October and pluck ripe fruit from the trees for a small fee.

Getting there
Capitol Reef is 3½ hours by car to Salt Lake City, which has international flights. The best way to travel through Southern Utah is by car, or 4WD to explore the backroads. Accommodations and services are in Torrey.

Events
Celebrate the 4th of July with Torrey Apple Days, a long weekend of events including a pie eating contest. In August, the Boulder Mountain Half-marathon and 5k is held.

Accessibility
There's wheelchair accessibility to the Visitor Center, Fruita Campground, scenic overlooks and the petroglyph panel.

Park in numbers

390 Area in sq miles
887 Plant species
2700 Fruit trees

Stay here...

 Fruita Campground
Welcome to your desert oasis. Set under sturdy cottonwood trees along the Fremont River, this park campground is also surrounded by historic barns and orchards planted by Mormon settlers. It's no wonder it's so popular. It's also central to hiking trails.

Torrey Schoolhouse B&B
Black-and-white portraits of fidgety generations of schoolchildren line the hallways of this restored 1914 schoolhouse. With antiques and country elegance, it's solid brick on the outside and full nostalgia on the inside. For today's guests it's a sound sleep and a gourmet breakfast with travelers from around the world.

Lodge at Red River Ranch
Modeled after the great Western ranches, this immense timber lodge in Teasdale invokes an upscale cowboy sensibility. Guests enjoy country quilts, Navajo rugs and a sprawling great room. The red-rock surroundings are sublime, especially if you want to take in the constellations from the outdoor hot tub.

Do this!

Mountain biking & driving
The best of the desert lies along its backroads. Long-distance mountain bikers and 4WDers love the bumpy, roughshod 58-mile (93km) loop route through Cathedral Valley. It's the ideal way to explore the park's remote north, with its alien desert landscapes, pierced by giant sandstone monoliths eroded into fantastic shapes.

Fruit-picking
The first Mormon homesteaders arrived here in 1880; Fruita's final resident left in 1969. Among the historic buildings, the NPS maintains 2700 cherry, apricot, peach, pear and apple trees planted by early settlers. Pick fruit in season or enjoy a picnic surrounded by deer and songbirds – a desert rarity.

Exploring ancient culture
Rock-art carvings (called petroglyphs) can be found at roadside panels or deep into the dusty backcountry. From bighorn sheep to horned beings and spirals, these riddles, clues or remnants speak to the 2000-year-old culture of the Fremont people. You can find the most accessible petroglyphs along Hwy 24 just east of the Visitor Center.

What to spot...

A variety of habitats, such as piñon-juniper, perennial streams, dry washes and rock cliffs, offer microhabitats and niches that allow for diverse plant and animal life in the park. Even the fragile biological soil crusts play a major role in the ecosystem. More than 300 animal species live here, including a number of lizards, snakes and reptiles in addition to deer, coyote and small rodents.

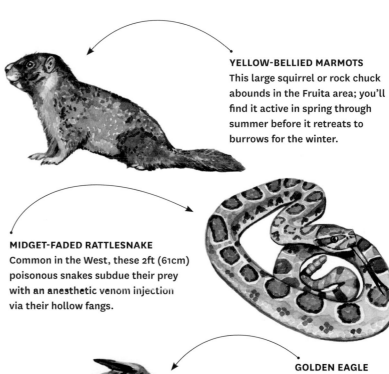

YELLOW-BELLIED MARMOTS
This large squirrel or rock chuck abounds in the Fruita area; you'll find it active in spring through summer before it retreats to burrows for the winter.

MIDGET-FADED RATTLESNAKE
Common in the West, these 2ft (61cm) poisonous snakes subdue their prey with an anesthetic venom injection via their hollow fangs.

GOLDEN EAGLE
Brown with golden neck plumage, this eagle is a prized sighting in the park. Agile and quick, it swoops down from the cliffs to claim rabbits and marmot as its prey.

Hike this...

O1 Grand Wash Trail
This 2.2-mile (3.5km) walk through the narrows grows dramatic as the canyon walls reach 80 stories high – and only a car's width apart.

O2 Navajo Knobs
For superb views of the park and beyond, follow a high slickrock ledge for 9 miles (14.5km) to these twin knobs perched on the edge of the Waterpocket Fold.

O3 Upper Muley Twist Canyon (overnight)
With arches and sculpted narrows, this twisting 15-mile (24km) route drinks in expansive views, and opportunities for exploration. Overnight camping permits are obtained at the visitor centers.

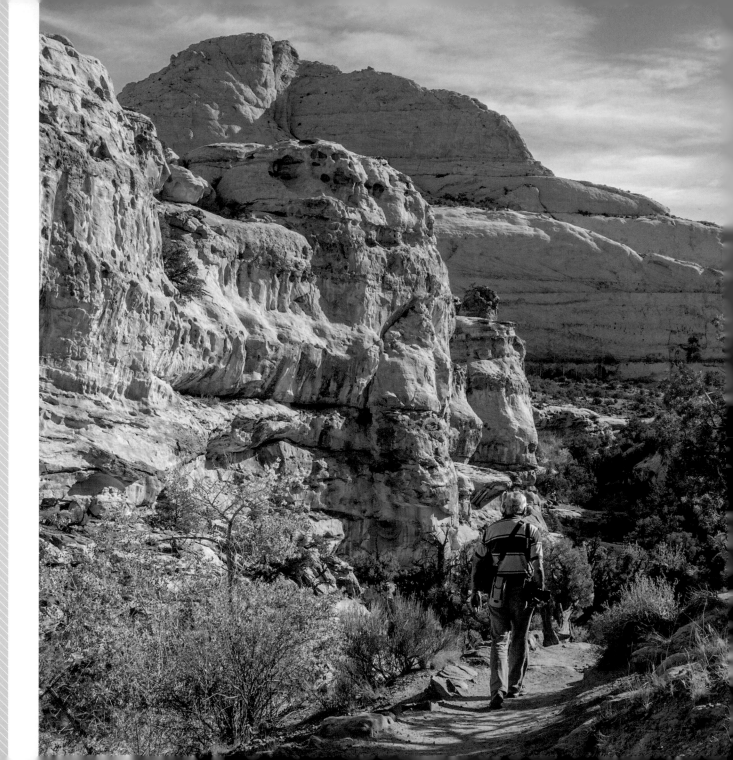

Itineraries

Whether you drive or hike, Capitol Reef's red rock art is a must-see. Combine it with some backcountry 4WD odysseys, fortified by Fruita's fruit pies.

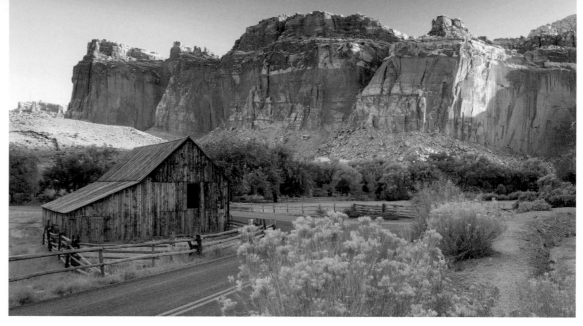

← Navajo Knobs; hiking Hickman Bridge trail.
→ A historic barn in Capitol Reef.

01
A day

In the heart of Utah's canyon country, Capitol Reef sits between Canyonlands and Bryce Canyon national parks along Utah Hwy 24. Many visitors do a pass-through. Do it justice by spending the day.

In the desert, first light is the coveted hour to hike. Much of the hiking here is shadeless, and sandy paths radiate heat. By noon, you want to be snoozing under a cottonwood or wading into the Fremont River. Start at Capitol Gorge Trail, a 2-mile (3.2km) round-trip through a sheer-walled canyon wash with petroglyphs, historic sites and secret watering holes. Break for lunch in the shade of the Fruita orchards.

Along Hwy 24, visit the petroglyphs. There's also a historic schoolhouse and the one-room 1882 Behunin Cabin, once home to a family of ten. The park's scenic drive was actually the main highway until 1962. This skinny, zig-zagging road gets you up close with the buckling Waterpocket Fold. Its final miles are the most stunning, passing Capitol Dome and the Golden Throne as it reaches deep passages of the gorge.

02
A weekend

Follow the one-day itinerary. Pitch your tent at Fruita Campground and pick up dessert from the small store next door – the fruit pies sell out daily. Catch the evening ranger program for insights on local culture or ecology. The next morning, hit the trail early.

How ambitious are you? If the answer is very, take Cohab Canyon and the Frying Pan link over the top of the Waterfold to reach Cassidy Arch – you'll find canyons within canyons, fragrant juniper forest and undulating slickrock criss-crossed by lizards. The Cassidy Arch is approached from above; walk it like a pirate-ship plank if you dare. It's 7 miles (11km) one-way, but easiest if you make it one-way and shuttle a car to the end at the Grand Wash parking area.

Finish the trip with a drive along 58-mile (93km) Cathedral Valley Loop in a 4WD vehicle. Late in the day is the golden hour for a photo safari: long shadows add to the drama of the many monoliths of Cathedral Valley and its hills banded with rainbow hues.

03
One week

Nothing says adventure like the lines of a topographic map. If you have the right set and know how to use it, backcountry hiking is awesome here, with solitary trails, sculpted landscapes and starlit nights.

Spend days one and two at Capitol Reef and Cassidy Arch. Stock up on supplies at Mesa Farm Market, the fresh cheese and artisanal bread justify the detour to Caineville, then sort out backcountry permits. Head north to the Cathedral district for roadless expanses marked by stunning monoliths with names like Temples of the Sun and Moon (it's all that). Or journey to the southern Waterpocket district to explore its diverse landscapes of slot canyons, arches and slickrock. There are lots of options, but all require hauling drinking water, and some a 4WD vehicle.

If you have time, drive Loop the Fold, a scenic, 124-mile (199km), part-paved trail that circles the Waterpocket by several iconic routes, including the burly Notom-Bullfrog Rd, an odyssey through curious formations and kaleidoscope colors.

11

NM

Carlsbad Caverns National Park

Hidden beneath the cactus-covered ridges of the Guadalupe Mountains lies a sprawling, subterranean wonderland of soaring chambers and otherworldly features.

Elaborately carved by the slow hand of time, the magnificent underground rooms and glittering passageways of Carlsbad Caverns feel like a portal into another realm. It's hard to imagine a more dramatic transition than to leave the desert air behind and step through the cool, utterly silent tunnels, with every twist and turn revealing a wondrous collection of artfully wrought formations.

The magic and mystery of Carlsbad becomes all the more apparent when you realize the extraordinary processes that created these sparkling chambers. It all began some 250 million years ago, when a large but shallow inland sea covered this area, along with a horseshoe-shaped reef that stretched for 400 miles (644km). As

the climate changed and the earth evolved, the reef was buried under deposits of salt and gypsum. A few million years ago, uplift caused the ancient reef to rise some 2 miles (3.2km) skyward, creating large cracks and fissures. Over the following millennia, rainwater seeped into the cracks, fresh water mixing with saltwater to create sulfuric acid, its corrosive power slowly shaping the massive underground chambers. The birth of the caves as a magnificent work of nature began about one million years ago, as rainwater, drip by drip, seeped through the layers of the earth, each droplet depositing a tiny mineral load of calcite – thus creating the spectacular array of stalactites, stalagmites, soda straws, helictites, draperies and cave pearls.

Although little early human evidence

has been found inside the caves, Native American tribes left their mark in the area, including a 1000-year-old pictograph near the main entrance. Carlsbad's fame, however, really began with Jim White, a 16-year-old cowhand who entered the caves in 1898 – a discovery that would change his life. He became the first to explore the caves and named many of its rooms and major formations (the Big Room, King's Palace, Bottomless Pit, Witch's Finger). He was also the cave's biggest promoter, leading members of a scientific expedition and later serving as the chief ranger of the caves.

⬆ Stalactites and stalagmites in Carlsbad Caverns, deep in the Guadalupe Mountains.
➡ The Chandelier.

Toolbox

When to go

It's worth planning a trip around the nightly bat flights, which happen May through October. Specific caving tours are offered only certain times of the week; advanced reservations are recommended. To beat the crowds, avoid coming on busy holiday weekends.

Getting there

Set in the southeastern corner of New Mexico, the park's closest airports are in El Paso, 140 miles (225km) southwest, and Midland, 160 miles (258km) east. Rental cars are available at either airport.

Events

Some weekends in December, the park stages 'The Rock of Ages', a lantern-lit tour with costumed performers.

Accessibility

An elevator gives access to the main cavern. Once there, the Big Room Trail is accessible. There's also accessible parking, picnicking and dining.

Park in numbers

73 Area in sq miles
1604 Deepest point (ft)
120 Number of known caves

Stay here...

The Trinity Hotel

Set against the big skies of southeastern New Mexico, this historic 1892 building was once a bank; you can almost imagine the row of horses saddled up out front. Overnighting here is a journey back to a bygone era, when the southwest was still a mysterious and little-known frontier. Except with great Italian-Amerian food to dine on.

Fiddler's Inn

You'll receive a warm welcome when you roll up to this tranquil B&B located a few blocks west of Lake Carlsbad. Julie and Tonk, who plays the fiddle (hence the inn's name), make you feel right at home, regaling you with stories of their own travels and sharing their favorite places in Carlsbad.

Backcountry camping

For a true back-to-nature experience, pitch your tent on national park land a short drive from the caverns. Gazing out over the landscape with no human presence in sight is pure magic; by evening you can catch dramatic sunsets, then watch the Milky Way light up the sky. Pick up a free backcountry permit at the visitor center (no reservations).

Do this!

Bat-watching

From May to mid-October, hundreds of thousands of Brazilian free-tailed bats roost in the caves. The nightly exodus happens just after dusk; you can watch from an amphitheater built near the cave entrance. Around sunset, rangers give a short presentation describing these fascinating mammals, before the bats take to the Chihuahuan Desert in search of food.

Stargazing

The night sky is exceptionally dark in this remote corner of New Mexico – seeing the Milky Way and hundreds of stars and constellations is not to be missed. The Caverns hosts periodic 'star parties,' where visitors can gaze through telescopes. Rangers also lead dark-sky wilderness walks to point out celestial wonders on short hikes into backcountry.

Hiking

Outside the caves, you'll find extensive hiking trails, from short, 0.5-mile (0.8km) ambles (like the Chihuahuan Desert Nature Trail) to more challenging multi-day treks, such as the 100-mile (160km) Guadalupe Ridge Trail that starts from Texas's highest point and ends in White's City, New Mexico, on the park's eastern border. The GRT takes you into real wilderness.

Explore this!

01 Big Room Trail

The jewel of the national park takes you on a 1.25-mile (2km) loop past astonishing formations of all shapes and sizes. Highlights include the Hall of Giants, the glistening Crystal Spring Dome and the soaring Temple of the Sun.

02 Lower Cave

Adventurers will enjoy this three-hour tour taking in an amazing array of formations, including cave pearls and the stalactite-filled 'Texas toothpick.' Descent is by 60ft (18.3m) of ladders and a knotted rope at the cave's entrance.

03 Rattlesnake Canyon

Take a break from the underground on one of the park's desert trails. This 5.5-mile (9km) out-and-back hike follows a steep descent into a side canyon, past the ruins of a 1930s homestead. Expect fabulous views.

What to spot...

Set in the Guadalupe Mountains and surrounded by the Chihuahuan Desert, Carlsbad Caverns has several distinct habitats, chief among them desert shrublands. Although this is a semi-arid environment, it is one of the wettest deserts in North America, with an average of 14.4in (around 37cm) of rain per year. This helps support a diverse ecosystem, including 67 mammal species, 357 bird species and more than 900 plant species.

BRAZILIAN FREE-TAILED BATS
The mammalian star of Carlsbad Caverns is the Brazilian free-tailed bat, which has a wingspan of 11in (28cm) and weighs just 0.5oz (14g) – about as much as three nickels. More than 400,000 of these insectivores roost in the caves.

TULIP PRICKLY PEAR This striking desert plant is found all across the southwest. The flowers grow atop flattened green, spiky pads, and typically have yellow petals with reddish coloration toward the base.

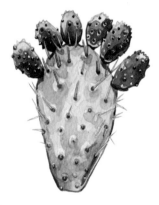

GIANT DESERT CENTIPEDE These impressive-looking creatures can grow up to 8in (20cm) in length and are capable of delivering a nasty (though not life-threatening) sting. Swift and agile, they typically hunt at night.

Itineraries

Bat cave or spider cave? There's plenty of both creatures to observe here, along with stunning cavern formations. Or just hike the trails under sunset desert skies.

← Stalactites drip down, stalagmites grow up.
→ Subterranean hiking.

01

A day

Get an early start by arriving at the caverns around opening time, at 8am. In the early morning, the winding drive in to the park can be magical, with the desert landscape bathed in a golden light. If you're in good shape, skip the elevators and make the long descent to the cave entrance on foot, as it gives a fine perspective on just how deep underground – 750ft (229m), or about 79 stories – you're going. Once at the entrance, paths lead to the mesmerizing Big Room – the largest single cave chamber in North America. It's a wonderland of glittering, sculpture-like formations of all shapes and sizes, from massive columns to elaborately carved stalactites and such curious depressions as the Bottomless Pit.

Once you finish the circuit, take the elevator back up to the surface and grab a bite to eat in the cafeteria. Then head out for a 9.5-mile (15.3km) scenic drive through the otherworldly landscape of the Chihuahuan Desert along the Desert Loop Rd. Keep an eye out for mule deer and javelinas, a small mammal also known as a collared peccary that, despite pig-like appearances, is only very distantly related to wild boar.

Around dusk, return to the cave entrance to watch the bat flight program, when huge swarms of Brazilian free-tailed bats fly out of the cave in the fading light of day for their nightly feeding: a mesmerizing end to the day and your cue to head on to Carlsbad.

02

Three days

After the self-guided tour, scenic drive and bat-watching on day one, spend your second day delving deeper into the caverns.

Sign up for one of the private ranger-guided tours. Peel back the centuries on a two-hour guide tour through Left Hand Tunnel. There you'll walk by candlelight (lantern provided) through a fascinating and undeveloped section of the cave.

Later in the afternoon, take a walk along the Old Guano Road, which was used for hauling out the phosphorous-rich deposits (aka bat manure) in the early 1900s. The 3.7-mile (6km) (one-way) desert trail takes you past the ruins of the old mining industry, while offering a sweeping panorama of the Guadalupe Mountains. Later, as the light-free skies fill with stars, end the day with guided stargazing (via telescope) led by a park ranger.

On day three, take a walk along the Rattlesnake Canyon Trail, one of Carlsbad's most scenic hikes. The 5.5-mile (9km) round-trip starts at the top of the mesa ridge and takes you into a bone-dry canyon, with dramatic views along the way. You'll pass a wide array of desert flora, and might hear the coo of a Bobwhite quail, stumble upon a few pronghorn, and spy a few spotted skunks slinking along the parched lowlands. End the day back at the visitor center, watching the desert turn an auburn glow at sunset.

12

Channel Islands National Park

Off SoCal's sunny coast, these islands – nicknamed 'California's Galapagos' – harbor abundant wildlife and memorable adventures by land and sea.

If you've ever dreamed of sailing off the edge of the world, this may be as close as you'll ever get. It's hard to believe these utterly remote islands were once populated. But when you step off the boat onto these ancient rocks, you will be following in the footsteps of indigenous people who arrived here more than 13,000 years ago. Chumash tribespeople paddled *tomols* (canoes carved out of redwood logs) across the channel and built villages here, followed much later by European explorers, seal and abalone hunters, livestock ranchers, shipwrecked sailors and smugglers.

Even more fascinating than the story of people in this place is the islands' remarkably varied wildlife. Many animals and plants that exist here are found nowhere else on the planet, making a vivid display of evolutionary biology. For other species endangered now or in the past, the islands have been a safe haven, including for such animals as northern elephant seals, northern fur seals (called 'sea bears' by 19th-century European explorers) and migratory gray whales, which pass by every winter. For visitors, the islands present an unequalled opportunity for wildlife spotting, whether you want to hike your way across windy bluffs or kayak around the coast.

Each of the park's five islands is unique. Anacapa, the island closest to the mainland, comprises three tiny islets totaling less than a square mile; in springtime thousands of nesting seabirds crowd every available inch of space here. Santa Cruz, the next island further west, is almost a hundred times larger, and features Mount Diablo, a 2450ft-high (747m) peak, and one of the largest sea caves in the world, Painted Cave. Santa Rosa, the second-largest island, abounds with archaeological sites and fossil finds – try to imagine what it looked like during the Pleistocene Epoch, when miniature mammoths roamed across the landscape.

Toolbox

When to go
Fair autumn weather brings calmer seas for water sports. Spring sees colorful wildflowers, but also fog and strong wind that may persist into summer. Late summer is hot and dry. Winter can be stormy, but it's spectacular for wildlife-watching.

Getting there
Most people arrive by boat, either on an organized tour or a boat ride from Ventura, off Hwy 101 in Southern California, between Los Angeles and Santa Barbara. Flightseeing planes depart from Camarillo, closer to LA.

Events
The Channel Islands Harbor Parade of Lights takes place every December. The whale-watching season runs from late-December to mid-April

Accessibility
The mainland visitor center in Ventura and the Santa Barbara contact station are both accessible but, due to the terrain, the islands are not readily accessible.

Park in numbers

390 Area in sq miles
145 Species found nowhere else in the world
5 Number of islands

Stay here...

The only way to stay overnight on the Channel Islands is to camp. No matter which island you choose to visit, advance reservations are required – both for campsites and boat transportation. Come prepared for a primitive wilderness experience, far from any of the creature comforts of civilization.

Backcountry camping
Both Santa Cruz and Santa Rosa islands offer limited backcountry camping by permit. The reward is isolation, big views and windswept solitude on the edge of the world.

Santa Rosa Campground
On Santa Rosa Island, this mid-sized campground is tucked into a windy canyon, where campsites are partly sheltered by lean-tos and eucalyptus trees. It's a flat 1.5-mile (2.4km) walk from the ferry dock.

Anacapa Campground
From the ferry dock, it's a steep 0.5-mile (0.8km) walk that ascends over 150 stairs to reach these sunny, exposed campsites with unforgettable ocean views. Don't forget to pack in all the water you'll need.

Do this!

Kayaking
Paddle your own kayak beneath sea arches and towering cliffs, or explore marine caves from the inside out. Beginners can start with a shoreline float around Santa Cruz Island, putting in at Scorpion Beach for easy access to sparkling clear waters.

Diving & snorkeling
Don a mask and plunk your face down into the ocean to peer at schools of brightly colored fish darting around kelp forests. The orange garibaldi, California's state marine fish, is particularly easy to spot. These islands also offer some of the best scuba diving in the US. Divers might even encounter a giant black sea bass weighing a whopping 800lb (363kg).

Tidepooling
Set far from the crowded, overdeveloped mainland, the islands' tidepools are protected by Mother Nature. Around every island's shoreline, rocky pools harbor a spectacular array of rainbow-colored marine critters, including hungry sea stars, spiny urchins, clinging barnacles and mussels, and tiny periwinkle snails.

← Playful California sea lions off Anacapa Island.
→ Gray whales are a common sighting in the Channel Islands.

Hike this...

O1 Inspiration Point
Soak up Anacapa Island's best views on this 1.5-mile (2.4km) trail, which passes Pinniped Point, where sea lions haul out to sunbathe.

O2 Cavern Point & Potato Harbor
On Santa Cruz Island, climb a steep 5.5 miles (8.9km) for clifftop vistas and whale-watching, then hike atop the bluffs to a picturesque harbor.

O3 Cherry Canyon
Traipse 3.5 miles (5.6km) through riparian wetlands on Santa Rosa Island, detouring to white-sand Water Canyon Beach or to summit Black Mountain.

What to spot...

California's Channel Islands were something of a primeval Garden of Eden before the arrival of humans. Their isolation spurred the evolution of marvelous biodiversity, just as Darwin observed in the Galapagos Islands. After centuries of environmental abuse, such as rampant livestock grazing, oil spills and military bombing practice, the islands are now on the road to recovery. In recent decades, ambitious conservation projects have restored lost habitat and protected rare wildlife, however the 'Scorpion Fire' in 2020 damaged Santa Cruz Island.

CALIFORNIA SEA LION The most playful of the islands' pinnipeds like to bark, bask on the sand and splash around in the surf, then dive deep for squid.

NORTHERN ELEPHANT SEAL Once in danger of going extinct, these enormous beasts are thriving again on the islands, where they mate and give birth in winter.

CALIFORNIA BROWN PELICAN These pouch-billed birds were officially endangered until 2009. Today, the only known breeding colonies are on Anacapa and Santa Barbara Islands.

Itineraries

Spend a day on Anacapa Island or several on Santa Cruz or Santa Rosa. There's plenty of snorkeling and swimming on offer.

 Purple sea urchins populate the ocean floor.
 Divers will spy wildlife large and small.

01

A day

Have a light breakfast before boarding the boat to Anacapa Island – the channel crossing can be a bit bumpy for landlubbers. Spy wild dolphins chasing your boat through the water as you sail toward Landing Cove, while iconic Arch Rock appears on the horizon. Arriving on the island, firmly grasp the metal ladder rungs and scramble up onto the wooden dock, then climb a steep stairway until you pop out atop the islet, where panoramic ocean views welcome you.

Drop by the island visitor center to watch a live scuba-diving broadcast or to join a ranger-guided program. When you're ready, 2 miles (3.2km) of hiking trails await outside. But there's no rush, because you can see it all in an afternoon – just don't miss the last boat back. Start hiking toward Inspiration Point, pausing at Pinniped Point to peer down at a noisy California sea lion colony. In spring, look for colorful wildflowers alongside the trail. On the return hike, detour to Cathedral Cove, another spectacular lookout over captivating rock formations.

02

Two days

See more than day-trippers ever do on an overnight camping trip to Santa Cruz Island. The morning ferry drops you off at curvy Scorpion Beach, where brightly colored kayaks are lined up on the sand. Heave-ho with your backpack for the 0.5-mile (0.8km) walk to the campground, where island foxes run around (note that you're not allowed to feed them). After setting up your tent and having a picnic lunch in the shade, head back to the beach for an afternoon of swimming and snorkeling when the ocean is calm.

Get up early the next day and step into your hiking boots. It's a huff-and-puff climb from the campground up to Cavern Point, but you'll be rewarded by stunning panoramas of cliffs and coves. Follow the rolling North Bluff Trail out to Potato Harbor. Passing through a eucalyptus grove, loop back to the campground and pack up your gear. Poke around the historic buildings of Scorpion Ranch on your way back to the beach to catch the last afternoon ferry.

03

Three days

After sailing 40 nautical miles (74 nautical km) off the California coast to Santa Rosa, you'll want to stay at least a night or two, especially with so many places to explore. The boat ride takes just over two hours – or you can pay more for a faster flight that touches down on the island's dirt airstrip.

Set up base camp at the sheltered canyon campground, then hoof it back to gorgeous, white-sand Water Canyon Beach. If it's not too windy, picnic tables fronting this 2-mile (3.2km) strand are a perfect spot for lunch before a bit of beachcombing. The next morning, pack a day-pack for a long hike through grassy Cherry Canyon and, if you're up for it, all the way to the top of Black Mountain.

On your third day, walk just as far as you feel like along the coastal road toward East Point, passing rare Torrey pine trees and hidden beaches. Pack up camp after lunch and go meet the afternoon boat to reluctantly return to civilization.

13

SC

Congaree National Park

Canoeing through the black waters of Congaree – Spanish moss dripping overhead, muffled bird-cries in the distance – is a journey into South Carolina's heart of darkness.

Congaree is 41 sq miles (106 sq km) of Southern Gothic landscapes. At the park's southern boundary, the wide, brown Congaree River snakes past forest and bluff, its waters alive with fish, turtles and snakes. The park's interior is the largest old-growth bottomland forest in the southeastern US. Here, you'll find a fairyland of floodplain trees: bulbous cypress with fluted trunks; towering swamp tupelo overgrown with emerald-hued lichen; water hickory with strips of peeling bark like wallpaper in an old mansion. These dark swamps hide a bestiary of reptiles, amphibians, insects and birds, as well as the occasional snorting feral pig – not to mention mosquitoes. (Bring your bug spray!)

The Congaree people who fished these waterways were largely killed off by smallpox introduced by European settlers around 1700. The new settlers tried their best to make the land farmable, but flooding washed away their efforts time and again. Eventually, in the early 1900s, logging operations bought up the land, cutting down the bald cypress and floating it down river. But logging, too, proved difficult, thanks to the bogginess of the land, and the loggers ultimately left the area to nature. Half a century later, high timber prices led private landowners to consider logging again. The Sierra Club, horrified at the thought of the pristine land being destroyed, led a campaign to have the land protected, and the Congaree Swamp National Monument

was established in 1976. In 2003, the monument became a national park.

A casual day-visitor will enjoy checking out the displays in Congaree's visitor center and ambling down the well-kept boardwalk trail nearby. But the swamp-lover who wants to take a deeper look can spend days paddling Congaree's shallow, vegetation-choked waterways, fishing in its still lakes and camping on its bluffs. At night, the hoots of owls and the guttural croak of frogs, pierced by the occasional coyote howl, makes civilization feel very far away indeed.

⬆ A boardwalk empire in Congaree National Park.

Toolbox

When to go

Congaree is open year-round, and the temperate climate makes it pleasant to visit any time. While it's rarely crowded, on weekends the campsites can play host to local scouting troops and college groups.

Getting there

Located in the state of South Carolina, Congaree is a 30-minute drive from the capital city of Columbia, home to a major airport. It's two hours from the popular vacation destination of Charleston. You'll need your own car.

Events

Fall foliage colors are a big draw from September through November.

Accessibility

The park's 2.4-mile (3.9km) Boardwalk Trail is entirely wheelchair accessible, as is the visitor center.

Park in numbers

41.5 Area in sq miles

167 Tallest tree (ft)

0 Park entrance fee ($)

Stay here...

Longleaf Campground

Congaree's accommodations are two primitive campgrounds; Longleaf ($10/night) has car access while Bluff ($5/night) does not. Get close to nature here, camping under the pines with no amenities (beyond a fire ring, picnic table and chemical toilet), waking to the hammering of woodpeckers. Water is available 24/7 at the visitor center. Reservations necessary.

1425 Inn

South Carolina's capital, Columbia, is the nearest non-camping place to stay when visiting Congaree. This sweet Southern B&B is about as far as you can get from a swamp, with its poster beds, claw-foot tubs and rocking chair–graced porch. The innkeepers earn high marks for Southern hospitality.

Hotel Trundle

Opened in 2018, this 41-room downtown boutique hotel has a whimsical vibe that seems made for Instagram: unicorn logo, bubble machines, eclectic, Art Deco-ish lobby. There's craft beer on tap at the check-in desk and gourmet popcorn at turndown.

Do this!

Canoeing

Paddling the dark waters of Congaree through primeval, old-growth forest is the number-one reason to visit the park. See otters, turtles, snakes and even (occasionally) gators as you pass beneath bald cypress trees dripping with Spanish moss. In the deliciously spooky heart of the swamp, it's almost possible to forget that civilization even exists.

Walking

Did you know that Spanish moss belongs to the same plant family as the pineapple? Learn fun facts like this on one of Congaree's 90-minute nature walks, led by volunteer naturalists every Saturday morning. Stroll the boardwalks as the guide points out air plants, wading birds and even the occasional snake while detailing what life is like in Congaree's 22 different plant communities.

Fishing

For a peaceful afternoon, paddle out into the middle of a wide brown Congaree waterway and drop a line. Fishing is allowed throughout the park (except for the Weston Lake overlook) with a South Carolina fishing license. Catches include largemouth bass and catfish – deep-water holes and undercut banks make the Congaree River good territory for the latter, which can grow as big as hogs.

Hike this...

01 Boardwalk Trail

You can't visit Congaree without strolling this 2.4-mile (3.9km) elevated boardwalk through the old-growth bottomland hardwood forest. Pass beneath cypress, tupelo and loblolly pine, keeping your eyes open for turtles and snakes.

02 Fork Swamp Trail

One of the park's newest trails runs for 0.6 miles (1km) along the edge of Bates Old River, an oxbow lake created by a hurricane in 1852. Expect snakes and the occasional gator.

03 River Trail

Hike 10 miles (16km) through dense bottomland forest and into the pines on the way to the wide, coffee-colored Congaree River. Bring binoculars for the excellent bird-watching.

What to spot...

Knobby-kneed bald cypress and water tupelo fringed with Spanish moss abound throughout the floodplain, while higher elevations are shaded with tall pines. The swampy waters are home to turtles and salamanders; the river teems with bass, bowfin and catfish; and the trees host screech owls and a huge variety of warblers. Don't be surprised to see a cottonmouth or an alligator glide by your canoe. This is a swamp – OK, technically a 'floodplain' – after all.

BALD CYPRESS These tall swamp trees are easily identified by their bulbous bases and 'knees' – root structures that stick up around the trunk like bent legs.

SPANISH MOSS
Technically a flowering plant rather than a true moss, it looks like a gray beard hanging off the branch of a tree.

EASTERN BOX TURTLE Identify these reptiles by their distinctive orange-and-black shells. Adults are usually around 6in (15cm) long; males have red eyes.

Itineraries

Canoe or kayak past alligators and armadillos or stroll through the cypresses on the Boardwalk Trail. It's misty, swampy serenity here.

◄ Kayaking the mangroves of Cedar Creek.
▲ A foraging raccoon and a watchful barred owl.

01

A day

Get your bearings by wandering the Boardwalk Trail through the eerie bottomland forest, where the cypresses grow so thick hardly a drop of sunlight reaches the ground in summer. The wooden walkway is only 2.4-miles (3.9km) long, but take your time to look for flocks of warblers flitting through the canopy, iridescent dragonflies landing amid the reeds, and red-bellied water snakes wriggling through the water. In the afternoon, hit the Weston Lake Loop Trail, meandering along a slough (dried riverbed) full of bulging cypress knees poking from the black water. If you get lucky, you'll see happy-go-lucky otters paddling around, and swamp birds racing across the water on spindly legs. Spend sunset fishing for catfish and crappie at Bates Old River (bring bug spray). Afterwards, camp by the pines at Longleaf Campground, waking early to see the mists rising over the swampland before heading out for a hearty Southern breakfast (we recommend the regional Waffle House chain, open 24/7).

02

Two to three days

The 50-mile (80.5km) Congaree River Blue Trail is one of the South's great weekend paddles. Launch your canoe or kayak in the city of Columbia, under the bridge at the West Columbia Amphitheater. Pass the turn-of-the-century Granby Lock and Dam, crossing via the lock on the right side, and glide into the Congaree Creek Heritage Preserve, with its stands of rare Atlantic white cedar. From here you'll mostly be on your own, passing the occasional ramshackle river cabin as you paddle deeper into the wilderness. The river is wide and sandy, with numerous sandbars perfect for a snack and a leg-stretch. Spend a night camping on the banks, watching the sun sink over the longleaf pines as the river turns from brown to black. On the second day you'll pass oxbow lakes, forested bluffs and muddy creek-mouths, spotting deer, turtles, egrets, snakes, alligators and maybe even an armadillo or feral pig. Spend a second night camping before finishing the paddle at Bates Bridge Landing on the third day.

14
OR

Crater Lake National Park

No matter how many times you've seen it, the stunning blue jewel that is Oregon's Crater Lake never fails to take your breath away.

Born of astonishing geological violence, the lake today radiates tranquility, while serving as a reminder of the fierce power of the natural world. It was created by the eruption of Mt Mazama some 7700 years ago. Over the course of just a few days, the mountain blew its top and then collapsed into itself, scattering ash across hundreds of thousands of miles and forming a caldera with sheer, steep rock walls. The caldera gradually filled with snow and rainwater to form Crater Lake. At 1943ft (592m), it's the deepest lake in the United States, and famous for the clarity and color of its water.

The lake and its surrounding area became a national park on May 22, 1902. It's one of the few places on earth where you'll find a volcano within a volcano: Wizard Island is a cinder cone that pokes up out of the water on the western side of the lake. Daily shuttles ferry visitors across to the island for hikes and exploration, but if you miss the boat you can also get good views from several vantage points along the rim. Look out too for the Old Man of the Lake, a floating tree stump – improbably vertical – that has been bobbing around the lake wherever the breeze takes it since at least the 1890s. The park is also home to the Crater Lake Science and Learning Center, which offers lab space and various facilities to support the study of natural resources by scientists, artists, students and teachers.

Whether you gaze out at the lake from the top of Rim Drive road, study it from a hiking trail along the rim, or cruise past volcanic islands on a ranger-led boat tour, Crater Lake is an experience you won't soon forget.

Toolbox

When to go
The lake is gorgeous in all weather but access is easier during summer. The park and main visitor center are open year-round; the Rim Visitor Center closes October to May, as do gas stations and most other facilities. Fire season is from July to August.

Getting there
Crater Lake is in southwest Oregon, about 65 miles (105km) northeast of Medford, 45 miles (72km) north of Klamath Falls. It's best reached by car.

Events
For 'Ride the Rim', East Rim Drive is closed to vehicles two Saturdays a year for cyclists and pedestrians.

Accessibility
Mazama Village facilities are accessible, as are Rim Village's lodge, café, picnic site, visitor center and most park restrooms. Godfrey Glen Trail is a 1-mile (1.6km) accessible loop trail.

Park in numbers

286 Area in sq miles
5 Volume of water in the lake (in trillion gallons)
6600 Years since most recent eruption

Stay here...

Crater Lake Lodge
Like many of its fellow lodges in national parks, this rustic 1915 beauty encourages lingering over a glass of wine at the fireplace in the Great Hall before retiring to one of its basic rooms. It's only a few steps from the caldera, so you can peer over the edge of the lake with minimal effort. Open from late May to early October.

Mazama Village Campground
Though it's huge, this campground near the park's south entrance is all nooks and crannies, arranged for privacy and surprisingly quiet. You'll wake up in what feels like remote wilderness, but you're only 7 miles (11km) from the rim of the lake, and as a bonus there are conveniently located services – gas station, grocery store, laundry, cafe – so you can gear up before venturing into the park.

Mazama Village Cabins
If you prefer comfy duvets, a hot shower and a roof over your head to sleeping in a tent, you're in luck: a bed and private bath await you in these cabins near the Mazama Village campsite. Best of all, from your hut you can poke your head out the door and smell the pine forest all around.

Do this!

Exploring
From the north side of Crater Lake, hike just over a mile (1.6km) along the steep Cleetwood Cove Trail down to the boat dock. A 45-minute shuttle ride takes you to Wizard Island, where you have three hours to hike around and explore on your own. The 75-minute boat trip includes rangers' explanations of the area's natural history. (The hike back up involves a 700ft (213m) elevation gain and can be strenuous.)

Cycling
The steep, narrow Rim Drive road circling the lake offers 33 miles (53km) of exciting bicycling. Start from park headquarters and make the loop clockwise to get the hardest part out of the way first. Elevation means the terrain can be challenging, and you may have to navigate traffic in busy periods.

Skiing & snowshoeing
In winter, nine trails of varying difficulty let skiers and snowshoers of all levels of experience and fitness explore the Crater Lake area. Ask for a map at the visitor center.

← In summer, Wizard Island in Crater Lake is accessible on two daily shuttle trips; there are also eight daily boat tours of the lake.
→ Western monkshood flower.

Hike this...

O1 Mount Scott
This 4.4-mile (7.1km) trail ascends the park's highest peak for epic views in all directions. For the best light, start early in the morning; the trailhead is on the lake's east side along Rim Drive.

O2 Garfield Peak
A steep, 3.4-mile (5.5km) round-trip hike delivers spectacular views of the lake and its surroundings. The trail starts near Crater Lake Lodge and heads east along the rim before ascending the peak.

O3 Pacific Crest Trail
A 33-mile (53km) stretch of this storied long-distance trail cuts through the park heading north to south, including an alternate route that hugs the rim for six miles.

Getty Images | Brinley Clark/EyeEm; Shutterstock | Robert Mutch

What to spot...

The high elevation of Crater Lake results in short summers and long, harsh winters, which means only the sturdiest of plants survive. Spring offers brief glimpses of early wildflowers, including Pasque flowers, lupine and Indian paintbrush. Animal life is plentiful and varied, but seldom seen: skittish deer, bear and pine martens inhabit the park's wild areas. Rainbow trout and Kokanee salmon live in the lake, introduced there by humans (no fish were native to the lake).

CLARK'S NUTCRACKER Not at all shy – and totally ignoring the 'Do Not Feed Birds' signs – these gray-and-black crows entertain visitors in hope of snacks.

SPOTTED OWL The lower-elevation conifer forests of the park are ideal for the spotted owl, a species made famous by its role at the center of debates between environmentalists and the timber industry in the 1990s.

MAZAMA NEWT Believed to be unique to Crater Lake, these rough-skinned amphibians have been threatened recently by the introduction of non-native crayfish to the lake.

78

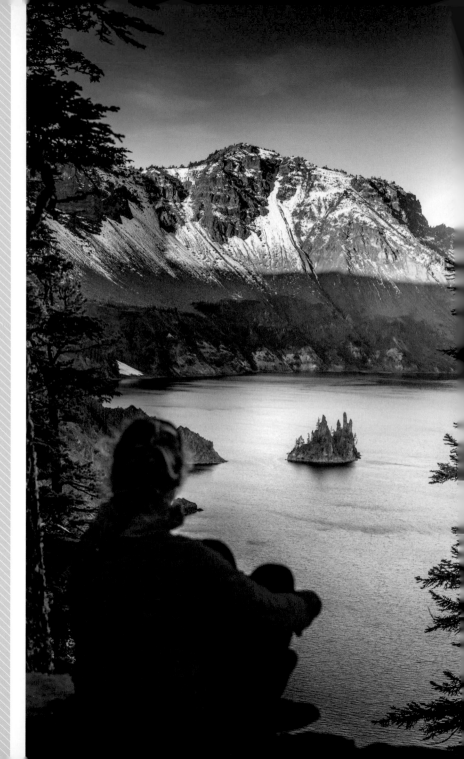

Itineraries

Whether you cruise Crater Lake or hike into Sky Lakes Wilderness, the birdwatching and scenic views reward. S'mores by a campfire are a perfect finish.

◄ Phantom Ship island in Crater Lake.
► Crater Lake Lodge dates from 1915.

01

A day

From the southern entrance at Mazama Village, drive to park headquarters in the Steel Visitor Center for a schedule of shuttle boats out to Wizard Island. Continue toward the lake, stopping near Crater Lake Lodge for a view of that famous blue water; fans of 'parkitecture' will want to check out the lodge itself, with its 1910s-era Great Hall. Then continue along West Rim Drive, stopping at Watchman Overlook for the first of many scenic views. About halfway around the loop road is Cleetwood Cove Trail, which takes you to a boat landing at the shore of the lake (be warned: it's a steep and difficult hike). If time and energy levels allow, walk down to the boat shuttle and take a cruise around the lake – they range from an hour or two to a full day with a stop at Wizard Island. Here you can spend three hours hiking, fishing or exploring. Afterward, head back the way you came or continue the drive along East Rim Drive, stopping at several overlooks, until you're back at park HQ.

02

A weekend

Stock up on cookout supplies (s'mores!) at the camping store in nearby Mazama Village, where you'll also want to top up the gas tank, fetch picnic supplies for the next day's lunch, and maybe pick up some souvenirs at the gift shop. Then follow the one-day itinerary, but instead of leaving the park at the end of the day, find a cozy campsite at Mazama Village Campground for the night.

Next morning, after a hearty breakfast at the Crater Lake Lodge, head out for a hike up to the rocky summit of Mount Scott, the highest point in the park, for gorgeous views – on a clear day you can see up to 100 miles. Leave plenty of time for birdwatching and scenic photographs, with a picnic lunch and, of course, a few selfies at the end of the hike. If you have time left over and want to rest your legs, hop onto a Crater Lake Trolley for a leisurely loop tour with a guide.

03

Three to four days

Up for a longer trek? Grab a map from the visitor center and aim for a spur trail heading southwest from Rim Village that connects to the Pacific Crest Trail, and extend your PCT exploration into an overnight backpacking campout. The trail heading south leads you into Sky Lakes Wilderness – be sure to carry a detailed topographical map and take all the usual backpacking precautions. Several intersecting trails allow you to turn this into a loop hike of various distances. Ask at the visitor center for details about trail conditions, where you can camp, whether there are campfire restrictions and what the weather forecast looks like. The recommended routes will vary from one year to the next, depending on things like snowpack and damage from the wildfires that ravage the area, so stay flexible and heed the rangers' advice. After your hike, celebrate with a night in a comfy bed, a hot shower and meal at the Crater Lake Lodge (book ahead).

15

OH

Cuyahoga Valley National Park

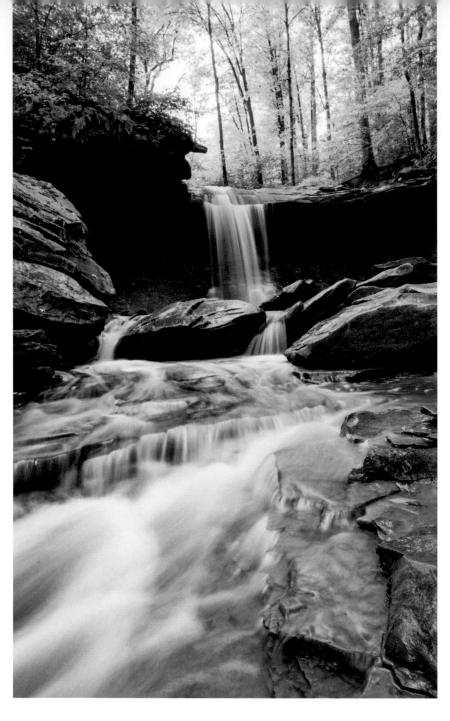

Amid the flowing curls of a crooked river, a verdant wonderland full of wildlife, waterfalls and historic trails transforms city folk into hiking, biking explorers.

Sandwiched between two cities and located in the middle of a geometric grid of freeways, Cuyahoga Valley National Park is an unlikely outdoor utopia – yet it offers 125 miles (201km) of hiking and horseback-riding trails, myriad cycling, camping and canoeing opportunities and a wealth of winter adventures. Even more surprising are the additional activities that can be enjoyed here, including golf, live concerts and even hitching a lift on a locomotive: Cuyahoga Valley is a park less ordinary.

Ohio's only national park lies between the cities of Cleveland and Akron. Over 12,000 years of human drama have played out in this valley, formed by the Cuyahoga River (the name means 'crooked river' in the Mohawk language) as it wends towards Lake Erie. Early occupants, Native Americans known as the Whittlesey people, mysteriously vacated the valley in the early 1600s. Beaver trappers, mountain men and new tribes moved in, but the Native Americans' claims to the area were quashed with the 1795 Treaty of Greenville, after which Ohio saw an influx of settlers.

Over the next 150 years, cities germinated and swelled, a canal was dug, a railroad built and roads developed. Granted easy access to the valley, urbanites fell in love with their wild backyard. Land was donated by Cleveland businessman Hayward Kendall, and during the Great Depression the Civilian Conservation Corps built most of the park's infrastructure.

Development threatened, and a petition began to push for park status. In 1973, the director of the NPS stated that it would become a park 'over his dead body,' but in 1974 President Gerald Ford approved the Cuyahoga Valley National Recreation Area, which was rebranded a national park in 2000. Its railways and fairways now form part of the patchwork of this peculiar park.

Toolbox

When to go

The park is open year-round, but spring and fall are the prettiest periods. Hiking and biking can be enjoyed most of the year, but in winter bring skis and sleds.

Getting there

Interstates I-80 and I-271 run through the park. Access is easy from Cleveland and Akron via the I-77 or Ohio State Route 8; visitor centers abound. Park entry is free.

Events

Catch live bands at the Cuyahoga Valley National Park Concert Series during the year. From November through mid-December, the Cuyahoga Valley Scenic Railroad transforms into the Polar Express.

Accessibility

All visitor centers are accessible, as are the park's top attractions: the Ohio & Erie Canal Towpath Trail, Everett Covered Bridge, Brandywine Falls (upper boardwalk), and the Scenic Railroad.

Park in numbers

51.3 Area in sq miles
125 Miles of hiking trails
39 Mammal species

Stay here...

🏕 Camping

Camping is no longer permitted within the park, although excellent places to pitch a tent lie within a 30-to 45-minute drive of Cuyahoga Valley. At Portage Lakes State Park (22 miles south), you'll find wooded sites, plus a beach and lake swimming. West Branch State Park (29 miles east) also offers lakeside adventures, plus 12 miles of hiking trails.

🏠 Shady Oaks Farm

Just one mile east of the park entrance, this family-run B&B makes for a rejuvenating getaway, no matter the season. The elegant rooms are furnished with antiques and period reproductions, and the wooded property has ample space to reconnect with nature – gardens, ponds, a walking trail, and views of a horse pasture. Expect a warm welcome and excellent cooked breakfasts.

🏠 The Inn at Brandywine Falls

Those who prefer a bit of pampering will luxuriate in the ambience and service at the Inn at Brandywine Falls. Overlooking Brandywine Waterfall, this historic building dates to 1848. Its hospitality is legendary.

Do this!

🚲 Cycling

Cycling the Ohio and Erie Canal Towpath Trail is virtually compulsory. Other bike-friendly paths include the Bike & Hike Trail. Rentals are available from Century Cycles in Peninsula. Most tracks are sealed, but the East Rim Trail, which opened in 2016, is oriented more for mountain bikers.

🎿 Winter sports

Once snow falls, Cuyahoga Valley becomes a wonderland for cross-country skiers, snowshoe-sporting trekkers and sled heads. Hire skis or snowshoes at MD Garage (across the river from the Boston Mill Visitor Center) and take to the park's many miles of snowy trekking trails. Off Quick Rd, the Kendall Hills offers prime conditions for sledding.

🪧 Scenic touring

Trains have been huffing and puffing through Cuyahoga Valley since 1880 and taking a ride on the scenic service is a highlight – especially when combined with a ride along the Towpath Trail. From the platform, hail the train by waving your arms in the air.

⬅ Blue Hen Falls after heavy rainfall in Cuyahoga National Park.
➡ Enjoy summer's wildflowers.

Hike this...

01 Ledges Trail

A slice of Middle Earth plunked into northern Ohio, this 2.2-mile (3.5km) loop has moss-covered rocks, lush forest, sandstone cliffs and a dramatic overlook.

02 Ohio & Erie Canal Towpath Trail

Around 20 miles (32km) of this historic route passes through the park, and hiking or cycling (or skating or skiing it) has become a must do experience.

03 Buckeye Trail

This epic, 1444-mile (2324km) circular walk around Ohio passes through the park. Combine one section of the Buckeye with the Towpath Trail to make an 8-mile (13km) loop starting and finishing at Red Lock, and passing scenic Blue Hen Falls en route.

What to spot...

The Appalachian Plateau and the Central Lowlands of America collide in the Cuyahoga Valley, creating a rich and healthy ecosystem. The skies above the park are busy with the activities of 194 species of birds, and in the forests and wetlands 900 plant species rustle as an eclectic collection of mammals, amphibians and reptiles go about their business. The river, too, is now in rude health, hosting 43 kinds of fish.

BALD EAGLE This iconic bird has returned to the park in numbers since the river's fish population rebounded. In November, watch them performing dramatic aerial courtship displays, diving and locking talons.

RACCOON Smart and crafty locals, raccoons can cope with the park's bitter winters, thanks to their dense underfur. Their distinctive face mask features in the mythology of several Native American tribes.

WANDERING GLIDER DRAGONFLY Ohio's wetlands are home to 157 species of dragonflies and damselflies, including the wandering glider (aka the globe skimmer), the planet's most common dragon.

82

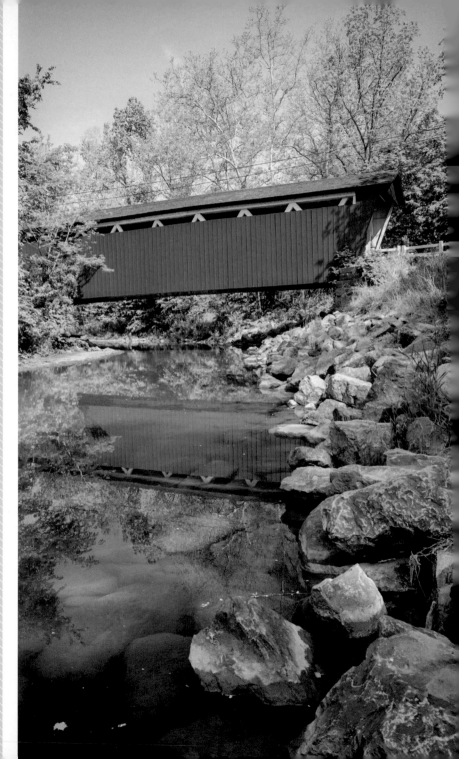

Itineraries

Brandywine Falls beckons with its boardwalks offering beaver spotting. Catch the Scenic Train or multitask on the Bike & Hike Trail.

◀ Covered bridges cross creeks in Cuyahoga Valley.
▶ The NKP-765 steam train on the Cuyahoga Valley Scenic Railroad.

01
A half-day

Free entry and easy access from surrounding cities make afternoon adventures entirely achievable in Cuyahoga Valley. Get a taste of the park's potential by wandering to one of the waterfalls, exploring a visitor center and spotting some wildlife.

The park's pin-up poster scene is Brandywine Falls, where the Brandywine Creek rushes off a 65ft-high (20m) drop in its haste to join the crooked river below. After an easy and short walk from the parking lot off Brandywine Road, you'll find boardwalks leading to observation platforms, where you can get close to the roaring cascade.

Grab lunch in the picnic area and then head west to the new Boston Mill Visitor Center, housed in a building dating to 1905. Interactive exhibits tell the tale of the Ohio and Erie Canal that runs through the valley, connecting Lake Erie to the Ohio River.

Finally, go looking for beaver, otter, muskrat and waterfowl along the wetland boardwalk that runs around Beaver Marsh, a stroll of 1.5 miles (2.4km) from the Ira Trailhead.

02
A day

The classic day trip to Cuyahoga Valley involves one thing: an adventure along the Towpath Trail. Twenty miles (32km) of the historic Ohio and Erie Canal passes through the park – a bit much for a day walk, perhaps, but ideal for a bike ride, especially since you can pedal one way and catch the Scenic Train back.

From Boston Mill Visitor Center, set off along the gloriously flat path. You could smash this in an hour or so, but with a packed lunch there's no point rushing – there are numerous picturesque picnic spots along the way.

Forests, fields, and wetlands line the trail as it flows through the Cuyahoga Valley. Occasionally the river itself makes an appearance, but the real highlight is spotting a couple of beavers in one of the wetlands.

Boarding the train at Rockside Station, grab a window seat and gaze out at the landscape you've just ridden through. It looks very different in winter, which might give you an idea – maybe come back in January to try skiing the Towpath...

03
Two or more days

To truly explore this ancient valley, you need to spend at least a night here, preferably under canvas – in blissful denial that the Ohio Turnpike is barely out of earshot.

Having spent the day in the saddle, cycling the towpath and circling back along the Bike & Hike Trail (one of America's first 'rails to trails' conversions), head to the Ledges in time for Cuyahoga's famous sunset –.all the more dramatic during fall foliage's fiery transformation.

Rise early the next day for a memorable foray along the Buckeye Trail, offering some of the state's finest scenery. Heading northbound from Boston Mill, you'll soon come across Blue Hen Falls – slightly smaller than Brandywine Falls, but every bit as impressive and with far fewer visitors. This sets the tone for a full-day hike, heading as far as you choose to go, before catching a train ride back to the Boston Mill Visitor Center. If you have another day to spare, consider getting out on the water. Just a short drive southeast of the park, you can kayak along the serene, forest-lined Cuyahoga River.

16

CA

Death Valley National Park

California's lowest, hottest and geologically oddest spot, Death Valley, is surprisingly full of life, especially when spring wildflowers bloom.

The air shimmers with heat. Looking out the windshield, you glimpse sand dunes on the horizon, as if this were a Hollywood adventure flick set in North Africa. Salt flats, where the earth cracks jaggedly open, look as if they could swallow a city whole. Stones secretively slip across the playa, leaving behind tracks in the dust of an ancient lakebed. Inside twisting canyons, rocks carved by eons of wind reveal a desert rainbow of shades: rust red, ochre, mauve, acid green and electric blue. Swirling around everything is an ocean of sand.

Driving through Death Valley, you'll miss subtle signs of life if you never stop the car. Get out and step close to a prickly pear cactus (look, but don't touch!). Spy on a desert tortoise sleepily emerging from its burrow, or spot a desert bighorn sheep, its curved horns proudly curling up into the sky, picking its way along a rocky ridge. The valley's fragile web of life all depends on water, hidden in springs or seeps. After winter and spring rains soak the parched ground, a profusion of wildflowers burst skyward, including purple Mojave asters, desert gold and orange globemallow.

Death Valley's name was bestowed by 19th-century emigrants in the gold rush, who became lost and almost died here. Later, prospectors moved in and dug mines for silver and other precious metals. The eerie relics of their endeavors stand along backroads through the desert, which preserves ghost towns as time capsules in its dry heat. Other unpaved roads lead to such spectacular vistas as Aguereberry Point, where you can see the 14,505ft-high (4421m) Mt Whitney, the USA's highest peak outside Alaska – then turn to look down over Badwater Basin, North America's lowest point, plummeting to 282ft (86m) below sea level.

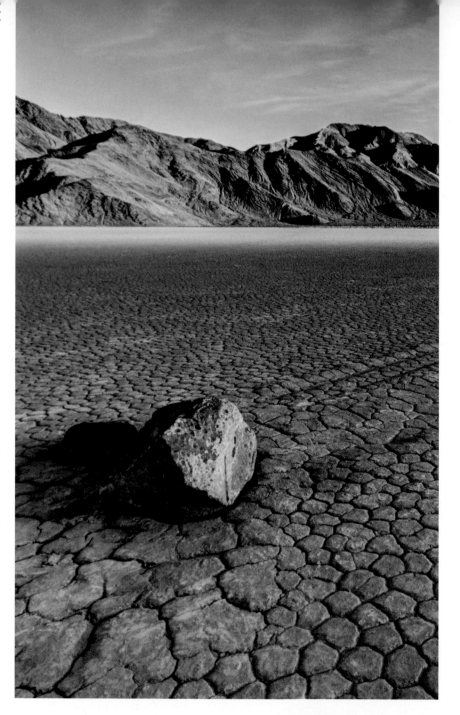

Toolbox

When to go
Spring is the busy season, when wildflowers bloom and temperatures are balmy. Autumn is another beautifully temperate time to visit. Winters remain mild at lower elevations, where summers are deadly hot.

Getting there
The park is located a two-hour drive from Las Vegas, Nevada, where you'll find the closest international airport. You'll need a car to get around this park.

Events
Billed as the toughest foot race on the planet, the 135-mile (217km) Badwater Ultra runs from Death Valley to Mt Whitney in baking July.

Accessibility
At Badwater Pool you'll find a ramp and boardwalk. With some assistance, you'll also be able to make it to the overlook at Zabriskie Point. Salt Creek, Dante's View and Harmony Borax Works all have accessible options.

Park in numbers

5347 Area in sq miles
134°F Highest recorded temperature (56°c)
282 Lowest elevation (ft below sea level)

Stay here...

🏠 **The Inn at Death Valley**
This completely renovated 1920s-era hotel has a tranquility spa, verandas with sweeping views, impossibly opulent gardens, spring-fed pools and amazing onsite amenities. Choose between tastefully updated rooms or one of the new private one-bedroom casitas.

🏠 **The Oasis at Death Valley**
Once a working ranch, this sprawling private inholding feels way more Palm Springs than Death Valley. There are gorgeously manicured lawns, pools and tennis courts, and a unique town square that feels straight out of a movie set. The mid-mod rooms feel swanky without being even a bit over the top. After all... this is California.

⛺ **Mesquite Springs Campground**
Campers who have visited the park before often head to this uncrowded spot first. Almost 2000ft (610m) above the valley floor, temperatures are refreshingly cooler here. With just 30 first-come first-served campsites, you'll feel like a pioneer when you pitch your tent beneath sheltering hillsides. Warning: winds may whip through, especially overnight.

Do this!

🪧 **Star Wars Tour**
The desert landscape might look familiar to Star Wars fans. Both *A New Hope* and *Return of the Jedi* had location shoots here. Top spots to geek out include Twenty Mule Team, Desolation and Golden canyons, Dante's View and the Mesquite Flat Sand Dunes.

🛞 **4WD driving**
To really get out and explore the wilderness, you'll need a high-clearance 4WD vehicle to tackle rough, rutted dirt roads, steep grades and sliding sands. The ultimate backcountry thrill is Titus Canyon, which slaloms downhill through the Grapevine Mountains, passing the ghost town of Leadfield and petroglyphs at Klare Spring. Rental 4WDs are available seasonally in Furnace Creek.

✨ **Stargazing**
Death Valley is officially the USA's biggest 'dark sky' national park. Roll out your sleeping bag, grab a star chart and contemplate eternity as you stare into the depths of the Milky Way and watch shooting stars (meteors) blaze overhead.

◀ Rocks wander the dry lakebed of Racetrack playa, moved by strong winds and ice. Previous page: Zabriskie Point.

What to spot...

Adaptation to a harsh, arid landscape has produced a spectacular diversity of flora and fauna in Death Valley. Over a thousand species of plants thrive here, along with more than 400 animals, ranging from the endangered pupfish – which is actually smaller than your thumb – to braying wild burros that roam the range, the descendants of pack animals set loose by mining prospectors. Desert wildlife is most active in the cool early morning and just after sunset.

DESERT TORTOISE Inhabitants of the Mojave Desert for millions of years, these slow-moving reptiles are now threatened by habitat loss, predators and disease.

DESERT BIGHORN SHEEP These elusive, sure-footed mammals are hard to catch sight of, but look for them on mountain ridges and sheer cliff faces.

CALIFORNIA BARREL CACTUS These spiny, portly and ribbed succulents bloom with yellow flowers in spring – and occasionally grow taller than a human being.

Hike this...

01 Cottonwood-Marble Canyon Loop
Best accomplished over three days, this 26 mile (42km) loop takes you into some of the wildest canyon country the park has to offer.

02 Mesquite Flat Sand Dunes
The lure of rolling, golden sand dunes is irresistible – take a 2-mile (3.2km) trek across them in dazzling sunshine, or at night under a full moon.

03 Wildrose Peak Trail
At cooler, higher elevations, a strenuous, 8.4-mile (13.5km) climb rewards hikers with awe-inspiring panoramas of the valley.

Shutterstock | Checubus; melissamn; Getty Images | Sebastien Mamy; Tracy Packer Photography; Mark Read

190 feet (58 m) below sea level

120°F

Itineraries

Explore ghost towns, the sunset palettes of Artist's Drive or hike to Badwater Basin, the continent's lowest point for the ultimate high.

 Sand dunes, Rhyolite Ghost Town, a coyote and Furnace Creek.
➡ Road-tripping Death Valley from Las Vegas.

01

A day

After a peek at the ghost town of Rhyolite in the morning, drive over Daylight Pass into the park and descend over 4000ft (1219m) to the valley floor. Turn north and motor past sand dunes, alluvial fan washes and wildflowers in spring. Step back in time with a look at the whimsical Scotty's Castle. Nearby, walk atop the volcanic pit of Ubehebe Crater. It's half a mile wide and 600ft (183m) deep and last exploded only a few centuries ago.

Get back on the road south to Furnace Creek, stopping for lunch and to take a dip in a springwater pool at the ranch. In the afternoon, detour down along Artist's Drive, where a sunset palette of soft colors warms the eroded hillsides. Your finish line awaits at Badwater Basin – snap a photo by the sign to prove you made it here. If you're lucky enough to arrive after a heavy rain, you might even find a temporary lake. Walk out over the salt flats at dusk when cool desert breezes blow, then wait for the night sky's star show.

02

A weekend

On an overnight desert escape, head into the park from the south, via Jubilee Pass. The road north to Badwater Basin shows this valley's vastness. Pull over by the Badwater salt flats. Continuing north, take a short hike through Golden Canyon, if it's not too hot. Pull into buzzing Furnace Creek and check into one of the park's gorgeous private hotels, or a campsite. Around sunset, head up to Zabriskie Point or Dante's View for more panoramas.

The next day, hop back in the car and head north for a spin through Mustard Canyon before turning west toward Stovepipe Wells. Next to the road, the Mesquite Flat Sand Dunes rise. You can walk across them, or continue west to scramble through cool, marbled Mosaic Canyon instead. After lunch, take a leisurely drive through the valley's most dramatic scenery. Nighttime is just as good in Death Valley. Take advantage of the dark skies with forays to Dante's View, Harmony Borax Works, Ubehebe Crater or the Mesquite Flat Sand Dunes.

03

Five days

With a week, you can poke into little-known corners of the park. Spend the first day in the south, hiking the salt flats of Badwater, the badlands of Golden Canyon and underneath the Natural Bridge, then visit viewpoints along Artist's Drive. Make Furnace Creek your base camp; spend the next day playing golf, horseback riding, or renting a 4WD. Head up to Zabriskie Point or Dante's View at sunset.

Head to Ubehebe Crater on day three then cross Nevada's state line to Rhyolite, a mining ghost town. Cool off at higher elevations on day four by following the Death Valley '49ers' escape route up Emigrant Canyon, taking turn-offs to ghost towns, viewpoints and hiking trails. On your last day, exit the park past Panamint Springs, pausing at Father Crowley Vista Point and hiking to Darwin Falls. Want something a little more wild? Over 90% of the park is protected as wilderness. With a backcountry permit, the right equipment, and a leave-no-trace attitude, you can experience rarely-seen corners of the park.

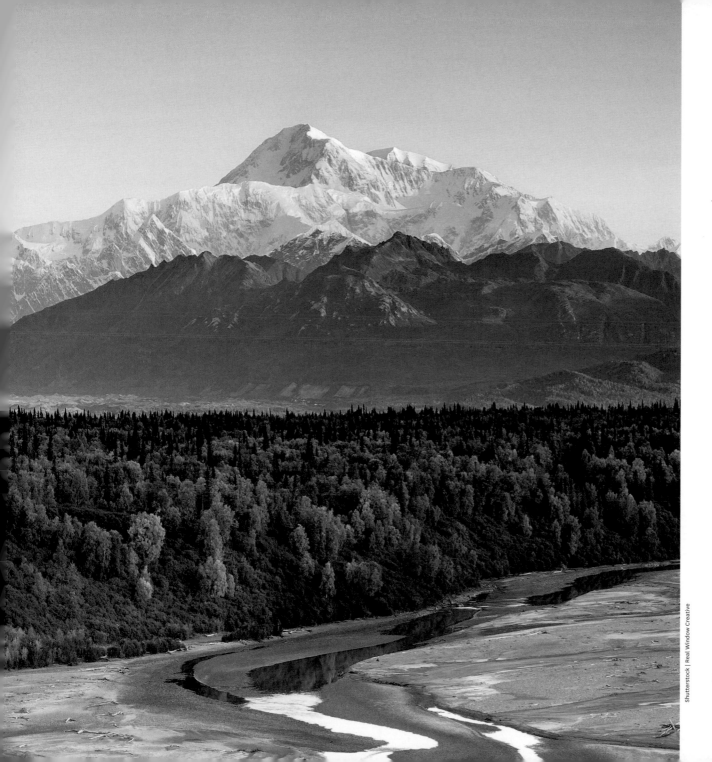

17

AK

Denali National Park

Denali National Park encapsulates everything that is great about the Alaskan wilderness. Under the sheltering subarctic sky, this majestic wild kingdom is vast, austere and exhilarating.

Denali

Here you'll discover nature in her most raw and at her most fierce. With over 6 million acres of intact wilderness, this massive park offers remarkable views and insights into the flora, fauna and active ecosystems of Alaska's immense interior.

Whether you take just a day to head up the Park Rd or plan a ten-day tromp across the virgin spaces of tundra, taiga forest, meadows, streams and hillsides that make this park so unique, a visit to Denali will not disappoint. With even the shortest of adventures, you are likely to see bear, moose, caribou and maybe a Dall sheep. Stay a while longer and you very well could spot a wolf or a fox, plus any number of avian species.

Hovering above it all is the 20,310ft (6190m) Denali, known as Mt McKinley until a presidential decree restored its original Athabascan name – which means 'The Great One' – in 2015. This hulking peak is the highest in North America. Wait for a clear day to see the glacier-capped summit massif unfurl her loving arms across this mindblowing stretch of firmament, and the true power of nature manifests itself with an immediacy and an intimacy not easily found in the continental US. It's just bigger here. And going big is what an Alaskan adventure is about.

Denali is alpha and omega, the beginning and the end, and under her watchful eye, the remarkably orchestrated, dramatic plots of nature unfold each spring when the snows melt. The grizzly bears emerge from a long winter's nap; the caribou and moose shed winter coats as their young struggle to find balance on wobbly legs; wildflowers bloom; fox and wolf fatten themselves on smaller prey; and visitors from across the globe move out through the wilderness,

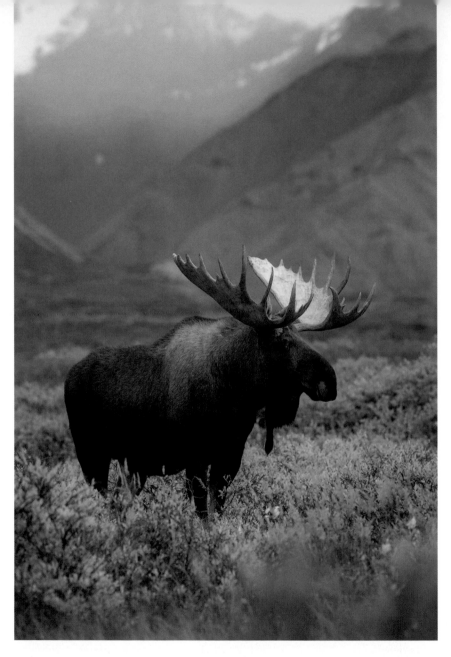

explorers in a foreign land, finding joy, balance and solitude in the whirl of life that spins around them.

⬆ A bull moose in autumn.
➡ Small planes are often the only way to reach Denali's glaciers.

Toolbox

When to go
Most people visit Denali from early June through early September for the best glimpses of wildlife, wildflowers and migratory birds. Come in winter or the shoulder seasons for solitude.

Getting there
Located along the road system in Alaska's Interior, the National Park entrance is accessed by car or train from Anchorage. From there, hop on the park shuttle for 92 miles (148km) of amazing wildlife viewing along the Park Rd.

Events
Park Rd is opened to private vehicles for just four days in the fall – apply to the lottery in June. In February, Winterfest is an icy party.

Accessibility
People with mobility challenges can drive the Park Rd in their own vehicle with a permit. In winter, let dogs do the work on a sled ride. Riley Creek Campground has accessible sites.

Park in numbers
9492 Area in sq miles
169 Species of birds
39 Species of mammals

Stay here...

Wonder Lake Campground Deep inside the park, this tent-only campground offers the best views of Denali. The mountain is shy, and sometimes it takes a day or two for her to come out from the clouds that usually drape her summit, so book well ahead to reserve three days.

Sheldon Chalet This is luxury at its finest. Start your all-inclusive stay at this five-bedroom private chalet with a helicopter tour – it's the only way to get here, there are no roads. From there you will be pampered with saunas, gourmet meals and plush beds. The chalet is located on the southern flank of Denali amid the glaciers and rocks, and outings include glacier snowshoes, crevasse exploration and more.

Backcountry camping Solace and solitude are hallmarks of Denali's 87 backcountry units. Rather than hiking on specific trails to backcountry campsites, you can head out here across trail-less terrain and stay wherever you like within your designated unit. It's a choose-your-own-adventure with a wild twist. Book permits in advance.

Do this!

Backpacking The park is roughly the size of Vermont, which means there's plenty of open space. Planning the trip is an essential first step; rangers can take you through the ins-and-outs of trail-less hiking, wilderness survival, bear safety and more. Once you hit the backcountry, it's a singular experience that will push your limits, challenge your senses and foster a deep connection with this great land. You need to know how to use a map and compass.

Cycling You can bike the entirety of the 92-mile (148km) Park Rd, a remarkable ribbon that bisects the park. A ride along its expanse takes you through low tundra, open spruce woodlands and meadows, black spruce forest, and white spruce and paper birch forest.

Flightseeing You think Denali looks big from your viewpoint at Wonder Lake? Take to the air for a change in perspective. From above, the immensity of this wilderness takes on new proportions that boggle the mind. No Alaskan adventure is complete without a flight.

◄ Touring cyclists pedal towards Denali. Opening spread: a panorama of the Denali Range.

What to spot...

The size and remoteness of Denali ensure a vibrant ecosystem that is intact and as untamed and real as it gets. You have a pretty good shot of seeing a handful of the park's most iconic megafauna with a simple bus tour along the Park Rd. Highlights include grizzly and black bear, wolf, caribou, moose and Dall Sheep. Migratory birds, and a startling diversity of plants, mosses, lichens and wildflowers add to the park's polychromatic eco-tapestry.

WOLF This is one of the best spots in Alaska to sight these fabled apex predators. There are generally 60 to 100 wolves within the park, though numbers dropped alarmingly to just 48 in 2015.

MOOSE These awkward ungulates, the second-largest mammal in North America, are found in forested areas by marshes and lakes. They're considered one of the most dangerous animals here.

GRIZZLY BEAR Mama bears often hang out by the Park Rd to protect their cubs, making this a great spot for grizzly viewing. Lacking a fish diet, they are smaller in size than their coastal cousins.

Hike this...

O1 Triple Lakes Trail
This 9.5-mile (15.3km) trail takes you across creeks, lush forests and alpine passes, with awesome views of the Alaska Range, to the gorgeous Triple Lakes.

O2 Horseshoe Lake Trail
Easily accessed from the Visitor Center at the park entrance, this simple 2-mile (3.2km) trail is a perfect intro to the park, taking in shimmering lake views on a looping series of trails that take you all the way down to lake level. Keep your eyes peeled for beaver.

O3 Trail-less Hiking
Choose your own adventure across brooks, past lakes, through tundra, meadow and wood. Stick to ridgelines and avoid thick brush and terrain traps to make the journey easier.

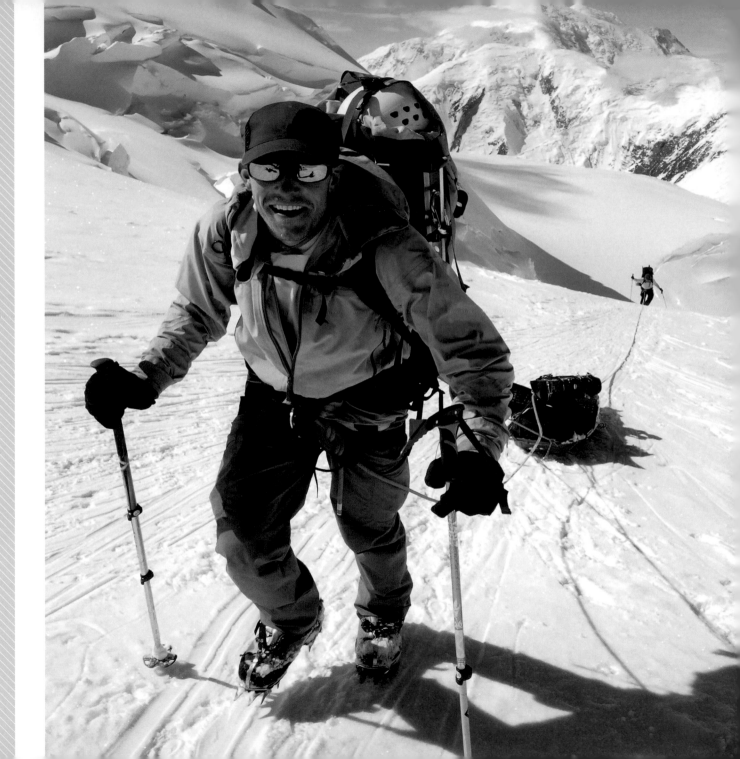

Itineraries

Whether you're into glacier hiking, rafting down canyons or the more sedate (but equally scenic) sightseeing from the Denali Star Train, strap yourself in.

← Dall sheep in Denali National Park. A ranger hauls his gear up to Windy Corner on Denali.
→ Country roads, Alaska-style, with far-off Mt Denali.

01
Two days

While you won't experience all that the park has to offer, you can easily see some amazing sights and a fair bit of wildlife in a day or two. The best start is aboard the Denali Star Train, a gorgeous sightseeing line that whisks you from Anchorage, past the Matanuska Valley and the Susitna River to the park entrance. While you're there, don't miss a trip to the kennels to visit the sled dogs that rangers use in winter to patrol the park. Stop for the night in Canyon, McKinley Village,

Carlo Creek or Healy, waking up early to get the first shuttle bus along the Park Rd. The shuttle takes eight hours just to get to the Eielson Visitor Center, so expect a full day. Some of the best views are had between Savage River and Eielson, where you can spot Dall sheep. At Sable Pass, marvel at the views of Polychrome Pass and head off for a short jaunt from the Visitor Center. You may choose to stop on the way back for an hour or two of trail-less hiking or outings on trails near Savage River.

02
A week

Denali National Park was created in 1917 with the mission of protecting the park's flora and fauna. In 1980, the US Congress tripled its size. Despite its massive scale, you can still see plenty of wildlands and wildlife in seven days. Plan well ahead to make backcountry and lodging reservations. If you miss out on the famed Wonder Lake Campground, try for the Teklanika River Campground. If you stay here, you are given special permission to drive your car in to mile 29 of the Park Rd.

If you want to lodge it, you can stay at Camp Denali, the Kantishna Roadhouse, Denali Backcountry Lodge or Skyline Lodge found at the end of the Park Rd in Kantishna.

Once you're fully acclimated, head back to park headquarters for your orientation for a multi-day wilderness trek. This is without a doubt a crowning highlight of any trip to Denali. Over three to seven days, you will walk through amazing untouched forests, meadows and tundra, and spot tons of wildlife.

03
Ten days

If adrenaline is your thing, there are some high-octane activities here to get your heart beating. Denali is about creating your own path, and there really is no limit to the number of off-the-wall adventures a serious outdoors person can have here. Start with some trail-less hiking for three or four days – the thrill of finding your own way in a roadless, trackless wilderness with map and compass is unlike any other.

If that's too tame for you, you can consider a flightseeing trip or some

guided glacier hiking. It's a three-week-long expedition-style ascent to get to the top of Denali. Over a thousand climbers attempt it every year, with fewer than half making it to the top. For river rats, there's some high-flying rafting on the nearby Nenana River, with Class III and IV water that features standing waves, bursting rapids and big holes down a sheer-cliffed canyon. Top off your trip with a few nights in nearby Talkeetna for bluegrass jams, killer fishing, zip-line tours and jet boats.

18

FL

Dry Tortugas National Park

Splashed across a remote archipelago, Dry Tortugas features a titanic 19th-century fort balanced on a tropical reef, surrounded by shipwrecks and sensational sea life.

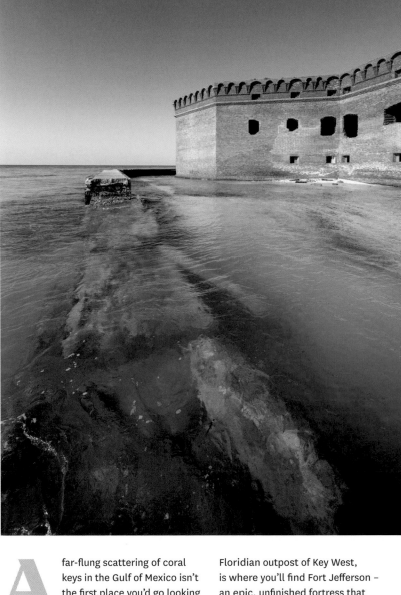

When Juan Ponce de León discovered Dry Tortugas in 1513, the Spaniard named the archipelago after the many *tortugas* (turtles) he encountered. (The word 'dry' was added to indicate the islands' lack of fresh water.) Nowadays, day-trippers come here to snorkel, dive and kayak around the reef and its seven atolls, spotting those languorous loggerhead turtles that are still numerous in these waters. But Dry Tortugas was originally scoped out for far less peaceful activities.

When the US acquired Florida from Spain in 1822, the strategic importance of Dry Tortugas was obvious. The keys' position at the mouth of the Bay of Mexico made them crucial for the defence of the young country's eastern flank. They were also considered for a base to combat the pirates of the Caribbean, though it wasn't until 1846 that construction finally began on the colossal coastal fortress.

During the Civil War, Fort Jefferson was used to hold Union deserters; it subsequently had a stint as a prison, famously hosting Dr Samuel Mudd after his conviction for involvement in Abraham Lincoln's assassination. Fortunately, though, since it never was properly finished, the only invasions the fort has witnessed have come in the form of flocks of birds that land here by the thousands while migrating.

The archipelago was made a national park in 1935, and these days the fort's sea wall and moat are popular with snorkelers.

A far-flung scattering of coral keys in the Gulf of Mexico isn't the first place you'd go looking for one of the largest brick buildings in the northern hemisphere. But here, 68 miles (109km) south of the famous Floridian outpost of Key West, is where you'll find Fort Jefferson – an epic, unfinished fortress that dominates Dry Tortugas, surely the most unusual of America's ever-surprising suite of national parks.

← The hexagonal Fort Jefferson in Dry Tortugas National Park, built with more than 16 million bricks.
→ Snorkeling around the coral reef.

Shutterstock | Ovidiu Hrubaru; Getty Images | Image Source

Toolbox

When to go

Visit in spring or fall to witness the twice-annual invasion of the islands by birds using Dry Tortugas as a stop-off on their migratory route between North and South America.

Getting there

Getting to Dry Tortugas is an adventure that involves either a sea ferry or a flight in a floatplane from Key West, Florida. Plane companies run half- and full-day experiences, while the *Yankee Freedom III*, a high-speed catamaran, offers day trips with 4-plus hours of island time (or you can camp overnight). Park entry is $15/person.

Accessibility

The ferry and dock are wheelchair accessible, as is the first floor of Fort Jefferson.

Park in numbers

101 Area in sq miles

16 Bricks used to build Fort Jefferson (in millions)

100,000 Number of sooty terns that arrive from March to September

Stay here...

Camping

This is possibly the only place on the planet where you can get an entire national park almost completely to yourself for the night. There are eight primitive, first-come-first-served campsites on Garden Key, near Fort Jefferson. There's nothing here but a star-studded sky, so it's basic – but when the last boat leaves, campers are the kings and queens of the islands.

Do this!

Snorkeling & diving

Meet Ponce de León's turtles and other marine life during a self-guided aquatic adventure around the park's coral gardens – home to goliath groupers, lobsters, squid, octopuses and reef sharks. The park is a ships' graveyard: divers can explore wrecks, including the *Windjammer*.

Kayaking

Confident paddlers can island-hop across the deep and sometimes challenging water between atolls, circumnavigating Bush and Long Key, or visiting Loggerhead Key and its beaches. Permits (free) required.

Birdwatching

Migration season brings nearly 300 species to spot. Spy magnificent frigatebirds, sooty terns nesting, and rare white-tailed tropicbirds soaring overhead.

Itineraries

Have catamaran, will travel – sail away to discover Fort Jefferson and its impressive moat, then snorkel the coral paradise of this park's seven atolls.

01

A day

It's not a bad way to start the day: skimming across the Gulf of Mexico in a luxury catamaran, past the Marquesas Keys and Boca Grande, on your way to a septuplet of islands that form one of America's smallest national parks. An on-board naturalist educates you about what to expect, and just over two hours after leaving Key West you're in the protected waters of Dry Tortugas National Park, itching to slide into the gin-clear tropical water that surrounds these remote coral atolls. First, though, you explore Fort Jefferson, one of America's biggest and most impressive 19th-century constructions – complete with a moat! – which has an extraordinary tale to tell. The afternoon is a different story altogether, though, as you embark on an aquatic odyssey of discovery in the park's underwater world, where an astonishing universe exists among the corals. Boarding the afternoon boat back to the mainland, it's hard not to cast an envious eye at the campers who are staying on.

Justin Foulkes

19

Everglades National Park

Vast marshes of swaying sawgrass stretching as far as the eye can see have earned the Everglades its nickname: 'the River of Grass.'

Imagine strolling the Anhinga Trail, an elevated boardwalk over the sawgrass marsh of Taylor Slough, broad-leafed marsh plants rippling gently in the brown water. You notice a large log, and then – wait! – the log moves! It's a 7ft (2m) gator, raising its primeval head for a yellow-eyed perusal of its surroundings before settling back into the mud. A minute later, a green snake whips its way through the water and disappears in the grass. A bubblegum-pink roseate spoonbill sticks its long, goofy beak into the water and yanks out a wriggling fish. This profusion of nature, in all its swampy, sticky, scaly glory, is what the Everglades are all about.

This is the largest tropical wilderness in the US, 2410 sq miles (6242 sq km) of wet sawgrass prairie, sun-dappled mangrove swamps, dense hardwood hammocks, pine forest and estuaries teeming with sea life. It's the third-largest national park in the lower 48, covering the entire southwest tip of Florida.

Indigenous people have roamed these swamps and forests for more than 10,000 years, leaving behind evidence of their existence in the form of shell mounds, piled up over many years of habitation. Over the centuries, various Native American tribes and escaped slaves have used the Everglades as a hiding place, secreting themselves deep within the swamp. A little more than a century ago, water in Florida flowed freely down the peninsula in a shallow sheet. This 11,000-sq-mile (28,490-sq-km) wetland was an intricate network of marshes, ponds, creeks and forest. But early settlers attempted to drain the land to make it farmable, destroying much of the delicate ecosystem in the process. Everglades National Park was

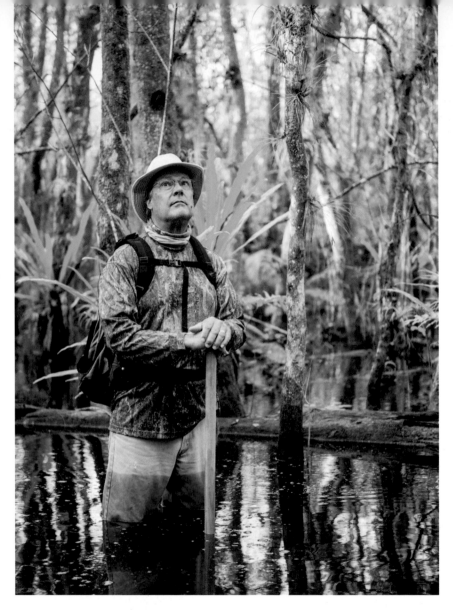

established in 1947 to protect what was left of the unique biozone. Today, the area around the park maintains an 'only in Florida' hint of wildness, with kitschy roadside attractions, tumbledown crab shacks and the occasional biker bar.

⬆ Hiring a guide can help you identify plant and animal species that you might otherwise miss. Previous page: the vivid and unique ecosystem of the Everglades' wetlands.

Justin Foulkes

Toolbox

When to go
The dry season runs from December through April, which is good for hiking and other land-based sightseeing, but bad for kayaking. Spring is better for watersports, but summer and fall bring heat, bugs and hurricanes.

Getting there
The park is less than an hour's drive from Miami. The two major access towns are Homestead/Florida City (southeast), and Everglades City (northwest). Both have accommodations and food. You'll need a car to get around here.

Events
The Everglades Seafood Festival is in February.

Accessibility
There are several wheelchair accessible trails. The Long Pine Key and Flamingo campgrounds have accessible sites. Some boat and tram tours are wheelchair accessible and offer listening aids.

Park in numbers

2410 Area in sq miles
15 Maximum adult size for an American alligator (ft)
60 Average yearly rainfall (in)

Stay here...

Hoosville Hostel
In a 1930s boarding house, this quirky Florida City hostel is big on atmosphere: mosaic floors, canopy beds, murals and book-filled dorms. But the real magic happens in the garden, a jungle Eden complete with a hammock, waterfalls, a rock pool and a gazebo. Accommodations range from dorm beds to private rooms to family suites. If there's no space, you can camp in the garden.

Flamingo Houseboats
Southwest of the park at sleepy Flamingo Marina, this NPS concessioner has safari-style eco tents and rents out houseboats that can accommodate up to six people. They also run boat tours, rent kayaks and speed boats, and were slated to open more lodging in summer 2021.

Long Pine Key Campground
Six miles from the Ernest Coe Visitor Center, this winter-only drive-in NPS campground has single and group sites, bathrooms and cold showers. What it lacks in amenities it makes up in cleanliness and proximity to nature. Wake in the morning to birdsong, the sun turning the water pink as it rises above the sawgrass. It's close to the Anhinga Trail – tops for gator-spotting – and other park sights. Bring bug spray!

Do this!

Kayaking
On Florida's southwest edge, the Ten Thousand Islands is an archipelago of tiny mangrove islands stretching some 60 miles (97km). Kayaking here will make you feel like Indiana Jones exploring a lost jungle. Paddle across stretches of pale jade water, alighting on an uninhabited white beach for a picnic lunch – before setting off beneath tunnels of mangroves.

Slogging
'What is slogging?' you ask, and why would you want to do it? Everglade-ese for 'walking through the mud,' slogging (or 'wet-walking') is a wonderfully messy way to get up close and personal with South Florida nature. Local companies offer guided slogs, where you'll be provided with special shoes for mucking through the wetlands, seeing swamp orchids, cypress trees, turtles and snakes.

Tram-touring
The Everglades' popular tram trip travels through the park's Shark Valley. Guides, all trained naturalists, point out wildlife – you're guaranteed to see gators here. In addition to gators, keep your eyes open for red-shouldered hawks, ibises and a plethora of snakes.

What to spot...

Famed for its alligators, the Everglades is home to so much more. The endless sawgrass prairie, tropical hardwood hammocks, mangrove swamps and swirling estuaries are home to a lush variety of birds, snakes (including some 150,000 invasive Burmese pythons), turtles and more. If you're incredibly lucky you might see a manatee in the waters of Florida Bay; dolphins are much more common, though. Rare orchids grow deep in the wetlands, colorful quarry for intrepid flower-spotters.

ALLIGATOR The big kahunas of the Everglades, gators are not hard to find. Spot them on the Anhinga Trail or, frankly, almost anywhere. They can blend in with logs; be patient.

FLORIDA BUTTERFLY ORCHID Green with a drooping lip of purple and white, these common orchids grow in hammocks and swamps, typically fixing themselves to oak, cypress or pine.

ROSEATE SPOONBILL Flamingo pink with a characteristic spoon-shaped bill, these large wading birds nest in mangrove trees and feed on crabs and small fish in shallow waters.

Hike this...

01 Anhinga Trail

You're guaranteed to see gators aplenty along this wheelchair- and stroller-accessible 0.8-mile (1.3km) boardwalk trail; look for cormorants along the stone wall and nesting roseate spoonbills in the trees.

02 Pinelands hiking and biking trails

The Pinelands, an area of high ground studded with stands of trees, are home to a 43-mile (69km) network of narrow old logging and fire roads perfect for long solitary hikes.

03 Snake Bight Trail

If the name doesn't scare you off, the mosquitoes might. But stay and be rewarded with a rugged, unmaintained 7.6-mile (12.2km) trek through hardwood hammock – keep your eyes open for flamingos.

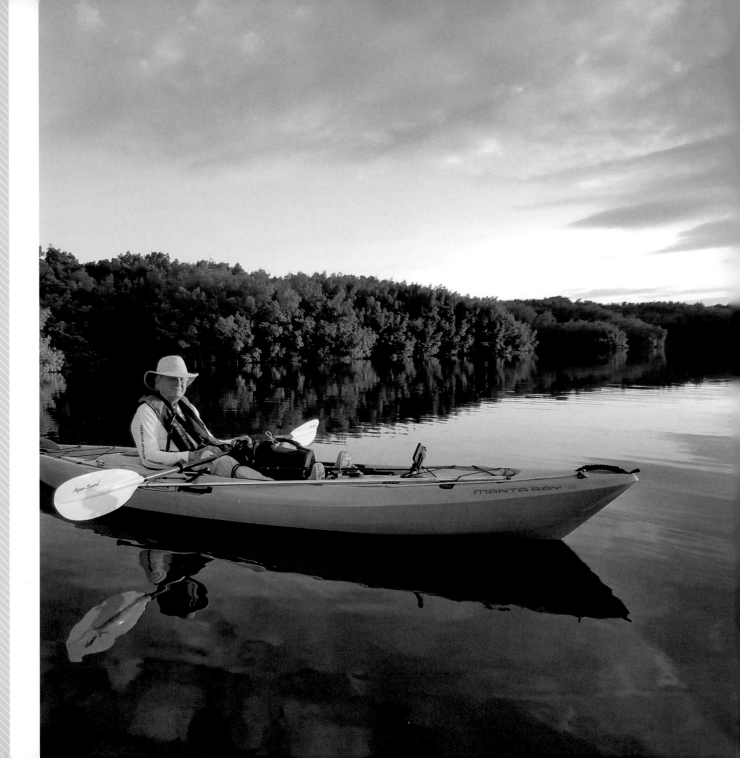

Itineraries

It's gators guaranteed here, whether you bike through Shark Valley or cruise through mangroved Ten Thousand Islands in the US' largest tropical wilderness.

 Mind the alligators. Kayaking a calm Coot Bay. 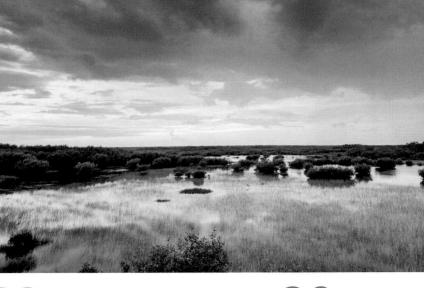 The campaign to create a national park here started in 1928 and the hope is to restore wetlands beyond the park.

01
A day

Stick to one area if your time is limited; in this case we recommend Shark Valley. The two-hour Shark Valley tram tours will give you an entertaining introduction to the area and its wildlife, and you'll certainly get to check 'spotting an alligator' off your life's to-do list. Afterwards, rent a bike and cruise the 15-mile (24km) paved Shark Valley tram road, passing cypress and hardwood forests and crossing creeks – with barely any elevation gain. (But bring more water and sunscreen than you imagine you'll need.

And food: there's nothing to eat in the park.) Picnic at the visitor center while looking for wood storks, great white herons and glossy ibises.

Afterwards, drive west to Big Cypress Gallery, where beloved Florida artist Clyde Butcher showcases his enormous B&W photographs of the swamps. Head back towards Miami with the sun sinking behind you, turning the wetlands pink and gold. Finish the day with a Cuban sandwich with house-cured ham and a *batido* (milkshake) at Sanguich De Miami in Little Havana.

02
Two days

Plan to spend your first night camping at Flamingo Campground, on Florida's isolated southern tip. You'll wake to the sight of dolphins arcing through warm waters dotted with tiny uninhabited islands. While it's still cool, stroll down the Guy Bradley Trail to the sliver of sand at Flamingo Beach, or take a spin around Bear Lake. In the afternoon, rent a kayak at Flamingo Everglades to explore the bights and paddle out to nearby wild keys. Spend your evening on the beach, looking up:

the area's remoteness makes this a world-class stargazing spot. On day two, chuck the tent in the car and hit the road. It's about half an hour north to the Pinelands, a unique ecosystem of slash pine- and saw palmetto-covered rocklands. Because it's on relatively high ground, the area is drier, making it a popular spot for hikers and bikers. You can get wet when you stop further on at the Ernest F Coe Visitor Center for a guided slog (check the NPS site for times and book ahead).

03
One week

On day one, hit the Ernest F Coe Visitor Center and take an introductory walk around the raised platform trails through sawgrass prairie. Then move towards Royal Palm Visitor Center for a gators-guaranteed hike on the Anhinga Trail. Day two, ride bikes or take a tram tour around Shark Valley, keeping your eyes peeled for roseate spoonbills; anhingas (a water bird); rare, iridescent indigo snakes; gators and more. On day three, opt for a guided boat trip through the mangrove stands of the Ten Thousand Islands area,

departing from the Gulf Coast Visitor Center. On day four, book a slog through the muddy waters of the cypress dome. Canoe the waters around Flamingo Point on day five, looking for wildlife. On day six, leave the Everglades for Biscayne National Park, which has the world's third-largest reef. Its crystalline waters, brimming with fish, make for world-class snorkeling. Spend day seven riding a glass-bottom boat around Biscayne and stare down at the jewel-colored reef, or dive one of the park's eerie shipwrecks.

20

AK

Gates of the Arctic National Park & Preserve

Endless summer nights, a primordial ecosystem that is untainted by roads, and far-flung adventures on the edge of the planet.

You don't know nature. That is, modern humans don't know true nature. Wherever we go – be it on a backwoods day-hike or a longer trek through the wilds of the Rockies – our modern invasive human imprint is everywhere. You'll see it in passing planes, roads, telephone wires, litter and smog. But up above the Arctic Circle, where the winds howl wild and the caribou run free, true wilderness still exists – this is arguably the most primitive, most raw, most born-free stretch of wilderness in all of North America.

Interestingly enough, humankind has lived in harmony within this 8.4-million-acre swath of wilderness for over 13,000 years. And the park and preserve has thousands of archaeological sites that preserve the semi-nomadic traditions of the Nunamiut and Athabascan peoples. To this day, the descendants of these original settlers – and a few non-native, modern-day back-to-the-Earthers – live, hunt and survive in this park. The days of nomadic hunting are over, but 11 small communities are associated with the park.

Non-native explorers first came to the Central Brooks Range in the 1880s, looking for gold, military high ground and improved opportunities. But their footprints have long faded. What's left is an adventure-seeker's Valhalla, with uncharted wilderness stretching to that northern horizon and beyond.

As with any hard-to-penetrate wilderness, rivers are natural pathways for human travel. And the six rivers of Gates of the Arctic – the Alatna, John, Kobuk, Noatak, North Fork of the Koyukuk and Tinayguk – provide miles upon miles of unspoiled wilderness, big views of precipitous, glacier-carved valleys, and a unique connecting point between humankind and the river wild.

Getting to and through the Gates of the Arctic requires serious outdoors skills. Its sheer remoteness is the stuff of legends for serious boaters and hikers looking to go beyond the everyday.

Toolbox

When to go
The summer is short here but having 24 hours of sunlight makes it easy to pack a lot into a short period. Come June through August, unless you have a dogsled team or pair of skis.

Getting there
Planes can take you to the gateway villages of Bettles (where you'll find park headquarters) or Anaktuvuk Pass, where you can get floatplanes to drop you at the put-in for your river trip or backcountry hike. You can also simply walk out from these villages (or from the Dalton Hwy at Coldfoot) to enter this roadless national treasure.

Events
The Northern Lights are best viewed in September.

Accessibility
This wilderness poses myriad challenges. You will need to think about loading and unloading from a small plane, as well as the lack of any health care. Boat or raft trips may be easier.

Park in numbers
13,238 Area in sq miles
6 Wild scenic rivers
145 Species of birds

Stay here...

Camping
There are no designated campsites here, which means you can basically camp anywhere – on the edge of a lake, up in the roaring winds of a jagged ridgeline, down by the river on the fringes of the boreal forest. Practise leave-no-trace travel.

Iniakuk Lake Wilderness Lodge
At the edge of the park, this fly-in luxury cabin offers all-inclusive stays in a 1974 log homestead. Trips include guided fishing, hiking and wildlife-watching but it's the intimacy and camaraderie that really make this place stand out. It also has 24-hour solar electricity, running water and a few remote cabins that will get you even further off the grid.

Bettles Lodge
Located in the community of Bettles, this log cabin lodge was built in 1952 and is recognized as a National Historic Site. It's a good jump-off point for adventures further afield. They also have a handful of remote cabins you should check out for fly-in adventures.

Do this!

Paddling
Serious river rats can raft, canoe or kayak these undammed and uncontaminated waterways – much as Alaska Natives have been doing for time immemorial – on trips that last from a few days to a few weeks. The Noatak offers amazing paddling and wildlife watching for trips that usually stretch up to ten days. The Kobuk takes you through some solid Class III water. Continue on for a longer adventure all the way to the Chukchi Sea.

Backpacking
On land, there's no end to what you can see and do – your own ambitions and abilities are truly the only obstacles in your path. Given that there are no trails, no roads and no cell-phone service, this challenging terrain is for expert outdoors enthusiasts only. Novices should hire a guide to lead them through this untamed wilderness.

Dog-sledding and skiing
Wintertime brings peace and solitude beneath the glowing aurora borealis. You can head out by dog sled or cross-country ski to explore around remote cabins.

← Backpacking Arrigetch Creek, with the peaks of Xanadu, Arial and Caliban in the distance.
→ Watch out for wolf prints in the Brooks Range.

See this...

O1 Flightseeing
You don't have to have MacGyver Swiss Army knife skills to enjoy the park. Hire a floatplane to take you across the park, spotting musk ox and caribou as you pass through the gates into the Brooks Range.

O2 Archaeology
The human imprint goes back 13,000 years and you can still uncover archaeological finds such as abandoned camps and mining cabins throughout the park. Go to Anaktuvuk Pass to learn about the lives of the native Nunamiut peoples in this small village.

O3 Birding
Stick near the waterways to spot osprey, eagles, yellow-rumped warblers, ptarmigan, snowy owl and any number of sparrows, longspurs, finch, grouse, gull and tern.

What to spot...

It doesn't last long, but the arctic summer catches fire. Birds migrate here to feed on the billions of mosquitoes; fish swim upstream; mammals fatten up for the long winter cold; caribou and moose take shelter in the boreal forest; and grizzlies eat until they're stuffed. While the migrating caribou, musk ox and big predators are highlights, it's the small rodents, birds and insect life that really bring this rich and diverse wilderness to life.

CARIBOU The largest caribou herd in Alaska runs right through here. These stately animals weigh up to 500lb (227kg). Their hides and meat are a staple for the Native Alaskans that still maintain a subsistence-hunting lifestyle.

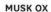

MUSK OX
These ice-age bearded beasts roam across the wild like sage prophets from a time long ago. Look for them in open fields and tundra.

ARCTIC TERN Artic terns stop here – after the longest migration of any bird in the world – to fill up on insects before heading south to Antarctic waters.

Itineraries

Take a flightseeing tour over the Arctic Circle, raft the remote Noatak River and maybe spot a grizzly bear or two in this raw, rugged wilderness.

← September and the depths of December are the best times to view the aurora borealis.
↑ Standing on a frozen Anaktuvuk River, looking towards Mt Napaktualuit; a brown bear fishes in Noatak River.

01

Five days

If you have limited outdoor experience or mobility (or just don't want to spend ten days freezing in a tent), this trip is for you. Begin with a day or two in Fairbanks, where you can take a flightseeing tour above the Arctic Circle, visit the Museum of the North, or just check out the ruined dredges, riverboats and more. Stop in at the Fairbanks Alaska Public Lands Information Center for an overview of options within the park. From there, hop an all-inclusive trip to Iniakuk Lake Wilderness Lodge. Fresh pastries will greet you every morning as you plan short forays into the wilderness. From here, you can do canoe trips, head out in search of wildlife or just watch the water as it reflects the blue arctic sky. Set aside a day or two to stay off the grid in one of the lodge's remote cabins. The Arrigetch Peaks Wilderness Cabin is a rustic log masterpiece with a big porch and even bigger views. Each day, challenge your guide to take you to a new corner of the Brooks Range in search of wildlife, rare birds and views that stretch as far as your imagination.

02

Ten days

Your rafting trip starts in Fairbanks with an afternoon pub-paddle on the Chena River, rising early the next day for a flight into Bettles. Check in at the park visitor center and arrange your gear or your guide, heading out into the wilds via floatplane along the southern flank of the Brooks Range to Walker Lake. As the floatplane buzzes away, the reality sinks in that you are alone in a wilderness double the size of Switzerland. You can spend a day fishing for trout, taking on an afternoon date-hike to the far edges of the shimmering body of water.

From there, head down the Kobuk River. Each day is different. You might take on 20 river miles in a day and a splashy Class III rapid, or have a lazy day and hike to a nearby ridge. The trip ends when you radio in and a bush plane (the first signs of civilization in days) whirrs over the horizon and picks you up. You ask the pilot to take one more sweep across the river, a grizzly is fishing along the banks. And you realize that you were just a traveler in a land ruled by the animal kingdom.

21
MO

Gateway Arch National Park

The tallest monument in America is both a lofty viewing platform and an engineering marvel — it's grander than ever following a massive five-year makeover.

Soaring 630ft above the swiftly flowing waters of the Mississippi River, the Gateway Arch is one of America's great public works of art. It earned national park status in 2018, following $380 million of upgrades that saw a vast expansion of its underground museum, the addition of more green space, and the building of a land bridge over the interstate to make the site more accessible (not to mention more attractive). Despite its new national park status, the Arch has been a symbol of St Louis since its completion back in 1965. The shimmering icon — all 43,226 tons of concrete wrapped in stainless steel — offers sweeping views over the river and downtown St Louis from the top. It's also a remarkable engineering achievement for its time.

Construction began at each base, with 60ft-deep foundations, a third of which was anchored into solid bedrock. The legs had to meet precisely at the summit — even an error of 1/64th of an inch would mean failure. It was built to withstand earthquakes and high winds (and is able to sway up to 18 inches up top) as well as lightning strikes. To access the top, a new mechanism had to be invented: an eight-car tram that's equal parts elevator and Ferris Wheel, which takes visitors to a lofty lookout in about four minutes.

Finnish-American architect Eero Saarinen designed the Arch in 1947, after winning a competition to create a memorial celebrating the vision of Thomas Jefferson to open the west to US expansion (among the 171 losing entries was one submitted by Saarinen's father, also a noted architect). Museum exhibitions do a fine job describing the history of St Louis and the early American explorers, as well as the indigenous people living out west who were given little consideration in the rush to fulfill Jefferson's continental ambitions.

⬆ The park was landscaped for the Arch's 50th anniversary in 2015.
➡ The Apotheosis of St Louis statue of King Louis IX of France in St Louis.

Toolbox

When to go

The park is open year-round. If coming in the peak summer months (June to early August) or on holidays, arrive early or late in the day to beat the crowds.

Getting there

Set in downtown St. Louis, 5 miles (8km) northwest of Lambert Airport, the park is reachable by MetroLink light rail (Laclede's Landing station).

Events

The park hosts a wide range of events, including holiday concerts, stargazing gatherings and natural history celebrations (like the Monarch butterfly migration in September).

Accessibility

The park grounds, parts of the Old Courthouse and the museum exhibits in the Gateway Arch complex are accessible. Unfortunately, the top of the arch is not, though there is a full-size replica of the keystone piece in the museum.

Park in numbers

91 Area in sq miles
30 Miles of visibility on clear days
630 Height (ft)

Stay here...

Camping

Just 10 miles northeast of the Arch, Horseshoe Lake State Park has 26 shaded campsites set on a small forest-covered lake island. The facilities are basic (water, pit toilets, no showers), but you can't beat the location, just 20 minutes from downtown St. Louis. It also has four miles of hiking trails and is a popular spot for fishing and boating (BYO canoe). It's open May through September, first come, first served.

Missouri Athletic Club

You can stroll to the Arch in a few minutes at this well-located hotel on Washington Avenue. It's set in a grand 1916 building with two fine restaurants and 75 classically furnished rooms. For an extra $12, guests can take advantage of the club facilities, which include a 25m indoor pool, steam rooms and sauna, and rooftop tennis court.

Casa Magnolia

Book well ahead to score one of the three rooms at this friendly B&B in the leafy Shaw neighborhood. The antique-filled Victorian home dates from 1906 and faces an expansive park. The Botanical Gardens are within walking distance, though it's a 15-minute drive to the Gateway Arch.

Do this!

Riverboat Cruise

The best views of the arch are out along the Mississippi, when you can take in the grandeur of its 630ft soaring above the St Louis skyline. Park rangers provide historical insight on one-hour cruises aboard replica 19th-century paddle-wheel riverboats. You can also see the arch by night on two-hour dinner cruises.

Cycling

Take in the majesty of America's mightiest river, the glittering Arch and the city's working waterfront on a spin along the Mississippi Greenway. In front of the park grounds, you can hop onto a trail and follow the river north for 15 miles all the way to the old Chain of Rocks bridge, a 1929 span that was once part of Route 66. Rent bikes from Urban Shark on Locust St.

Urban walking

One of America's largest urban parks offers a heady dose of greenery, with walking and biking trails, scenic lakes and public artwork – including an iconic statue of the city's namesake, King Louis IX of France – plus several major museums and a massive (free) zoo. It's reachable by public transit (take the Metrolink from Lacledes Landing station near the Arch).

Hike this...

01 Cliff Cave Park

A 30-minute drive south of St Louis, this riverfront park has scenic trails, including a 7-mile (11km) paved path along the Mississippi and a short River Bluff trail offering fine views across America's mightiest waterway.

02 Rockwoods Reservation

This forested park has springs, ravines and rock formations. The seven trails offer plenty of variety, from half-mile rambles to the more challenging 9-mile (14.5km) round trip Green Rock Trail. It's a 40-minute drive west of St Louis.

03 Powder Valley

For a nature fix, go 17 miles (27km) southwest to the Powder Valley Conservation Nature Center for three short trails through oak and hickory forest (one trail is wheelchair accessible).

Itineraries

An urban park this may be but you can still explore indigenous culture and a grand river before checking out the city's architecture and history.

Shutterstock | Sean Pavone; photo.ua

← A birds-eye view of St Louis from the top of the Arch.
↑ The historic Old Courthouse is undergoing renovations.

01
A day

Beat the crowds by arriving at opening time and taking the first tram ride to the top (note you can purchase tickets online up to three days in advance). Once there, you can linger as you long as you like, enjoying the fine views (weather permitting) over the city skyline, east to Illinois and west across Missouri.

After you head back down, check out the subterranean Museum at the Gateway Arch, set just below the soaring monument. Exhibits delve into the history of the region, looking at the indigenous and Creole cultures before the Louisiana Purchase, St Louis' development as an early trade hub, and Jefferson's vision for westward expansion. Other sections cover the city's big growth in the riverfront era and more recent times when Eero Saarinen's design forever changed the city skyline. Cap your visit with a viewing of the 28-minute documentary Monument to the Dream, which gives fascinating insight into the arch's complicated construction.

In the afternoon, walk up to the Old Courthouse, which is also part of the national park. The striking 19th-century building boasts an Italian Renaissance-style cast iron dome (modeled on St Peter's in Rome). Inside, a small museum provides an elucidating account of the Dred Scott case that was tried here, as well as the larger issue of slavery in the United States in the decades leading up to the Civil War.

22

MT

Glacier
National
Park

Everything in Glacier is larger than life, from the ancient snowy mountains and the deep navy lakes to the fearless mountain goats.

Shutterstock | Freedom 2 Dream

↓ Avalanche Lake.
→ Most trails are open to horses.
Previous page: Saint Mary Lake
in Glacier National Park is a
widescreen wonder.

Driving along Glacier National Park's famed Going-to-the-Sun Rd feels rather ordinary at first. You drive through pine forest. You pass a lake. Then – whoa! – you turn a bend and you're 1000ft (305m) above the valley floor, surrounded by prehistoric granite peaks straining towards the clouds. You turn your head to see a wall of waterfalls streaming down an ancient rock face. Turn again and spot mountain goats leaping along flower-fringed crags so high they seem to touch the sun. This is Glacier National Park. Words like 'pretty' don't apply. Words like 'massive,' 'electrifying,' and 'fierce,' however, do.

Signed into existence by William Howard Taft in 1910, Glacier didn't become a major tourist destination until two years later, when the Great Northern Railway began building magnificent hotels and advertising the region as 'America's Switzerland.' WWII brought activity in the park to a screeching halt, and many of the chalets fell into disrepair. Today, nine of the original thirteen have been revived.

The 53-mile-long (85km) Going-to-the-Sun Rd was finished in 1932, ushering in the era of automobile travel. Traversing some of the park's most spectacular terrain via switchbacks and hairpin turns, it's considered by many to be one of the finest scenic drives in America. It's named for Going-to-the-Sun Mountain, which the local Blackfeet tribe considered a sacred spot. Today, it's closed for much of the year due to snow, sometimes not opening until as late as July.

In 1932, Glacier joined with Waterton Lakes National Park across the border in Alberta, Canada, to create the world's first International Peace Park, a symbol

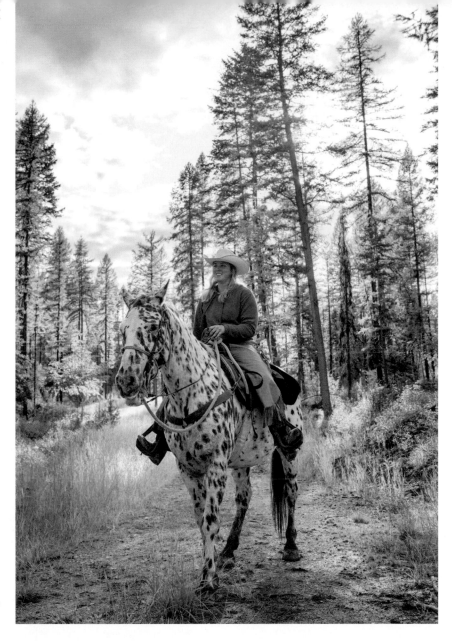

of the friendship between the US and Canada. Today visitors can hike or take a boat ride across the US–Canada border. In fact, this is the only place you can cross the border without clearing customs, but do bring your passport – hikers crossing the border by foot will get a unique mountain goat stamp.

Justin Foulkes

Toolbox

When to go
This park is freezing most of the year. Many facilities don't open until July, and roads are often closed after the snowfalls in early fall. Late August or early September has the best blend of warm weather and solitude.

Getting there
Lying in northern Montana, Glacier Park Airport is about 30 miles (48km) west in Kalispell. Amtrak's Empire Builder train stops at East and West Glacier stations on its trip between Seattle and Chicago. A public bus plies the park's main areas. Seven-day pass: $35/car, $20/pedestrian or bike.

Events
Summer brings ranger-led programs and the Native America Speaks series.

Accessibility
Several trails and campsites are accessible, as are shuttles and bus tours with advance notice.

Park in numbers

1583 Area in sq miles
6646 Highest point on Going-to-the-Sun Rd: Logan Pass (ft)
1500 Number of mountain goats in the park

Stay here...

🏠 Many Glacier Hotel
Everything about this rickety Swiss-style chalet charms, from the valets in lederhosen to the vintage tiled bathrooms and the library full of bird-watching books. Built in 1915, the lodge is far enough from Going-to-the-Sun Rd to be quiet even in mid-July. Rooms are basic but comfy. In the evening, pull on a sweater for drinks overlooking Swiftcurrent Lake.

⛺ Many Glacier Campground
First-come, first-served sites at Many Glacier Campground fill up fast, and no wonder – this is one of Glacier's loveliest campsites. Arrive early to snag a spot with good views.

Easy access to showers, laundry and a camp store means you won't be roughing it too much – and proximity to some of the park's finest hiking means you can roll right out of your sleeping bag and onto the trail.

🏠 Lake McDonald Lodge
Built in 1913, this pretty chalet is perched on the shore of Lake McDonald. The lobby is an example of early-20th-century 'parkitecture,' with half-timbered walls and a stone fireplace. Stay in the main lodge or a cabin, save money with a hostel-style dorm or splurge on a suite. Like all the park's lodgings, it books up early.

Do this!

🎡 Scenic driving
Bisecting the park diagonally from southwest to northeast, the engineering marvel that is Going-to-the-Sun Rd gives drivers dizzy views across the range and to the valley floor far below. Drive your own car, ride the park shuttle, or – our favorite – join a tour in one of Glacier's vintage red buses, complete with a guide.

🐴 Horseback riding
See Glacier from the back of a horse: Swan Mountain Outfitters has corrals throughout the park, where their cowboys and cowgirls will lead you on a half- or whole-day ride through the pine forests to mountain

lakes and streams. You'll learn neat facts about the park's flora and fauna (sometimes because your horse is busy trying to eat a poisonous bush!).

✋ Learning about Native American culture
In the summer, the Native America Speaks program brings people from the local Blackfeet, Salish, Kootenai,and Pend d'Oreille tribes to teach about native history and culture. Find programs at campgrounds, lodges and ranger stations throughout the park. Or join the Sun Tours bus to see the park through the eyes of a Blackfeet guide.

What to spot...

Glacier teems with wildlife, especially when the summer thaws mean hibernating creatures come out to play. Chubby yellow-bellied marmots scurry across rocky pinnacles, majestic moose graze peacefully on the upper slopes of mountains, lumbering grizzlies forage for huckleberries in the lush meadows. The eastern side of the park is blown by dry chinook winds, making it drier and browner. The west side is wetter and more primeval, home to dark, dew-dripping cedar and hemlock forests.

MOUNTAIN GOATS
The park's official symbol, the fluffy, white mountain goat can be found scrambling up steep slopes – often they use the same hiking paths humans do.

GLACIER LILY In summer the avalanche slopes are carpeted in delicate yellow glacier lilies, which look like tiny six-pointed stars.

CANADIAN LYNX The silvery-brown lynx looks rather like a large housecat and it takes work to spot them. Their numbers are threatened, and they are generally active at night.

Justin Foulkes

Hiking Logan Pass Trail to Hidden Lake; expect wildflowers in summer.

Hike this...

O1 The Highline
The park's most iconic hike cuts a narrow path along the famed Garden Wall (handholds included) before winding 7.5 miles (12km) into the mountains towards the rustic Granite Park Chalet.

O2 Avalanche Lake
Popular with families, this steady 4-mile (6.4km) round-trip traverses dense forest to the banks of a pretty blue alpine lake.

O3 Boulder Pass
Keen backpackers will relish the 31-mile (50km) trek between Kintla Lake and Goat Haunt. Backcountry camping permits and bear spray necessary.

Itineraries

Ready for some life-changing hikes? Try Iceberg Lake or Logan Pass for glacial views, stunning vistas and bonus wolf sightings.

 Kayaking on glacier-gouged Lake McDonald, the park's largest.
➡ Backcountry cooking in Glacier National Park.

01

Two days

Wake early on your first day and inhale the piney air as you embark on the length of Going-to-the-Sun Rd. Heading southwest to northeast, stop first at Lake McDonald for a photo session and a peek at the timber lobby of iconic 1913 Lake McDonald Lodge. Ascend the hairpin turns of The Loop, where the road cuts across the continent-dividing Garden Wall. Keep your eyes open for the cascades at Bird Woman Falls and the Weeping Wall, then stop at Logan Pass Visitor Center to stretch your legs and gaze down across the valley from 6646ft (2026m). Descend to the viewpoint of Jackson Glacier Overlook, then head to your campground on the shores of St Mary Lake. Finish up with a bison burger and a thick slice of huckleberry pie at the Park Cafe in St Mary. On day two, hit the Many Glaciers area for a plunge into the park's wilder side. Fortify yourself with lunch at the Ptarmigan Dining Room in Many Glacier Hotel before embarking on the 9-mile (14.5km) hike to impressive Iceberg Lake.

02

Four days

On day one, drive Going-to-the-Sun Rd as described in the two-day itinerary, but this time park at Logan Pass for the life-changing hike along the Highline Trail. You'll almost certainly spot a mountain goat or three along the trail; in spring and summer they sometimes have their fluffy white kids in tow. On day two finish Going-to-the-Sun Rd and stop at the mirror-smooth St Mary Lake for an afternoon of canoeing. On day three, head to Many Glacier and hike to either Iceberg Lake or Grinnell Glacier; both trails are stunners, full of sweeping vistas and sparkly snowcaps. Dine at Two Sisters Cafe near Babb, beloved for their goofy-bumper-sticker–lined walls and their huckleberry milkshakes. On day four explore the more remote precincts of the park at Two Medicine Valley, where you're just as likely to see a wolf as another person. Upper Two Medicine Lake is a good day hike, passing through dense, ferny forest to reveal achingly beautiful mountain views.

03

One week

Get the lay of the land on day one with a bus tour – choose from the iconic red 'jammer' bus or the Blackfeet-run Sun Tours. On day two, hike to icy McDonald Falls, then have a photo op at historic Lake McDonald Lodge. In the evening, check out one of the summertime Native America Speaks programs, from dance demos to language lectures. On day three, gawp at gargantuan trees on Trail of the Cedars, then continue on to Avalanche Lake.

On day four, proceed to Logan Pass for the Highline Trail, bringing lunch to eat at Granite Park Chalet, then descend to stargaze that evening at the new St Mary observatory. On day five head to the Swan Mountain corral at Many Glacier for a day-long trail ride through the dense forest to one of the area's milky-blue glacial lakes. Plunge into the wild Two Medicine Valley on day six for a scenic boat tour across the ice-cold, glassy lake. On your final day, pack your passport and cross the border for a day trip of hiking and boating in Waterton Lakes National Park in Canada.

23

AK

Glacier Bay National Park & Preserve

Quintessential Alaska, Glacier Bay is a forceful reminder of the strength, tenacity and power of Mother Nature.

Eleven tidewater glaciers cascade down from the mountains here and fill the sea with icebergs of all shapes and sizes imaginable. The park itself covers a wide variety of terrain over 3.3 million acres, from mountains and ice fields to temperate rainforest and secluded fjords, but it's the glaciers, with their dramatic calving events, towering grandeur and visceral appeal, that are the star attraction.

The natural history of this bay is revealed in the deep fjord that was formed by rapidly retreating ice. When Captain George Vancouver sailed through here in 1794, Glacier Bay was little more than a mountain of ice. The next century, John Muir discovered that the ice had retreated within the bay by some 20 miles (32km) from the icy strait. Today, it goes back more than 60 miles (96.5km), revealing a hydrological history that is both fascinating and perhaps a little alarming.

You are unlikely to visit this rugged bay – marked by the thunderous roar of falling icebergs and the spirited vaults of migrating humpback whales – by land. In fact, no roads go here. Instead, you'll probably see it from the deck of a cruise ship – or, if you're lucky, from the water aboard a sea kayak. Two large cruise ships are permitted to enter the bay every day, and it's a highlight of many Southeast Alaska cruises. Independent adventurers can visit the park from Juneau, with stops in the remote offbeat village of Gustavus and park headquarters at Bartlett Cove. From aboard your vessel, you are likely to spot any number of remarkable sea mammals, such as whales and harbor seals; you might also spot a bear or moose paddling their way across a narrow section of bay. Part of the even larger 25-million-acre World Heritage Site found here, this wilderness is rough and wild, untamed and unrelenting.

Toolbox

When to go
The park is open year-round, but the peak season is late May to early September. It rains up to 70in (178cm) a year here, regardless of the season, so expect it to be wet and cold.

Getting there
Most of the 300,000 yearly visitors get here on a cruise. If you're traveling independently, start from Gustavus, an off-the-grid backwater so remote it didn't get electricity until the 1980s. From there, arrange a cruise or kayak from park headquarters at Bartlett Cove.

Events
Huna Tribal House, memorializing the Huna Tlingit clan houses that once dotted these shores, has rotating arts and culture exhibits and programs.

Accessibility
Glacier Bay Lodge is accessible from a wheelchair ramp and most large cruises provide easy access.

Park in numbers

5156 Area in sq miles

11 Tidal glaciers

40 Weight of a humpback whale in tons

Stay here...

National Park Service Campground
Set in a ridiculously lush forest steps from the shoreline, this free campsite has a bear cache and little warming shelter. It's just 0.25 miles (0.4km) from Glacier Bay Lodge, where you can grab meals and warm up.

Glacier Bay Country Inn
A cozy inn set on a 160-acre property in Gustavus, this fine collection of wood-hewn cabins features a game room, theater and welcoming hot tub. Come with your appetite, the family meals are legendary.

Glacier Bay Lodge
The only hotel and restaurant in Bartlett Cove, this granddaddy of a lodge has a warm, cozy air. The broad stone fireplace and restaurant are center-stage, where backpackers, just-back-from-the-wild kayakers, and well-heeled sightseers all gather. Nightly slideshows, guided day trips, ranger talks and the occasional movie upstairs add to the mix.

Do this!

Kayaking
Take to the water, where the snap-crackle-and-pop of melting icebergs overpowers your senses. With a sea-taxi drop off you can explore a good bit in a day. Take a few more to further explore the Muir Inlet and West Arm, staying away from the open waters of the Bay. A fun overnight takes you to Beardslee Islands, where you can camp, spot birds and search for wildflowers.

Flightseeing
The majesty of this world of ice, water and forest takes on new perspectives aboard a small airplane. You can head out from Haines to see the glaciers, bays and oceanfronts of the park. Numerous routes, running from 1 to 2½ hours, take you over the most dramatic scenery of the park.

Boat touring
Two-day tours to the park include an overnight at the Glacier Bay Lodge, and a long, eight-hour boat tour out to the glaciers. For something a little different, consider a whale-watching tour.

◀ A glacial landscape on a clear day is a fun geology lesson.
▶ Brown bears enjoy berries too.

Hike this...

01 Nagoonberry Loop
For huge fields of wildflowers, spend a morning cruising this short, 2.2-mile (3.5km) trail. You'll pass from meadow to old-growth forest, giving great perspective on area flora.

02 Tlingit Trail
It's just a half mile to the Huna Tribal House from Glacier Bay lodge; stop in to learn about Tlingit culture and art before continuing on for the four-hour round trip on the Bartlett River Trail.

03 Point Gustavus
You can walk along the beach from Bartlett Cove to Gustavus on this 12-mile (19km) trek, which usually takes two days. Look for pods of orca at Point Gustavus.

What to spot...

Most of your wildlife viewing will be from the sea, so expect plenty of maritime species and birds. There are Steller sea lion, harbor porpoise, harbor seal and mischievous sea otters. In the forested areas near the mouth of the Bay, you might sight brown or black bear; look to the cliffs for mountain goats. But the real stars are the whales that call this bay home and who are regularly spotted lobbing their tails on the water's surface.

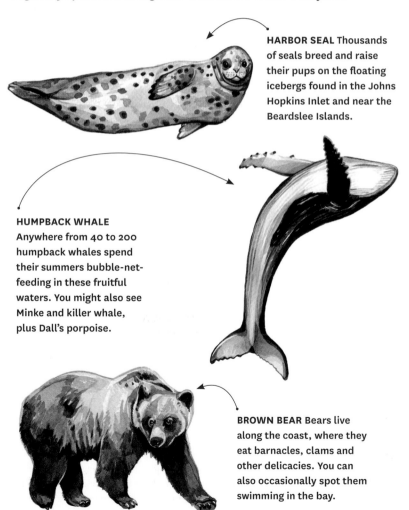

HARBOR SEAL Thousands of seals breed and raise their pups on the floating icebergs found in the Johns Hopkins Inlet and near the Beardslee Islands.

HUMPBACK WHALE Anywhere from 40 to 200 humpback whales spend their summers bubble-net-feeding in these fruitful waters. You might also see Minke and killer whale, plus Dall's porpoise.

BROWN BEAR Bears live along the coast, where they eat barnacles, clams and other delicacies. You can also occasionally spot them swimming in the bay.

124

Itineraries

Spot puffins and Steller sea lions on a Glacier Bay boat tour or take it up a notch with a multiday paddle on the Alsek River.

← Humpback whales can be viewed from the shore of Glacier Bay National Park.

↑ A tree carving by indigenous Tlingit people. Photographing Margerie Glacier.

01

Two days

If you aren't here on a cruise ship, you'll need to do a little pre-planning – and a lot of saving to get here. There are regular flights from Juneau, Alaska's capital, to Gustavus, or you can hop on a ferry aboard the Alaska Marine Highway, which offers beautiful sightseeing on its own. Stay at the Blue Heron B&B in Gustavus, sampling organic rolled oats with blueberries the next morning. Grab a picnic lunch at Sunnyside Market and hitch a ride over to Bartlett Cove. Stay the night in the campsite, with a little afternoon jaunt on the Forest Trail. The next day, get up early for a seven-hour boat tour of Glacier Bay. A park ranger provides commentary on the 130-mile (209km) circuit. At South Marble Island, expect to see tufted and horned puffins, along with Steller sea lions. You'll start seeing icebergs 20 miles (32km) out; after lunch is the pièce de résistance – close-up views of the tidewater glaciers that make this bay famous. If you're lucky, you might just see a chunk of ice the size of a building fall and crash into the water.

02

One week

With a heightened sense of adventure – and no aversion to risk, cold or wet – you can see and do remarkable things here. It all starts on the water. Begin from Gustavus and Bartlett Cove, where you can arrange sea taxis, guides and gear. The Glacier Bay Boat Tour will drop off independent parties, or a number of guided operations can take you for day-long or multiday paddles. All but the most experienced of paddlers should consider going with a guide (if for nothing else but the companionship).

You can do a short warm-up trip to Beardslee Islands to get your toes wet; another day trip takes you to Point Adolphus, a great spot for humpback sighting. Go bigger with a weeklong paddle up the East or West Arms. On your way home, continue north of the park to Glacier Bay National Preserve, a remote corner of wilderness best accessed from Yakutat, where you can raft the Alsek River, learn more about subsistence living, or find your own adventure in a wilderness without boundaries.

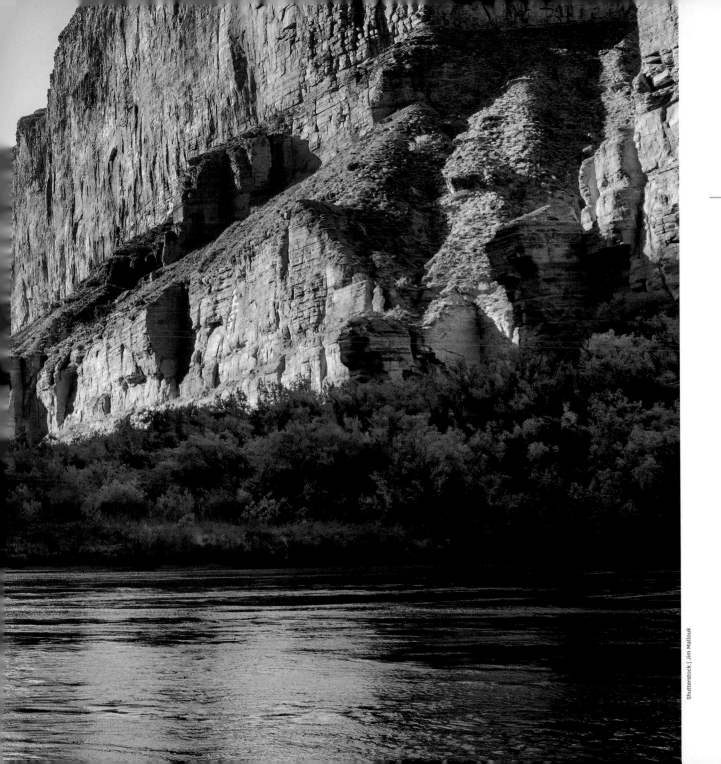

24
AZ

Grand Canyon National Park

To catch your first glimpse of this epic rent in Earth is to understand that some things are just as grand as they're billed.

Grand Canyon

Shutterstock | Jim Mallouk

The Grand Canyon, with its hypnotic folds of gold and red cliffs, its mesas rippling endlessly towards the horizon, is one of the most magnificent wonders of this planet. A mile (1.6km) deep, 18 miles (29km) wide and 277 miles (446km) long, its scope is truly hard to appreciate until you've seen it yourself. Come here to hike narrow trails down sandstone cliffs, to raft the roiling waters of the Colorado, to ride a mule through fragrant stands of piñon and sagebrush. Or just come to stand on the rim, camera in hand, marveling at the wonder of it all.

Some 90% of visitors come to the canyon's warmer South Rim, with its arid summers, silver falls, snowy fairyland winters and cool blue springs. The higher, colder North Rim is far more difficult to access, but is deeply rewarding for its crowd-free trails and silent nights powdered with stars. Further-flung areas are administered by Native American tribes – including the psychedelic blue falls of the Havasupai and the vertiginous glass Skywalk of the Hualapai people.

The wild Colorado River has been sawing away at the Arizona landscape for some six million years. Along with wind, ice and continental drift, it has slowly cut through the earth, revealing a layer cake of Kaibab limestone, Coconino sandstone, Hermit shale and many other types of rock, creating the vast chasm we see today.

Home to various Native American groups for more than 10,000 years, the canyon's first European visitors were Spanish explorers in the 1540s. In the 1870s, geologist John Wesley Powell led expeditions through the canyon, drawing national attention to its beauty via a series of early photographs.

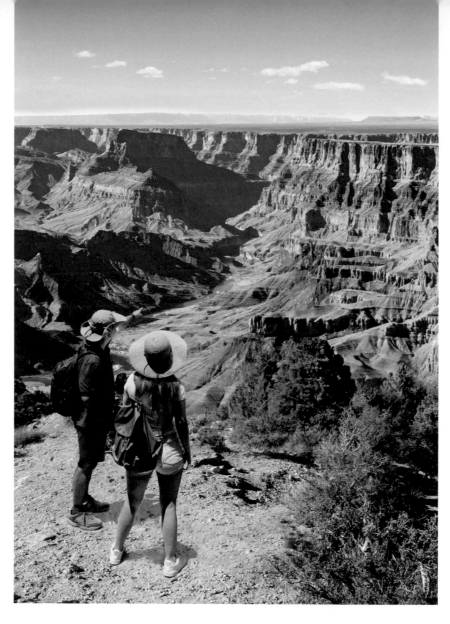

By the early 1900s, tourists were arriving in earnest via the Santa Fe Railroad. Today, some five million people from all over the globe come to be stunned by the canyon's epic size and beauty.

⬆ A clifftop lookout on the South Rim. Previous page: rafting the Colorado River is a lifetime ambition fulfilled for a lucky few.

Toolbox

When to go
The South Rim is open year-round, but summer crowds and winter cold make spring and fall the most pleasant times to visit. The North Rim has a more limited season of May to October.

Getting there
The South Rim is an hour north of Flagstaff, on I-40. Grand Canyon West, with the Skywalk, is a four-hour drive from South Rim. Four hours south is Phoenix airport. The North Rim entrance is 30 miles (48km) south of Jacob Lake.

Events
Summer means ranger-led stargazing nights and a July 4th parade. November is Native American Heritage Month, with special events.

Accessibility
Shuttle buses are equipped to carry most wheelchairs. While many viewpoints are accessible, hiking trails into the canyon itself are not.

Park in numbers
1902 Area in sq miles
8800 Highest point: Pt Imperial (ft)
2 Age of oldest rocks in the Canyon, Vishnu Schist, in billions of years

Stay here...

Grand Canyon Lodge
The grand dame of the North Rim, this 1928 National Historic Landmark is built of local timber and Kaibab limestone. Sleep in rustic cabins and dine in the splendid Main Lodge dining room. There's free shuttle service to the Kaibab trailhead. As with other park lodges, book six months or more in advance. is the colors of a desert sunset. Its 'geologic' fireplace features all the rock layers of the canyon. Rooms range from doubles with shared bathrooms to log-lined suites.

Bright Angel Lodge
Pioneering female architect Mary Jane Colter created this and other landmark park buildings, inspired by the local landscape and native traditions. Made of stone with bright-painted trim, the 1935 lodge

Phantom Ranch
Overnighting at the Phantom Ranch is a true 'bucket list' experience. You can only get here by hiking, rafting or riding a mule, so forget about dodging tour bus crowds. Designed by Mary Jane Colter, these cozy stone cottages are tucked into the trees on the north side of the Colorado River. After a long day of tramping, there's nothing like sharing a beer with fellow travelers in the dining room.

Do this!

Sunset-watching
You won't be alone seeing the sun set over Lipan Point, but there's a reason for the crowds. Watching the light go red and violet over the Palisades of the Desert and the Echo and Vermilion cliffs is a lifetime experience. You'll also have a terrific view of Unkar Rapid to the west. Arrive early and stay until the last drop of purple drains from the walls.

Mule trips
Ride a steady-footed mule along the South Rim for a three-hour trip, or descend to the canyon floor for the overnight trek to Phantom Ranch. It's an incredibly popular experience: book up to 15 months in advance. Shorter horse and mule trail rides are also available.

Rafting
Wannabe rafters often wait for a year or more to run the powerful Colorado, but the occasional lucky traveler gets a last-minute booking. However you get in, a rafting trip along the floor of the Grand Canyon is an experience you'll be telling your grandkids about. Trips range from about four to ten days, complete with riverside camping. Some sections are glass-smooth, while others will hurtle you over 30ft-plus (9m) rapids. Whee!

What to spot...

With an 8000ft (2438m) elevation gain from the Colorado River to the North Rim, the Grand Canyon hosts a startling variety of habitats. Gray foxes, mule deer and bighorn sheep inhabit the piñon forests of the South Rim, while the cooler Ponderosa pine and blue spruce forests of the North Rim are home to mountain lions, bobcats and goshawks. The river itself is a habitat for endangered humpback chub and razorback suckers, while beavers, canyon tree frogs and coyotes can be found among the cottonwoods on its banks.

KAIBAB SQUIRREL
The entire habitat of this tassel-eared squirrel is the Kaibab Plateau, along the Canyon's North Rim and just beyond.

CALIFORNIA CONDOR The largest land bird in America, this bald, black vulture became extinct in the wild in 1987. It was reintroduced to the Southwest, but there are still fewer than 300.

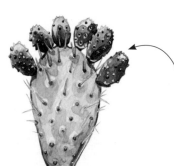

PRICKLY PEAR CACTUS These common cacti have wide, paddle-shaped pads and grow stunning pink, orange or yellow flowers and bulbous purple fruits.

Hike this...

O1 Rim Trail
If you're not into altitude changes, this semi-paved, 12-mile (19km) trail covers the best viewpoints on the South Rim in one family-friendly walk.

O2 Bright Angel Trail
See the canyon walls up close and personal on this popular stair trail, which descends 7.8 miles (12.5km) to the Colorado. There are several easy turning points for day-hikers.

O3 Rim to Rim
Snag a backcountry camping permit for this overnight trek from the North to South Rim along the North Kaibab to Bright Angel trails (24 miles (38.6km).

Itineraries

Whichever itinerary you choose, don't miss a sunset over the canyon. The hiking, mule trips and gorging on prickly pear are a bonus.

 Taking time to appreciate the natural grandeur of the Grand Canyon; hiking the North Rim.

 Horse-riding tours are popular.

01

A day

Arrive at the South Rim as dawn is breaking pink and lavender over the Painted Desert. Hit the best viewpoints in the most efficient way by walking the 12-mile (19km) Rim Trail. Stop first at the Pipe Creek Vista to gawk at the endless mesas' sea of red and purple waves. Then onward to the Yavapai Observation Station, where plate-glass windows offer panoramic views and topographic relief models explain the canyon's geology. Nearby Grandeur Point lets you look down at the hikers moving ant-like along the ribbon that is the Bright Angel Trail; stop here for a picnic lunch amid the pines. A bit further on, Mission-style Verkamp's Visitor Center is one of the park's oldest buildings, while the Mary Jane Colter–designed Hopi House was modeled after an old Hopi pueblo and built largely by Hopi tribespeople. Today it's a primo spot to pick up Native American jewelry and crafts. Several vistas later is Hopi Point – the place to see sunset drip its Crayola colors down the canyon walls (though nearby Mohave Point is a contender as well).

02

A weekend

Wake early amid the smell of piñon and juniper at one of the South Rim's campgrounds and fortify yourself with a hearty breakfast before hitting the Bright Angel Trail (with plenty of snacks and water). Wind your way down the canyon's rust-and-orange limestone and sandstone walls, passing mule trains as you go. Go as far as Indian Garden, an oasis of lush trees and waters 4.6 miles (7.4km) down. When you drag yourself, exhausted, back above the rim, have a shower and treat yourself to dinner in the dark-wood environs of the El Tovar Dining Room – locally ranched filet mignon tastes even better after so many miles of hiking. The next day, rest your aching calves by driving the 25-mile (40km) Desert View Dr. Start at Mather Point, where you can see the Bright Angel Trail winding into the rosy canyon. Don't miss the panoramas of Lipan Point or the 70ft (21m) climb up the Watchtower. End the day watching the sun sink like a red penny behind the cliffs.

03

Five days

On day one, take in the multi-hued vistas along the 25-mile (40km) Desert View Dr, stopping to learn about the canyon's geologic and cultural history at the Yavapai Geology Museum and the Tusayan Museum.

On day two, plunge in with the steep 1.5-mile (2.5km) hike into the canyon's deep red folds on the Grandview Trail. On day three, pack your backpack and set out down the Bright Angel Trail, winding your way down the piñon-shaded track, past the chartreuse oasis of Indian Garden and onto the canyon floor, overnighting at Phantom Ranch. On day four, do the same thing, but in reverse! Harder that way, isn't it?

On day five, rest your tired legs with the park's newest activity: e-biking along greenway trails, then, plunge into the canyon like an eagle with a skydiving trip, newly available from concessioner Paragon Skydive. For your last two days, make the 4.5-hour drive to the North Rim for a different (and chillier) perspective on the canyon's eternal majesty.

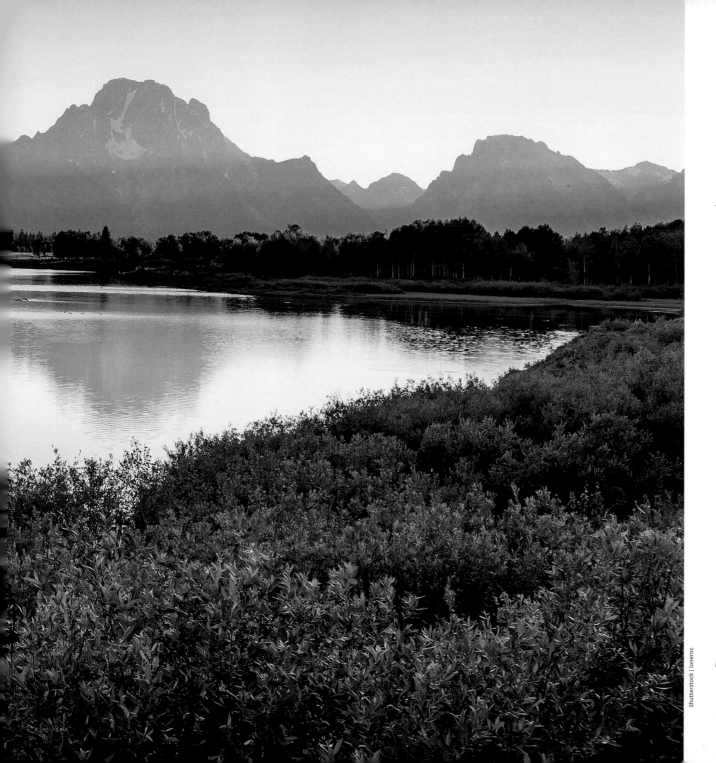

Shutterstock | loneroc

25

WY

Grand Teton National Park

Yellowstone's lesser-known southern neighbor is a high-altitude stunner, with peaks, meadows and back roads that offer unbelievable views and blissful solitude.

Grand Teton

Grand Teton isn't a 'drive-through' park, where you can see the best parts without straying more than a hundred paces from your car. Though it certainly does have some stunning scenic drives, this is a park for exploring. It's for hiking quad-burning trails up craggy peaks dotted with jade-green high-altitude lakes. It's for kayaking the choppy waters of Jackson Lake or rafting the undulating curves of the Snake River. It's for sitting silently in the tall grass watching pronghorns and bison graze in the wheat-colored afternoon sunlight. So if you're looking for an active, immersive park experience, the peaks and valleys of Grand Teton will make an unforgettable trip.

The sharp-spined Teton Range is the centerpiece of Grand Teton National Park. French fur trappers called its three main peaks *les trois tétons* – 'the three breasts.' (While we're not sure what Medusa-like creature has breasts as jagged as the Tetons, the name stuck.) In the early 1900s, the Jackson Hole area became crowded with tourist-centric development, from gas stations to dance halls to racetracks. Standard Oil heir John D Rockefeller Jr, concerned with the land's degradation, began secretly buying up property throughout the valley with the intent of giving it away as national park land. When the public found out, they revolted, angry about possible lost tax revenue. Though the park was established in 1929, it took more than 50 years and numerous acts of Congress to finalize its boundaries.

The terrain of Grand Teton varies vastly, its *Lord of the Rings*-like mountains erupting suddenly from the calm valley floor. Within the same day you can swim in a glacier-created mountain lake, hike through

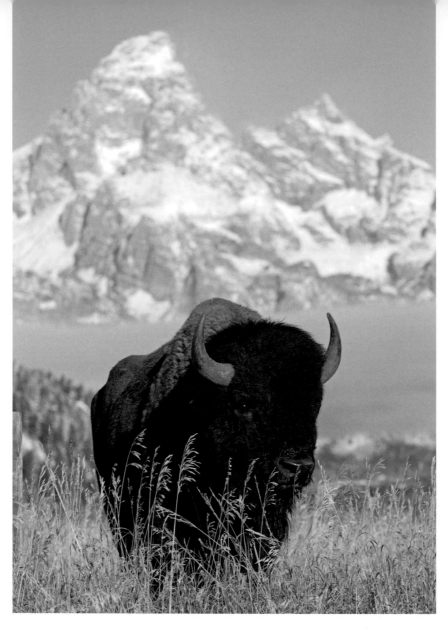

dripping conifer forests, picnic beneath the cottonwoods of swift-flowing rivers and drive along the flat golden meadows of the valley. Watch the stars at night, or head to Jackson for a luxe bison-steak dinner.

⬆ Large ungulates in the park include bison and moose, look for them around Snake River. Previous page: fishing from a kayak on Snake River. ➡ John Moulton barn.

Shutterstock | moosehenderson; Mark Read

Toolbox

When to go
Grand Teton is open year-round but it is more crowded in the summer, when wildflowers bloom and high temperatures are in the comfortable mid-70s F (low 20s C). Winter is gorgeous, though some roads may be closed due to snow.

Getting there
Grand Teton is just outside the town of Jackson, in Wyoming's northwest. The Jackson Hole Airport is actually inside Grand Teton. You'll need a car to explore.

Events
May is Old West Days in Jackson Hole. Hundreds of classical musicians arrive in July and August for the Grand Teton Music Festival.

Accessibility
Most park lodgings have accessible units. Wheelchair accessible trails include the Colter Bay headwall, Jackson Lake Dam overview, Menors Ferry Historic District and the Jenny Lake shore trail.

Park in numbers
485 Area in sq miles
13,770 Highest point: Grand Teton (ft)
173 Average snowfall (in)

Permits are required for all boating, including canoeing on Jackson Lake.

Stay here...

Jenny Lake Campground
In summer, campers circle this lakeside haven as early as 6am, hoping to snag a coveted spot as the previous night's residents leave. We think it's worth the dawn wake-up to sleep under the evergreens at this central campground. With only 51 tent-only spots and no showers or dishwashing facilities, this is definitely not glamping – but that's the point.

Jenny Lake Lodge
The luxe log cabins go quickly at this upscale-rustic resort, which often books up nearly a year in advance. Guests have been burrowing beneath Jenny Lake Lodge's handmade quilts since the 1920s. The high prices include breakfast, a five-course dinner as well as such activities as horseback riding and bike trips.

American Alpine Club Climbers' Ranch
Climbers and mountaineers retire to this rustic co-ed cabin complex to cook up big pasta meals over the camp stove, share beers with new friends, and even break out the guitars for impromptu singalongs. Though remote, down a winding road at the base of a glacial moraine, it's got showers, a boon after a long day on the crag.

Do this!

Rafting
Raft down the Snake River as it wends its way through the valley, watching beavers and otters splash as eagles and osprey glide overhead. On the shore, you might spot pronghorn or elk grazing as you pass beneath green-gold willow trees. A number of outfitters offer this rafting trip, which lasts about 10 miles (16km). No white water here, just a peaceful meander, as guides point out animals.

Boat cruising
In summer, passenger boats shuttle between the Jenny Lake Visitor Center and the base of Mount Teewinot every 10 to 15 minutes. Alight on the west side of the lake for the short-but-stunning hike to Hidden Falls. Or opt for one of the thrice-daily scenic cruises, which ply the lake's glassy waters for an hour.

Cycling
A car-free multi-use path extends from Jackson to Jenny Lake, running parallel to major roads (get a permit by the Moose entrance). Rent a bike at Moose then cruise the valley. Don't be surprised to spy a moose munching the grass as you fly by, especially early in the morning. In Jackson, fuel up on haute cowboy meals like bison burgers or elk steak before riding back.

What to spot...

Grand Teton has two major ecosystems: the mountains and the valley. The valley floor is blanketed in silvery sagebrush, a favorite snack of pronghorns and deer. On the riverbanks, cottonwood trees and willows give shade as otters frolic and elk stop for a drink. The lower slopes of the mountains are cool and green with conifers, the boughs of which are home to a plethora of songbirds. Further up, marmots and pikas scramble across rocky exposed peaks.

YELLOW-BELLIED MARMOTS Resembling beavers without the paddle-shaped tails, goofy-cute marmots are always a crowd-pleaser. They're easy to spot on the higher slopes of the Teton Range.

HUCKLEBERRY BUSHES In late summer, huckleberries begin to ripen on their spindly-branched bushes. Resembling darker, glossier blueberries, they're a favorite of humans and bears alike.

ELK In warm weather, elk graze in the park's valley. As the snow sets in, they make their way to the National Elk Refuge, just southeast of the park.

Hike this...

O1 Surprise & Amphitheater lakes

This lung-burning 9.6-mile (15.5km) round-trip hike follows switchbacks up the wildflower-spangled side of Disappointment Peak to these two chilly mountain oases.

O2 Teton Crest Trail

At 40 miles (64km), this epic route crosses much of the park and beyond, with jagged vistas, backcountry lakes, and glacier-carved gullies as far as you can see. Permits necessary for backcountry camping.

O3 Hidden Falls

A popular family hike, this 1.5-mile (2.4km) meander begins at the western dock of the Jenny Lake shuttle and leads to this much-photographed 200ft (61m) waterfall.

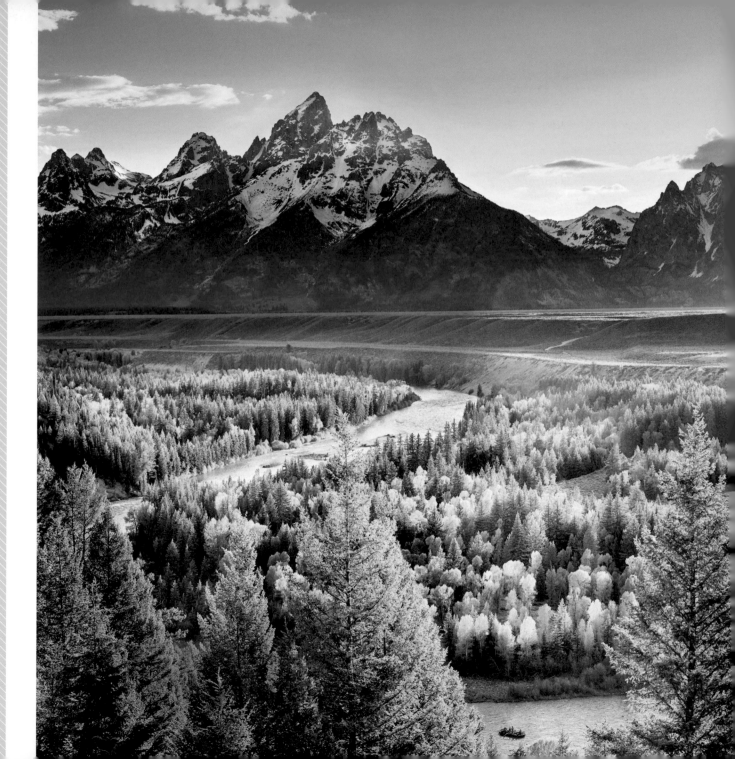

Itineraries

Raft down Snake River, cruise tranquil Jenny Lake or hike alpine heights to Surprise and Amphitheater lakes. Binoculars and a camera are a must for bird-watching.

← Hidden Falls; Snake River flows west through the park.
→ A bull moose in the sage brush.

01
A day

Drive in from Jackson early in the morning to make the most of your day. Arrive in the valley as the sun is just beginning to kiss the valley floor with golden light, looking for grazing elk and moose. Take advantage of the good light to photograph the atmospherically decaying barns of Mormon Row in the park's southeast corner, home to a tiny community of Mormon homesteaders in the late 1800s. As the day begins to warm, make your way to Jenny Lake to ride the passenger boat across the mirror-smooth waters, snapping pictures of the jagged Teton Range as you near them. On the lake's western edge, take the 1.5-mile hike (2.4km) to the pounding waters of Hidden Falls. Spend the afternoon paddling along the shores of Jackson Lake. Don't forget your binoculars; this is a primo bird-watching spot. By now you've worked up an appetite for the chuckwagon dinner at Dornan's in Moose; enjoy plates of fire-cooked mashed potatoes, corn on the cob, BBQ beef, blackened fish and more at a picnic table under the starry sky.

02
Two days

Awaken in your tent (or in your lodge, if you've been lucky enough to snag a room) and take the first shuttle of the morning across Jenny Lake to the beat the crowds to the trailhead of Cascade Canyon. Spend the next six or seven hours traversing mossy forests, beach-like riverbanks and alpine meadows straight out of *Heidi* until you reach the icy waters of Lake Solitude. Then head back down in time for dinner with a view at the Mural Room in the Jackson Lake Lodge. The next morning, arrive at your pre-booked rafting trip down the Snake River, and spend the day drifting beneath the endless skies as birds sing in the background. Hit the chuckwagon dinner at Dornan's in Moose, or roast some wieners on an open fire. Set your alarm for a middle-of-the-night wake-up to marvel at the star-powdered sky. If you're ambitious, stay up for a dawn photo session of grazing mammals in the valley fields – early morning is the best time to catch them in action.

03
A week

Warm up on your first day with one of the park's most lung-blasting hikes, the 10-mile (16km) round-trip trek to Surprise and Amphitheater lakes. On day two, canoe around Jenny Lake and enjoy a couple of easy hikes on the west side. The next day, cycle the dedicated trail all the way to Jackson, purple mountains majestic in the background. Splurge on dinner at Coelette, a buzzy new spot in a historic cabin specializing in food from the world's mountain regions.

On the fourth day, saddle up with a trail ride from Colter Bay in the morning, then enjoy a little solitude and wildlife-watching in the Laurance S Rockefeller Preserve. On the fifth day, book a guided climbing trip with Exum, America's oldest climbing guide service. They'll take you up the serrated summit of Cube Point, or create a bespoke adventure based on ability.

On day six, take a town day to relax at a Jackson spa. On the seventh day, make your own souvenirs with a wildlife photo safari: if you're looking for moose try Gros Ventre; for bears Pilgrim Creek.

Grand Teton

26

Great Basin National Park

An imposing peak stabs into a star-splattered sky in central Nevada, surrounded by unbelievably ancient trees, incredible caves, an endangered glacier and awesome arches.

Less than 300 miles (483km) from the lairy neon glare of Las Vegas, Great Basin National Park is almost entirely free of light pollution, offering a spectacular window into the night sky – where five of our solar system's eight planets are often visible to the naked eye.

The White Pine county park sits almost a mile above sea level in Nevada, its elevation accentuating the clarity of the heavens above. The Snake Range climbs towards the stars here, reaching its zenith with Wheeler Peak, a high-flying horn sculpted by ice over many millennia, which shelters a tenacious glacier, laced with moonmilk and gypsum. This was the old hunting ground of the Fremont people and, later, Shoshone tribes. It lay on the route of the California Trail, which saw heavy wagon traffic when gold-rush fever began spreading like a contagion across America from the west coast in 1848.

The imposing Wheeler Peak overlooks an array of natural features that fall within the boundaries of an extraordinary park, named for the basins (valleys) that pockmark the region. Above ground you'll find stone arches, thousand-year-old wall paintings, and trees that began growing from cones when Egypt's Great Pyramid was still being built.

But the discovery of the park's most famous feature is credited to Absalom Lehman, a wandering miner and sometime rancher who chanced across a great marble subterranean cavern in the early 1880s. Lehman Caves, a chamber that burrows into the side of the Snake Range, is a treasure trove of stalactites, stalagmites and rare speleothems.

These caves brought the region its first layer of protection, with President Warren G Harding creating Lehman Caves National Monument in 1922. The surrounding area was made a national park in 1986.

Toolbox

When to go
Great Basin is open year-round. Summer is best for hiking. Cross-country skiing is great in winter, but only one campground stays open all year. Lehman Caves stay a steady 50°F (10°C).

Getting there
The park is 290 miles (467km) north of Las Vegas and 235 miles (378km) south of Salt Lake City. The visitor center is in the east of the park on Hwy 487. It's easily accessed by car via the I-15 and US 50 highways. There is no public transportation in the park.

Events
The three-day Astronomy Festival in mid-September offers star-gazing hikes and photography workshops.

Accessibilty
The Island Forest Trail is a wheelchair-accessible path. Visitors in non-motorized wheelchairs can join the first thirty minutes of a cave tour.

Park in numbers

121 Area in sq miles
13,065 Height of Wheeler Peak's summit (ft)
4900 Age of 'Prometheus,' a Great Basin bristlecone pine felled in 1964 (years)

Stay here...

Lower Lehman Creek
Fittingly, for a place with such a stellar reputation for its night sky, there's only one way to stay in Great Basin: you have to sleep out under the stars. Of the park's five developed campgrounds, only this one is open year-round. Facilities include vault toilets, picnic tables, tent pads, and campfire grills. The creek runs through the ground.

Wheeler Peak
At 9886ft (3013m), this is the highest of the park's campgrounds – temperatures can be cool. Open on a first-come-first-served basis between May and October (depending on conditions), it's great for tent campers, but large RVs will struggle. The views here are stunning, and trails leading to the park's top peak are close by.

Backcountry camping
Shortly after the generators are switched off, a peaceful darkness descends on the primitive campgrounds along Snake Creek Rd, and the entire universe seems to rise above the brooding silhouette of Wheeler Peak. There are picnic tables and fire rings here, but little else – save for the million-dollar view.

Do this!

Stargazing
Cloudless nights in Great Basin offer an astonishing panoply of stars. Five planets can be seen with the naked eye, plus the Andromeda Galaxy, the Milky Way and meteor showers. Numerous nocturnal adventures can be enjoyed: take a tour through outer space with a laser-wielding ranger or, if there's a full moon, join a guided night hike.

Caving
Lehman Caves is a colossal marble cavern featuring a staggering collection of formations, including stalactites, stalagmites, helictites, flowstone, popcorn, and over 300 rare shields. There are two tour options: the 60-minute Lodge tour and the slightly more demanding 90-minute Grand Palace tour, which takes in the famous Parachute Shield.

Scenic drives
The Wheeler Peak Scenic Drive climbs 4000ft in 12 miles (19km), passing sagebrush, piñon pines and Douglas firs as it rolls through several ecological zones. At each hairpin turn the mountain-and-basin vistas expand. The Summit Trail awaits at 10,000ft near the end of your drive. .

◀ ▶ A bristlecone pine tree in Wheeler Peak Grove, some of the world's oldest-living organisms.

Hike this...

01 Lexington Arch Trail
A six-story limestone arch is your destination on this 5.4-mile (8.7km) round-trip hike that begins south of Baker. You may need to add a mile or two of walking depending on where you park. The road is washed out near the trailhead.

02 Bristlecone & Glacier Trail
With global temperatures rising, the park's glacier is expected to melt away within 20 years – see it while you can on this 4.6-mile (7.4km) trail. Nearby, bristlecone cone trees have been growing for millennia.

03 Wheeler Peak Summit Trail
Hike to the roof of the park and the summit of the Snake Range for stunning views. The 8.6-mile (13.8km) route follows the ridge from the Summit Trail parking area.

What to spot...

As a place where the desert meets the mountains in the midst of a great tract of largely untouched wilderness, the ecosystem here is vibrant. Great Basin is home to some of the world's most ancient lifeforms – bristlecone pine trees – plus another 800 species of plant and tree. Mammals here range from mountain lions to ground squirrels; snakes slither past prickly pear bushes; and birds such as Clark's nutcrackers flit around collecting pine nuts.

GREAT BASIN BRISTLECONE PINE
This species of tree can live for thousands of years. The oldest non-clonal organism ever found was a Great Basin bristlecone pine tree, felled near Wheeler Peak and dated at 4900 years old.

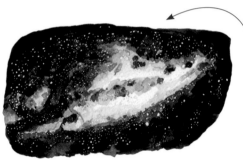

THE MILKY WAY
Our galactic neighborhood burns brightly above Great Basin at night, with 100 to 400 billion stars creating a great white smudge across the sky.

PYGMY RABBIT
The world's smallest rabbit is a resident of Great Basin; it's one of only two American species of rabbit to dig its own burrow.

RING-TAILED CAT A relative of the raccoon (and not actually a cat at all), ring-tails are shy, nocturnal creatures who live very solitary lives, meeting only to mate.

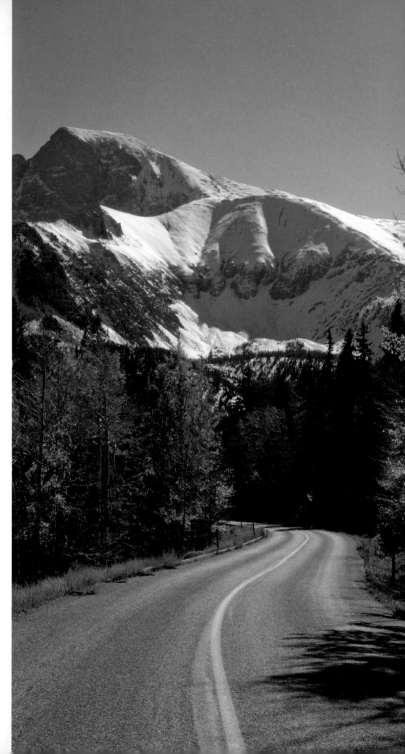

Itineraries

*Take a guided tour of Lehman Caves,
trek the mighty Wheeler Peak or
tackle the backcountry along the
Baker Lake Loop Trail.*

 12 miles (19km) of beauty on
Wheeler Peak Scenic Drive.
 Lehman Caves feature hundreds
of rock formations.

01

A half-day

If you're driving I-15
between Salt Lake
City and Vegas and
want to break up the
journey with compelling
natural scenery, a quick
exploration of Great Basin
is the perfect antidote to
freeway fatigue.

After exploring the
visitor center, join a park
ranger for a 90-minute
guided tour of Lehman
Caves, marveling at the
natural grandeur of the
Grand Palace and spotting
century-old signatures on
the walls of the Inscription
Room.

Back outside, consider
your schedule. If you're
short on time, take an
easy stroll through a
pinyon-juniper forest
on the .3-mile (.4km)
Mountain View Trail beside
the Lehman Caves Visitor
Center. If you're not in a
rush, hop into your car for
a spin along the 12-mile
(19km) Wheeler Peak
Scenic Drive, drinking
in inspiring views of the
mountain and panoramic
vistas of the valleys as you
climb through five distinct
ecological zones. Travel as
far as time allows.

02

Two days

Follow the half-day itinerary,
but pitch your tent at the
Wheeler Peak Campground
at the end of the scenic
drive. Stake a spot then hike
the Bristlecone Pine Trail,
which leads to the oldest
lifeforms on the planet –
some of them thousands
of years old. It would be a
shame to be so close and not
see Nevada's only glacier,
especially since it could
be gone within a couple of
decades. Carry on beyond
the pines to find the park's
most endangered feature.

In the evening, attend
a ranger-led stargazing
talk. These are offered on
Saturday nights from May
though October, and on
Tuesday and Thursday nights
from June through early
September.

Early the next morning,
begin the 8.6-mile (13.8km)
trek to the top of Wheeler
Peak from the Summit Trail
parking lot. Start early to
minimize the risk of getting
caught in the open during
one of the storms that
sometimes blast this park.
The trail traces the ridgeline.
By the time you reach the
summit you'll have earned
the vista before you.

03

Three or more days

After two days exploring the
heart of the park, its time
to venture further afield. If
you're interested in the lives
of the region's early settlers,
head to the excavated
Fremont Indian Village at
Baker Archaeological Site,
inhabited in the late 13th
century. You can search
for rock art created by
the Fremont people at
Pictograph Cave, where
images were cut into the
rock and then painted.

To admire a six-story
limestone arch, drive 25
miles south of Baker for a
5.4-mile (8.7km) out-
and-back hike to rugged
Lexington Arch. Note that
the road is very rough
and you may have to park
and walk an extra mile to
the trailhead depending
on conditions and the
clearance level of your car.

The biggest adventure,
though, promises to be the
backcountry escapade along
the Baker Lake/Johnson
Lake Loop Trail. Come
armed with a lightweight
tent, and break the 13-mile
(21km) hike with some
primitive camping. Just you
and the stars – a heavenly
experience indeed.

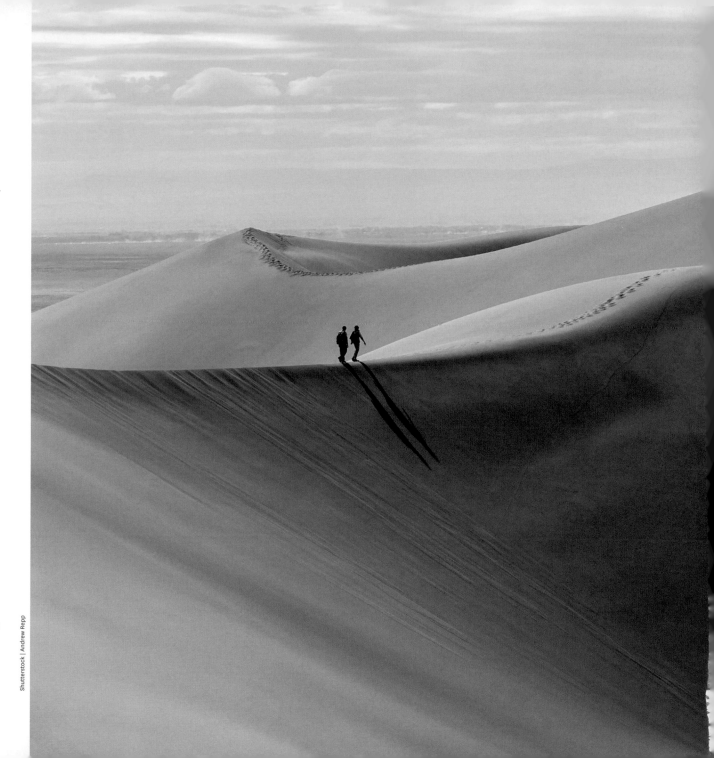

27

CO

Great Sand Dunes National Park

This sea of sand banked up against snow-dusted peaks is no optical illusion. It's nature at its most whimsical and surreal.

Shutterstock | Andrew Repp

After a long approach through the flats of the San Luis Valley, this shimmering Saharan landscape seems like a mirage. The dunes stretch for 30 sq miles (78 sq km), flanked by the steep Sangre de Cristo range on one side and glassy wetlands on the other.

It's a place of stirring optical illusions. The ceaseless wind works like a disconsolate sculptor, constantly creating or erasing elegant ripples underfoot. One can lose all perspective in the shadow of the dunes – the largest of which rises over 700ft (213m). In this monochromatic landscape, the only reference to judge distance is the sight of other hikers, like ants on the faraway dunes.

The Great Sand Dunes are a playground for both grown-ups and children alike, who can glide down dunes in saucers and on snowboards, build castles, bury limbs and rejoice in the joys of this unusual gift. Hold a grain under a magnifying glass to see the spectrum of its shapes and colors: 29 different rock and mineral types – from obsidian and sulfur to amethyst and turquoise – are represented in the sand's makeup.

Where did all this sand come from, and why does it stay here? The answer lies in the unique geography and weather patterns of the San Luis Valley. For millions of years, streams, snowmelt and flash floods have been carrying eroded sand and silt out of the San Juan Mountains, about 60 miles (96.5km) west, to the valley floor. From there, prevailing southwest winds gradually blow the sand into the natural hollow at the southern end of the Sangre de Cristo range. At the same time, streams and stronger prevailing winds from the eastern mountains reciprocate, causing the sand to pile up into what have become the highest dunes in North America.

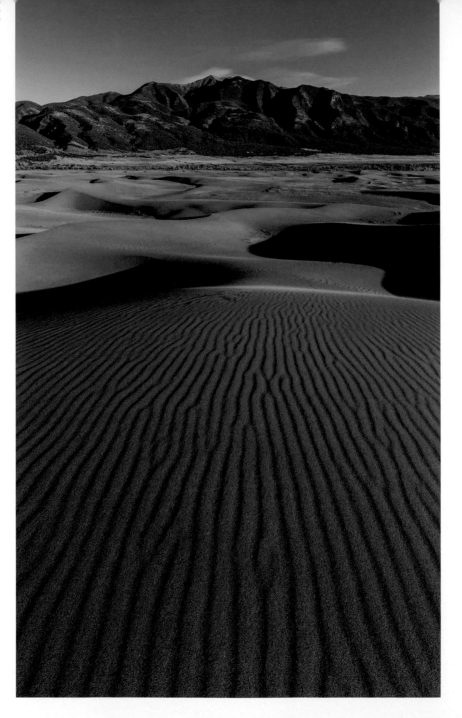

Toolbox

When to go
The moderate temperatures of late spring and early fall are best for visitation. (In summer, the sand can reach 140°F/60°C during the heat of the day.) It's also exquisite during a full moon. The campground is open May through mid-November.

Getting there
Colorado's Great Sand Dunes National Park is 33 miles (53km) northeast of Alamosa and 240 miles (386km) from state capital Denver, which has an international airport. There's no public transportation, so a car is necessary.

Events
The Alamosa Round Up Rodeo is held the last week in June, with barrel racing, broncs and bareback riding.

Accessibility
A specialized dunes wheelchair can be reserved in advance at the visitor center, for a child or adult.

Park in numbers

132 Area in sq miles
140°F/-20°F High and low dune temperature (60/-29°C)
750 Tallest dune (ft)

Stay here...

Piñon Flats Campground
The park's official campground boasts a great location not far from the dune field. Pitch your tent, gather around the campfire and take advantage of the star-riddled sky of the valley for amazing nighttime views. When Medano Creek hits peak flow in late May to early June, campsites are booked months in advance.

Zapata Falls Campground
Perched high in the Sangre de Cristo range, these secluded sites south of the national park offer glorious panoramas of the valley and tranquility in spades, but campers must bring their own water supply. With a steep access road.

Orient Mine & Valley View Hot Springs
Offering campsites and affordable cabins that sell out in summer, this off-the-grid, hot springs resort is a magical place snuggled into the foothills of the Sangre de Cristo mountains. Geothermal waters flow downhill through a series of natural ponds in one of Colorado's most beautiful hot springs. It's also clothing optional. The location is 66 miles (106km) from the Sand Dunes.

Do this!

Sledding
The heavy wooden sled may seem like a bad idea when you're trudging out to the dunes, but the gleeful rush down the slopes is worth every footstep. Conditions are best after recent precipitation. Sandboards can be rented at the edge of the park.

Tubing
The snowmelt stream of Medano Creek flows down from the Sangre de Cristo Mountains. At times, you can even float down the creek on an inner tube, right besides the dunes. Peak flow is usually in late May or early June. Water rippling over the sand creates a temporary beach popular with families.

Wildlife viewing
Alamosa National Wildlife Refuge hosts bald eagles, elk and coyotes. In the spring and fall look for migrating sandhill cranes. Visit at dawn or dusk, when wildlife is the most active – and when you'll hear the amazing auditory soundscape of bird calls and whistles. It's 3 miles (5km) from Alamosa.

← Sand dunes and the Sangre de Cristo mountains. Previous page: it can be energy-sapping to walk on the sand dunes.

What to spot...

The sand dunes are a strange centerpiece in a diverse landscape of grasslands, wetlands, conifer and aspen forests, alpine lakes, and tundra. The unique high-altitude desert environment is a place of extremes, with big fluctuations in temperature. Constant moisture from precipitation allows some species, including kangaroo rat, blowgrass and various beetles, to survive on the actual dunes. Scientists estimate that the dunes are about a half-million years old.

RIO GRANDE CUTTHROAT TROUT
With a flaming belly stripe, this lovely native trout survives well in Medano Creek because exotic fish cannot invade the closed drainage system.

PEREGRINE FALCON This monitored and once-endangered falcon is the fastest bird in the world. It nests in cliffs and swoops down on these grasslands in search of prey.

ROCKY MOUNTAIN BEE PLANT During wet summers, pink patches of this wildflower attract diverse pollinators to damp grasslands and woodlands. Locals call it 'skunkweed' for its signature stink.

Hike this...

O1 Great Sand Dunes
There are no trails through these expansive dunes, but hiking's still the star attraction. It's hard – trudging hills of sand, you'll feel like an ant in a sugar bowl. Try for High Dune, a 2.5-mile (4km) round-trip with panoramas.

O2 Mosca Pass Trail
A moderate, 7-mile (11km) round-trip hike up into the Sangre de Cristo Wilderness through meadows and aspen stands along Mosca Creek.

O3 Zapata Falls
This short, 0.5-mile (0.8km) family hike scrambles through ankle-deep, ice-cold water and over slippery rocks to the end of a slot canyon.

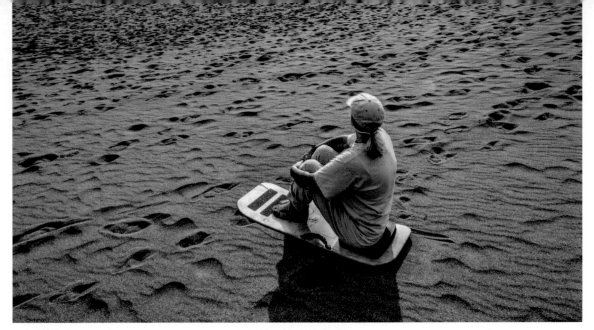

← There's a display of night photography in the visitor center.
→ Bring or borrow a sandboard for sliding down the dunes.

Itineraries

Hike the dunes, sled down them or take on daunting Blanca Peak. Cool down your adrenaline in Mosca Creek or get steamy in Valley View Hot Springs.

01

A day

Arm yourself with good sunblock, a hat and plenty of water. If it's summer, an early start on the dunes will help you avoid both heat and afternoon thunderstorms. Although sandals might seem ideal, closed-toe shoes provide a firmer grip and better protection against the heat.

Hike the dunes in any direction. There are no trails or obstructions – this is free hiking at its best. Keeping track of landmarks, such as distant peaks, will help with orientation. Bring a sled and you have entertainment for as long as your calves can drag it uphill. If you can't resist goal-setting, head for High Dune and Star Dune, which is, at 750ft (229m), the tallest dune in the park.

At lunchtime, take a break at the picnic area and cool your heels in Mosca Creek. In early summer, the flow is usually high enough to float in inner tubes. Spend your afternoon exploring the other facets of the park. That's right – the dunes make up less than half of it. Head south 10 miles (16km) for a short, scrambling hike at Zapata Falls.

02

A weekend

Spend your first day on the dunes. Sleeping over at the Pinyon Flats Campground earns you the privilege of photographing the dunes in the moonlight. Keep an eye out for nocturnal wanderers: kangaroo rats, toads, coyotes, bobcats and owls.

On day two, head further afield. The Zapata Falls hike can be extended to reach the alpine South Zapata Lake (8 miles/13km round-trip). Look for chirping marmots and pikas on the slopes.

And then there's the obvious staring you down. Blanca Peak (14,344ft/4372m) is the tall, diamond-shaped summit that's the backdrop to the sand dunes. While for most it will just be a photo op across the valley, experienced hikers will want to take it on. From the Lake Como trailhead it's a full-day odyssey with an early start. The 11-mile (17.7km) round-trip has 3900ft (1189m) of elevation gain. Access requires a 4WD vehicle.

Cap your weekend off with a soak in the nearby Valley View Hot Springs. Hike into these natural rock ponds to soothe your muscle aches.

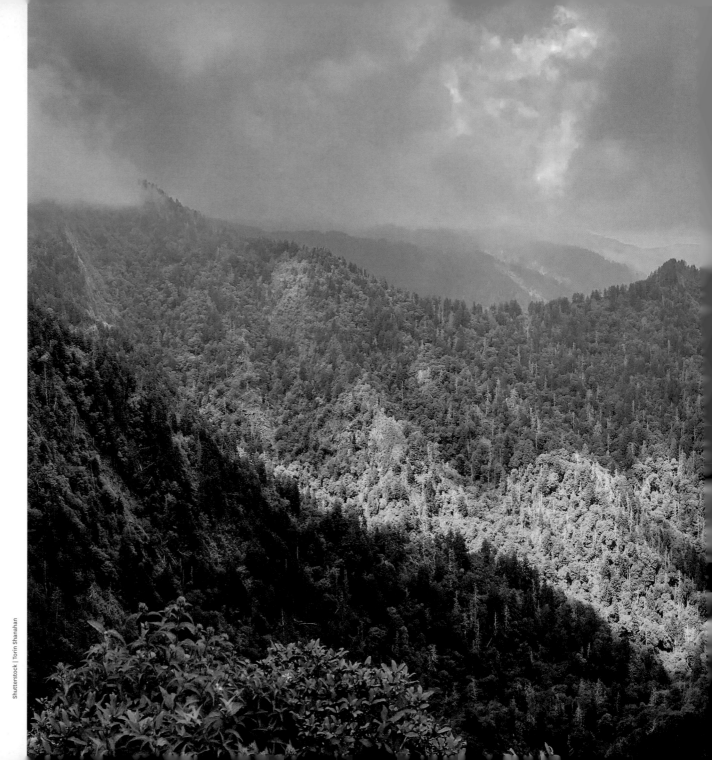

28

NC
TN

Great Smoky Mountains National Park

The Rockies may be dramatic, but the mist- and moss-shrouded peaks of the ancient Appalachians have mystery.

Shutterstock | Torin Shanahan

Imagine watching the sky go from ink-black to periwinkle-blue as pink dawn clouds ripple across the endless, wrinkled chain of peaks stretching towards the horizon. It's like nowhere else on earth. From the fog-choked summit of Clingmans Dome to the photogenic ghost town of Cades Cove to the tinkling music of a dozen silvery waterfalls, there's something deeply magical about these mountains. Experience it by hiking the park's trails, sleeping in its many remote campgrounds, splashing in its icy swimming holes and driving its craggy back roads.

The Cherokee people who called this land home for thousands of years were forcibly removed by President Andrew Jackson's decree in the 1830s, marching to Oklahoma along what's now known as the Trail of Tears. But some decided to stay behind, hiding in the mountains in what is now the national park; some of the ancestors of these rebels still live outside the park, in the Qualla Boundary area.

White settlers arrived in the early 1800s, homesteading, building railroads, and cutting timber from the deep primeval forests. Worried the logging would spoil the landscape, private citizens, the US government and Standard Oil heir John D Rockefeller Jr banded together to buy up land and evict those living in the park in the 1920s.

Unlike most national parks, Great Smoky Mountains charges no admission to visitors, thanks to a proviso in the park's original charter as part of a grant from the Rockefeller family. Its lack of entry fee and its convenient location to many Eastern cities make Great Smoky Mountains America's most visited national park, with more than 10 million travelers a year. But

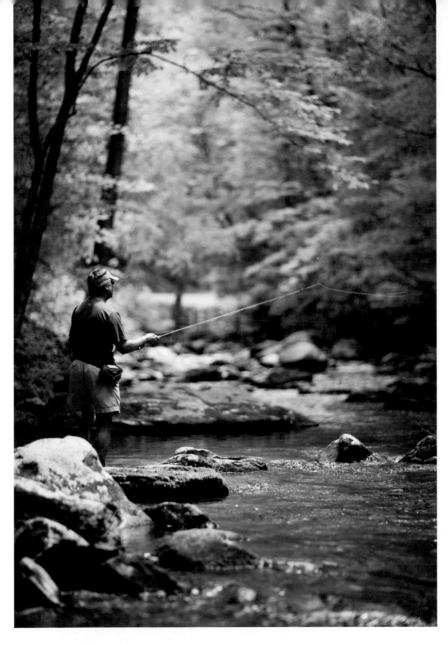

most visitors don't stray far from their cars, which is their loss – once you get a few hundred steps away from the road you're in your own personal fairyland.

◄ The watermill at Roaring Fork.
▲ Fishing in the park's streams is permitted year-round. Previous page: viewpoints abound.

Toolbox

When to go
The park is open year-round, but is most crowded in summer. Fall is stunning. In winter, some roads and facilities may be closed.

Getting there
The park straddles eastern Tennessee and western North Carolina. In Tennessee the major hub is Gatlinburg. In North Carolina it's the town of Cherokee; the city of Asheville makes a good base: it's about two hours' drive away and has an airport.

Events
September brings the two-day Music of the Mountains Appalachian music festival

Accessibility
Mountain Farm Museum, Mingus Mill, and much of Cades Cove are partially accessible. Cades Cove, Elkmont, and Smokemont campgrounds have accessible sites, as does the Big Creek Horse Camp. Sugarlands Valley Nature Trail is fully accessible.

Park in numbers

816 Area in sq miles
907 New plant and animal species discovered here
78 Preserved historic buildings

Stay here...

 LeConte Lodge
LeConte is no ordinary hotel. Perched on the summit of Mt LeConte, this electricity-free lodge is reached on foot. Supplies are packed in on llamas (see them hoofing it up Trillium Gap Trail on Monday, Wednesday and Friday mornings). Hikers dine by the light of kerosene lamps before retiring to bunks to doze through the silent Appalachian night.

 Cades Cove Campground
Cades Cove has a social vibe, with summer ranger programs, bike rentals and a camp store. The 160 campsites are shaded by forest, with flush toilets nearby. The trailhead to Abrams Falls is outside your tent flap, as is a stable offering trail and carriage rides through the valley. Cades Cove is heavenly during fall.

Balsam Mountain Campground
In a forest 'island' of red spruce and balsam fir, this small campground is off the beaten path – watch bunnies hop past your tent. The overlook offers one of the most stunning sunsets in the Smokies. Lack of RV hookups keep Balsam Mountain peaceful, and the high elevation keeps things cool – bring a sweater!

Do this!

 Cycling
Cades Cove, a mountain valley ('cove' in Appalachian-speak), was settled by gritty English, Welsh and Scots-Irish pioneers in the 1800s. Today, the area is a photogenic ghost town of mills and homesteads. An 11-mile (17.7km) loop road gets slammed with traffic in the high season; rent a bike and ride on a Wednesday, when it's car-free.

 Vista-viewing
At 6643ft (2025m), foggy Clingmans Dome is the Smokies' highest peak. A drive and a 0.5-mile (0.8km) hike lead to an observation tower that looks rather like a flying saucer. On a clear day, you can see 100 miles (161km) and seven states from its panoramic platform. It's also a primo sunset-viewing spot, with wispy clouds turning the sky into a pink-and-purple watercolor painting. In fall, views over the gold and red mountains are absolutely luscious.

Waterfall-hopping
More than 85in (216cm) of rain fall every year in the high country, ideal conditions for lots of waterfalls. Near Cades Cove, Abrams Falls plunges down 20ft (6m) of rocks, sending mist high into the air. You can walk behind bridal-veil-like Grotto Falls, deep within the old-growth hemlock forest. At Mingo Falls, silvery water streams down for 120ft (36.6m).

What to spot...

The Smokies are home to such an astounding richness of plant and animal life they've been declared an International Biosphere Reserve. Mountain meadows light up with trillium, columbine, violets and fire pinks in spring. In summer, mountain laurels, rhododendrons and azaleas bloom wildly on heath balds. Deep spruce, pine and hemlock forests shelter a profusion of mosses and ferns, some yet unnamed by science. Throughout the territory, black bears, owls, brook trout, salamanders and hundreds of other animals make their homes.

BLEEDING HEART
Just as their name suggests, these pink wildflowers are shaped like valentine hearts with a drop emerging at the bottom. Look for them on slopes in April and May.

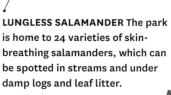

LUNGLESS SALAMANDER The park is home to 24 varieties of skin-breathing salamanders, which can be spotted in streams and under damp logs and leaf litter.

YELLOW BIRCH These common trees can be identified by their bronze bark, which smells faintly of wintergreen. In fall their leaves turn a stunning gold.

Sunset at Clingmans Dome mountaintop observation tower.

Hike this...

O1 Laurel Falls
This classic, 2.6-mile (4.2km) round-trip hike climbs gently through oak and mountain laurel to an 80ft (24.4m) cascade with two wading-friendly pools.

O2 Chimney Tops
This 4-mile (6.4km) quad burner ascends steeply through rhododendron thicket and across several streams, finishing at two knobs of metamorphic rock known as 'the chimneys.'

O3 Newfound Gap to Charlies Bunion
Climb steadily through spruce-fir forest and traverse view-packed ridges before ending at the 'bunion' – a stone outcrop 5500 feet (1676 m) above sea level (8 miles).

Itineraries

Waterfall fans are spoiled for choice: look for black bears near Laurel Falls, hike Abrams Falls or hit Townsend Wye to jump off rocks into Little River.

← Purple phacelia flowers.
The view from Charlies Bunion mountain via Newfound Gap.
→ Spruce Flats Falls.

01
A day

Concentrate on the park's main artery, 30-mile (43km) Newfound Gap Rd, which winds through forest so deep it feels like a tunnel on the way from Cherokee, North Carolina, to Gatlinburg, Tennessee. Starting from the North Carolina side, you'll hit Mingus Mill, a restored 1886 gristmill, and Mountain Farm, a collection of 19th-century buildings giving visitors a peek into the life of Appalachian homesteaders. Gawk at the patchwork quilt of the Oconaluftee River Valley from the overlook, then take the turnoff for Clingmans Dome for 100-mile (161km) views across the mid-South. At Newfound Gap you'll cross from North Carolina into Tennessee; a few miles later you'll hit the trailhead for Alum Cave Bluffs – take it if you fancy a hike through misty alpine forest. Do the loop-de-loop at The Loop, a section of road that goes through a tunnel and crosses over itself. Near the Tennessee-side exit you'll have opportunities to snap the iconic stone peaks of Chimney Tops. Top the day off with pancakes in delightfully cheesy Gatlinburg.

02
Two days

Drive Newfound Gap Rd as in the first itinerary, but when you get near the Tennessee border, hang a left onto Little River Rd to find the trailhead for Laurel Falls, one of the park's most popular waterfall overlooks. It's not uncommon to see a black bear snuffling in the bushes beyond this 80ft (24.4m) torrent. Splash around in the chilly base pool here, or head a little further to the beloved Townsend Wye swimming hole, where families jump from rocks into Little River. Camp amid the fragrant pines at Cades Cove Campground.

In the morning, wake early to drive (or cycle!) the Cades Cove loop, poking into old log cabins, watching a grist mill in action and climbing the hill to the old graveyard to get a feel for life in this mountain valley in the 1800s. Later, take the 5-mile (8km) hike to Abrams Falls, a short but wild waterfall deep in the cool forest. Finish the evening hanging out outside the camp store with fellow travelers, swapping tales of trails hiked and bears seen.

03
A week

Begin your journey in the North Carolina access town of Cherokee, where you can ignore the fast food and cheesy gift shops in favor of the top-notch Museum of the Cherokee Indian. To appreciate these mountains you should learn about the people who named the region Shaconage ('land of the blue smoke'). On day two, skirt the park's edge to the entrance for the remote Cataloochee Valley, where you can spend the next day and a half elk-spotting and exploring 19th century settler buildings, camping overnight at Cataloochee Campground. On day four return to (relative) civilization with a trek up the Trillium Gap Trail to Mt LeConte (why yes, you've reserved this wildly popular lodge a year in advance – good planning!), passing through virgin hemlock forest and stands of prehistoric-looking ferns. Coming back down on the fifth day, check out the historic valley of Cades Cove before making the drive to the park's far southwest, where Fontana Lake's chilly waters are a boating and fishing mecca.

Great Smoky Mountains

29

TX

Guadalupe Mountains National Park

Soaring high above the desert floor, the untrammeled wilderness of the Guadalupe Mountains is one of the best-kept secrets in Texas.

Mountain, forest and desert intersect in this rugged landscape wilderness, which attracts only a handful of visitors each year, despite its diversity. Gazing out across the shimmering Chihuahuan Desert from the tallest peak in Texas, it's hard to believe that this national park remains so little known. On even a one-day hike, you can get a taste of Guadalupe's unusual features, traversing arid, cactus-lined open country, then dipping into woodland-lined canyons and crossing trout-filled streams before beginning a steep ascent past windswept grasslands to craggy ridges with the scent of pine all around you.

Hidden in a small pocket of the southwest, you could almost miss this

place if it weren't for the sheer, 8085ft-high (2464m) rockface of El Capitan, one of the park's most dramatic features. But in fact there's more to this region than meets the eye. The mountains here comprise one of the finest remnants of an ancient fossil reef. Around 250 million years ago, when the world was dominated by a single supercontinent called Pangaea, a vast tropical sea covered this area. This reef might have remained forever entombed were it not for uplift, with powerful geological forces creating sheer canyons and jagged mountains – as well as exposing huge sections of the reef and its age-old fossils, which today draw scientists from across the globe.

Fast-forward to 10,000 BC, when the

Guadalupe Mountains played a crucial role for early indigenous populations, who hunted mammoth and other animals in the waning days of the Ice Age. They also gathered edible vegetation and lived in caves in the range, where they left behind pottery, baskets and rock art. Later on the scene were Apaches and gold-seeking Spaniards, followed by pioneers in the 19th-century. The mountains were also the unlikely setting for a station on the Butterfield Overland Mail Route, a 2800-mile (4502km) run that connected St Louis with San Francisco.

⬆ El Capitan in Guadalupe Mountains, once used as a signal peak by early inhabitants.

➡ Pratt Cabin, McKittrick Canyon.

Toolbox

When to go

A spectacular time to visit the park is in late October and early November, when you can see a blaze of colorful fall foliage. Spring (March to May) has cooler temperatures for long hikes.

Getting there

The park is in Texas' northwest corner. Dog Canyon is accessed via NM137 in New Mexico, while McKittrick Canyon and Pine Springs are on US62 in Texas. There are no roads inside the park; it's a 120-mile (193km) drive between north and south entrances. The closest airport is in El Paso, 100 miles (161km) west.

Events

There are occasional guided night hikes as well as ranger-led star-gazing sessions.

Accessibility

Pine Springs, Dog Canyon and McKittrick Canyon visitor centers are accessible. Each campground has one accessible tent site.

Park in numbers

135 Area in sq miles
8751 Highest point: Guadalupe Peak (ft)
1000 Number of plant species

Stay here...

Dog Canyon Campground
Located in tree-covered canyon on the north side of the park, this is the more appealing of Guadalupe's two established campgrounds. Sites are in a scenic, well-protected location beneath steep cliff walls. The 6290ft-high (1917m) elevation can make nights cool here, so plan accordingly.

White's City Cavern Inn
In a tiny settlement some 32 miles (51.5km) northeast of the park entrance, this budget-friendly motel has well-equipped rooms and a small pool that's most welcome after a hot day of hiking. The restaurant next door serves good southwestern fare. The location is also quite handy for visiting nearby Carlsbad Caverns, seven miles (11km) west.

Hotel El Capitan
Named after the dramatic rockface in the Guadalupe Mountains, El Capitan is a historic Mission-revival style hotel built in the 1930s. The best rooms are spacious, with French doors opening onto private balconies overlooking a courtyard. The restaurant serves up some of the best cooking in a hundred-mile radius. It's located 65 miles (105km) south of the park in Van Horn.

Do this!

Bat-watching
The unique ecosystems of the Guadalupe Mountains make them attractive for a wide range of birds migrating through the Chihuahuan Desert. You can spy such desert dwellers as canyon towhees and roadrunners, with golden eagles soaring overhead. Early evening in riparian areas yield other rewards: violet-green swallows flitting over springs; broad-tailed hummingbirds feeding on nectar; and black phoebes hunting insects over the water.

Backpacking
The Guadalupe Mountains are an ideal destination for a multiday trek. You'll find 10 backcountry campgrounds spread along some 85 miles (137km) of trails. The variety of terrain means that you can get a taste of the low-desert country, riparian woodlands and pine-covered mountains all in one trip.

Wildlife-watching
No matter what time of year you visit, the park offers some fine opportunities to view wildlife. The few permanent water sources in the park (McKittrick Canyon, Smith Springs and Manzanita Spring) are the best places to look for creatures – as well as signs of animal life (tracks, scat, burrows and dens).

Hike this...

01 Guadalupe Peak
This challenging, 8.4-mile (13.5km) out-and-back hike takes you up the highest peak in Texas – 8751ft (2667m) – and includes a 3000ft (915m) elevation gain.

02 McKittrick Canyon Trail
One of the most popular trails in the park is a 7-mile (11.3km) round-trip hike that leads though scenic canyon woodlands to a historic cabin and out to the Grotto, set beside a gurgling stream.

03 Devil's Hall Trail
From Pine Springs, a 4.2-mile (6.7km) round-trip hike leads you past soaring peaks, with great views along the way. Ancient seafloor layered like stairs and a narrow slot ravine make for a dramatic finish.

What to spot...

Rising up out of the desert landscape, the Guadalupe Mountains encompass several varied ecosystems. Its rocky canyons, lush wooded streams and forest-fringed mountaintops provide habitats for 60 mammal species, 55 reptile species and some 300 bird species. There are also nocturnal desert creatures, such as coyotes, badgers and 16 bat species. Many of Guadalupe's reptiles can be spotted in the daytime (such as the crevice spiny lizard).

TRILOBITE FOSSIL
Trilobites were an arthropod group that flourished some 400 million years ago before dying out in the mass extinction that happened at the end of the Permian era (250 million years ago).

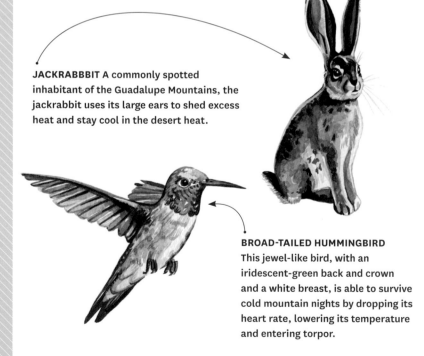

JACKRABBBIT A commonly spotted inhabitant of the Guadalupe Mountains, the jackrabbit uses its large ears to shed excess heat and stay cool in the desert heat.

BROAD-TAILED HUMMINGBIRD
This jewel-like bird, with an iridescent-green back and crown and a white breast, is able to survive cold mountain nights by dropping its heart rate, lowering its temperature and entering torpor.

Itineraries

Hike the highest point in Texas, admire the cactus and agave on the iconic Canyon Trail, or picnic by a grotto.

← The summit of Guadalupe Peak, the highest point in Texas.
↑ A spotted owl and a river-side cypress tree.

01

A day

Start the day at opening time (8am) at the McKittrick Canyon entrance. The crisp, early morning air is a fine time to spy wildlife so head off on the iconic Canyon Trail without delay. The route leads across a scrubby desert landscape sprinkled with cactus and agave to reach a stream where the woodlands begin; after the open desert, walking in the shade of oak and maple (beneath a canopy of fiery colors in fall) is bliss. A few miles further on, arrive at the Pratt Cabin, the old family dwelling of Wallace Pratt, a petroleum geologist and conservationist who fell in love with the area and built this home in the 1930s (later donating it to the national park). Although you can stop here for lunch, it's worth pressing on to the Grotto for a scenic picnic beside a stream; it's a lush setting, and you can even spy rainbow trout in the water. After the return hike, drive down to the Pine Springs Visitor Center, to peruse exhibits on the park's natural history and fauna and watch a short film on the Guadalupe Mountains.

02

A weekend

First, discover the origin story of the park. Tour the exhibits at the Frijole Ranch History Museum, look for wildlife on the easy Smith Spring Trail, then visit the ruins of a stagecoach station on Pinery Trail. Before sunset, head out to one of the most remote corners of the park, the Salt Basin Dunes, a 50-mile (80km) drive north and west of Pine Springs. Backed by distant mountain peaks, the white gypsum dunes are most striking at sunset or sunrise. It's a roughly 1.5-mile (2.5km) hike to the dunes from the parking lot.

On day two, tackle the challenging ascent of Guadalupe Peak. The views will impel you onward. Along the way, you'll pass through a cool forest of pine and Douglas fir, which flourish on the north slopes. This is the highest point in Texas, and the panorama over the desert below is sublime. Allow six to eight hours for the hike. Alternatively, spend the weekend hiking a section of the new 100-mile (160km) Guadalupe Ridge Trail, a fifth of which traverses the park.

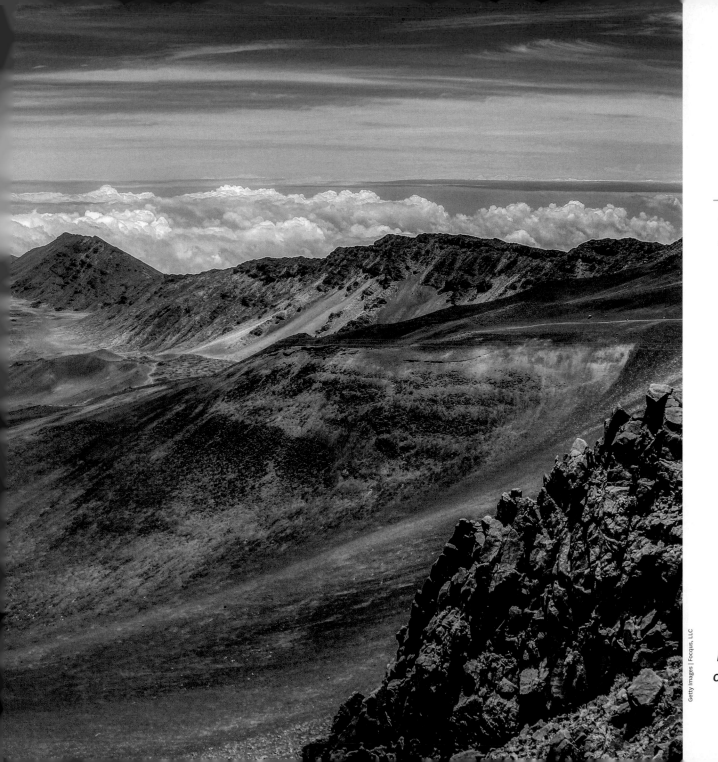

30

HI

Haleakalā National Park

Step inside what Native Hawaiians named 'The House of the Sun,' an ancient volcano spreading from sky to sea.

Haleakalā

S tanding on the edge of Haleakalā's summit crater, you'll shiver in the pre-dawn cold as you peer down into what looks like an ancient battlefield of cinder cones and lava rocks. But you won't give the chilly temperature another thought once the sun finally blazes over the eroded edge of this ancient volcano, its rays slanting across a colorful cinder desert and lighting up an ocean of clouds floating as far as you can see. It's a spiritual experience in a spot that is sacred to Native Hawaiians, who tell a story about how the demigod Maui lassoed the sun from this peak, giving light and life to his people.

Soaring over 10,000ft (3048m) high, Haleakalā Volcano is the park's resplendent centerpiece. Its summit is a winding 37-mile (59.5km) drive uphill from Maui's paradisiacal beaches, making a higher ascent in a shorter distance than on any other road on earth. Hiking trails dive into the volcanic crater's wilderness, where rare, endangered wildlife such as the Haleakalā silversword plant and the nēnē (Hawaiian goose) thrive. Wild summit weather can change in a heartbeat, from blisteringly sunny to icy cold, windy and rainy – yet the volcanic landscape remains an alien beauty. For an unforgettable night, camp out or sleep in a primitive cabin on the crater floor as the Milky Way glows overhead.

Though the volcanic summit is Haleakalā's most famous attraction, there's another side to this park. Follow the jungle road beyond Hāna to coastal Kīpahulu, an ancient Hawaiian village site on the volcano's lower slopes. There, in 'Ohe'o Gulch, stream-fed pools tumble downhill into the Pacific Ocean; their chilly waters as green as the surrounding jungle. Afterward, trek uphill through a forest of green bamboo, which rustles musically in the wind, to lacy Waimoku Falls.

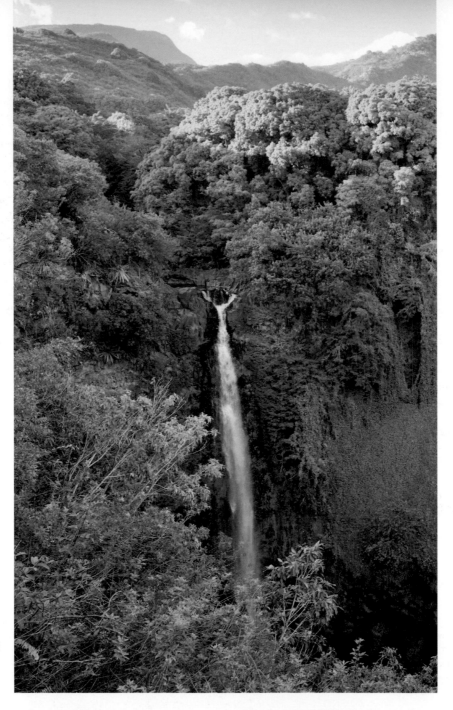

Toolbox

When to go
Visit at any time of year. Winters are cooler and wetter and rainstorms can close the park's summit and coastal areas. The weather atop the summit is fickle, so check the forecast before driving up.

Getting there
To the summit, it's a 1½-hour drive from Kahului, Maui's main airport, where domestic and inter-island flights land, and rental cars are available. To Kīpahulu, it's a 60-mile (96.5km) drive via the slow road to Hāna; allow 2½ hours.

Events
Summer brings a variety of ranger-led activities and cultural demonstrations from the local community

Accessibility
Park trails are unpaved and inaccessible. The visitor centers are wheelchair-accessible, as is the Hosmer Grove picnic area. Braille brochures can be found at the visitor center.

Park in numbers

52 Area in sq miles
10,023 Highest elevation (ft)
19 Size of summit crater (sq miles)

Stay here...

 Hōlua Cabin & Wilderness Campground
From the park's summit road, Hōlua is less than a 4-mile (6.4km) hike into the crater via the switchbacking Halemau'u Trail. Book ahead to stay in a cabin built by the Civilian Conservation Corps or pack your own tent and gear for a wilderness campsite (permit required).

Kapalaoa Cabin
If you're lucky enough to score a reservation for this basic, bunk-bedded wilderness cabin, you'll sleep inside the belly of the beast: the crater's cinder desert. Stargazing and sunrises are unbelievably awesome here. It's a 5.5-mile (8.9km) hike downhill via the Keonehe'ehe'e Trail from the summit road.

Kīpahulu Campground
Of the park's two drive-up campgrounds, one is near the summit and one is by the coast – and Kīpahulu wins for its ocean panoramas and open, grassy camping area. Bonus: it's free. Just bring your own water.

Do this!

 Birding
Traipse along the 0.5-mile (0.8km) Hosmer Grove Loop Trail through a forest high on the volcano's slopes and spy myriad birds. Expect to spot 'i'iwi, 'apapane, 'amakihi and 'alauahio, all native Hawaiian honeycreepers. If you're exceedingly lucky you'll catch the rare kiwikiu (Maui parrotbill), only found in a tiny patch of Haleakalā's windward slope.

Stargazing
The skies are so clear over the summit of Haleakalā that solar observatories have been built there. Skywatching after dark is equally good. Bring your own binoculars, which can be rented from island dive shops. Rangers often lead stargazing programs at Hosmer Grove Campground in summer.

Swimming
As long as rain isn't in the forecast, you can realize your tropical fantasy of swimming in jungle pools along Pīpīwai Stream, which falls in cascades as it makes its way downhill into the ocean. To swim in the sea, head to idyllic Hamoa Beach – less than 10 miles (16km) away from the park's Kipahulu district.

◄ Makahiku Falls, reached via Pīpīwai Trail – stop at the pool at the top for a swim. Previous page: the view from the peak of Haleakalā crater.

What to spot...

As elsewhere in the Hawaiian Islands, Maui's endemic flora and fauna have evolved into an astonishing array of species, many found nowhere else on the planet. Along with Hawai'i Volcanoes National Park, its sister park on the Big Island, Haleakalā has been designated a Unesco International Biosphere Reserve for its diverse ecosystems and rare wildlife – which is under threat from habitat loss, global climate change and invasive species brought by the first Europeans and Americans who landed on Hawaiian shores.

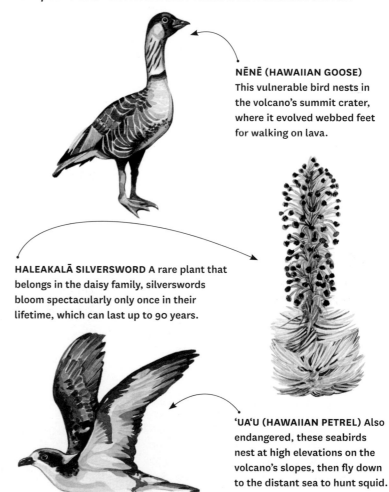

NĒNĒ (HAWAIIAN GOOSE) This vulnerable bird nests in the volcano's summit crater, where it evolved webbed feet for walking on lava.

HALEAKALĀ SILVERSWORD A rare plant that belongs in the daisy family, silverswords bloom spectacularly only once in their lifetime, which can last up to 90 years.

'UA'U (HAWAIIAN PETREL) Also endangered, these seabirds nest at high elevations on the volcano's slopes, then fly down to the distant sea to hunt squid.

Hike this...

O1 Halemauʻu Trail
Starting from cloud level, descend 1000ft-high (305m) cliffs into the volcano's crater. Don't miss the fascinating Silversword Loop detour (plants bloom July-October). The trail ranges from 2.2 to 9.2 miles (3.5 to 14.8km).

O2 Keoneheʻeheʻe Trail
Nicknamed 'Sliding Sands,' this thrilling trail wraps around cinder cones as it switchbacks from the summit to the crater floor. The trail ranges from 0.5 to 11.2 miles (0.8 to 18km)

O3 Pīpīwai Trail
In the coastal Kīpahulu district, this family-friendly 4-mile (6.4km) hike climbs through lush bamboo forest to stop beneath 400ft-tall (122m) Waimoku Falls.

Itineraries

Circle the grand loop of the volcanic crater, marvel at the pools of ʻOheʻo Gulch or trek to a jungle waterfall. Colorful cinder sunsets come for free.

 A silversword. Banyan trees are common but not native to the islands.
➡ An ʻIʻiwi bird, a variety of honeycreeper, in Haleakalā National Park.

01
A day

Sunrise-watching permit at the ready, wake up in the silent blue dark – don't you dare hit snooze! It may be a long drive, depending on where you're staying, and you'll want to be standing on the crater rim well before dawn breaks, when the sun performs its light show among the clouds and cinder cones. Evade the crowds huddled at the summit overlook by climbing a short way up Pa Kaʻoao (White Hill) for a better perch.

After sunrise, hike down the Keoneheʻeheʻe (Sliding Sands) Trail into the utterly wild cinder desert, then head out across the crater floor, bordered by cliffs, to wilderness Kapalaoa Cabin. Eat your lunch at the picnic table outside the cabin (but please don't feed or give any water to the nēnē, no matter how sweetly they beg!). If you've got energy to spare, detour north toward the most striking cones in the crater area, nicknamed Pele's Paint Pot after the Hawaiian goddess of fire and volcanoes. End your hike where it began, back uphill at the summit.

02
Two days

Follow the first day's itinerary, starting with sacred sunrise-gazing and moving on to an afternoon of Sliding Sands hiking. On day two, hit the road early for an adventure in the park's coastal Kīpahulu district. Drive the serpentine highway, which passes over 54 one-lane bridges, to sleepy Hāna town. Stop here for a takeaway 'plate lunch' – the iconic Hawaiian meal of rice, macaroni salad, and meat such as taro leaf-wrapped pork or Japanese-style teriyaki beef.

Entering the Kīpahulu district, pull over at coastal overlooks to spot monk seals, sea turtles and – in December through April – humpback whales. Then wander to ʻOheʻo Gulch, also known as the Seven Sacred Pools, a series of deep green pools connected by waterfalls (swimming is common here but discouraged by the NPS), eyes open for critters like the rock-climbing goby. The family-friendly 4-mile (6.4km) Pīpīwai Trail, heads uphill through a bamboo tunnel to a waterfall.

03
Four days

For hikers and backpackers, the ultimate park experience is making a grand loop on foot around the volcanic crater. Organize wilderness cabin bookings well in advance, or bring all the gear you'll need for camping at high elevations in highly variable weather. On day one, after watching sunrise at the summit, drop into the crater on the Keoneheʻeheʻe (Sliding Sands) Trail and head to Kapalaoa Cabin (no camping). Take time to explore the colorful cinder desert just north of the cabin before sunset. The next day, strap on your pack for the hike over to the wet, windy side of the volcano, where you can camp outside or sleep inside Palikū Cabin. On day three, trek back across the crater floor, winding through the cinder desert to reach the campsite and cabin at Hōlua, which boasts the crater's best sunrise views. On your last day, hike up the switchbacks of the Halemauʻu Trail back to the crater rim, reluctantly leaving the volcanic wilderness behind.

31

HI

Hawaiʻi Volcanoes National Park

Newly born earth churns and fiery lava glows in the chaotic realm of Pele, the Hawaiian goddess of volcanoes.

Hawaiʻi Volcanoes

For over 70 million years, volcanoes in the deep have been giving birth to the Hawaiian Islands. After emerging as bare rocks from under the sea, the islands later become oases for unique plant and animal life, then eventually tumble down into flat coral atolls flung over thousands of miles of open ocean. Today Hawai'i, also known as the Big Island, sits directly atop a 'hot spot' deep beneath the Earth's crust. This majestic park on the island's southeast shore includes the summits of two of the world's most active volcanoes: Kīlauea and Mauna Loa.

Life and the landscape here are never static. Kīlauea began erupting continuously in 1983, when lava fountains dramatically spewed into the sky. In 2008, its Halema'uma'u Crater, home of the hot-tempered Hawaiian trickster goddess Pele, was transformed into a lava lake, just as it was when famous 19th-century travelers Isabella Bird and Mark Twain ventured here on horseback. In 2018, eruptions caused the Kīlauea summit to collapse, destroying some 700 houses and shutting down much of the park temporarily. When the smoke cleared, the 35-year-old eruption was officially declared over. Today, atop jet-black lava flows, vibrant green ferns, lichens, moss, 'ohelo plants with bright-red berries and 'ohi'a lehua trees (blossoming with pom-pom flowers) colonize the new terrain.

Whether you come for a startling geology lesson or to get in touch with living Hawaiian traditions, this park doesn't disappoint. Native Hawaiians first walked this land, etching petroglyphs and burying the *piko* (umbilical cord) of newborns in lava rocks. They left behind footprints fossilized in the volcanic ash and performed sacred

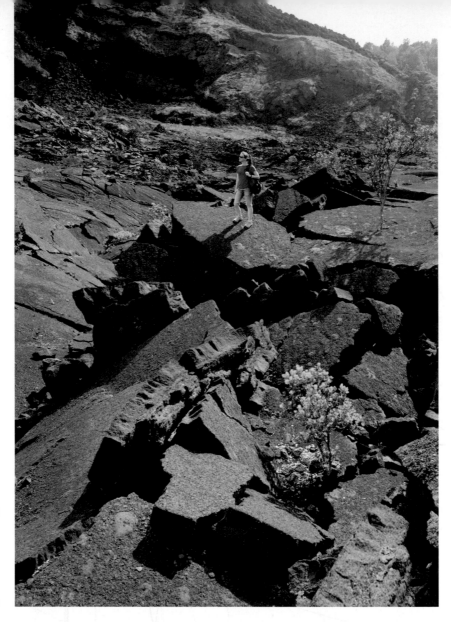

hula dances on the crater rim. They also summited Mauna Loa, at 13,680ft (4170m) the world's most massive shield volcano – which is higher than Mt Everest when measured from the ocean floor.

⬆ Lava rock on Kīlauea volcano, the most active on the island (and molten on the previous page).

➡ Lava hardens when it reaches the Pacific Ocean.

Shutterstock | MNStudio; Jo Crebbin

Toolbox

When to go
Open year-round, the park experiences wetter, cooler winters. Before visiting, check for eruption updates, which can close some viewpoints, roads and trails.

Getting there
On the east side of the Big Island, the park is an hour's drive south of Hilo airport, or 2½ hours from busier Kailua-Kona airport on the west coast. Interisland flights from the state's main airport in its capital Honolulu are fast and frequent. Rent a car in Hilo or Kona to get around.

Events
There's an annual festival of Hawaiian culture each July at Kahuku Unit.

Accessibility
Kīlauea Visitor Center has wheelchairs available. Most of Ha'akulamanu (Sulphur Banks) Trail is wheelchair accessible, as is the short trail to Steaming Bluff (Wahinekapu)

Park in numbers
505.4 Area in sq miles
2018 Year of last eruption of Kīlauea volcano
875 Acres of new land created by 2018 eruptions

Stay here...

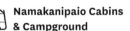

Volcano House
Being the only hotel in this national park (and, being founded in 1846, actually predating the park) means that nowhere else can you wake up to views of the Kīlauea Caldera and a rainforest through your window. Even if you don't stay overnight at this historic (and recently renovated) venue, stop for an epicurean meal at the hotel's Rim Restaurant or for a drink in Uncle George's Lounge, where Hawaiian musicians play.

Namakanipaio Cabins & Campground
Nestled within a peaceful grove of eucalyptus trees, this park campground will let you pitch a tent – if you rent one from them, they'll even set it up for you – or bunk down in a rustic cabin with a barbecue grill and fire pit outside.

Kīlauea Lodge
Just outside the park, this 1938 YMCA children's camp is now a character-filled inn and restaurant. The main lodge has a scout-chic vibe, all rustic wood and stone, while rooms are light-drenched and encircled by native ōhiʻa trees. Day trips from this base can include black-sand beaches.

Do this!

Driving tours
There are two classic volcano-spotting drives in the park: Crater Rim Drive and Chain of Craters Road. Stop at overlooks for thrilling views over craters and calderas, lava plains and roiling ocean. Short side hikes will take you deeper into the alien landscape of cinder cones and dried lava flows. The section of Crater Rim Drive past Kīlauea Overlook is currently closed.

Caving
When molten lava erupts, it leaves behind lava tubes. Some are even big enough to drive a school bus through! You can walk right into Nāhuku (Thurston Lava Tube), which is hidden in a fern forest just off Crater Rim Dr.

Learning about Hawaiian arts & culture
Traditional *hula halau* (schools) dance and Hawaiian artisans demonstrate their crafts at the Volcano Art Center Gallery, next door to the park's visitor center. Sign up in advance for art classes and workshops.

◄ Entering 500-year-old Nāhuku, also known as the Thurston Lava Tube cave on Kīlauea Crater.

What to spot...

Both a Unesco World Heritage site and an International Biosphere Reserve, the park protects unexpectedly diverse habitats: lava deserts, rain forest, coastal beaches, and even an alpine mountain summit. More than 50 threatened or endangered species find refuge here. Birds are especially abundant, from petite, rainbow-colored Hawaiian honeycreepers that flutter through rain forest oases to the solitary royal Hawaiian hawk (ʻio) swooping overhead as its hunts for prey.

ʻOHIʻA LEHUA Growing as a plant, a shrub or a tree, ʻohiʻa is easily recognized by its twisting stems, and branches with flowers that vary in color from cream to red.

ʻAPAPANE This Hawaiian honeycreeper sports crimson feathers and a curved black beak for drinking flower nectar.

HONUʻEA (HAWAIIAN HAWKSBILL TURTLE) This endangered amphibian hauls out on remote beaches to lay eggs. Hatchlings dig themselves out of the sandy nests, emerging only at night and heading straight back into the sea.

Hike this...

01 Kīlauea Iki Trail Trek 4 miles (6.4km) from the crater's rain forest down across a lava moonscape on this loop trail through a recent volcanic eruption.

02 Puʻu Loa Petroglyphs Off Chain of Craters Rd, a short, 1.4-mile (2.3km) hike leads to an archaeological field of ancient Hawaiian rock art.

03 Mauna Loa Experienced backcountry hikers will relish the dizzying climb up this 13,680 foot (4,170m) volcano, its surface covered in slippery loose volcanic rock. Permits necessary for backcountry camping.

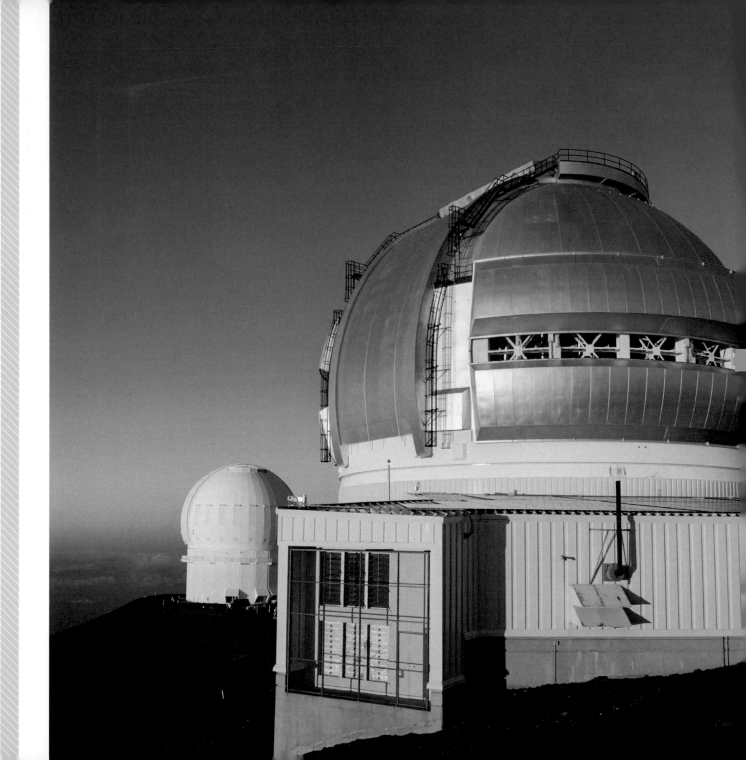

Itineraries

Take a night walk through spooky Thurston Lava Tube, hike Devastation Trail or opt for sheer wilderness and native birds on the Kahuku Unit.

 A nēnē goose. The Gemini Observatory on the summit of Mauna Kea. ➡ Inside Nāhuku (or the Thurston Lava Tube cave).

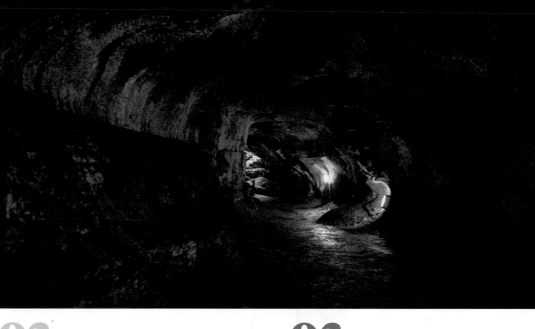

01
A day

Don't fret if rain clouds greet your early-morning arrival at the park – the mercurial weather at the volcanic summit could just as easily bring sunshine later in the day. Stop by the park visitor center and get oriented inside its educational museum. Cruising west along Crater Rim Dr, park at Sulphur Banks, where volcanic gases have left colorful mineral deposits, then goggle Kīlauea Overlook, the 'Ailā'au shield on the horizon. Backtrack for lunch at the historic Volcano House (try a 'POG' juice – passionfruit-orange-guava). In the afternoon, you'll feel like an astronaut exploring another planet on the Kīlauea Iki Loop Trail, which dips from the rainforest into a volcanic crater. After sunset, take a spooky walk (bring flashlights!) through Thurston Lava Tube, just across the road. Then return to your rustic digs at the Namakanipaio Cabins & Campground for an evening of tall tales around the fire pit.

02
Two days

Start with the day one itinerary then get a leisurely start after breakfast in Volcano town. Drive back into the park and wind downhill toward the ocean on Chain of Craters Rd, passing evidence of violent past eruptions – craters, cinder cones, and lava shields. Take some short nature hikes, including the Devastation Trail and the walk out to the Pu'u Loa petroglyph field, one of many archaeological sites protected by the park. Of all the viewpoints overlooking the park's lava flows, don't skip Kealakomo Overlook, where a picnic table makes the perfect lunch spot. About 1000 feet (300m) past the end gate of Chain of Craters Rd, look offshore for the landmark Hōlei Sea Arch.

Drive back uphill to the park entrance, then head west to little-traveled Mauna Loa Rd. It begins as a one-lane paved road near Kīpukapuaulu (Bird Park), where birders hike along a forested loop trail, then climbs partway up Mauna Loa volcano to a mesmerizing lookout.

03
Three days

Proceed as per days one and two. On your third day in the park, take some time to get off the beaten path and explore the Kahuku Unit, the newest addition to this already massive park. To get there, follow the island's belt road south through the Ka'u district, known for its small coffee farms and the sea turtles that haul out on the beach at Punalu'u. You'll drive past the turnoff to Ka Lae, the southernmost point in the US, and Papakōlea (Green Sands) Beach, whose khaki tint comes from the mineral olivine; both are worth a detour. Back on the belt road, keep driving toward Ocean View. The turnoff to the Kahuku Unit will be on your right, and the gates are usually open daily (check website ahead of time for hours).

On the grounds of an historic ranch, this pocket of wilderness is a place of peaceful pastures, lava flows and dense forest. On any of several short hiking trails, you may be the only person crunching over these ancient lava flows and listening for the songs of the islands's native birds.

32

AR

Hot Springs National Park

A small park surrounding a natural wonder – people have been soaking in the curious, curative waters of this steamy sanctuary for centuries.

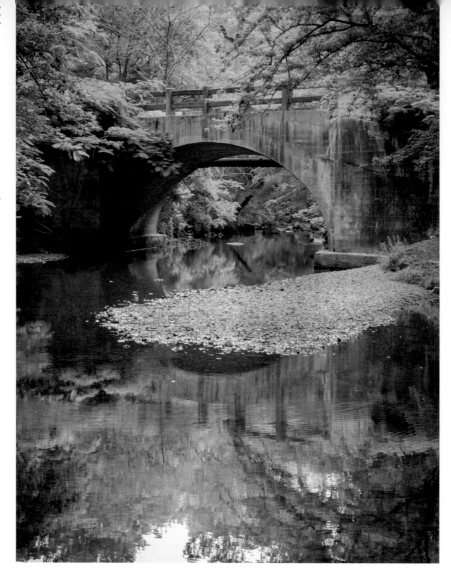

The smallest (and arguably the oldest) of America's national parks, Hot Springs revolves around 47 boiling brooks of geothermally warmed water that once enveloped this corner of Arkansas in an ethereal cloak of steam – and are invested, many people insist, with healing powers.

The water is regurgitated rainfall, deep-heated during a dramatic 4000-year journey from mountaintop into the bowels of the earth and back again. Hot Springs doesn't suffer from the sulfur stink that most spa towns have to endure, and the colorless water is pumped to 'jug fountains,' where you can taste the famous magic mountain juice with rumored restorative qualities.

Font of youth or simply nature's gift, the spring has been phenomenally popular for centuries, and the area has attracted human activity for millennia. Native American tribes – including the Caddo, Choctaw and Cherokee – were drawn to the 'Valley of the Vapours' long before Europeans arrived. Spanish Conquistador Hernando de Soto stopped for a soak in 1541, beginning a long-standing tourist tradition, and Dunbar and Hunter visited during their mission of discovery after the US acquired the region in the 1803 Louisiana Purchase. The first American settlers arrived by 1807.

But it's also caused some hot debates, not least about its place in the history of the country's parks. Yellowstone is commonly considered the world's first national park, but the Hot Springs Reservation, predecessor of Hot Springs National Park, was signed into being by President Andrew Jackson in 1832 – four decades before Yellowstone received protection. Numerous generations of buildings have housed hot tubs here over the years, until the current Bathhouse Row was built between 1912 and 1922 – by which time Hot Springs was officially a national park.

The confusion is understandable. This isn't what most people picture when they imagine a national park – no grizzly bears, but instead bare bodies in the Buckstaff Bath House – but there are indeed outdoor adventures to be enjoyed in this historical setting.

← There are many creeks to cross in Hot Springs, the only national park that is also a town.

Toolbox

When to go
The park is open all year, but gets very busy in the summer months, especially July. Winters are mild and wildflowers bloom from February.

Getting there
The park is found downtown in the Arkansas city of Hot Springs – 300 miles (483km) east of Dallas, Texas, and 200 miles (322km) west of Memphis, Tennessee.

Events
Hot Springs hosts several music and arts festivals from September through November, a popular music festival in June, a jazz festival in August, and the 'World's Shortest St Patrick's Day Parade' in March.

Accessibility
The Fordyce Visitor Center is wheelchair accessible and offers loaner wheelchairs. Gulpha Gorge Campground is accessible too.

Park in numbers

8.6 Area in sq miles
143 Average temperature of the hot springs' water (°F)
700,000 Gallons of hot water collected each day in the reservoir

Stay here...

Gulpha Gorge
The park's only campground is beautifully positioned on a creek (with crawfish) and connected to the trail network that leads to Hot Creek Mountain. There are no showers – but you're located next to the most famous bathhouse in America.

Hotel Hale
Dig the Gilded Age vibes at this splendidly renovated bathhouse, the only hotel in the park. Opened in 2019, it occupies the Classic Revival-style 1892 Hale Bathhouse. Each suite has a soaking tub with mineral water pumped directly from the springs.

Do this!

Bathing
Two of the eight original Bathhouse Row spas are in use. Roman Gothic-style Buckstaff Bathhouse has offered traditional water treatments since 1912. And the Spanish Colonial Revival-style Quapaw Baths, opened in 1922, has a dazzling mosaic dome.

Hiking
The park has 26 miles (42km) of trails, mostly short and steep options. For a bigger challenge, hike the 10-mile (16km) Sunset Trail, which traverses West Mountain, threads the hardwood forest of Sugarloaf Mountain and crosses Fordyce Mountain to end in Gulpha Gorge Campground.

What to spot...

Hot Springs has a mild climate and the park features forests populated by pine, oak and hickory. Bird species include ruby-throated hummingbirds and golden eagles.

RED RIVER WATERDOG
This local mudpuppy uses feathery gills to breathe underwater. Like other salamanders, they retain the freaky – but useful – larval ability to regenerate lost limbs and even repair parts of their brains.

Itineraries

For geothermal good times, hike Hot Springs Mountain before immersing in a traditional spa treatment.

01

A day

Wake to a dawn chorus of bird chatter in Gulpha Gorge Campground. This might be America's smallest national park, but there's still plenty to fit into a day.

A perfect start is to hike Hot Springs Mountain. From outside your tent a choice of paths all lead to Mountain Tower, where, before heading down via the Oertel Trail, you see the city flicker into life.

Wander past century-old spa buildings on Bathhouse Row to imagine the scene that would have greeted Dunbar and Hunter when they arrived in 1804. Back then the 47 steaming springs would have been open to the elements; now the only 'Open Spring' can be seen behind Maurice Bathhouse.

Stop by the visitor center in the old Fordyce Bathhouse to see how the place looked in 1915, before braving the Buckstaff to experience what a traditional spa treatment feels like. You had intended to hike the Sunset Trail later, but such energetic plans get entangled with the hot-water vapors and begin evaporating – maybe stay another night...

33
IN

Indiana Dunes National Park

A patchwork mosaic of marshes, forest, grassland and dunes on the edge of Lake Michigan holds astonishing biodiversity: welcome to the birthplace of American ecology.

Wedged into an industrial corridor in northern Indiana, this 15,000-acre coastal reserve seems at first glance an unlikely setting for a national park. But once you make peace with the surrounding area — the Chicago skyline shimmering across the lake in one direction, a distant view of a power plant off in another — you can appreciate this protected landmark for all its surprising allure. Towering dunes, meandering rivers, oak savannas, windswept prairies, verdant wetlands and 15 miles of ocean-like shoreline all form the backdrop to one of America's most biologically diverse national parks.

The Indiana Dunes experience is about many things: walking up forest-covered dunes to magnificent lookouts over the lake, breathing in the scent of wildflowers along the Little Calumet River, or spotting hundreds of bird species during the twice yearly migration. The park is also a living record of the last Ice Age. Some 11,000 years ago, vast mile-thick glaciers melted and retreated, leaving behind Lake Michigan and the other Great Lakes. Various successive shorelines formed during the slow glacial melting process, and you can travel back in time as you go inland from sandy beach to progressively older dunes, passing a still active shoreline. The extraordinary variety of vascular plants in differing habitats attracted

the attention of botanist Henry Cowles in the early 1900s. Cowles and other scientists made groundbreaking studies in the newly emerging field of ecology, and put the region on the map, ultimately saving it from destruction over the next half century.

The park has many unusual highlights: Mount Baldy, the largest 'living' dune in the area moves about four feet inland each year, consuming grasses, shrubs and even trees in its path. There are rare plants – like the fringed polygala, which grows only on the north slope of one particular dune and nowhere else in Indiana – and more orchids than in all of Hawaii. The Indiana Dunes are full of wonder, and reward those willing to discover what lies behind the shoreline.

Toolbox

When to go
The park is open year-round, with camping available from April through October. June through early September is crowded, though mid-week is quieter. Try May (spring flowers) or October (changing fall colors).

Getting there
The park is a short hop from Chicago (50 miles northwest) and lies between the once industrial towns of Gary and Michigan City. It's easy to reach by train – the South Shore Line has four stops in the park: Miller, Ogden Dunes, Dune Park and Beverly Shores.

Events
In June, Chellberg Farm hosts a summer solstice festival to celebrate the region's Swedish immigrants.

Accessibility
The Paul H Douglas Center is fully accessible with access to two marsh areas and a picnic area. There is also a variety of mobility devices you can borrow.

Park in numbers

23.5 Area in sq miles
370 Bird species
1130 Flowering plant and fern species

Stay here...

 Riley's Railhouse
Set in a converted railroad freight station, Riley's offers a unique stay in imaginatively furnished rooms and common areas dotted with vintage train memorabilia. Avid train spotters should book the Upper Berth, which has a small balcony overlooking the tracks where trains still rumble past.

 Duneswalk Inn
In an 1881 three-story brick mansion, this family-friendly inn has handsomely furnished guest rooms with wood floors in a great location just a few minutes' drive to the lake. The best rooms have fireplaces and small kitchen units. Soundproof windows dampen the noise of the busy road out front.

Dunewood Campground
On the eastern side of the park (and an easy stroll from Beverly Shores train station), Dunewood Campground has 67 forested decently spaced sites, 12 of which are in a more secluded walk-in section. There's a fine walking trail nearby, though it's a 1.3-mile (2km) stroll to the lakeshore.

Do this!

Birdwatching
Amid dunes and wetlands, the Indiana Dunes offers outstanding birdwatching. Its location at the foot of Lake Michigan makes a prime spot for migrating birds. In the autumn, you can see thousands of sandhill cranes, or spot hawks in the spring. Another highlight is the Heron Rookery, home to nesting warblers, kingfishers and woodpeckers.

Biking
An interconnected trail system covers 37 miles (60km) across the national park, and takes in dunes, prairie and forested stretches. Memorable jaunts include the 10.3-mile (16.5km) Prairie-Duneland Trail, which takes in ponds, dunes and woodlands along a disused rail line. Various outfitters rent bikes, including one next door to the Indiana Dunes Visitor Center.

Beach going
For summer fun, West Beach is a big draw, with a lifeguard station, plus a mile-long boardwalk past interdunal ponds. Further east, Porter Beach is backed by dunes where you can spy a variety of birds. At Central Avenue Beach the shoreline is backed by a forest of partially buried trees.

◄ Crossing the dunes into Kemil Beach on Lake Michigan.
► The Dune Succession Trail.

Hike this...

01 Dune Succession Trail
In the west of the park, the short but challenging 1.1-mile (1.8km) trail takes you up 270 steps for a view of the lake, with Chicago in the distance. Then dig your heels in the sand on West Beach or link up with the Long Lake Trail.

02 Cowles Bog Trail
An overview of the wetlands' biodiversity, this 4.7-mile (7.6km) trail passes ponds, marshes and black-oak savannas. Climb down to the beach for a tranquil view over the lakeshore.

03 Little Calumet River Trail
This 3.4-mile (5.5km) hike winds along a stretch of the Little Calumet River and takes you through prairie for a view of grasslands that once blanketed the region. You'll pass a 19th-century homestead and a farm.

What to spot...

Despite its small size, the Indiana Dunes National Park is home to a wide variety of living creatures, including 46 species of mammal and 60 butterfly species – not to mention over 1000 plant varieties. Migrating birds fill the skies in April and September, while even the sands are filled with life – keep an eye out for six-lined racerunners (a type of lizard) and a native species of prickly pear cacti.

WOOD FROG How does a small, cold-blooded amphibian survive the harsh winters? By letting its hibernating body freeze nearly solid, while producing large amounts of sugar in its liver to keep its cells from being damaged by ice.

SCARLET TANAGER Among the most striking birds in the eastern US, male scarlet tanagers have fiery red bodies, with dark black wings and tail (females are yellow and olive). Keep an eye on the treetops for the telltale flash of brilliant red as this medium-sized songbird flits after insects.

PURPLE PITCHER PLANT One of several carnivorous plants in the park, the pitcher plant collects rainwater in its hollow gibbous leaves that lure (and later trap) insects. You can spot them at Pinhook Bog.

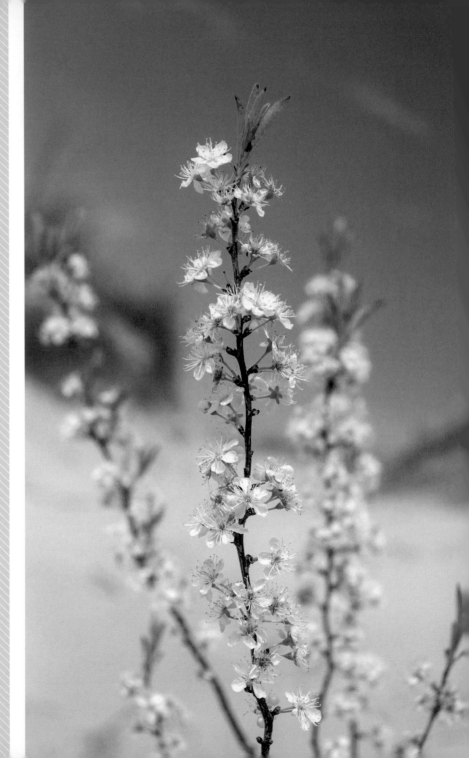

Itineraries

Hike up to the top of a forest-dotted dune for sweeping lake views, hike a wetlands trail in search of birds and beavers or just relax on the beach while listening to the 'singing sands'

◀ Great Lakes sandcherry grows in sandy areas of the park.
▶ Boardwalks protect many of the park's dunes.

01

A half-day

With just half a day at your disposal, make your way to the lakeshore for a day of basking on the gorgeous lakefront (marred only slightly by the steaming power plant to your right).

Some 15 miles of shoreline park hugging Lake Michigan means you won't lack for options. A perennial favorite is West Beach, which is great for swimming (with a lifeguard station in the summer), with an expanse of sand for beach combing and relaxing by the water's edge. After getting your fill of the shoreline, hit the trail for an up-close look at the park's striking beauty. The Dune Succession Trail takes you up many steps (270 to be specific) to a lofty perch with views of the Chicago skyline on clear days.

The mile-long walk shows you the stages of dune development, from bare beach to a forested section growing right out of the sands. If time allows, there are more trails to explore, and you can stroll the Long Lake Trail or even onto the Marquette Trail, passing stretches of hardwood forest and wetlands.

02

A day

Start the day at the Visitor Center to learn about the ecology and history of this biodiverse region. Rangers can advise on highlights for the day (what's in bloom; birds to spot).

Then head to the Bailly Homestead area. In 1822, Joseph Bailly established one of the first fur-trading posts in the area, and it served as a crossroads for Native Americans and Euro-American colonists. Next door, the Chellberg Farm also spins you back into the past, via a beautifully preserved home founded by a Swedish immigrant family in the 1880s. Out back you can get your barnyard fix, with chickens, pigs, cows, goats and more. Nearby, enjoy the Dunes' wilder side with a walk on one of the interconnected trails. The Little Calumet River Trail takes you past the Mnoké prairie, through forest, and over tiny bridges, with plenty of opportunities to spy wildlife. End the day at Central Beach. This stretch of sand is backed by dune and forest, and is a fine spot for catching the sunset.

03

Three days

Make the most of Indiana's star attraction by camping at the Dunewood Campground. This will give you prime dune access at sunrise and sunset, blissfully free of the day-tripping crowds. To be even closer to the lakeshore, book a site in the Indiana Dunes State Park. After taking in the full-day itinerary, start day two with a hike along the Cowles Bog Trail. Named after one of America's ecological pioneers, the trail harbors habitats home to unique species (including orchids and carnivorous plants). It also abuts a beachfront reachable only on foot or by boat (bring a picnic). In the afternoon, visit a quiet corner of the park. The Heron Rookery is a great spot for birdwatching. In springtime the forest is blanketed with wildflowers.

On your last day in the park, it's worth exploring some of the sections just outside the park boundaries. You can undertake the three-dune challenge at Indiana Dunes State Park (sandwiched between the national park) or go mountain biking on a top-notch 10-mile trail at Imagination Glen Park.

34
MI
Isle Royale National Park

A wild kingdom of moose and wolves in the middle of Lake Superior, Isle Royale is the least-visited national park in the Lower 48.

Everything about Isle Royale is intriguing. The world's fourth largest lake island – surrounded by 450 smaller satellite islands – is thick with spruce and birch and sits in the middle of the biggest and coldest of the Great Lakes. It may look like pristine wilderness, but Isle Royale's abundant natural resources have been mined for centuries. Native Americans were hammering chunks of copper out of bedrock using smooth stones found along the shoreline 4500 years ago. After the US took possession of the island from the French in 1783, commercial fishermen used gillnets to catch whitefish, lake trout and

siskiwit off the shore. In the mid-1800s, workers set fire to satellite islands to prospect for copper and logged off the massive white pines on the mainland to make way for human development. In the early 1900s, Isle Royale was such a popular summer haven for wealthy families from St Louis and Chicago that Belle Isle, off the northeast shoreline, had a nine-hole golf course.

Today, the trees have grown back and 99% of the island is designated as wilderness. In that wilderness, zigzagged by hiking trails and dotted with campsites, lives a constantly fluctuating number of wolves and moose. It's not likely a visitor

will see one of the 15 or so elusive wolves on the island, but it is relatively common to see a massive bull moose, its antler rack spanning 6ft (1.8m), crashing through the lowland swamps and diving the inland lakes to eat the roots of water lilies.

For the last 50 years scientists here have been conducting the longest-running study of a predator-prey system in the world. The wolf population had shrunk to just two by 2018 (leading to an unsustainable increase in the moose population), but the park has had recent success in reintroducing wolves to the island – with more planned in the years ahead. Some of the wolves wear radio collars so you can track them online.

Toolbox

When to go
The park is open from mid-April until mid-October. Fog or rough water can delay flights or ferries. The park is most crowded in August. For a quiet trip, go in May. For the most reliable weather, visit in July or August.

Getting there
Isle Royale belongs to Michigan and is 55 miles (88.5km) northwest of its Keweenaw Peninsula, but the island is only 22 miles (35.4km) east of Minnesota and even closer to Canada. Four ferries and one seaplane provide service from Houghton or Copper Harbor, Michigan, or Grand Portage, Minnesota.

Events
A range of unique ranger-led hikes and boat tours are offered from June to mid-September.

Accessibility
The three visitor centers, the ferries *Ranger III* and *MV Sandy*, and most of the parks ranger-led programs are accessible.

Park in numbers

850 Area in sq miles
256 Number of bird species
18,200 Annual visitors

Stay here...

 Rock Harbor Lodge Housekeeping Cottages
Tucked in the woods behind the main lodge, the cottages can sleep up to six, and have a fully equipped kitchenette, a bathroom, and a wall of picture windows that overlook placid Tobin Harbor. The quality of the serenity in these cabins is priceless.

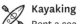 **Three Mile Campground**
Three miles (5km) east of the main park entrance of Rock Harbor, this campground sees a lot of hiker traffic. But it also sits on a gorgeous southern shoreline of pebbly beaches and granite rocks that slope straight into Lake Superior. There are at least two screened-in camping shelters right on the water and an overnight dock for campers arriving by private boat.

Moskey Basin Campground
Rise early to see the sunrise at this magical spot that's set with two waterside tent sites and six shelters. You might see moose, beavers and numerous birds, including nesting loons. It's reachable on foot (Lake Richie or Rock Harbor trails) or by kayak/canoe via Rock Harbor Channel.

Do this!

Kayaking
Rent a sea kayak from the Rock Harbor marina and spend at least a half-day exploring the archipelago, where hundred-year-old cabins sit on granite sloping down to the lakeshore. Beware: the weather here is very changeable and currents around Blake Point, the easternmost tip of the island, can be tricky.

 Backpacking
One of the best ways to experience the park is on a multiday backpacking trip. With 165 miles of trails, you won't lack for options, and the park's 36 campgrounds (accessible by foot or boat only) make fine bases for the adventure. Experienced travelers can go further afield cross-country camping (camping outside of established campgrounds).

Scuba diving
The waters off Isle Royale are riddled with ten major wrecks, all relatively easy to see in Lake Superior's clear water. With surface water temperatures rarely above 55°F (13°C) and deeper water falling to 35°F (2°C) degrees, a dry suit is mandatory. Isle Royale Charters runs diving trips.

◄ Dusk gathers over Rock Harbor.
◢ Not all the wildlife is large here.

Hike this...

01 Feldtmann Lake Loop
This challenging 33-mile (53km) trail takes you from Windigo up Sugar Mountain (1362ft) to Sisikwit Bay for water views then on to Feldtmann Lake where you can often see moose. Allow three to four days for the trip.

02 Greenstone Ridge Trail
The main 40-mile-long (64.5km) island thruway barrels along the backbone of Isle Royale and tops out at 1300ft (396m), with glorious views to Lake Superior. Plan three to five days to do the whole thing.

03 Scoville Point Loop
It may be short, but this 4-mile (6.4km) loop trail starting in Rock Harbor offers some of the most gorgeous scenery on the entire island. Time the hike for sunrise to spot moose, or sundown over Tobin Harbor.

What to spot...

A classic, second-growth northern boreal forest, Isle Royale is thick with spruce, pine and birch, and riddled with freshwater inland lakes lined by water lilies and the occasional purple orchid. Moose, wolves and fox live here, but the island has no bears or raccoons, making it unnecessary to hang food at night in the backcountry.

MOOSE Standing six feet high (1.8m) at the shoulder, moose can weigh over 1000lbs (454kg). They're most active at dawn and dusk, and frequently feed at inland lakes. If you see a sow with a calf or a bull in rutting season (mid-September to late October), steer clear.

PILEATED WOODPECKER Yellow-eyed, black-bodied, scarlet-headed woodpeckers are a delight to spot as they dart from tree to tree, pecking away at dead trunks for carpenter ants. Their signature calling card: a rectangular hole.

WOLF The odds of spotting the very elusive Isle Royale wolves are not great – but one can always hope. Interestingly, the most frequent recent sightings have been on the east end of the island, close to the most populated part of the park in the summer.

184

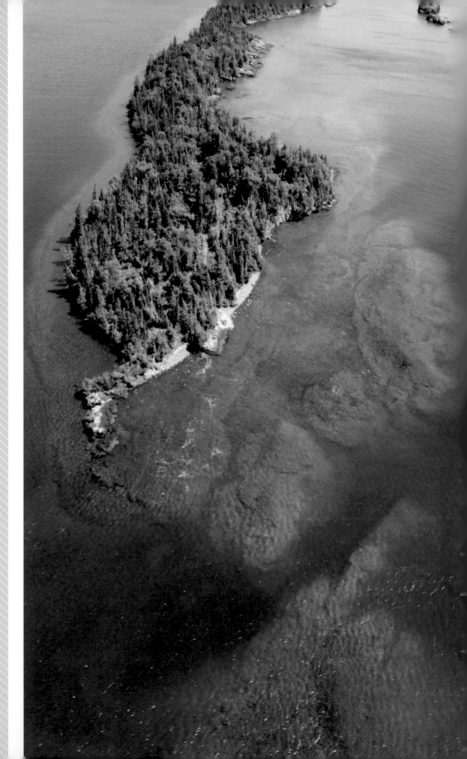

Itineraries

Sail the thrice-weekly ferry for a classic overview of the island, kayak or canoe Rock or Tobin harbors, or the truly adventurous can hike the whole island.

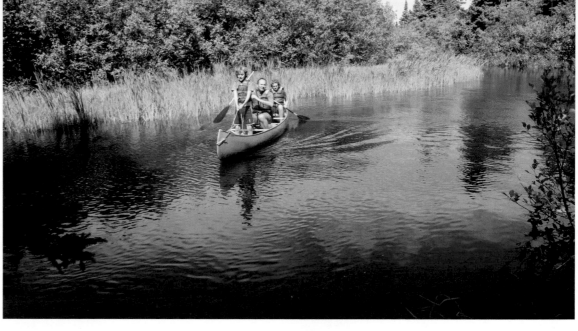

⬅ Isle Royale from the air, largest of the national park's islands.
➡ Check the weather forecast before exploring Isle Royale's inlets.

01

Two days

For a grand overview of the entire island, buy a ticket on the *Voyageur II*, a comfortable and sturdy 65ft (20m) aluminum ferry that leaves three times a week from Grand Portage, Minnesota. By 7:30am the boat is well underway to Windigo, the first stop on Isle Royale. Traveling clockwise around the densely wooded shore, the next stop is McCargoe Cove, where the boat picks up hard-core hikers who have toughed the Minong Ridge Trail. After rounding Blake Point, the boat turns southwest toward Rock Harbor. Check into a lakeside room at Rock Harbor Lodge, take a quick 4-mile (6.4km) round-trip hike to Scoville Point, and then dine on fresh lake trout at rustic Lighthouse Restaurant. The next morning, catch the sunrise from your northeast-facing room before boarding the ferry to see south-shore highlights, such as an old commercial fisherman's cabin and a classic lighthouse. If the weather cooperates, the boat will have fully circumnavigated the island and get back to Grand Portage by 3pm.

02

Four days

If time is of the essence, opt for the rock-star entrance: a round-trip floatplane flight from Houghton, Michigan, with Isle Royale Seaplanes. It's more expensive than a ferry, but takes just 35 minutes and the flight lands right at Rock Harbor. Book a stay in a cottage, buy a map of the park at the park service office, then set off on foot for the 9.4-mile (15km) roundtrip hike to Mt Franklin, an island high point that rises more than 1000ft (305m) and has glorious views of the north shore and Lake Superior beyond.

On day two, if the weather is right, rent a kayak, canoe, or outboard and troll Rock or Tobin harbors for lake trout, brook trout or whitefish. On day three, make the 5.5-mile (9km) round-trip hike along the southern shoreline toward Three Mile Campground, There you'll find some fine swimming spots before drying off in the sun. On your last day, delve into the island's past on a tour of the historic Eden Fishery and a visit to the 1855 Rock Harbor lighthouse.

03

Six days

The rite of passage on Isle Royale is to hike the length of the island. Five nights is ample time to complete the 40-mile (64km) hike along the Greenstone Ridge Trail. Take the *Voyageur II* from Grand Portage, start in Windigo on the west side of the island and hike 6 miles (9.6km) to Island Mine or 12 miles (19.3km) to South Lake Desor. The campgrounds, which are nicely spaced out at 6- to 10-mile (9.6 to 16km) interims, are first-come, first-served. On the fourth night, hang a right at Mt Franklin and hike the 2 miles (3.2km) to Three Mile Campground, hopefully getting there in time to secure a lakeside campsite, which includes a screened-in shelter.

The last day will be an easy lakeside stroll into Rock Harbor, where a hot shower and a cold draft beer will be waiting. Just remember: this may be the flat Midwest, but there are eight points along the trail that rise above 1300ft (396m). (Be prepared for sore feet and legs!) On the morning of day six, hop on the ferry at Rock Harbor.

35

CA

Joshua Tree National Park

Twisted trees pointing skyward, epic playgrounds of rocks and rare palm oases beckon you to this Southern California desert crossroads.

Joshua Tree

This untamed park propels even the most mild-mannered to go wild. As you scamper up jumbled rock heaps, with evocative names like 'Skull Rock,' or trek out deep into the desert, the myth and mystery of this truly divine place will reveal itself… piece by piece, rock by rock.

The park's bizarrely bent namesake trees stand out against the serene landscape. Under the light of the moon, these trees take on new dimensions as they cut across the desert sky full of stars and wonderment. Climbing through the parched rocky hills here, you may stumble upon the biggest surprise of all: a cool spring shaded by California fan palms, trees that can live for up to 200 years.

Joshua Tree is uniquely placed, with one foot in the higher, cooler Mojave Desert and the other foot in the lower, hotter Colorado Desert. The latter is part of the Sonora Desert that stretches into Mexico – you can sometimes see that far from the park's Keys View. On the road to Cottonwood Spring, watch through your car's windshield as these landscapes collide, winding you down finally through Pinto Basin, an area that has been inhabited for over 8000 years. Native Americans, including the Serrano, Chemehuevi and Cahuilla tribes, still call this desert home, traditionally gathering its plants for food, medicine and for weaving baskets with bold patterns. Along dirt trails, historical artifacts abound – look, but resist the urge to take them home, they are sacred to this place.

Gun-slinging American miners arrived in the 19th century seeking silver and gold, though most never found it. Homesteaders also tried to make a go of it here, but left when the rains disappeared. Today, rock climbers come to test world-class routes up granite monoliths and slabs of 'J-Tree.' These eye-catching features are the result of plutonic hard-rock

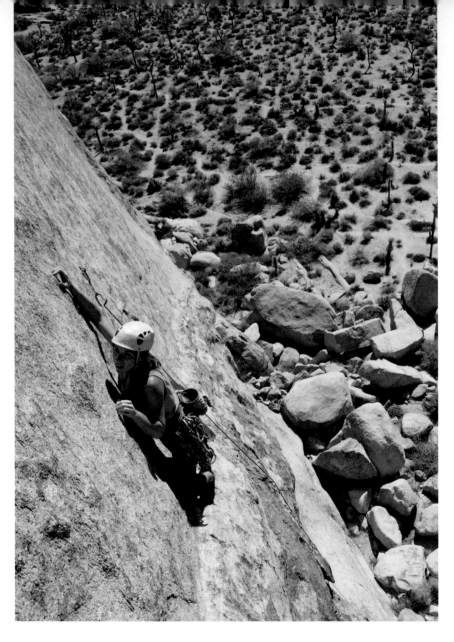

intrusions uncovered and sculpted over the millennia by wind and rain. The terrain is crisscrossed by dozens of earthquake faults. California's famously shaky San Andreas Fault is easily spotted from Keys View. While the fault lies outside of the park, several smaller branches are found here, creating the very springs and oases that make life possible here.

Toolbox

When to go
The biggest crowds arrive in spring, when wildflowers are in bloom. Temperatures are mild in both spring and autumn, perfect for activities. Winter can be cold, but with clear skies.

Getting there
The park is in Southern California, an hour's drive northeast of the resort town of Palm Springs. It's at least two hours by car east of Los Angeles and its airport. The main visitor center is in the nearby town of Joshua Tree.

Events
Generally peaking in July and August, the Perseids meteor shower of sparkle and awe takes on new levels in the clear night skies of Joshua Tree.

Accessibility
The Oasis of Mara Trail and Lower Keys View Overlook have paved trails that are accessible for wheelchairs. Jumbo Rocks and Black Rock have accessible campsites and restrooms.

Park in numbers
1235.5 Area in sq miles
8000 Rock climbing routes
5 Desert fan-palm oases

Stay here...

Backcountry camping
You can camp almost anywhere in Joshua Tree's 792,000 acres. Make sure you are a mile from the road, 500 feet from trails and water sources, and not in day-use-only areas. Outside that, the world is your oyster. Pick the best rock outcrop around and go wild.

Jumbo Rocks Campground
Are you dreaming of sleeping under the stars next to the park's iconic rock formations? This reservation only campground is smack dab in the middle of all that gorgeous scenery. Show up early to get a site, especially on weekends. Don't forget to bring your own water.

Harmony Motel
A simple roadside motel has one big claim to fame: the rock band U2 stayed here while working on their groundbreaking album *The Joshua Tree*. Unwind in the outdoor hot tub or cool swimming pool after a satisfyingly long day of hiking and climbing. Book the Jack Kerouac Cabin for a more private getaway.

Do this!

Rock climbing
Monzogranite boulders, slabs and sheer faces issue a siren's call for you to climb, whether you're an enthusiastic novice going with a guide or an expert going it alone. Outdoor outfitters in the town of Joshua Tree rent and sell climbing gear and teach hands-on lessons. Before you head out on your own, though, join the park's climbing ranger for morning coffee during the climbing season (roughly October to April).

Dirt-road driving
Some of the most fun you can have in a desert park is bumping down dirt roads into the wilderness (never leave the actual roads, it will destroy this delicate ecosystem). Follow the 18-mile (29km) Geology Tour Rd for a sped-up version of 100 million years of natural history, or explore Covington Flats, where the park's biggest Joshua trees grow.

Guided touring
Buy tickets for a tour of fascinating Keys Ranch, where homesteaders staked a claim, or take a full moon hike guided by a ranger naturalist (free!).

◄ Joshua Tree National Park attracts rock climbers of all ages. Previous page: the park's eroded rocks provide plenty of handholds.

What to spot...

Uniquely positioned at the boundary of two deserts, this park offers visitors an astounding collection of plants and animals to look for. To the south, the Colorado Desert is earmarked by ocotillo plants, with their spiky red blooms, and cholla cactus, whose spines seem to 'jump out' at passersby (watch out!). Further north, the milder Mojave Desert provides habitat for rare Joshua trees, as well as desert tortoises and migratory birds stopping over along the Pacific Flyway.

JOSHUA TREE Growing up to 40ft (12m) high and instantly recognizable by their twisted branches, these yucca plants bloom with creamy white flowers in spring.

GREATER ROADRUNNER One of the park's most famous resident avian species, these tan cuckoos can run over 25mph (40kph) and are fast enough to kill attacking rattlesnakes.

MOJAVE COLLARED LIZARD Look for the distinctive black-and-white rings around the neck of this reptilian predator found in rocky areas of the park.

Hike this...

01 Hidden Valley
Children will enjoy this short, 1-mile (1.6km) nature trail, an all-in-one introduction to the park's geology, flora and fauna.

02 Mastodon Peak
This moderate 3-mile (4.8 km) hike in the Colorado Desert part of the park scrambles all the way to the top of a craggy granite peak, finally looping around an old gold mine.

03 Lost Palms Oasis
Become an explorer of a lost world on this remote, 7.2-mile (11.6km) hike to a California fan-palm oasis.

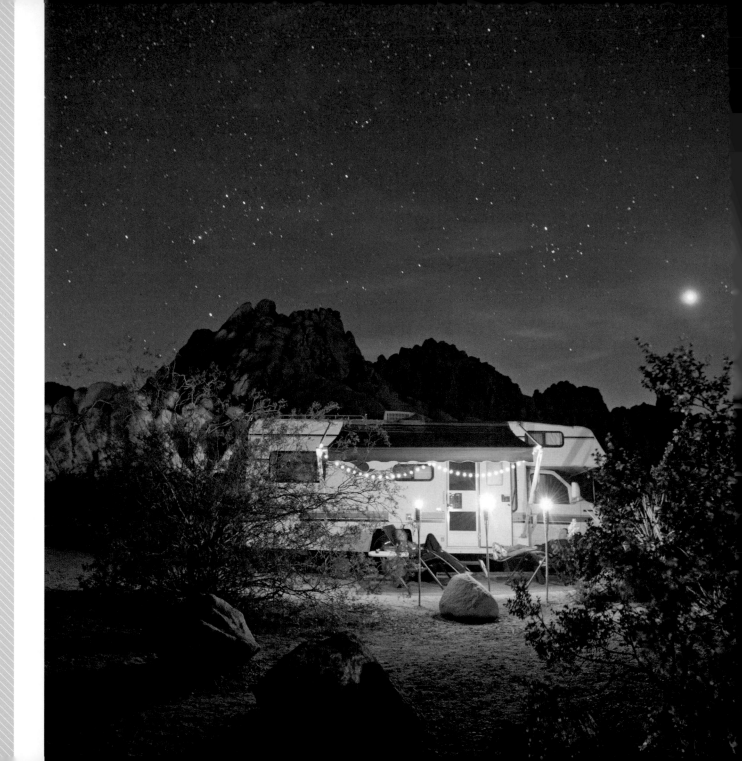

Itineraries

Visit the ruins of Lost Horse Mine, hike Hidden Valley and Barker Dam, and don't miss the Keys View sunsets over the iconic Joshua trees.

◀ A coyote. Park up to admire the Milky Way; there's an annual Night Sky festival in the park.
▶ The Joshua tree is a variety of yucca.

01
A day

It may leave you wanting more, but one day is still enough to hit the highlights of this desert park. Driving in from Palm Springs through the Yucca Valley, the tiny town of Joshua Tree is your last chance for food, water and gas – there are no tourist services inside the park. Driving down Park Blvd, you'll spot those iconic Joshua trees even before you reach the park's entrance station. Inside the park, hop out of the car at Hidden Valley for a brief nature walk and a picnic lunch. Nearby, a short trail rounds the cool reservoir at Barker Dam and passes Native American petroglyphs and the Wonderland of Rocks. Head up to Keys View for panoramic photos, then drive east past glorious gardens of granite boulders are heaped up in every conceivable shape – kids especially love Skull Rock. Peruse educational exhibits inside the visitor center by the Oasis of Mara, then take a late afternoon hike over a hill to Fortynine Palms Oasis, where California fan palms shade a clear pool of water that attracts wildlife.

02
Two days

If you've got two days to spend, make more time for the heart of the park. Reserve your place for a historic ranger-led tour of Keys Ranch or hike into a desert wash to visit the ruins of Lost Horse Mine. Bump down Geology Tour Rd, passing rock climbers clinging to rock slabs. With some advance planning, you can snag a prime campsite (or even better go for a backcountry trip), and later watch the stars twinkle high above your sleeping bag.

The next day, drive south through Pinto Basin, stopping to walk around the cactus garden of succulents, including crooked ocotillo plants and fuzzy-looking 'teddy bear' cholla cactus (which are, in fact, painfully barbed). Dropping into the Colorado Desert, the road finally reaches Cottonwood Spring, which has a small visitor center and campground. Gear up and bring plenty of water for the meditative hike to Lost Palms Oasis, a native fan-palm grove standing in a canyon, where desert bighorn sheep might be your only companions.

03
Three days

Three days give you plenty of time to explore this park. With three million visitors a year, it's good to get off the beaten path: grab a permit and head into the backcountry. If you want to stay closer to the roads, spend a day around Hidden Valley and Barker Dam, hiking, picnicking, and taking a rock-climbing lesson from a local guide. A great sunset perch is Keys View, although the top of Ryan Mountain offers equally magnificent vistas with more solitude, if you're up for a hardy ascent. Pitch your tent at Hidden Valley for the first night.

The next day, tour Keys Ranch or head out into Queen Valley (you are allowed to ride a bicycle on the park's roads), where you can inspect the remains of a huge mine. Before sunset, head to Black Rock Campground and drive the dirt roads around Covington Flat to see gigantic Joshua trees – you'll need a high-clearance 4WD for this one. On day three, drive down to Cottonwood Springs, where you can hike to fantastic Lost Palms Oasis before leaving the park.

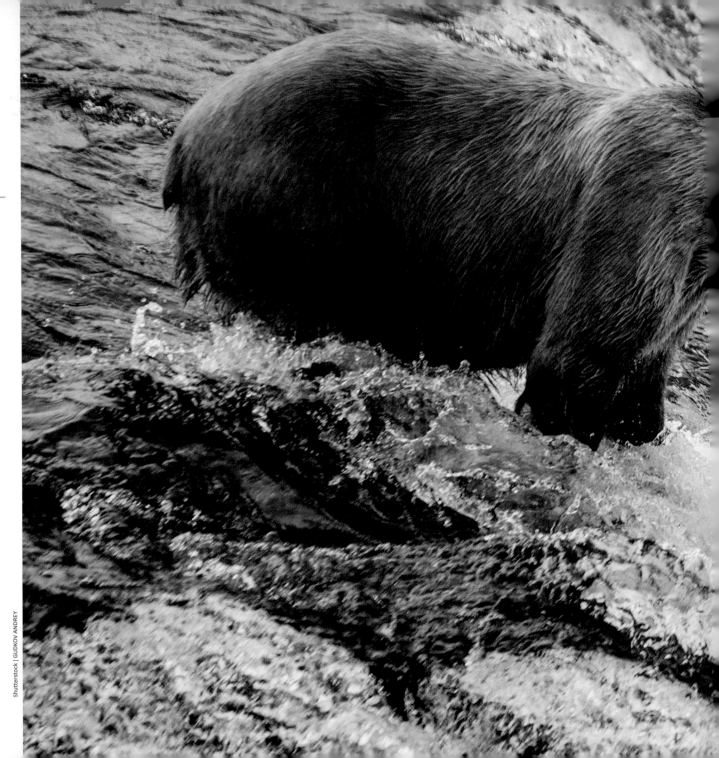

36

AK

Katmai National Park & Preserve

Some of the best brown bear-watching in the world can be found at this remote park on the hazy-bayed Alaskan Peninsula.

Shutterstock | GUDKOV ANDREY

Remember watching wildlife shows as a kid and seeing a 1000-pound (454kg) brown bear scooping salmon from a waterfall? That was shot – almost without a doubt – in Katmai National Park's Brooks Camp. If you have the money to get here, you can see this postcard-perfect scene from wild America play out in real life and in living color.

Head a little further afield in the 6400-sq-mile (16,576 sq km) park – that's about the size of the country of Wales – to explore lost lakes, revel in Alaska Native cultural traditions that go back thousands of years, enjoy some excellent fishing and visit the enchanting and evocatively named Valley of Ten Thousand Smokes.

Formed as a national monument in 1918, Katmai was recognized as a national park in 1980. Its original purpose was to study the active volcanism of the Valley of Ten Thousand Smokes and the extensive coastal habitats that make this ecosystem so rich. The Valley of Ten Thousand Smokes is a 40-sq-mile (103.6 sq km) ashflow that resulted from the eruption of Novarupta in 1912. For years the entire valley was filled with smoking fumaroles; today, only a few remain on the nearby hillsides. What's left behind is a naked moonscape that's powerful, bleak and just a little surreal.

The real reason you go here is to see bears – big ones. Fattened up from massive salmon runs, the brown bears of Katmai are immense, powerful and awe-inspiring. While most people head to Brooks Falls to sight these ursine masterpieces, you can spot bears throughout the park. You'll also find excellent canoeing and kayaking on the hundreds of miles of river, lake and stream

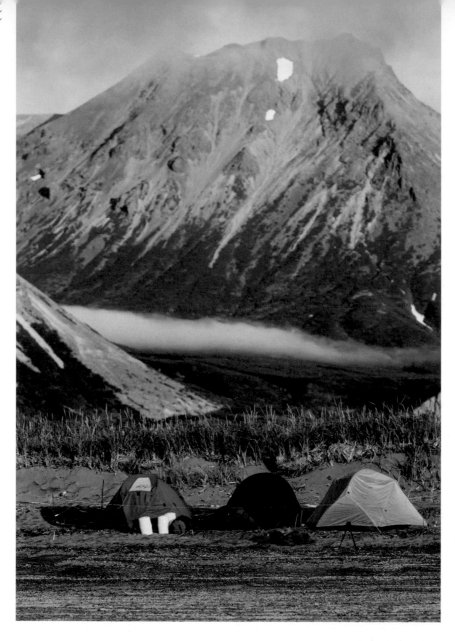

that crisscross this coastal environment. Backcountry explorers can easily extend their trip into the wilderness that marks this untrammeled corner of the earth.

There are only 5 miles (8km) of trail in the park. With a bit of wilderness know-how, or a qualified local guide, you can extend your adventures here for weeks.

Getty Images | Scott Dickerson / Design Pics

Toolbox

When to go
July and September are the best months for bear viewing at Brooks Camp; come in July to see the salmon fighting their way upstream. Park services run from June to mid-September but you can visit at any time.

Getting there
Set on the Alaska Peninsula, it's not easy to get here. Fly to King Salmon then take a floatplane to Brooks Camp. With a bit of planning, there are unlimited backcountry hikes and paddles.

Events
From June 7 to September 17 the rangers here run programs, from cultural walks to tours of the Valley of Ten Thousand Smokes.

Accessibility
Most of the buildings in Brooks Camp are accessible, but you may need some help to navigate the trails that access the wildlife viewing platforms. Getting in and out of float planes can be challenging.

Park in numbers

6400 Area in sq miles
2200 Brown bears
9000 Years of human habitation

Stay here...

Hallo Bay Bear Camp
Specializing in bear-watching, this eco-minded tour operator has a safari camp on the coastal edge of the park. You'll sleep in tents and get plenty of proximity with guided nature tours. The groups are small, making for intimate encounters with the big bears that roam the park.

Brooks Lodge
Just a short walk from Brooks Falls, this lodge offers easy access to fishing and bear-viewing, plus awesome views of Naknek Lake. It's a rustic yet expensive treat. Expect to stay on bunk beds in one of 16 modern rooms – and stay up late swapping tales with fellow travelers.

Fure's Cabin
On Naknek Lake's Bay of Islands, this public-use cabin was the home of famed trapper Roy Fure, who built the cabin in 1926 from hand-hewn spruce logs. It's a welcome, simple stopover for kayakers and canoers adventuring into the further reaches of the park. Book at www.recreation.gov.

Do this!

Canoeing & kayaking
Hop in a kayak or canoe to paddle any number of scenic waterways through the Katmai backcountry, long navigated by Native Alaskans on these aquatic corridors. Take all the recommended pre-float precautions – this is an adventurous land.

Fishing
For thousands of years, fishing has been a central part of the culture and commerce of the region. Within the park, you can fish for rainbow trout, arctic char, Dolly Varden trout, arctic grayling, char, and of course the five species of Pacific salmon that run through here.

Bear-watching
This is the reason around 40,000 people make it here every year. The best viewing is of course at Brooks Falls, where in high season you can see around 10 bears gathered by the falls, where salmon make dramatic leaps and the bears happily claw them out of the air and into their bellies. Go further afield for smaller crowds, and always – always – practice good bear safety.

◀ Camping on Hallo Bay, where sedge meadows attract bears (note the fence!). Previous page: a coastal brown bear catching salmon at Brooks Falls.

What to spot...

Alongside the hallmark brown bears, 42 species of mammal inhabit the park. Brown bears and moose are found in the coastal and lake regions. You can also spot caribou, red fox, wolf, lynx, wolverine, river otter, mink, marten, weasel, porcupine, snowshoe hare, red squirrel and busy little beavers. Along the coast, red salmon are the region's lifeblood, but you can also spot barking sea lions, sea otters and the occasional whale or porpoise along the Shelikof Strait, just beyond the park borders.

BROWN BEAR
Weighing in at over 1000lbs (454kg) at the end of the summer – when they can down up to 30 salmon in a day – brown bears are one of the world's most iconic apex predators.

BEAVER The lakes, ponds and marshes of this coastal area attract an amazing variety of animal life. Watching beavers build their lodges and ponds is a wonderful afternoon activity.

SEA LION
Head to the coast to spot seals and sea lions, and the ever-endearing (and sadly endangered) sea otters. The large sea lion colonies are a sight (and sound) to behold.

Hike this...

01 Brooks Falls
It's just a 1.2-mile (2km) hike from the drop-off to Brooks Falls. Along the way are three viewing platforms and the final deck, where camera-toting tourists battle for the best shot.

02 Dumpling Mountain
The only developed trail, this half-day trek takes you to the top of 2440 ft (744m) Dumpling Mountain, where you catch superlative views of the surrounding lake country.

03 Three Forks Overlook
There aren't many trails in the park, but you can ask to be dropped off at this overlook of the famous Valley of Ten Thousand Smokes, where you can trek into the rugged backcountry.

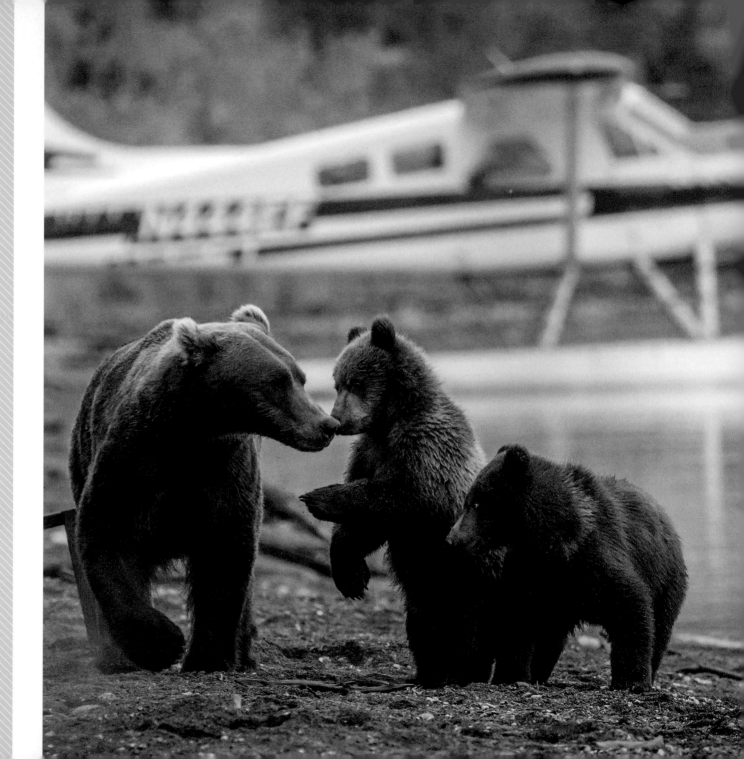

Itineraries

Bear-watching around Brooks Camp, roadtripping to Three Forks Overlook, kayaking the Savonoski Loop – this park has it all, and Ten Thousand Smokes views.

◄ Family time at Naknek Lake, which is accessed by floatplane.
► Brooks Falls campground; track bear prints, big and small in Katmai's mudflats.

01

Three days

It's expensive staying at Brooks Camp, so you may wish to limit your time and focus on just the essentials. Fly into Brooks Camp on floatplane from the gateway village of King Salmon. On a budget, you can either set up shop in King Salmon, with day trips to the park, or enter the lottery to stay at the Brooks Camp Campground (which is, understandably, surrounded by an electric fence). For a bit more expense, stay at the rustic Brooks Lodge or Hallo Bay Bear Camp. Every trip here starts with a mandatory bear safety talk. And you'll want to spend most of your first day watching bears on the platforms around Brooks Camp. Every day you will probably end up spending at least a few hours on the platforms waiting for that perfect shot. On day two, hop on the 23-mile (38km) road (the only one in the park) to the Three Forks Overlook, for arching views of the Valley of Ten Thousand Smokes. You can head off here for some killer trail-less hiking. On your third day, consider a short kayak or spring for a flightseeing tour.

02

Ten days

Time, budget and outdoor experience permitting, you can do some once-in-a-lifetime activities. Start with bear viewing at Brooks Camp, where you can gather information and solidify plans for a backcountry expedition. From there, paddlers can hop in a kayak or canoe for a five- to 10-day circuit on the Savonoski Loop. The full trip takes you through some of the best of Katmai across 86 miles (138km). In just two or three days, you reach Fure's Cabin in the Bay of Islands. Then it's on to Grosvenor Lake and the Savonoski River. Expect high winds and rough waters on big lakes, and some class I and II rapids on the river. If you aren't wiped out already, venture from the Valley of Ten Thousand Smokes for backcountry hiking, using riverbeds and ridgelines to traverse this trackless terrain. A few operators offer all-inclusive trips that include hiking, paddling and bear-watching. For an added kick, end your trip with a journey to Lake Clark National Park & Preserve, a seldom-explored park of hills, glaciers and more.

3.7

AK

Kenai Fjords National Park

With cascading glaciers, sky-high fjords teaming with bird and sea life, and easy access, this maritime park is an enchanting mix of sea, ice and mountainside.

The nearly 40 glaciers that carve their way through stone and rock down to the rugged fjords are the crowning jewels of this popular national park.

Alas, due to global warming, these glaciers are in retreat. But they are still massive, incredible, awe-inspiring and remarkably forceful. Atop it all is the Harding Icefield. This majestic glimmering block of ice, created more than 23,000 years ago, covers 700 sq miles (1813 sq km) of Alaska's Kenai Mountains. From it, glaciers flowed to the sea, carving the deep fjords you see today in such legendary waters as Resurrection and Aialik bays.

The *de rigeur* trip here is a boat tour from the lyrical fishing village of Seward. Along the way, you will see fjords, glaciers and a remarkable tapestry of marine wildlife that includes sea otters, Dall's porpoise, harbor porpoise, Steller sea lion, harbor seal and orca. Whalewatching is also spectacular, with opportunities to sight fin, gray, humpack, minke and sei whale.

For another perspective on this watery world, get closer to nature on a kayak tour – paddling between icebergs and listening to the crackle of melting ice is magical. Head out for a day amid the bergs or scale-up your adventure with multiday paddles.

The Exit Glacier is the most often-visited land area in the park. You can hike here easily in a day, even extending your trip to make it to the top of the world on the Harding Icefield. From here you can also access a trail that traverses the entire Kenai Peninsula. This broad spit of land on the southern coast of Alaska is home to black and brown bear, mountain goat and moose. You might even sight a marmot or northern bog lemming if you look close enough.

Toolbox

When to go
In these northern latitudes, the best time is during the summer months of June to August. On the shoulder season, you may catch some good weather, but the visitor centers aren't open.

Getting there
From Anchorage, hop on the Alaska Railroad to get down to the gateway city of Seward. It's an easy two-hour drive down if you have your own wheels. Boat and kayak trips into the park depart from here, or you can head inland for a hike to the Exit Glacier.

Events
The grueling Mount Marathon Race 5k race takes you up 3000 feet (914m) to the top of Mt Marathon and back on the Fourth of July.

Accessibility
Most, but not all, of the boat tours are wheelchair accessible. At Exit Glacier, a one-mile (1.6km) accessible loop takes you to views of the glacier.

Park in numbers
940 Area in sq miles
191 Species of bird
545 Miles of coastline

Stay here...

🏠 Public-use cabins
For a back-to-nature treat, book one of the two public-use cabins located along the fjords for a long weekend. The Aialik Cabin sits on a beach, offering great whalewatching. From the Holgate Arm Cabin, you can wonder at the nearby glacier. Willow Cabin is located at the Exit Glacier.

🏠 Kenai Fjords Glacier Lodge
The only wilderness lodge within the park, this all-inclusive lodge on a glorious lagoon has 16 rustic cabins that exude just the right balance between modern comfort and Alaska-backwoods atavism. A series of boardwalks connect your cabins, and everything is included – guided boat trips, kayaks, gourmet meals and transport from Seward.

🏠 Nauti Otter
For lodging on the cheap, check out this fun collection of cabins, hostel rooms and a yurt village just outside the town of Seward. The Otter has two kitchens and an outdoor area with gas grills for self-catering. The bus service from Anchorage to Seward will drop you at the Nauti Otter.

Do this!

🛶 Sea kayaking
While you can go on a short day paddle, multiday blue-water excursions here are where it's at. From Seward, you can hire a boat to take you out to Aialik Bay, spending three or four days paddling south past Pedersen Glacier and into the Holgate Arm. Aboard a kayak, with the wind in your hair and the water lapping at your side, you'll feel an intimate connection with the water and nature that makes this place special.

〰️ Boat touring
From a boat, you'll see plenty of birds and coastal wildlife, also taking in the dramatic sights, waterfalls and calving glaciers of Resurrection Bay, Holgate Arm and the Northwestern Lagoon. This experience takes you close to the wild, steep fjords of the park. Trained naturalists offer running commentary and, when it's cold, hot chocolate.

🪧 Glacier touring
Strap on some crampons, ready your ice ax and tie-in for adventure with an ice-climbing excursion onto the Harding Icefield. Guided trips take you past crevasses and ice caves, where remarkable blues shine in the bright Alaskan sun.

◀ The rock spikes of Porcupine Bay.
▶ Puffins feed and nest here.

Hike this...

01 Exit Glacier
From the Exit Glacier Nature Center, head out for a ranger-guided trek to a viewing point above this glacier (one of the few spots accessible by land in the park). The hike takes just an hour or two round-trip.

02 Harding Icefield Trail
It's only 4 miles (6.4km) to the top, but because of the 1000ft (305m) of elevation gain, it can take you up to eight hours' round-trip to make it to the Harding Icefield.

03 Resurrection River Trail
Outside the park, this trail is a spectacular backwoods romp. Strap on a backpack for a multi-day hike from Seward to the village of Hope on the northern coast of the Kenai Peninsula.

Shutterstock | Sekar B; CSNafzger

What to spot...

If you love sea life, then Kenai Fjords is the place for you. Top on nearly everybody's list is sighting marine mammals such as various whales or porpoise – in fact the park's mission includes protecting these sea animals and maintaining their breeding areas. You'll want your binoculars and mega-zoom lens to spot some of the signature bird species, including tufted and horned puffins, bald eagles and oystercatchers.

ORCA There are approximately 250 orca in 15 pods roaming the waters of Prince William Sound. In May and early June, you might just spot them cruising at 35mph (56km/h) past your bow.

PUFFIN These fanciful birds with their colorful beaks nest here starting in mid-May. They are incredible swimmers and, like penguins, they mate for life.

SEA OTTER Playful, hilarious to watch and curious as anything, these water weasels are seen throughout Alaska's southern coasts. You will most certainly see a handful on your trip.

200

Itineraries

Take a boat tour of the fjords, a guided ascent of the Harding Icefield or meet the challenge of Mt Marathon before dining on the world's freshest halibut.

◀ A stand-up paddle board lets you get close to an iceberg canyon on Bear Lake in Kenai Fjords.
➡ Snack time at Bear Lake.

01
Three days

Head down to Seward from Anchorage on the Coastal Classic Train, stopping to view beluga whale running up the Turnagain Arm mid-July through August. Once you get here, stroll through town, enjoying the murals that add color to every corner. Have dinner dockside at Chinooks, and hire your boat tour for the following day. Two major operators run the boat tours. You won't see much on the three-hour tour, so splurge instead on the full eight-hour deal to see more of the fjords. A naturalist will provide running commentary. Keep your eyes on the horizon for whale, orca and other sea mammals. Party that night Alaskan-style at the rough-and-tumble Thorn's Showcase Lounge, which serves some of the best halibut around. The next day, get up early for the guided ascent to Harding Icefield, stopping on the way home at the Exit Glacier Salmon Bake. On day three, consider taking a guided sea-kayak trip, or else head out for a long day-hike in the wild countryside that surrounds the village of Seward.

02
Five days

The best way to explore this water-bound national park is aboard a sea kayak. You'll get closer than you ever imagined to the sights, sounds and energy of this place. It requires planning, as only expert paddlers should tackle the waters outside of Resurrection Bay. For the rest of us, you'll need to hire a sea-taxi to drop you in the relatively calm waters of Aialik Bay. It's always better to go with a guide: they know the local flora and fauna and they will keep you from dying. Expect to be cold and wet most of the time. A dry top or splash top is essential. Stay in a public-use cabin in Aialik or one of dozens of remote campsites. Over the next four days, you can slowly make your way past Pedersen Glacier and into Holgate Arm, where another public-use cabin awaits. Don't be tempted to get too close to the icebergs, they can flip at any moment. A sea-taxi can pick you up after day five, or continue on, exploring the seldom-viewed corners of this remote park. Finish your trip with beers and dinner at Ray's Waterfront in Seward.

03
Seven days

Start with the essentials, then move out into new ground with a little improvisation. After you've exhausted the tours and kayaks of the park, there's still plenty to do in and around Seward. The Lost Lake Trail goes up 13.8 miles (22.2km) and offers some of the most spectacular views of Resurrection Bay you will ever see.

If that's not enough, really challenge yourself with an ascent of nearby Mt Marathon, where loco locals run a killer footrace every July 4th. The following day, rent a fat-tire mountain bike to ride some way along the Iditarod National Historic Trail.

In the afternoon, you can spend three hours ziplining through the treetop canopy of Sitka spruce at Stoney Creek Canopy Adventures just north of Seward. To treat yourself on the final day, hire a flightseeing tour, or go one step further with a glacier hike out onto the Harding Icefield. Top off everything with some deep-sea fishing for halibut and salmon.

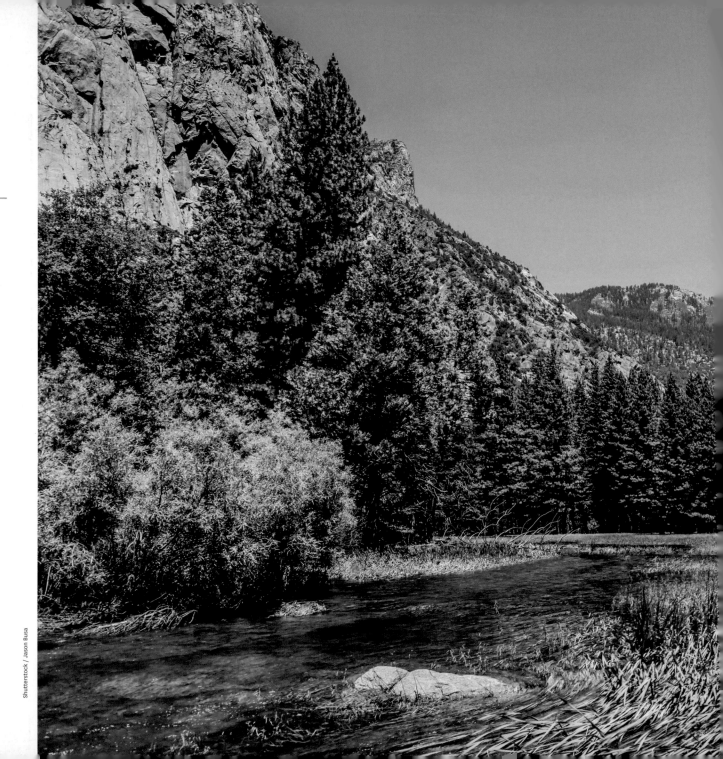

38

CA

Kings Canyon National Park

Giant sequoia trees, sheer granite cliffs and a dizzyingly deep river canyon all combine in this hidden Sierra Nevada beauty.

Shutterstock / Jason Busa

The poet and conservationist John Muir once called Kings Canyon 'a rival to the Yosemite.' You'll understand why as you drive down the serpentine Kings Canyon Scenic Byway, cut narrowly into the edges of canyon walls carved by glaciers and polished by rushing water and creeping time. At roadside vista points like Junction View, steel your nerves and peer over the precipice toward the roaring white-water river far below. Arriving at the end of the road in Cedar Grove, get out and ramble beside the powerful Kings River, where Muir himself gave impromptu lectures while standing atop an enormous rock.

Only a fraction of the crowds that swarm Yosemite National Park, found further north in the Sierra Nevada, make their way to Kings Canyon. As you hike deep into the peaceful forest to a tumbling waterfall, the only sounds along the trail may be birdsong, canyon breezes, and your own footsteps. Down by the Kings River, you can go for a dip in summertime swimming holes, or show up in spring to spy black bears grazing in wildflower meadows. In winter, strap on snowshoes and tramp among some of the world's largest trees, including the towering General Grant Tree, the official Christmas tree of the US.

Backpackers revel in the wilderness of the High Sierra, so readily accessible from Cedar Grove. One classic route is the Rae Lakes Loop, which follows the famous John Muir Trail and Pacific Crest Trail over mountain passes and past alpine lakes that will leave you awestruck by nature's majesty. Expert rock climbers find epic challenges – without the crowds of Yosemite's El Capitan – in the park's backcountry, too. For kids, camping next to trees that measure over 20 stories tall is a thrill not soon forgotten.

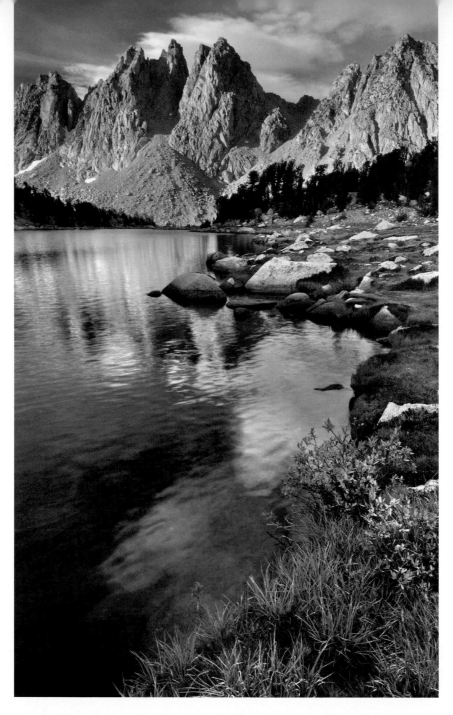

Toolbox

When to go
Summer is a crowded time to visit. Waterfalls peak in late spring. Early fall is still warm enough for camping. In winter, the Kings Canyon Scenic Byway closes.

Getting there
The park is a four-hour drive southeast of San Francisco via Fresno. In summer, buses to Grant Grove stop at Fresno's airport and train and bus stations. You'll need a car to drive the Kings Canyon Scenic Byway.

Events
The Dark Sky Festival for stargazers is in early September. The Trek to the Tree event on the second Saturday in December includes holiday carolers

Accessibility
Free wheelchair loans are available at the Lodgepole Visitor Center and the Giant Forest Museum. The Grant Tree Trail is paved but steep and not designated as wheelchair accessible.

Park in numbers
721.7 Area in sq miles
8200 Maximum depth of Kings Canyon (ft)
268.1 Height of General Grant, tallest tree (ft)

Stay here...

John Muir Lodge
In Grant Grove Village, secluded down a side road away from the crowds of campers, this woodsy inn is the best place to bed down in the park. Relax in a rocking chair on the front porch in summer, or cozy up by the fireplace in winter.

Paradise Valley
Numerous backpacking trips beeline from the Road's End Trailhead in Cedar Grove into the tree-and-granite-lined Paradise Valley, which hugs the Kings River.

A wilderness permit is required for overnight camping; check the park website for current requirements.

Azalea Campground
Within walking distance of the General Grant Grove, this forested, family-friendly campground allows you to camp quite close to giant sequoias. It's a quick shuttle ride to the Grant Grove Village market, which sells all the supplies you'll need to make s'mores in the crackling fire pit at your campsite.

Do this!

Swimming
When the Kings River water levels drop in mid-summer, swimming holes appear. Look for them near Roads End in Cedar Grove, especially around the beach by Muir Rock and underneath the Red Bridge. Always check with park rangers before taking a dip, just to be sure current conditions are safe. Spring and early summer are the most dangerous times to be around rivers due to melting snow.

Horseback riding
Saddle up for a short trail ride among giant sequoia trees at Grant Grove. Drive all the way down into the canyon to the rustic Cedar Grove Pack Station for trots beside the Kings River and multi-day wilderness trips to High Sierra lakes and meadows.

Skiing & snowshoeing
When the Kings Canyon Scenic Byway is closed in winter, you can still rent snowshoes in Grant Grove Village and trek among the giant sequoias. Try sledding at Big Stump, also in the Grant Grove area. In the nearby Sequoia National Forest, family-friendly Montecito Sequoia Lodge rents snowshoes and cross-country skis and has miles of groomed ski trails.

◧ A wintry Kearsarge Lake. Previous page: verdant Zumwalt Meadow is a favorite foraging spot for bears.

What to spot...

Kings Canyon has all the diversity of more famous Sierra Nevada national parks, and then some. Black bears, mule deer and yellow-bellied marmots inhabit mixed conifer forests, high mountain meadows, granite peaks and the canyon's slopes. So do 150 rare and unusual species, such as the endangered mountain yellow-legged frog, which survives only by alpine lakes in the High Sierra. The park is also a paradise for birders, with more than 200 varied species thriving here.

BLACK BEAR
Ursus americanus is the king of the forests. Don't let the name fool you, though: their fur can be black, brown, golden or even cinnamon-colored.

GIANT SEQUOIA These venerable trees grow in abundance in Grant Grove and in historically misnamed Redwood Canyon, where few people now go.

CALIFORNIA SPOTTED OWL
Count yourself lucky if you see this nocturnal hunter with inky dark eyes – Kings Canyon is one of its few protected strongholds.

Hike this...

01 **General Grant Tree Trail**
Amble past giant sequoias and peek inside the Fallen Monarch, a tree so big it once served as horse stables. The trail is 0.4 miles (0.6km).

02 **Zumwalt Meadow Loop**
Tramp 1.5 miles (2.4km) along the boardwalk through a grassy meadow, where wildflowers bloom next to the Kings River.

03 **Rae Lakes Loop**
Climb a shady forest through Kings Canyon's granite walls. You'll pass Mist Falls at 4.6 miles (7.4km) on the way to alpine lakes. The loop is 41.4 miles (66.6km).

Itineraries

Hike to a waterfall in aptly named Paradise Valley, see the world's second largest tree at General Grant Grove or tour the marble magic of Boyden Cavern.

◄ The mountain yellow-legged frog. Giant sequoia are the world's largest living organisms and can live for more than 3000 years.
➤ Setting up camp in the Sierras.

01

A day

From the park's Big Stump entrance station, it's just a few more miles to the park's visitor hub, Grant Grove Village. Step inside the Kings Canyon Visitor Center for natural history displays and to pick up hiking maps and information; there's even an educational play room at the back for kids. Drive to General Grant Grove, where an easy nature walk loops past fine specimens of giant sequoias, including the world's second-largest living tree and the hollowed-out Fallen Monarch. After a pleasant picnic lunch in the sun-dappled forest, head over to Grant Grove Stables for a short horseback or mule ride. If you crave more solitude while hiking among the giant sequoias, drive south to Redwood Canyon for its interlocking network of trails.

Before sunset, return to Grant Grove Village and follow Panoramic Point Rd as it winds narrowly upward; on foot, hike up a short hill for sweeping views of Kings Canyon – at its best when the fading sunlight paints the rocks in serene pastels.

02

Two days

Wake up to the smell of pine trees at your forest campsite in Grant Grove. After breakfast, swoop down the Kings Canyon Scenic Byway, which drops deep into the canyon for 35 miles (56.3km), passing through the Giant Sequoia National Monument on its way down to Cedar Grove. Stop at Junction View for unbelievable vistas of one of North America's deepest canyons and to take a tour of Boyden Cavern, a marble cave set in the canyon's walls. Pulling into Cedar Grove Village, grab some cold drinks and ice cream at the market or lunch at the grill, then kick back on the riverside deck. Afterward, drive 6 miles (9.6km) down the road, passing Roaring River Falls and pretty Zumwalt Meadow, a favorite haunt of black bears.

From aptly named Roads End, set out for gorgeous Mist Falls. Follow the sandy riverside trail for two miles before joining the Paradise Valley Trail for a 2.7-mile (4.3km) climb to the falls. Afterwards, return to your Grant Grove campsite.

03

Three days

Follow the two-day itinerary then pack up your tent early and get pumped for a day of whitewater rafting with the long-running, family-owned Kings River Expeditions. You'll meet your guides at the company's base camp deep in the Sequoia National Forest. From here, a shuttle takes you to the drop-in point where you'll begin a four-hour adventure on the Kings River. The class III rapids are perfect for beginner and intermediate paddlers (wetsuits provided).

From here, it's a winding drive through the forest on the Generals Highway to your overnight digs: the eco-minded High Sierra Sequoia Camp, an all-inclusive luxury resort (in nearby Sequoia National Park). But you can't drive to your door. From the Marvin Pass Trailhead it's a one-mile (1.6km) hike to your canvas tent cabin, which is kitted out with a pillow-top mattress, feather pillows and wool rugs. Ahhh. Overlooking Kings Canyon from 8,282ft, the resort – and you – are sitting on the top of the world.

39

AK

Kobuk Valley National Park & Preserve

Discover sand dunes, massive herds of migrating caribou and mile upon glorious mile of remote solitude in this Great Land park.

Above the arctic circle, the wilds of Alaska get just a little wilder. And the remote Kobuk Valley National Park and Preserve – with its patches of oddly placed sand dunes, the rambling Kobuk River, bookended mountain ranges, and lasting Alaska Native cultural imprint – is as wild as it gets. The Baird and Waring mountain ranges encircle this park, protecting unique geological features, such as the 25-sq-mile (64.8 sq km) Great Kobuk Sand Dunes, which formed over millennia as particles of fine sand produced by the grinding action of nearby glaciers were blown into the valley.

'Kobuk' translates to Big River, and adventures both big and small are had along the park's waterways. Along the 61-mile (98km) stretch of the Kobuk River, you'll find 150ft-high (46m) river bluffs marked by the ages with permafrost ice and fossils dating back to the ice age. The Little Kobuk and Hunt River dunes add to this Technicolor mix.

Twice a year hundreds of thousands of caribou from the Western Arctic Caribou Herd migrate through the park: north in the spring and south in the fall. You'll find their tracks along the lofty sand dunes and in the surrounding wetlands wilderness. Witnessing this great migration is a spectacle on par with the great movements of the Serengeti – except, of course, it's a lot colder.

At Onion Portage, Alaska Natives have gathered for at least 9000 years to hunt these migrating herds as they ford the stream. To this day, subsistence hunters remain active in the park, harvesting caribou to feed their families over the Alaskan winter.

Kobuk is hard to reach and remote, presenting a challenge for experienced backpackers, boaters and wildlife watchers. In America's least-visited national park, you'll be rewarded with solitude, endless vistas and 24 hours of sunlight. A visit to the top of the world is about reconnecting to Earth as it was – before human progress affected the courses of our waterways, the shapes of our mountains and grandeur of our valleys.

Toolbox

When to go
Flightseers and wildlife enthusiasts time trips around the great caribou migrations in spring and fall (changing temperatures may be affecting migration patterns). For boating and backpacking come in the summer.

Getting there
There are no roads into the park and getting here will require planning and patience. From Anchorage, fly to Kotzebue, then take a puddle-jumper to the Native villages near the park or get dropped off on a chartered floatplane to see the Kobuk River and sand dunes.

Events
Bring a camera and tripod for expert-led Northern Lights photography expeditions in the winter.

Accessibility
There are no accessible trails or roads. Bush planes also pose a challenge for some people with limited mobility.

Park in numbers

2736 Area in sq miles
400 Plant species
162 Bird species

Stay here...

Bettles Lodge
This vintage 1952 lodge is a National Historic site. The six rooms are back-to-basics, but you get a spirited dining room and bar with the requisite moose-antler decorations. They also offer tours, unguided wilderness outfitting, and operate a number of remote cabins. Come in winter to experience the Northern Lights and dog sledding.

Camping
Camping in the Great Kobuk Sand Dunes – just a 2-mile (3.2km) hike up from your floatplane drop-off on the river – is an otherworldly experience that will last a lifetime. Find a corner of sand to pitch your tent and set off for miles of exploration in this out-of-place sandscape on the edge of the Arctic.

Kobuk River Lodge
After floating the Kobuk River for several days, nothing feels better than a hot shower. Overlooking the confluence of the Kobuk and Ambler rivers, this homegrown lodge has simple rooms, plenty of taxidermy (including a big-tusked walrus) and enough hot water to warm away the day's shivers. It offers guided day hikes to Onion Portage and the Great Kobuk Sand Dunes.

◄ A caribou herd crosses Kobuk River in fall.
► Locals can get around by dog-sleds.

Do this!

Kayaking
From Walker Lake in the Gates of the Arctic National Preserve, you can travel some 115 river miles (185km) down to your take-out in Kobuk village; the trip takes from five to eight days. You'll start with some big-time Class IV water in Gates of the Arctic, moving into floatable Class I. Entering the park, you'll encounter fishing camps and hunting parties, along with a rich variety of wildlife. It's a gorgeous adventure.

Flightseeing
Book a half-day flightseeing tour from Kotzebue or Bettles to see the park from the air, a good way to spot migrating caribou and other wildlife. Or hire a floatplane to drop you off for backcountry hiking (along the ridgelines in the Baird Mountains).

Itineraries

Go flightseeing for migrating caribou or day trip to Great Kobuk Sand Dunes.

01

Five days

This is one of the least-visited national parks. There are no roads, no established trails, no official campsites – so whether you come here on a one-day flightseeing tour or spend eight days on the river, you'll need to plan ahead. Start with a flight from Anchorage to Kotzebue, where you can stay at the Nullaġvik Hotel and check out the Northwest Arctic Heritage Center, which also serves as park headquarters. From there, take a flightseeing tour of the park, hoping for views of migrating caribou. The next day, transfer to Kobuk. From here, take day tours to Onion Portage and the Great Kobuk Sand Dunes, where you can spot caribou, climb through the dunes and search out wildlife. Spend your final day angling for Dolly Varden trout, sheefish, salmon, grayling and pike near Kobuk.

40

AK

Lake Clark National Park and Preserve

This under-the-radar, four-million-acre park is the epitome of Alaska, with coastal bays, glaciers, active volcanoes, tundra, deep freshwater lakes, wildlife, and centuries of Native American history.

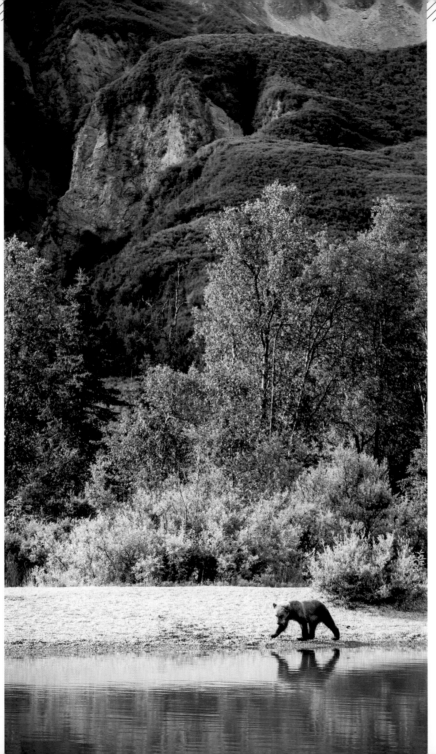

The abundance in Lake Clark National Park is over the top, even for Alaska. Two major mountain ranges, the Neacola and the Chigmit, merge here; Lake Clark Pass, which separates them, was once surrounded by 24 glaciers. While most have since receded, left in their wake are glacial lakes and streams swimming with such a bounty of salmon that the park has one of the highest concentrations of brown bears in the world.

Descendants of the Dena'ina Athabascan Indians have been fishing Lake Clark, a 128-sq-mile (332 sq km) haven for salmon and trout, for 12,000 years. The lake's native name, Qizhjeh Vena, means 'a place where people gathered.' In the early 20th century the Dena'ina abandoned their village of Kijik, which they had occupied for almost a thousand years; today the ghost town is the largest Athabascan archaeological site in the state of Alaska. The surviving Dena'ina descendants still live in Nondalton, a village of 130 residents on the southwestern shoreline of Six Mile Lake at the southern tip of Lake Clark.

Accessible only via floatplane (or a beach-landing bush plane), the park may seem out of reach for short hops, but it's only 100 miles (161km) southwest across the Cook Inlet from Anchorage, and many exciting regions are accessible via a 70-minute flight. The park's marquee attraction is its 130-mile-long (209km) coastline along the Cook Inlet, where mother bears and their cubs migrate every June in search of sedge, razor clams, and fish.

Humans can migrate to the park to fish for salmon, too. Anywhere from 150,000 to 3 million sockeye salmon migrate here annually. Beyond fishing, visitors can hike high-alpine tundra of the western slope, kayak-camp in Lake Clark, or take a day trip to view bears along the coastline.

Toolbox

When to go
There is no official park entry, but its visitor center in Port Alsworth is open from late May to mid-September. Camping is good within that window, but plan ahead: June for bear-viewing, or July or August for fishing.

Getting there
Unconnected to the Alaskan road network, the park is 100 miles (161km) southwest of Anchorage and is accessible via floatplane from Homer, Kenai and Anchorage. Weather and tides permitting, the east side of the park along Cook Inlet is accessible via boat.

Events
The salmon run comes to a peak in July and August, making for out-of-this-world fishing and bear watching.

Accessibility
Port Alsworth Visitor Center has a wheelchair accessible ramp. They also have big-wheeled all-terrain chairs in Port Alsworth, Silver Salmon Creek and Chinitna Bay ranger stations.

Park in numbers

6297 Area in sq miles
0 Number of roads
6000 Miles of waterways

Stay here...

 Redoubt Mountain Lodge
This six-cabin lodge spread over five acres and surrounded by an electric fence to keep out the brown bears, is the only property on Crescent Lake, a glacial-fed lake in the shadow of 10,197ft (3108m) Redoubt Volcano. It's a boat ride away from some of the best sockeye, coho, chinook, and king-salmon fishing in the world.

 Backcountry camping
Lake Clark has an infinite number of superb places to pitch a tent. Close in, there are two public use cabins on the northwest shore of Lake Clark. One highly coveted spot, which requires a short flight from Port Alsworth, is the spit of land that juts out of Turquoise Lake – tucked between 8000ft (2438m) snow-studded peaks to the east and high-alpine tundra to the west.

Silver Salmon Creek Lodge
Set between volcanic peaks and tidal marshes beside Cook Inlet, this cozy lodge with a communal lounging area and bedrooms with sleigh beds is a wilderness oasis. The lodge's tented camp, 10 miles (16km) to the south, operates from July to September.

Do this!

Fishing
Fishing here is a full sensory experience. As if fly-casting in the shadow of 10,000-foot peaks isn't enough, there's also the very real possibility that a brown bear is lurking on the shoreline, waiting for you to reel in your catch. Luckily, the salmon are so abundant here, that there's plenty for everyone.

 Bear-viewing
It would be nearly impossible to visit Lake Clark in June and not see a brown bear (the same as a grizzly except that it lives along the coastline instead of in the interior). It's an easy hop from Anchorage, Kenai or Homer to the Cook Inlet shoreline to watch the largest land-based predator on earth forage, fight and play.

Kayaking
This 42-mile (68km) lake lined by the Chigmit Mountains is an ideal place to experience backcountry Alaska on a budget. With advance planning, campers can fly into Port Alsworth and rent a kayak, then hop a water taxi to take them to a campsite furnished with a tent, firewood and a pit toilet – and a killer view. There are three wild rivers worth exploring while you're here as well.

◄ A young brown bear forages by Crescent Lake.
► Fireweed is found in the park.

Hike this...

01 Tanalian Mountain
It may be only 4.1 miles (6.6km) to the top, but the trail climbs 3600ft (1097m) from Port Alsworth to the top of 3900ft (1189m) Tanalian Mountain, with views of Lake Clark.

02 Turquoise to Twin lakes
This 25-mile (40km) point-to-point hike loops through high-alpine tundra. The payoff for an 8000ft (2438m) ascent is possible sightings of bear, sheep, caribou, eagle or moose.

03 Portage Creek Trail
Combine a paddle and a hike on this remote hike accessed by boat from the Joe Thompson Public Use Cabin. From the cabin (stay overnight, it's amazing), you have a short 3-mile (4.8km) hike through birch and spruce forest on up to alpine tundra.

What to spot...

BROWN BEAR Black and brown bears wander throughout the entire park, but the most impressive numbers can be found along the park's coastline in June. Watch *Wild Kingdom* unfold before your eyes, with mamas teaching cubs how to dig for razor clams and males catching up to 30 fish per day.

SOCKEYE SALMON This brilliant red fish is what has kept brown bears, sea mammals and humans alive in this harsh region for centuries; one of the main reasons for the park's existence is to protect the fish's spawning grounds. The sheer numbers of sockeye that enter the park's watershed through the Newhalen River each year are staggering – from 1.5 to 6 million.

ALDER Better known as 'tanglefoot,' the densest clusters of this silvery-green shrub are so thick that it's almost impossible to hike through them. If hiking is your objective, stick to the park's western slope, where the alder is less intrusive.

212

Itineraries

Prepare to see bears, not to mention glaciers and snow-capped volcanoes. Hiking is tough but mix it up with whitewater rafting and easy fishing.

◀ Horned puffins live in Lake Clark National Park.
▶ River crossings are a regular pleasure (and risk) in the park.

01

A day

With its trifecta of nutritional sources – razor clams, sedge and salmon – Chinitna Bay, a coastal salt-marsh habitat, is a magnet for brown bears, who congregate along the beach. There are two vantage points from which guests can photograph them digging for clams, catching salmon or chasing each other down the beach.

Bear-watching requires a few wilderness smarts. You will want to make some noise so you don't surprise a bear on your visit, and never get between a mama and her cub. The bears are so busy foraging for food that unless you disturb them, they will not disturb you. And no, bears don't like taking selfies with tourists, so resist any urge to try to get close to the world's largest land-based predator.

From Homer, you can access Chinitna Bay via boat. It's about a five-hour one-way trip. What you get are views of glaciers falling to the sea, snowcapped volcanoes, sea birds and other marine life. The full-day tour includes a few hours with the bears, plus the option of halibut fishing or clam digging.

02

Five days

When the red Cessna from Anchorage-based Rust's Flying Service touches down on Crescent Lake, the scenery seems almost too impossibly Technicolor to be true. On the northwest end of the turquoise glacial lake is snowcapped Redoubt Volcano; to the southeast is the 2-mile-long (3.2km) Lake Fork Crescent River, a world-class sockeye and silver salmon fishery. In between are precipitous, mountain-fringed shorelines where brown bears troll for easy prey. Photograph them fishing from the distant comfort of a flat-bottomed boat, or drop a line in to catch lake trout. Hiking here can be a little tough as the alder along the shoreline is dense and catchy, but there are at least seven treks that spur off of the lake, one of which ends at a 60ft (18m) waterfall. Every night guests gather at the rustic Redoubt Mountain Lodge, where the chef serves up a fresh catch of the day, followed by a fireside nightcap and an early bedtime in one of six cozy log cabins with tin roofs – an ideal place to bunk down in a rainstorm.

03

Seven days

Considering that the park is four million acres and you can camp just about anywhere in it, there's a lot of backcountry to explore – but if you don't have extensive Alaskan wilderness skills, it's best to travel with a guide who does. Dan Oberlatz, the owner of Alaska Alpine Adventures, has been exploring the park since 1992: 'I get to be the exploratory guy, backpacking, running rivers, or mountaineering,' he says. One of his most interesting offerings in the park is a seven-day hiking-and-kayaking trip that starts with a drop-off on Lower Twin Lake and includes unlimited explorations of the waterways of the Upper and Lower Twin Lakes.

The trip continues with hiking in the Hope and Beech Creek valleys, a heart-pumping climb up to Low Pass (which doesn't feel so low), and a loop through Death Valley. It's not uncommon to see wolves, bears and caribou en route. The last night includes a hot shower and a cozy bed at a lodge on Lake Clark.

Lake Clark

41

Lassen Volcanic National Park

Where the Sierra Nevada mountains, Cascade Volcanoes and the Great Basin Desert collide, this geologically active spot is exhilarating to explore.

Pristine lakes sparkle in the sunshine and wildflowers bloom in forest meadows. Found way off the beaten path in Northern California, nearly three-quarters of the park is designated as wilderness. It's threaded by hiking trails, chains of lakes for exploring by boat, and the remnants of ancient lava beds and cinder cones. Half a million people visit this volcanic zone each year. At night, the only sounds you're likely to hear from inside your tent are the spine-tingling howls of wild coyotes. Come in winter for skiing and snowshoeing in a winter wonderland.

The park rests at the northern edge of the Sierra Nevada range and the terminus of the Cascade Range. Lassen Peak is one of the southernmost volcanoes in the mountain range that extends north to the Pacific Northwest. Astoundingly, four of the world's different volcano types – shield, dome, cinder cone and composite – are found here, along with boiling mud pots, steaming vents and sulfurous hot springs. Geologically speaking, the hubbub began 825,000 years ago – and it's still going on. Lassen Peak's last major eruption occurred in 1915, just one year before it became a national park. Witness the chaos of a morphing landscape in the park's unique hydrothermal areas, which still hiss and bubble dramatically today.

At the boundary of three distinct ecological regions, Lassen has long been a meeting point for Mountain Maidu, Yahi, Yana and Atsugewi people. Various resources from the land within the park are still essential to the health and traditions of these cultures. Tread softly and leave no trace. You are only visitors here. During the 19th century, wagon-train emigrants to California passed through; later still, fortune-hunting miners, loggers and ranchers all made their way here. You can learn more about the park's cultural history inside the Loomis Museum and at Kohm Yah-mah-nee Visitor Center; which is the Mountain Maidu name for Lassen Peak.

Toolbox

When to go
Most visitor facilities are open during summer only. The main road through the park typically closes after the first major snowfall in October and doesn't reopen until the snow melts the following year – usually sometime in June.

Getting there
Located off the I-5 Fwy in Northern California's mountains, the park is less than a four-hour drive from San Francisco. You'll need a car to get here and around.

Events
Held every August, Lassen Dark Sky Festival includes activities for kids, and occasional talks by the bright folks at NASA

Accessibility
The visitor center, Loomis Museum and Discovery center all have interactive tactile exhibits and good accessibility. Sulphur Works is the most accessible hydrothermal area.

Park in numbers

166.3 Area in sq miles
10,457 Height of Lassen Peak (ft)
1915 Last major volcanic eruption (May 22)

Stay here...

 Manzanita Lake Campground
Sprawling at almost 6000ft (1829m) in elevation, this family-friendly campground near the park's northern entrance stays open from early summer until the first snow falls. Book ahead for a cozy, tent cabin that can sleep a family of up to six people.

Drakesbad Guest Ranch
Hidden in the pastoral Warner Valley, this old-fashioned mountain resort dates from the late 19th century. It rents accommodations in the ranch's historic lodge, cabins and bungalows, and serves three gourmet meals a day. You can keep kids busy here with swimming, horseback rides, campfire sing-alongs and stargazing.

Summit Lake Campground
In the middle of the park, these woodsy campgrounds are great for families. They're ideally positioned for day hikes, lake swimming and peak climbing too. Rangers give talks in the outdoor amphitheater nearby. It's smart to reserve a site in advance at this always-popular campground, which is open only during summer.

Do this!

 Swimming & boating
In summer, the park's higher elevation lakes call to swimmers, especially those who are willing to hike out to more secluded spots off the park's main road. Paddlers can rent kayaks, canoes, 'catarafts' and stand-up paddle boarding (SUP) sets from the camper store at Manzanita Lake.

Stargazing
One of California's best dark sky parks, the heavens above Lassen are barely impacted by artificial light pollution, thanks to the park's distance from major urban areas. Rangers give free astronomy programs in summer.

 Cross-country skiing & snowshoeing
When the main park road is closed in winter, you can still go snowshoeing or cross-country skiing if you bring your own equipment. Ungroomed trails start from both the south and north park entrances, leading to frozen lakes and up mountain peaks – the latter for the experienced. Be sure to have proper training and carry appropriate avalanche gear, including a beacon, shovel and probe.

← Lassen Peak and Lake Helen at 8200ft (2500m), named after Helen Tanner Brodt, the first woman to summit Lassen Peak. → A local jay.

Hike this...

O1 Bumpass Hell
Follow the 3-mile (4.8km) hike to a boardwalk through a netherworld of wildly colored, steaming pools and mud pots, with inspiring views of Brokeoff Mountain.

O2 Pacific Crest Trail
Some 17 beautiful miles (27km) of this world-class through-hike run through the park. Get a permit and build your own adventure.

O3 Echo Lake
Starting from Summit Lake Campground, it's a refreshing 4.4-mile (7km) hike through the forest to find this blue-green gem, where folks picnic and swim.

Lassen Volcanic National Park's Painted Dunes are visible from the challenging Cinder Cone trail.

What to spot...

The contrast of cool forests and hot cinder deserts, along a mix of craggy volcanic and mountainous terrain, results in an unusual variety of resident wildlife. More than 200 species of birds have been spotted, including those that stop over during annual spring and fall migrations, as well as more rarely seen birds, such as bald eagles, peregrine falcons and California spotted owls. The mixed conifer forests and alpine peaks here provide habitat for a rainbow of wildflowers too.

SIERRA NEVADA RED FOX Lassen is one of only three places in California where you may spot this small mammal, one of the state's most endangered species.

RED FIR These mighty trees can live for a few hundred years; they grow over 175ft (53m) tall in Lassen's dense forests.

WHITEBARK PINE These stunted, twisted conifers growing at the edge of the tree line are easily recognized, but they're threatened by climate change.

Itineraries

Kayak Manzanita Lake, hike the volcanic summit of Lassen Peak or get some 4WD action out to the turquoise Juniper Lake for stunning views from Mt Harkness.

◄ The Milky Way reflected in Summit Lake.
► Bumpass Hell is the largest hydrothermal area in the park with some of world's hottest fumaroles.

01
A day

The Kohm Yah-mah-nee Visitor Center should be your first stop. Peruse the natural and cultural history exhibits and catch a free nature film in the auditorium. Keep driving uphill on the main park road to the Sulphur Works, where stinky vents hiss steam into the air. Pull over at Bumpass Hell to hike out along a wooden boardwalk into the heart of the park's biggest hydrothermal area – its eerie landscape is unforgettable. Be careful on the hike. Picnic on the shores of nearby Lake Helen, above which rises the awe-inspiring dome of

Lassen Peak that seems to be pulled straight from a Bob Ross painting, complete with 'happy little trees' at its base.

The road continues toward the park's northern entrance, passing through the scars of the volcano's 1915 eruption, where an accessible trail leads around the Devastated Area, and a pullout affords views of Chaos Crags and Jumbles. Spend the rest of the afternoon by Manzanita Lake, taking a dip or paddling a kayak or canoe in the placid waters. Bed down in a camping cabin or pitch a tent in the nearby campground.

02
Two days

Follow the itinerary for day one then, on the morning of day two, get up early and backtrack south along the main park road to the trailhead for Lassen Peak. Starting out from a breathtaking elevation of 8500ft (2591m), this adventurous trail tops out on the volcanic summit at 10,457ft (3187m), where you can peer down over the evidence of 800,000 years of eruptions that have shaped this park. Beware icy patches. Back at the trailhead, hop in your car and drive north

to Summit Lake North for a picnic lunch and maybe a quick sunlight snooze by the shore. If you're up for it, take a gentle hike out to tranquil Echo Lake, which is less than 2 miles (3.2km) away. You could spend the whole day hiking this chain of lakes, including jaunts to larger Upper and Lower Twin Lakes (if you didn't already while away the morning on Lassen Peak). Before sunset arrives, set up camp at Summit Lake, then join a ranger-led program after dark.

03
Three days

For three days in the park, follow the two-day itinerary then pack up camp at Summit Lake and get back on the main park road heading south. Exit the park and loop east (via Hwys 89 and 36) over to the park's remote Warner Valley; it's at least a 90-minute drive from Kohm Yah-mah-nee Visitor Center. In a grassy valley fed by Hot Springs Creek, you'll find the historic Drakesbad Guest Ranch, along with easy trails to lakes and steaming hydrothermal areas that are more serene and less often visited than those along the

main park road. Call ahead for reservations to treat yourself to a hearty lunch at the ranch. In the late afternoon, backtrack out of the valley, then take the dirt road out to turquoise Juniper Lake, with its beautiful shoreline campground. It's less than a 4-mile (6.4km) round-trip hike from the lake up to the fire lookout on Mt Harkness, affording views over the countryside. You can't swim in any of the park's hot springs (only the lakes), so on your way back to civilization, stop at the Feather River Hot Springs.

42

KY

Mammoth Cave National Park

With stalagmites as tall as trees, cathedral-sized chambers and subterranean rivers full of strange, blind cave creatures, visiting Mammoth is like being on another planet.

Descend into an eerie underground world, walking down a damp pathway into a long, dark corridor of rock. Here, hundreds of feet beneath the earth's surface, rock formations bloom like exotic flowers. There's delicate cave coral; striated 'cave bacon'; long, fluted frozen waterfalls; and walls striped and swirled like taffy. The longest known cave system in the world, Mammoth has more than 400 miles (644km) of explored passages. It's all due to water drip-drip-dripping its way through the porous limestone for millions of years.

Native American remains have been found in the cave, leading archaeologists to believe the first humans entered here about 4000 years ago. According to legend, the cave was rediscovered by settlers at the end of the 18th century, when a hunter chased a wounded bear right up to the cave entrance. Entrepreneurs soon realized Mammoth was full of saltpetre – which is used to make gunpowder – and began mining here during the War of 1812. Later, a doctor bought the cave and turned it into a tuberculosis hospital, believing the cave air would cure his patients. Some died, and the rest left; no one was cured. Noting the great acoustics, locals began holding Christmas singalongs here in 1883; the tradition continues today.

Tourists have been visiting since the 1810s, making this one of the oldest American tourist attractions. Early cave owners used enslaved people as tour guides; one such guide, Stephen Bishop, became one of the first people to map the cave and name its features. The limestone hills in the Mammoth region are riddled with caverns; in the early 20th century, local farmers tried to lure tourists heading to Mammoth to their own caves, planting fake signs or claiming Mammoth was closed. The resulting skirmishes became known as 'the Cave Wars'. Today, there are numerous caves to visit in the area, but you can't miss Mammoth itself.

↑ Throughout the year, park rangers lead subterranean tours of varying degrees of difficulty in Mammoth Caves. ➜ A wild turkey.

Toolbox

When to go
While the outside temperature fluctuates, inside the cave it's a steady 54°F (12°C). Fall is the nicest season for hiking. Reserve cave tours ahead of time, especially in summer.

Getting there
Mammoth Cave is in central Kentucky. Louisville and Nashville, both with major airports, are both about two hours' drive away. The access town of Cave City has numerous motels and restaurants, but isn't much to look at. You'll need a car here.

Events
Winter means tours are limited, but the Christmas holidays bring the annual Cave Sing.

Accessibility
There's a fully wheelchair accessible cave tour and several accessible trails, including the newly improved Echo River Springs Trail.

Park in numbers

82.6 Area in sq miles
1941 Year established
105 Depth of the cave's 'Bottomless Pit' (ft)

Stay here...

The Lodge at Mammoth Cave

Right next to the visitor center, the park's only lodge is freshly renovated with sustainable touches like LED lights and reclaimed wood, and a dining room serving Southern-style comfort fare. There are spare but comfy historic cottages perfect for families – some are even pet-friendly. There's also an on-site day-boarding kennel for dogs and cats.

Rock Cabin Camping

Less than 10 minutes from the visitor center, these cool historic cabins were built from local stone in the late 1920s. Today they're kitted out with modern amenities. Kids (and grown-up kids) will love roasting marshmallows under the stars on the fire pit. An adjacent campsite has tent and RV spots, with showers and toilets nearby.

Mammoth Cave Campground

Spitting distance from the visitor center, this basic NPS campground has more than 100 tent and RV sites, including wheelchair-accessible ones. You won't be roughing it, with hot showers, a seasonal camp store and an amphitheater for ranger programs.

Do this!

Cave touring

At any time of year, there are a dozen different cave touring options at Mammoth. All are wonderful. The Historic Tour takes you through the old tuberculosis ward; the Violet City Tour is guided by lantern-light to recreate the experience of visiting the cave in the 1800s; and the Wild Cave Tour has you slithering on your belly through narrow passageways.

Horseback riding

Saddle up to roam 60 miles (97km) of horse trails north of the Green River. Several Cave City-based outfitters offer trail rides through the Mammoth Cave hills, traversing grasslands and sun-dappled oak and hickory forests. The trails are particularly photogenic in autumn, when the leaves turn gold and russet. There's a horse-friendly campground.

Canoeing & kayaking

The Green and Nolin rivers wind through the park, offering opportunity for canoeing and kayaking; bring your own watercraft or book a trip with a local outfitter. You'll cruise through hardwood forests, passing sandbars, islands and bluffs. The waters teem with bass, crappie, bluegill and catfish, so bring a fishing pole if you're so inclined. Look up to see hawks, bald eagles, kingfishers and herons flapping their way through the blue Kentucky sky.

Hike this...

01 Sal Hollow Trail

One of the park's several dozen backcountry trails takes you 8.6 miles (13.8km) across creek crossings and several small waterfalls. Look out for deer and wild turkeys.

02 Mammoth Cave Railroad Trail

Following the old Mammoth Cave Railroad line, this flat 5-miler (8km) runs through hardwood forest. Ideal during fall, when the leaves put on a show.

03 Cedar Sink Trail

Descend into the valley to a neat limestone sinkhole surrounded by rocky outcroppings – if you're lucky, you'll spot some bats. It's 2 miles (3.2km) round-trip.

What to spot...

Even within the depths of Mammoth Cave, life abides. Far below the surface of the earth, creatures such as Kentucky cave shrimp, eyeless cave fish and blind cave beetles are perfectly suited to their subterranean surrounds. Above ground, the limestone hills, hemlock ravines and forest swamps support white-tailed deer, opossums, bobcats, coyote and bats, as well as a plethora of birds and fish. In spring, the valleys and ridges are carpeted in rue, bluebells, wood poppy and larkspur.

CAVE CRAYFISH These creepy crustaceans look like small, nearly translucent lobsters. They live in cave streams, though they can travel on land if need be.

LITTLE BROWN BATS These small flying mammals were once abundant in Mammoth, but recently an epidemic of a fungal disease called white-nose syndrome has been killing them off and they're now officially endangered.

TULIP POPLAR Kentucky's state tree is a tall hardwood that blooms with yellow, tulip-shaped flowers in spring. Look for them in rich, well-drained soil.

Itineraries

Descend into the depths on the Domes and Dripstones Tour, hike the Mammoth Cave Railroad Trail or learn about settlers' history.

01
A day

Get the most cave in the shortest time period by doubling up on your tours. Park rangers say the Historic Tour and the Domes and Dripstones Tour are an ideal duo, as they cover very different territory. Start off early by descending into the darkness on the two-hour Historic Tour. See the cave through the eyes of a 19th-century visitor, learning about saltpetre mining and passing remnants of the old tuberculosis hospital (spooky!). Afterwards, enjoy a picnic lunch outside under the oaks before plunging back in with the Domes and Dripstones tour. This two-hour trip takes you through the most lavishly decorated parts of the caves: stalactites like icicles; spiky stalagmites; colorful pillars; intricate, frozen waterfalls. Emerge blinking in the afternoon sunlight, in time for a quick hike down to where the River Styx emerges from the cave, its milky jade waters flowing into the Green River. Refuel with fried chicken, catfish and cobbler at the Watermill, a beloved Southern buffet in Cave City.

02
Two days

Follow the one-day itinerary to get the best of the cave's spooky and spectacular depths. Then spend your second day above ground. Hike the Mammoth Cave Railroad Trail along the route 19th-century visitors used to take into the park – you can still see Engine Number 4. Pay respects to Stephen Bishop, the young enslaved man who made some of the cave's earliest maps. He's buried in the Old Guides Cemetery near the main entrance, along with several patients from the ill-fated TB hospital. Two preserved historic churches – Mammoth Cave Baptist and Joppa Missionary Baptist – offer a peek into early settler life in these hills. After a picnic lunch, put your kayak in at the newly improved Green River Ferry ramp and spend the afternoon paddling the park's cool brown waterways. End your day with a ranger-led stargazing program before nestling into your tent for a long sleep beneath swaying maple trees.

→ More than 30 miles (48km) of the Green and Nolin Rivers wend their way through the park.

Shutterstock | Sopotnicki

43
CO

Mesa Verde National Park

In an arid corner of southern Colorado, these green mesas loom above the valley, with ancient dwellings etched into their cliffsides.

Mesa Verde

Mesa Verde is not your typical national park. Though it's a stunner, visitors don't come for its natural beauty, biodiversity or rare species. Instead, they flock to see an astonishing fragment of ancient America. Up until around the year 1300, Ancestral Puebloans had inhabited this area and beyond for some 700 years. In that time, they created 600 cliff dwellings, among them homes, *kivas* (ceremonial centers) and storage bins set on alcoves slit into sheer rockface, often hundreds of feet above the valley floor. Ancestral Puebloans were no stranger to adventure.

In some cases, you can't just walk into the past at Mesa Verde. You scramble up ladders, scale rock and crawl through tunnels to enter these ancient homes. Even with helpful railings and rangers, it's exploration at its gritty best. Today there still isn't a full understanding of why the Ancestral Puebloans left this site some seven centuries ago. Browsing the rooms, puzzling over the relics and gazing out over the expansive views is the best way to enter into their long-ago lives.

From 1849 to 1850, a US Army lieutenant documented these spectacular ruins; some 25 years later a pair of cowboys herding stray cattle stumbled upon Cliff Palace, discovering its hundreds of rooms. They soon became guides, leading archaeologists into the site until a Coloradan campaigned for its preservation, leading Congress to enact the Antiquities Act in 1906.

Archeological sites are found throughout the canyons and mesas, perched on a high plateau south of Cortez and Mancos. While much of the park can be explored on your own, some key attractions allow only limited visitation, and others remain off-limits. While hiking takes a back seat, it's still worthwhile, if only to escape the crowds. It's also a great way to search for petroglyphs etched into the rock face.

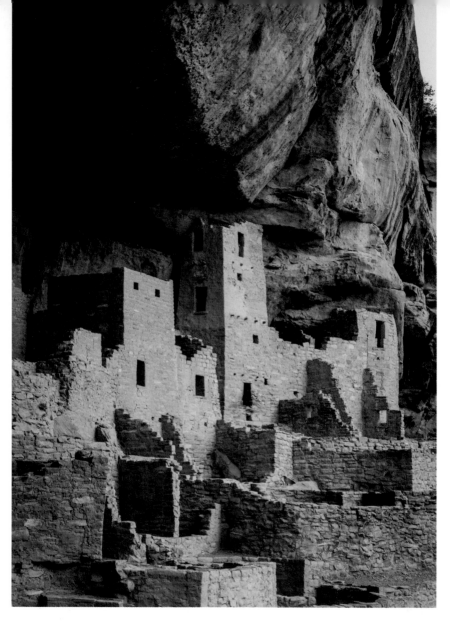

⬆ Mesa Verde is a World Heritage Site. Previous page: the Cliff Palace would have been an important ceremonial building.

Chip Kalback; Shutterstock | Rob Crandall

Toolbox

When to go
The park is open year-round; ranger stations may be closed from mid-September to mid-May. Camping runs from May through September and lodging from April through September. Summers are hot and winter offers snowshoe and cross-country ski access.

Getting there
Flights serve Denver, 370 miles (595km) away, with connections to Durango, 36 miles (58km) from the park. There is no public transportation here; rent a vehicle in either city.

Events
The Holiday Open House & Luminaria is a free evening in December. The Four Corners Lecture Series brings experts to speak on various topics.

Accessibility
Mesa Verde has limited accessibility. Wheelchairs with wide rim wheels are recommended on trails.

Park in numbers
81 Area in sq miles
8571 Highest point: Park Point (ft)
300–400 Number of occupants once living at Cliff Palace alone

Hike this...

01 Petroglyph Loop Trail
It's a challenge to spot all the mystical images on this 2.8-mile (4.5km), family-friendly loop, the only park trail with readily viewed rock art.

02 Spring House
Fit explorers should lace up for the all-day, ranger-led, 8-mile (12.9km) hiking tours to Spring House, a remote alcove that's the largest unexcavated cliff dwelling in the park. Fee required.

03 Spruce Canyon Loop Trail
Explore the shady canyon bottoms via this 2.1-mile (3.4km) loop; it begins at Spruce Tree House, the park's most accessible ruin.

⬆ A 13th-century tool in Crow Canyon Archaeological Center.
➡ Ascending to the Long House on Wetherill Mesa; there's a popular ranger-led tour of the site.

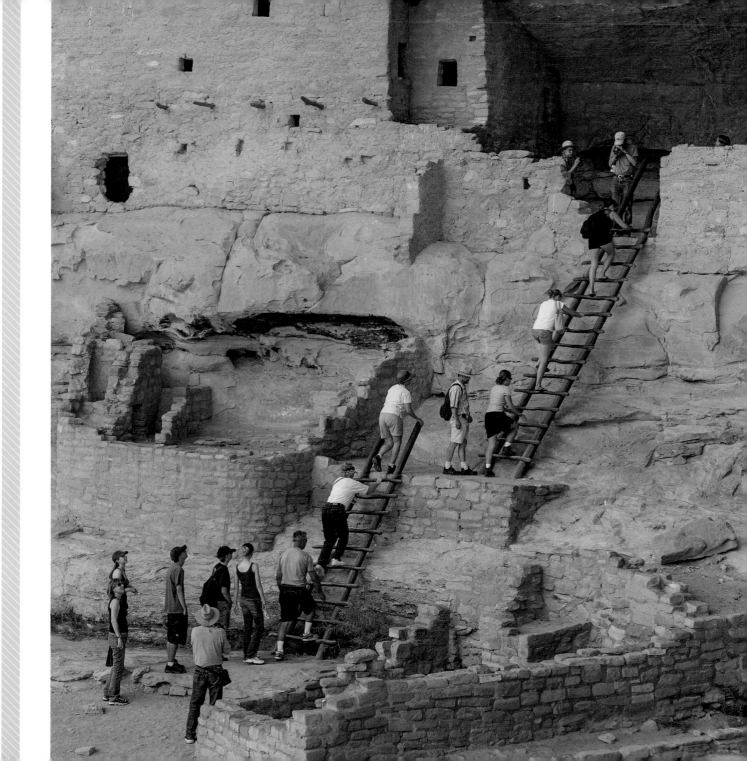

Stay here...

Willowtail Springs
These lakeside cabins are snuggled into ponderosa forest in Mancos. Highlights of their warm and exotic decor include clawfoot tubs and the owner's fabulous original art. There's a canoe hitched to the dock and a hot tub for guests. It's also a wildlife sanctuary that releases raptors. Slow yourself down to the pace of the pond's largemouth bass.

Morefield Campground
Mesa Verde National Park's only camping option sits on the mesa top, with well-spaced sites on grassy grounds replete with grills and picnic tables. With over 200 sites, it's rarely full. Morefield Village offers services, including a cafe and grocery store.

Jersey Jim Lookout Tower
From Jack Kerouac to Edward Abbey, some of America's best writers did stints in fire towers, so why not you? This former fire-lookout tower stands 55ft (16.7m) above a meadow at an elevation of 9800ft (2987m). Up to four adults can bunk down here, though it must be reserved online long in advance. Open late May through early October. Set near Mancos.

Do this!

Exploring Cliff Palace
The only way to see this grand engineering achievement with hundreds of rooms and dozens of *kivas* is to take the hour-long tour (fee required). However, it's well worth it. Ranger guides help illuminate the day-to-day experience of Ancestral Puebloans for visitors who follow in their footsteps more than seven hundred years later.

Exploring Balcony House
Indiana Jones, eat your heart out. To tour the 40 rooms of the Balcony House (one hour, fee required) you'll descend a 100ft (30m) ladder, crawl through a tunnel and negotiate even more ladders and stone steps. The adventure earns you outstanding views of Soda Canyon from Balcony House's large sandstone alcove. Tours are available from late April to early October.

Cross-country skiing & snowshoeing
In wintertime, the cliff dwellings become snowbound and sparkly and there's nary a tourist in sight. Cliff Palace Loop Rd also closes to vehicle traffic, so when the sun comes out strap on some snowshoes or cross-country skis to make the 6-mile (10km) loop, and look closely for rabbit tracks.

What to spot...

With great changes in elevation, Mesa Verde has unique geography along with diverse plant and animal life. Ancestral Puebloans made brilliant use of the park's seep springs and alcoves. There are 640 plant species, the most common being Gambel oaks, juniper, sagebrush and the edible serviceberry. In the park's mostly arid expanse, exuberant plant life lines the Mancos River corridor, attracting birdlife and black bears in berry season. Elk, mule deer and wild turkey frequent the campground.

MEXICAN SPOTTED OWL These owls prefer old-growth forests with high canopies, which are ideal for nesting. They are easily identified by their uniquely dark eyes.

PORCUPINE Arrayed in some 30,000 quills, these nocturnal herbivores are found in cottonwood trees; by day they rest in hollow trees and logs.

ABERT'S SQUIRREL With white tails and big, tufted ears, the small Abert's squirrel feasts on Ponderosa pine cones, dropping leftovers that are later enjoyed by mule deer.

Itineraries

Hike Petroglyph Loop Trail to Park Point for panorama magic, tour grand Cliff Palace or head for mountain biking mayhem at Phil's World.

→ Mountain biking at Phil's World, a network of trails atop a mesa just outside Cortez.

01
A day

With Ancestral Puebloan sites scattered throughout the canyons and mesas of Mesa Verde, a day trip is a tall order, so give yourself an early start. Begin at the Chapin Mesa Museum, where prehistoric artifacts help put this group's 700-year habitation of Mesa Verde into context. Next up is Spruce Tree House, a sloping 0.5-mile (0.8 km) walk to an alcove structure dating from 1210. This is the only dwelling that visitors can walk through without a ranger-led tour and it's well worth checking out.

Bring an appetite to the Metate Room, where the innovative menu is inspired by Native American foods. Spend the afternoon hiking the Petroglyph Loop Trail or just exploring the views of the many other sites of Chapin Mesa, searching for the tell-tale alcoves. On your way out, stop at the fire lookout at Park Point; at 8571ft (2612m) it's the highest point in the park. Drink in the panorama of the San Juan and La Plata mountains, the sloping plateau, and the volcanic plug known as the Shiprock.

02
A weekend

Begin your first morning at the Mesa Verde Vistor and Research Center to obtain tickets for a ranger-led tour of the limited-access cliff dwellings. These are hot tickets, so aim to take the tour the following day. Continue on to Chapin Mesa, following the itinerary for the day trip. Make the most of your night in the park by attending one of the campfire programs at Morefield Campground.

Start the second day in the park with the ticketed tour to Cliff Palace or Balcony House. While the grandeur of Cliff Palace cannot be beat, Balcony House is a blast for the intrepid – but not for agoraphobes or claustrophobes! Stop for lunch at the Far View Terrace Cafe, where Navajo tacos are the house specialty. Pass the afternoon visiting peaceful Wetherill Mesa, the less-frequented western side of Mesa Verde. Stroll the mesa top Badger House Community and descend to the Step House; these sites from different eras offer clearer views on how the native culture developed.

03
Four days

Four days in Mesa Verde offer ample time to fully explore the park and bask in its surroundings. Follow the weekend itinerary for the first two days and consider a break from camping with a stay in nearby Cortez or Mancos. Cortez is convenient to Ute Mountain Tribal Park, the jumping-off point for fascinating Ute and Ancient Puebloan sites. Ute tribal members lead active small group tours with 4WD jeeps.

On your last day, return to Mesa Verde for an all-day hike to Spring House, exploring remote sites along the way. (Remember to reserve this ranger-led tour in advance.) Or if you want an adrenaline fix, return to the Cortez area, where world-class mountain biking awaits at Phil's World, with 32 miles (51.5km) of singletrack rolling through piñon-juniper trees.

Satiate your appetite later at one of Cortez's wonderful downtown restaurants – our pick are the grass-fed burgers with tomato jam at Farm Bistro.

44

WA

Mount Rainier National Park

Glacier-capped Mt Rainier, surrounded by waterfalls and meadows, may be among the snowiest places on earth but it's also one of the most sublime.

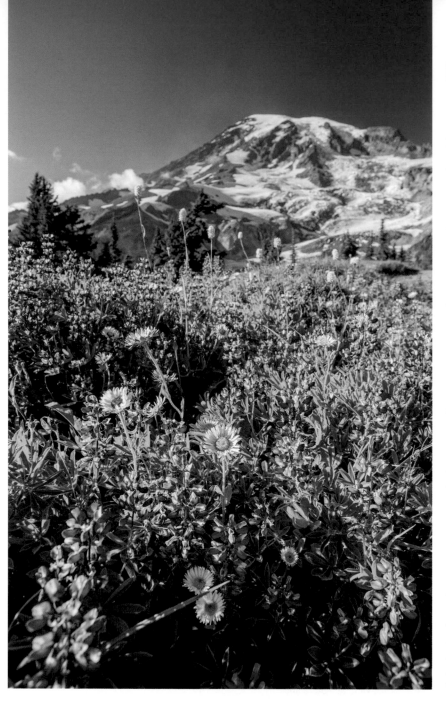

There you are, rounding a bend on a secluded alpine trail, when suddenly you glimpse brown fur in the bushes. You freeze. Is it a bear? OK, so it's probably just a marmot. If you're on a hike in Mt Rainier National Park, odds are good that you'll run across more than one wild creature along the way.

The mountain's name, surprisingly, has nothing to do with the weather: Rainier was named by the British Navy's Captain George Vancouver for his friend, Rear Admiral Peter Rainier, in 1792. The earliest documented ascent of Mt Rainier happened in 1870; the area was dedicated as a national park in 1899. Fifteen years later, the first cars came trundling along the road between Paradise and Longmire. As with many US national parks, Rainier benefited from the work of the Civilian Conservation Corps, which built and repaired most of its structures in the 1930s.

The park is a wilderness hiker's dream, with more than 260 miles (418km) of established trails. Rainier is the highest peak in the Cascade Range; since the 1960s, it has also served as a mountaineering training ground, especially for attempts on Mt Everest, thanks to its challenging terrain. It's an active volcano, formed some 500,000 years ago and then reduced by a few thousand feet in an eruption 5700 years ago. Since the 1800s, however, it's remained relatively calm.

Today Mt Rainier supports more than 35 sq miles (90 sq km) of glaciers spreading out from its summit. The glaciers move up to 3ft (1m) in a day, depending on weather. Emmons Glacier is easily seen from the viewpoint at Sunrise, the highest car-accessible point in the park. Nisqually Glacier and the Nisqually Icefall are even more accessible: use the Glacier View overlook on the road from Nisqually to Paradise.

Toolbox

When to go
Most roads in the park are closed in winter, except for the stretch between the Nisqually entrance and Paradise. Snow sometimes closes the entrances; check online (www.nps.gov/mora). Even in summer, when the temperature averages 70°F (21°C), wear layers and carry rain gear.

Getting there
Mt Rainier is in west-central Washington, about 87 miles (140km) from Seattle and 136 miles (219km) from Portland, Oregon. It's best reached by car as there's no public transportation.

Events
RAMROD (Ride Around Mt Rainier in One Day) is organized each July by the Redmond Cycling Club.

Accessibility
Picnic areas and visitor centers are accessible. Several trails from each visitor center are accessible; wheelchairs are available.

Park in numbers
369 Area in sq miles
700 Thickness of Carbon Glacier (ft)
14,410 Height of Mt Rainier (ft)

Stay here...

 Paradise Inn
This beautiful and imposing building, listed on the National Register of Historic Places, was built in 1917 but underwent a major remodel that finished in 2019. Rooms are basic (no phones or TVs; many have shared baths) but the huge lobby and comfy dining room both have massive fireplaces and killer views. This historic inn, like others in the park, has accessible rooms and dining areas. Open from mid-May through early October.

National Park Inn
This historic 25-room inn in Longmire is open year-round and has something of a ski-lodge vibe (indeed you can also rent cross-country ski equipment and snowshoes here). There's a casual restaurant and lounge.

Cougar Rock Campground
Many of the sites at this lovely, wooded campground have views of the mountain; the outdoor amphitheater features ranger-led programs in the evenings. About half of the sites here are first-come, first-served. There are four wheelchair accessible sites. Closed in winter.

Do this!

 Mountain climbing
Summiting Mt Rainier is one of those lifetime experiences you plan a whole vacation around. And it does take some planning: you'll need a permit to climb above 10,000ft (3048m), and of course you'll need the right training and equipment. If you'd rather not go it alone, there are several guide services available, most of which include training seminars.

Cycling
The steep, winding park roads around Mt Rainier make for thrilling, if rigorous, cycling. September and early October are best for this, with fall colors and reduced car traffic. Electric bikes (with motors of less than 750 watts in power) are now allowed anywhere traditional bicycles are permitted in the park.

Cross-country skiing
In winter, the town of Paradise becomes a base for snow sports – primarily cross-country skiing and snowshoeing, but there's also sledding and tubing in a designated play area. You can find trail maps and rental equipment in Longmire.

◁ Wildflowers at Mt Rainier.
▷ From the Skyline Trail hikers can occasionally see as far as Mt Hood in Oregon.

See this...

01 Trail of the Shadows
This family-friendly, wheelchair-accessible hike is a good way to see the highlights. It starts near the National Park Inn and takes you through the original Longmire settlement.

02 Cayuse Pass / Stevens Canyon
This 15-mile (24km) round-trip hike along a section of the storied Wonderland Trail has a bit of everything: steep climbs above timberline, lush wildflower meadows, snowfields and waterfalls.

03 Skyline Trail
A challenging 5-mile (8km) hike, the Skyline starts at Paradise and follows a high ridge with a 1500ft (457m) elevation gain for views of Mt Adams and Mt St Helens.

What to spot...

Abundant wildlife inhabits Mt Rainier and the surrounding area, including adorable and hard-to-miss marmots, black bears, foxes, rabbits, ptarmigans and snowshoe hares (the latter two likely to be spotted in winter, when they're most active). Plant life includes alpine wildflowers, cedar, fir, hemlock and pine trees, mushrooms, heather and huckleberry shrubs and mountain bunchgrass. The park's elevation changes mean there are several ecosystems, resulting in unusually varied flora and fauna.

DOUGLAS FIR These magnificent conifers live all across the Pacific Northwest (it's the Oregon state tree). Fun fact: strictly speaking, it's not a fir tree – its scientific name means 'false hemlock.'

DOUGLAS SQUIRREL You'll have no trouble spotting these chirruping cuties. They hang out in forested areas all over the park, collecting seeds to eat, and having what must surely be fascinating conversations.

CASCADE RED FOX Small and bushy-tailed, this rare subspecies of red fox lives at the highest elevations in the Cascade mountain range.

Shutterstock | Tpt: Roman Slavik.com

Itineraries

Whether you hike the short Trail of the Shadows or the challenging Wonderland Trail, views of Mt Rainier and its glaciers won't fail to impress.

➡ Mt Rainier beckons from downtown Seattle, promising adventure ⬅ Spray Falls on the Wonderland Trail.

01
A day

Stop at a visitor center near the park entrance where you came in. Here you'll find a schedule of programs and talks for the day, including nature hikes and films, and you'll also be able to ask about weather, hiking conditions and wildlife (any recent bear sightings?) and get a map. A good place to start is the Longmire Museum; originally the park's headquarters, it still functions as a visitor center, but is also home to several exhibits on the area's natural history. From here, take the short and easy loop hike along the Trail of the Shadows for views of Mt Rainier and the mineral springs that first inspired development of the Longmire area. Be sure to explore the Longmire Historic District while you're here. Drive on to Paradise for refreshments and to scope out the gorgeous lodge. Got some time left? Hike the 1.2-mile (1.9km) round-trip Nisqually Vista Trail, which should take about 45 minutes; it starts from the lower parking lot at Paradise and offers views of Nisqually Glacier and the slow-motion Nisqually Icefall.

02
A weekend

Take the first day's itinerary to get a feel for the area. Stay the night at the historic Paradise Inn (you'll need to reserve well ahead of time), enjoying its enormous stone fireplace and rough-hewn glory. In the morning, pack a lunch and make your way up the Skyline Trail, starting from the upper parking lot at Paradise. This fairly strenuous four-hour, 5-mile (8km) hike ascends the Alta Vista Ridge for excellent views of the surrounding glaciers and peaks, including Mt Adams and Mt St Helens. Be sure to check in at the visitor center first and make sure trail conditions are OK; it's wise to be flexible with your day-hike plans, as some trails may be closed and others busy, depending on time of year. After your hike, have dinner and stay the night at the National Park Inn, Rainier's other historic lodge (again, reserve well ahead); it's in Longmire, convenient for exiting the park at Nisqually the next morning.

03
10 to 14 days

With this much time, you can backpack the 93-mile (150km) Wonderland Trail circling Mt Rainier – and you should! Apply for backcountry permits through the online lottery system in advance, and make the usual preparations for a multi-day backpacking trip: plan your route with topographical maps, talk to rangers and be sure your hiking buddies are prepared, mentally and physically, for the duration and difficulty of the hike.

Making the full loop requires careful planning and a skills assessment, particularly in choosing the distance between your camping spots. It's a challenging route and not ideal for brand-new backpackers: the ups and downs along the trail are fairly extreme, with elevations ranging from roughly 2300ft to 6400ft (701m to 1951m). Parts of the trail are snowpacked from October through at least June; meanwhile, you may find a lot of competition for campsites in July and August (the busiest months), especially on weekends.

45

WA

North Cascades National Park

Dramatic and daunting, remote and challenging, this eerie wilderness in the Northwest attracts adrenalin-seekers like no other.

Shutterstock | Andrew Bertino

That only-person-on-earth feeling happens a lot in the North Cascades. Huge swaths of the landscape feel completely untouched, even though native peoples have lived in this area for thousands of years. The whole region somehow feels newly made, the glaciers on its jagged peaks creating streams and rivers before your eyes, the deeply carved valleys presenting you with gem-colored lakes. If what you're after is a sense of awe and a true appreciation for the land in this part of the world, you've come to the right place.

Established in 1968, the park is bisected by Ross Lake National Recreation Area. At the southern tip of the park is 50-mile-long (80km) Lake Chelan, most of which can only be reached on foot or by boat. The whole park complex, including the Ross and Chelan recreational areas, forms the core of more than 2 million acres (8094 sq km) of federally designated wilderness, the immense variety of which supports an unparalleled diversity of habitat. Among other things, it's a fantastic place to study an ecosystem in the raw and to monitor the effects of climate change.

The North Cascades is home to 312 glaciers, a third of all the glaciers in the lower 48 United States. All these glaciers and lakes feed into thousands of miles of rivers, providing great fishing and some epic waterfalls.

The subalpine region of the park historically was home to many Northwest Coast Indian settlements; archaeological digs have found 260 prehistoric sites, including homesteads, mines, and sheep farming settlements. On the cliffs around Lake Chelan there are ancient pictographs made with red ocher (see the replica panel at the visitor center in Newhalem). The study of archaeological sites here has led to new understanding in several areas of human activity across the centuries.

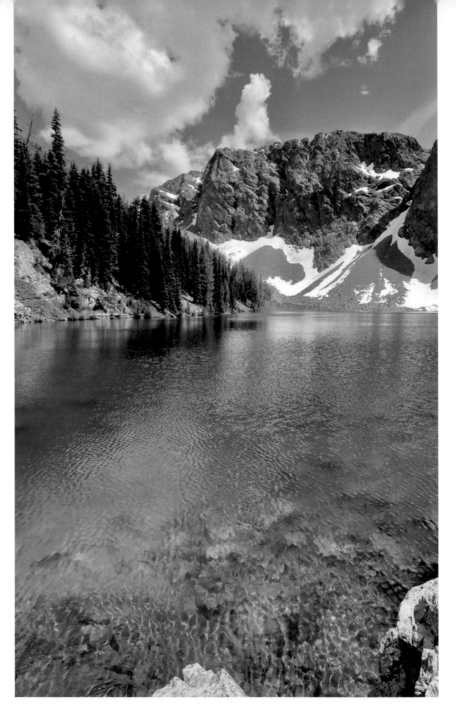

Toolbox

When to go
The park is open all year, but parts of the North Cascades Hwy are closed in winter (usually mid-November to mid-April). The Information Center in Sedro-Woolley is normally open year-round. In July and August, wildfires may close roads and trails.

Getting there
State Hwy 20 (the North Cascades Hwy) provides the main access route through the park; the Golden West Visitor Center at the north end of Lake Chelan is accessible only by ferry or floatplane. Otherwise the park is best visited by car.

Events
Skagit Eagle Festival is held during eagle-watching season (January). The Nature of Writing speaker series takes place each fall.

Accessibility
Restrooms at visitor centers and most campgrounds are accessible. Several scenic trails are accessible.

Park in numbers
1068 Area in sq miles
9206 Highest point: Goode Mountain (ft)
400 Lowest point: Skagit River (ft)

Stay here...

 Ross Lake Resort
Getting here really is half the fun: a night at this tranquil, isolated resort means a steep 2-mile (3km) hike from Hwy 20 down to a ferry dock. At the dock you'll find a mysterious telephone; pick it up to summon a water taxi, which will fetch you across the lake to the resort's string of floating wooden cabins. Once there you can also rent kayaks and rowboats for further exploring.

 Stehekin Valley Ranch
You don't have much to worry about if you stay here: the ranch takes care of everything, from all your meals to transportation across the 50-mile (80km) Lake Chelan. On arrival, settle into a cabin with a private bath, or perhaps a more rustic tent-style cabin, and explore the surroundings by horseback. Haven't had enough of the lake? Opt for a guided kayak tour.

Colonial Creek Campground
Set in an old-growth forest at the edge of Diablo Lake, this campground is hard to beat. Kids and grown-ups alike will find the evening programs led by rangers both educational and entertaining, and during the day you can walk around the lake or choose from several other hiking trails that showcase the area's natural wonders.

Do this!

 Boating
Take a cruise on the Lady of the Lake to the historic town of Stehekin, set at the headwaters of Lake Chelan. Catch the boat in the town of Chelan for either a day trip or a few days of backpacking. Gear up before you go: Stehekin is tiny and remote, reachable only by boat, hiking trail or floatplane.

Fishing
The Skagit River has trout, salmon and char. In Lake Chelan you can catch trout, kokanee and freshwater cod, while the Stehekin River is home to rainbow and cutthroat trout. You'll need to get a Washington state fishing license.

Learning
Get the kids hooked on nature with a fun and educational program organized through the Environmental Learning Center at the North Cascades Institute, an ecofriendly residential campus on Diablo Lake. Arrange for a day trip, long weekend or backcountry excursion with the family.

◀ There are more than 500 lakes in the park. Previous page: solitude at sunset in the Cascades.

What to spot...

The wildly varying terrain of the North Cascades – from lowland forests to glacial peaks – supports a huge amount of biodiversity. The park boasts 75 mammal species and 200 types of birds, as well as plentiful fish. In terms of diversity, however, its plant life is where the park really shines: it has over 200,000 acres (809 sq km) of old-growth forest and more than 1600 different vascular plant species (no one seems to have counted all the fungi).

BALD EAGLE The national bird of the United States and sacred in many Native American cultures, the bald eagle is always thrilling to spot, even in places where it's relatively common.

BLACK-TAILED MULE DEER These are the most common hoofed animals native to the park.

CHINOOK SALMON During fall, the Chinook and other salmon fight their way up the Skagit River to spawn. This is also your best time for seeing a bald eagle.

Hike this...

O1 Easy Pass Trail

This deceptively named 3.5-mile (5.6km) trail gains 2800ft (853m) elevation, but the payoff for the climb is a 360-degree view, plus wildflower meadows and frequent mountain goat sightings.

O2 Thornton Lake Trail

A fairly steep one-way 5-mile (8km) hike to a subalpine lake, this trail ascends through mature woods to alpine heather and huckleberry fields before reaching a high ridge.

O3 Bridge Creek Trail

This 12-mile (19.3km) stretch of the Pacific Crest Trail provides the easiest hiking route to Stehekin.

Shutterstock | Chris Mayhew; Tobin Akehurst; Marina Poushkina

Itineraries

Hike the Diablo Lake Trail for exquisite waterfall and lake scenery, boat around Lake Chelan or do a little dusk fishing for maximum serenity.

◀ Thornton Lake and Trappers Peak; you can make this an overnight hike. ▶ Come equipped for adventure in winter.

01
A day

Cruise through the park on the North Cascades Hwy (State Hwy 20), starting from Marblemount along the Skagit River. Stop at the North Cascades National Park Visitor Center in Newhalem for a slew of information on the area; if you're lucky, you'll arrive in time for a ranger-led nature walk or presentation. If not, choose a self-guided hike from the many short trails that start at Newhalem, all of which make for scenic walks in the woods. Afterward, continue along Hwy 20 to Diablo Lake, where you'll find excellent picnic sites as well as more hiking; if time allows, take the Diablo Lake Trail, just over 7 miles (11km) round-trip, which climbs through old-growth forest and along dry creek beds to a steep gorge with impressive waterfalls, all the while featuring views of the turquoise lake below. If you're all hiked out, opt for some fishing in the lake, followed by an educational visit to the Environmental Learning Center, which offers programs and classes focusing on the ecosystem of the North Cascades. (Reverse this route if you're driving east to west.)

02
A weekend

Start your weekend just south of the park complex in the town of Chelan; load up on supplies here, park your car at the ferry dock, then hop on board the Lady of the Lake boat and head out onto beautiful Lake Chelan. The 50-mile (80km) boat ride to the tiny, historic settlement of Stehekin (the population is about 80 permanent residents) is an experience all of its own.

Spend the night in Stehekin – you'll want to have booked accommodations well in advance – where the isolation and majesty of the surroundings combine to create an atmosphere you won't soon forget. You might do some fishing at dusk, or just relax and enjoy the quiet. The next day, do a loop hike heading out from Stehekin (ask for recommendations at the Golden West Visitor Center first; fauna and flora includes woodpeckers and western red cedars) before catching the boat back to Chelan in the evening.

03
A week

In a whole week, you have time to do both the previous itineraries and then some. Start with the Stehekin overnight trip, then head back onto Hwy 20 and find the Bridge Creek trailhead, at milepost 159 east of Rainy Pass. From here, find the short connector trail to the Pacific Crest Trail south of the highway; this segment is called the Bridge Creek trail, and it makes an excellent 32-mile (51km) multi-day backpacking loop with the McAlester Lake, Rainbow Lake and Rainbow Creek trails. There are hundreds of miles of hiking routes in the park, which means you can put together an epic backpacking loop for hikers of just about any level of fitness and ambition – this is just one of many options. Note that backcountry permits are required, and numbers may be limited, so reserve ahead.

After your hike, head northwest along Hwy 20 to explore Diablo Lake and Newhalem. If you have an extra day, take the short, steep hike up to Thornton Lake for a lofty picnic lunch overlooking the lake before exiting the park complex.

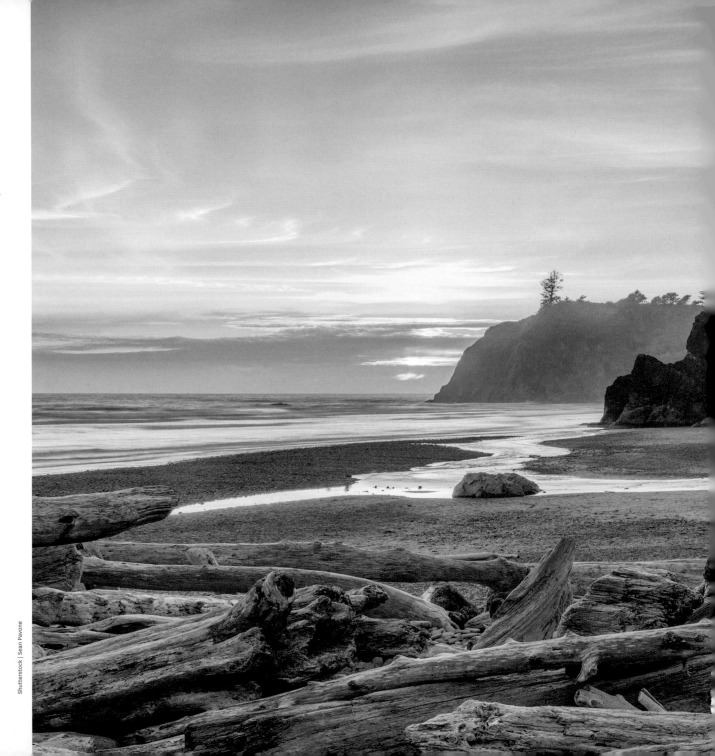

46

WA

Olympic National Park

This park truly feels like another world – or rather, three other worlds: mossy rainforest, lonely coastline, craggy peak.

Each of this park's environments is so distinct that it really isn't much of a stretch to imagine that Hwy 101, which connects them, is some sort of interplanetary roadway. But in fact this otherworldly beauty is all right here in the same park – easily reached, no spaceship required.

The core of the park is Mt Olympus and its namesake Olympic mountain range. Flowing west from the mountain and into the Pacific Ocean is the Hoh River, surrounded by deep green rainforests full of huge trees draped in moss. And northwest of the river's mouth lie about 62 miles (100km) of the wildest coastal habitat left intact in the world.

Olympic National Park occupies the center of the remote, roughly triangular Olympic Peninsula and is adjacent to the reservations of several American Indian tribes: the Skokomish, Makah, Hoh, Quinault, Quileute, Jamestown S'Klallam, Port Gamble S'Klallam and Lower Elwha Klallam all have strong cultural ties to the land here. Traditions of the coastal tribes include the potlatch, an elaborate feast and social gathering. Most of the visitor centers in the park offer schedules of tribal cultural events and programs.

The Spanish explored this area in the 1770s, setting up a beachhead at Neah Bay in 1792. (They abandoned it after only a few months.) Pioneers of all sorts followed them here through the 1800s. The first pioneer settlement to be permanently established on the Olympic Peninsula was Port Townsend, in 1851.

A presidential tag team established the park: first, President Theodore Roosevelt decreed Mt Olympus a National Monument in 1909. Then in 1938, President Franklin

D Roosevelt signed the Olympic National Park into existence. Coastal wilderness was added to the park later, in 1953. The park is 95% wilderness and is officially protected from most development, including building, timber cutting, mining and hunting.

Toolbox

When to go
Many areas are unreachable in winter; most entrances are open all year, but roads may be closed. At high elevations, it can snow year-round. Summer is relatively warm and dry, but be ready for rain and sub-70°F (21°C) temperatures. December and January are the wettest.

Getting there
Olympic National Park is about 90 miles (145km) west of Seattle. Access is via US Hwy 101. It's best reached by car, although Clallam Transit (www.clallamtransit.com) has local bus routes.

Events
Olympic Music Festival is an annual summer classical music program in Port Townsend. For beer and bivalves try Oysterfest in early October. Olympic Bird Festival is a mid-April event in Sequim.

Accessibility
Some beaches and viewpoints have paved trails and picnic areas.

Park in numbers
1442 Area in sq miles
73 Length of wilderness coastline (miles)
300 Bird species

Stay here...

Lake Quinault Lodge
Perched on the shore of Lake Quinault, this grand lodge blends a 1920s park vibe with Native American design elements. The dining room is named for Franklin D Roosevelt, who visited here in 1937. There are ranger talks, interpretive hikes and evening programs in summer, as well as boat tours and boat rentals.

Kalaloch Lodge
This impressive coastal lodge has rooms, cabins and kitchenettes, all with private baths, and a restaurant-bar with stellar views. It's right at the edge of a marine wildlife sanctuary, so look for otters and various tidepool inhabitants. The lodge is 36 miles (58km) south of Forks along US 101.

Kalaloch Campground
The only one of the park's three campgrounds to accept reservations (the others are first-come, first-served), this forested area is situated high above the ocean on a bluff. Many of its sites have ocean views. It's open all year and has great access to coastal hiking trails.

Do this!

Hiking
The whole park is hiker heaven, but for something unusual, take a self-guided walk from the Hoh Visitor Center through the Hoh Rain Forest, or join a ranger-led nature walk to learn even more about the area's unique features and natural history. Don't forget to bring your rain gear!

Learning
The Makah Museum in Neah Bay holds hundreds of artifacts from archeological research into a Makah village near Ozette that was partially buried in a mudslide around 1750. There are also guided tours and demonstrations of traditional weaving and carving practiced by native peoples.

Soaking in hot springs
Cap off a hike or a long drive with some relaxing in Sol Duc's three mineral hot springs pools. You can also book a massage. Sol Duc Falls are an easy 3-mile (4.8km) hike from the hot springs resort (and if you're really in relaxation mode, you can drive two of those miles and only hike the last one).

◄ Roosevelt elk are the largest variety of elk in America. Previous page: Ruby Beach on the southwest coast of Olympic peninsula.

What to spot...

The wildly different environments that make up the Olympic National Park – mountain, coast, temperate rainforest – result in equally diverse habitats and wildlife. Much of the coastline is a protected marine-life sanctuary: exploration of tidepools here is extremely rewarding. Bears, deer and elk roam from the lowlands to the alpine meadows of the Olympic mountain range, while the rainforests between mountains and coast teem with plant and animal life.

OLYMPIC MARMOT Found only on the Olympic Peninsula, these cat-size creatures are friendly and social. They eat mostly flowering plants and hibernate in winter.

SITKA SPRUCE These stately old trees, usually draped in moss, are the dominant species in the temperate rainforest. They can be hundreds of years old and up to 60ft around.

ROOSEVELT ELK The park is home to the largest wild group of Roosevelt elk in the US. They like to graze the forest floor in the temperate rainforests.

Hike this...

O1 Hurricane Hill Trail
Get the most bang for your buck with this 3-mile (4.8km) round-trip paved route on Hurricane Ridge, which offers views of the Olympic mountains, plus the Strait of Juan de Fuca, the San Juan Islands and Victoria, BC.

O2 Ozette Lake to Sand Point
From the Ozette Visitor Center (off US 112), a 3-mile (4.8km) boardwalk path leads to the beach at Cape Alava; continue along the coastline to Sand Point for a 9.3-mile (15km) round-trip.

O3 North Wilderness Beach Hike
The only way to access parts of the coastal wilderness, this 20-mile (32km) trail goes from Ozette Trailhead to Rialto Beach, taking two to three days. Permits required.

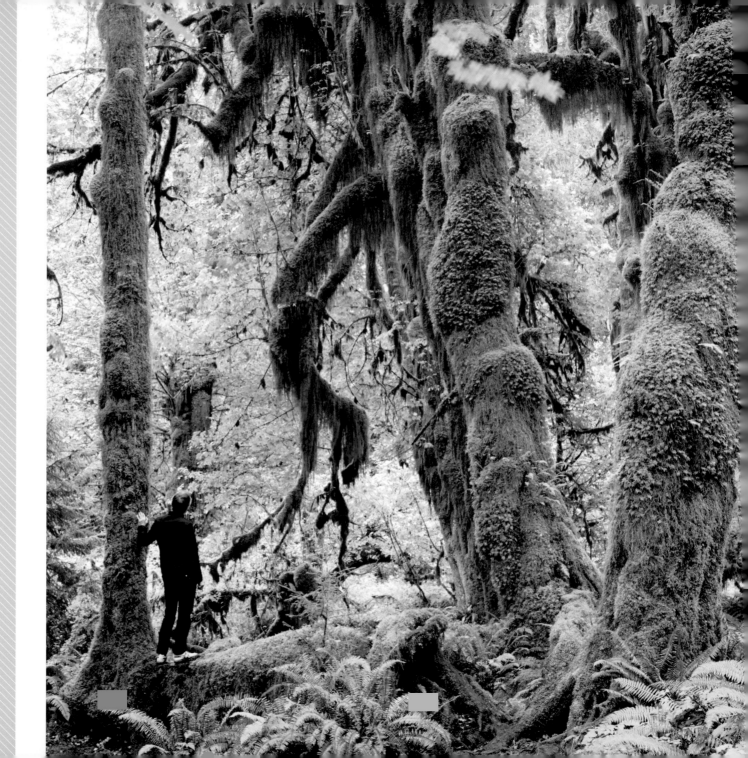

Itineraries

Hurricane Ridge's views will make the blood rush, the Hoh Rain Forest will soothe your soul, and a soak at Sol Duc Hot Springs relaxes hike-weary muscles.

◀ Olympic deer. Hoh Rain Forest, one of the wettest places in the US. ▶ Woodland adventures.

01
A day

Even with only a day to explore, you can make inroads into this massive park. Start at the Olympic National Park Visitor Center in Port Angeles. Behind the visitor center is an interpretive trail that makes a good appetizer for the park. From here, drive up the spur road to Hurricane Ridge (off Hwy 101). The views from this road are absolutely dizzying, and there's a gorgeous field of wildflowers sloping down from the top in spring and summer. Hikers should take the short Hurricane Hill Trail for hundred-mile views all around. If you're here in winter, ask about ranger-guided snowshoe and cross-country ski tours that depart from Hurricane Ridge Visitor Center. The center is open Friday through Sunday in the winter and also offers snowboarding and tubing. In summer, if you're up for a little more driving (and possible vertigo), venture along the 8-mile (13km) gravel Obstruction Point Rd, which goes east from Hurricane Ridge, for views of Mt Olympus.

02
Two days

Start as per day one, but when you return to the base of Hurricane Ridge, continue driving west on US Hwy 101. You'll pass Lake Crescent, which makes a good place for a picnic lunch. From here, head toward Sol Duc, which is just past the lake on a spur road bearing south. Settle into a cabin at the Sol Duc Hot Springs resort for the night; you can soak in the resort's powder-blue hot-spring pools. Start the next day with a short hike through old-growth forest to the Sol Duc Falls before heading back out.

03
A week

In a week you can see many of the park's highlights and gain an appreciation for the huge variety of terrain here. Follow the two-day itinerary, but after your Sol Duc hike, return to Hwy 101 and head west to Ozette Lake. (Keep in mind that driving between points on Olympic Peninsula often takes much longer than you might think. Be sure to refuel at every opportunity.) Stay the night at a lakeside lodge or campsite, then set out the next morning on the trail from Ozette Lake to Sand Point. Return to Ozette for another night, or push on northward to Neah Bay. The next day, spend some time at the extremely worthwhile Makah Museum in Neah Bay, and be sure to try some fry bread, the local specialty. From here, head inland to the Hoh Rain Forest Visitor Center for a radical change of scenery. Take a ranger-guided tour, or set out on your own into the dark and mysterious woods along the Hall of Mosses trail. If you have time, plan on extending the hike by following the Hoh River Trail, which is 18 miles (29km) in total, as far as you like; there are waterfalls along the way.

Spend the night at the Hoh Campground. Next day, head back toward the coast, where Kalaloch Lodge and campground await. This is an ideal base for exploring the wild coastline, most of it accessible only by foot or boat. Kalaloch Ranger Station will have details and a schedule of walks and talks, or you can hike around on your own. There are also boat rentals and guided tours available. Spend the night here at the lodge or campground before meandering back to your entry point the next day.

47

AZ

Petrified Forest National Park

Time travelers from the Triassic Period, petrified trees now rest comfortably on windswept grasslands flanked by brilliant badlands and intricate petroglyphs.

It takes a moment to comprehend the Crystal Forest. At first glance, the fossilized logs scattered across the landscape look like charred bales of hay. Or maybe they're embers left in the sand from a campfire built by giants. But a short walk on the Crystal Forest Trail reveals the true magic of the park's namesake treasures – each ancient tree hides a kaleidoscopic core of fiery reds, oranges and purples. Some even sparkle with crystals.

Rivers carried the trees to the floodplain here 225 million years ago. Silica-rich volcanic ash buried the trees before they could decompose. Groundwater dissolved the silica, which seeped into the logs and eventually crystallized into quartz. Iron, manganese and other colorful minerals joined the party. The 'forests' scattered across the southern reaches of the park began as log jams millions of years ago. Old Faithful, almost 10ft (3m) across, basks in the sun behind the Rainbow Forest Museum.

The rest of the park is a cabinet of curiosities writ large. Scenic overlooks and spur trails on the 28-mile (45km) scenic drive spotlight an amazing diversity of sights. At sunset, the Painted Desert, in the northern sector of the park, glows in a broad palette of colors. The Painted Desert Inn shares the region's history. Just south, a weathered jalopy memorializes Route 66, which bounced through the grasslands here in the mid-1900s. Ancestral Puebloans called the region home between AD 650 and the early 1400s – their eye-catching petroglyphs at Newspaper Rock suggest that social media is not a modern invention.

President Theodore Roosevelt established Petrified Forest National Monument in December of 1906, pursuant to the Antiquities Act, which had been created to protect Native American sites in the Southwest. The monument became a national park in 1962. Today, there is a breezy, unhurried vibe to the place. So ease off the pedal and relax – those rocks aren't going anywhere soon.

Toolbox

When to go
Spring can be windy and summer is high season. For the most pleasant weather and conditions, visit in fall.

Getting there
The park straddles the I-40 in northeast Arizona. Flagstaff is 115 miles (185km) west; Albuquerque is 204 miles (328km) east. Sky Harbor Airport in Phoenix is 260 miles (418km) southwest via I-40 and I-17. To prevent backtracking, westbound travelers should exit I-40 at exit 311; eastbound travelers should take exit 285 to Hwy 180 south.

Events
Wildflower season runs from March through May. Check the online Wildlfower Report for what's out there.

Accessibility
Most park trails are paved although sections may be too steep to meet ADA requirements.

Park in numbers
346 Area in sq miles
650 Number of Newspaper Rock petroglyphs
1250–1400 Human occupation of Puerco Pueblo (AD)

Stay here...

🏕 Backcountry camping
There are no developed campgrounds in the park, but you can set up your tent in the surrounding Petrified Forest National Wilderness Area. All that's required is a permit, which is free, and a one-mile (1.6km) walk from one of two designated parking areas. This means you can sleep in the Painted Desert!

🏠 Wigwam Motel
To get your kicks on Route 66, drop your bags inside a concrete tipi at the beloved Wigwam Motel in Holbrook. Rooms are furnished with 1950s logpole furniture, and each tipi squeezes in a bathroom with a shower. Vintage cars in the parking lot add to the mid-century mood.

🏠 La Posada Hotel & Gardens
Art, history and architecture merge elegantly at La Posada, a grand hacienda in Winslow that originally opened in 1930. Designed by Mary Jane Colter, La Posada was the last of the grand railroad hotels commissioned by the Fred Harvey Company along the Santa Fe line.

Do this!

✋ Cultural learning
Swirls. Footprints. Wild animals. Were Ancestral Puebloans leaving messages about local game? Were their shaman transcribing their visions? Or maybe the petroglyphs are no more than the doodles of a daydreamer. Make your own guesses from the catwalk overlooking the rocks at Newspaper Rock. For up-close views, check out the carvings beside the Puerco Pueblo Trail.

🗺 Route 66 touring
The Painted Desert Inn no longer hosts overnight guests, but the 1920s-era building does welcome travelers interested in learning about Route 66, which passed this way. Exhibits spotlight the famous road as well as the Civilian Conservation Corps and the inn's history and architecture. Drive south on the Scenic Road to an outdoor exhibit about the famous route, complete with a vintage car.

🚲 Cycling
The 28-mile (45km) Scenic Road curves past the Painted Desert, then passes semi-arid grasslands, forests of petrified wood, Ancestral Puebloan ruins and crumbling badlands. Plan your trip for spring or fall, when traffic is lighter. Bike rentals are available in Flagstaff.

← → Fossilized trees from the Late Triassic period lie throughout the park.

Hike this...

01 Devil's Playground
A playground for the devil or Dr Seuss? The park issues only three permits per week for this backcountry hike, which takes in colorful hoodoos and striking rock formations. The hike is a 7–8-mile (11–13km) round-trip.

02 Long Logs & Agate House
The largest collection of petrified trees in the park fronts a partially restored prehistoric pueblo. The hike is 2.6 miles (4.2km) round-trip.

03 Painted Desert Rim
The Painted Desert struts its stuff at sunset, when layered deposits of clay and sandstone put on a luminous show. An easy 0.5-mile (0.8km) trail between Tawa and Kachina Points provides a lofty view.

What to spot...

The lofty Colorado Plateau stretches across northern Arizona and parts of New Mexico, Colorado and Utah, a region collectively known as the Four Corners. Semi-arid native grasslands blanket the national park, which is dotted with mesas and badlands. Plants and animals here are a hardy breed, having adapted to an extreme range of temperatures. Early morning and dusk are best for wildlife viewing.

BLACK-TAILED JACKRABBIT
That pair of black-tipped ears – all 6in (15cm) of them – is to aid heat loss. These athletic hares can run up to 40mph (64km/h) and jump 20ft (6m).

PRONGHORN The fastest land animal in the country, these graceful antelopes can run about 60mph (97km/h). The backward-facing horns of male pronghorns can extend 12in (30cm).

GREATER SHORT-HORNED LIZARD
With a face only a mother could love, this flat and stocky lizard is noted for its spiky horns and pointy scales. When threatened, they may squirt blood from their eyes or poke at predators with their horns.

248

Itineraries

Take it easy with an Eagles tribute in Winslow, hit the Painted Desert for Hopi murals and sunsets or take a scenic drive to Crystal Forest.

◀ A collared lizard warms itself on a fossilized log. ▶ Looking out over the Painted Desert in the Petrified Forest National Park.

01

A day

As you drive past the ranger booth at the southern entrance, it feels like you're entering a prehistoric *Land of the Lost*. You won't see any dinosaurs lumbering about, but the giant petrified logs and the parched grasslands evoke a more dangerous age. The skeletons of giant lizards, stalking across the Rainbow Forest Museum, add to the menacing vibe. Join the ranger-led Triassic Talk, then walk the Giant Logs Trail.

From the museum, the 28-mile (45km) scenic road ribbons north, with pull-offs and spur trails along the way. The petrified trees scattered across the Crystal Forest were once part of an ancient log jam. Just north, on the Blue Mesa Loop Trail, the blue-tinged badlands are photographic fodder for your Instagram feed. On the Puerco Pueblo Trail, a shaft of sunlight hits a spiral-shaped pictograph every year on June 21st, accurately marking the summer solstice.

Continuing north, the scenic drive rolls past I-40 into the northern section of the park, home to the Painted Desert badlands. Just beyond the highway, a rusted vintage car and an interpretative marker celebrate Route 66 – this is the only national park that's home to a stretch of the Mother Road. Enjoy a picnic lunch and views of the Painted Desert at Chinde Point Overlook.

Hopi murals are a highlight in the historic Painted Desert Inn. From here, take your pick of overlooks to watch the Painted Desert change colors as the sun drops on the horizon.

02

Two days

Follow the one-day itinerary, except you'll be backpacking into the Painted Desert Wilderness in the afternoon. A free permit is required – available at the Painted Desert Visitor Center – as is a 1-mile hike (1.6km) from Kachina Point. On your hike, look for the Onyx Bridge, a Triassic conifer tree preserved in the Black Forest. It's about 210 million years old! Continue on, then set up camp for a night under the stars – the park earned an International Dark Sky designation in 2018.

On day two, enjoy the sunrise then return to Kachina Point. Leave the park and drive one hour west to Winslow where breakfast at the Turquoise Room in the La Posada Hotel isn't for the timid: orange marmalade crepes, green-chile eggs, bread pudding slathered with prickly pear syrup. After breakfast, take photos at Standin' on the Corner Park, which celebrates the song *Take it Easy* by The Eagles. Return to the park, pulling into Jim Gray's Petrified Wood Company, 1 mile (1.6km) south of Holbrook, for keepsakes.

In the afternoon, stroll the combined Long Logs & Agate House trails, a 2.6-mile (4.2km) out-and-back that passes the largest collection of petrified trees in the park as well as the ruins of a pueblo. Ancestral Puebloans carved petroglyphs into the rocks at Newspaper Rock up to 2000 years ago. For the adventurous, several hikes head deeper into the backcountry. The 8.5-mile (13.7km) Red Basin Clam Beds Loop passes petrified logs, petroglyphs, hoodoos and fossil clam beds.

48

CA

Pinnacles National Park

With its craggy volcanic peaks, condors and wide-open skies, one of the USA's newest national parks offers up a big punch in a little package.

Rocks jutting up toward the sky define Pinnacles' topography of peaks, canyons and caves. The park is all that remains of an ancient volcano born over 20 million years ago and far away, near the modern city of Los Angeles. Tectonic plate movement along California's earthquake-prone San Andreas Fault slowly dragged the volcano almost 200 miles (322km) north of its original location – incredibly, it keeps moving another 1in (2.5cm) every year. Over eons, wind and water eroded the volcano – which was once almost as tall as Mt St Helens – into the unusually shaped terrain you'll see today.

You might not expect such rich wildlife packed into a territory so small but above the tangled chaparral that covers the valley floor and rolling hills, vertical cliffs and spires reach hundreds of feet into the air, making Pinnacles an ecological island. As you hike and climb among the jagged high peaks, where bears and wolves once prowled, you might be lucky enough to spot a California condor soaring overhead. The park is the only NPS unit that manages a release site for captive bred California condors, which is vital to species conservation and recovery efforts. Back down closer to earth, over a dozen kinds of bats roost in in the park.

More than a century after President Theodore Roosevelt declared it a national monument, Pinnacles became a national park in 2013. It's also one of the smallest US national parks, and often overlooked because California superstars like Yosemite and Death Valley get more press. Yet finding this hidden spot is part of the fun. Pinnacles lies east of the agricultural Salinas Valley in rural Central California. It's a slow drive inland from US Hwy 101, which traces El Camino Real, the 18th-century road built by Spanish colonists between their Catholic missions, the first European settlements in what was then a province of Mexico.

Toolbox

When to go
A Mediterranean climate makes spring and fall ideal. Summers are hot and humid, with daytime highs over 100°F (38°C). Winter temperatures may slip below freezing overnight.

Getting there
Pinnacles is about two hours' drive southeast of San Francisco. The park's east and west entrances are not connected by road – the only way to get between them is on foot. The main visitor facilities are on the park's east side.

Events
In early spring crowds of ladybugs come here on their annual migration. In the fall, male tarantulas can be seen crossing roads as they search for a mate.

Accessibility
Both of the visitor centers are ADA accessible. Many of the paths are steep and rocky but check out Bench and Prewett Point trails.

Park in numbers

41.6 Area in sq miles
3304 Highest point: Chalone Peak (ft)
337 Wild California condors in the world

Stay here...

Pinnacles Campground
Near the park's east entrance, this family campground opens its outdoor swimming pool seasonally. Campsites are spacious and often partly shaded by oak trees, with a campers' general store just a short walk away. Watch out for wild turkeys strutting through your campsite in the morning!

Inn at the Pinnacles Only a 5-minute drive from the park's west entrance, this B&B inn is set among vineyards in Monterey County. Swim in the outdoor salt pool, sink into a deep-soaking tub in your suite, or grill dinner on the back patio. Rooms are simple, but some have gorgeous views of the surrounding countryside.

Joshua Inn Bed & Breakfast
About 30 miles (48.2km) northwest of the park's east entrance in the town of Hollister, this updated lemon-yellow, turreted 1902 Queen Anne Victorian is full of character, complete with a croquet set on the lawn, penny candies and themed rooms. The gourmet organic breakfast is to die for.

Do this!

Rock climbing
Rock jocks scale walls and cliffs and tackle boulders alongside trails. Options range from top-roping for beginners to expert multi-pitch climbs. (Our favorite climbing route name? 'Tourist Trap.') Climbers should be aware of closures due to raptor nesting in sensitive areas from January through July.

Caving
Talus caves filled with jumbled rockfall are perfect for beginning spelunkers, because you can walk right up to them and step inside (bring a flashlight). The Bear Gulch caves are closed in late spring and summer, when bats roost inside. During the rest of the year, they are accessible to hikers via gentle trails that kids can manage.

Nighttime exploring
Check the park's online calendar and make reservations to secure your spot on a moonlight or dark-sky hike, a nighttime cave exploration or a stargazing party with telescopes pointed into the Milky Way. These special, ranger-guided programs usually take place on weekends.

◀ Bear Gulch reservoir in the Pinnacles National Park.
▶ Pass through Tunnel Rock on the High Peaks Trail.

Hike this...

01 High Peaks Trail
Make a thrilling, 6.7 mile round trip (10.8km) ascent of the park's iconic rock formations on this steep, narrow trail, with steps and railings to help you.

02 Balconies Cliffs-Cave Loop
An easy 2.4-mile roundtrip (3.8km) route from Chaparral in West Pinnacles, this route takes you to Balconies Cave. In the winter, you might have to do some wading.

03 Chalone Peak Trail
For eye-popping vistas, make a strenuous, 9-mile (14.5km) climb to the top of the park's tallest mountain, gaining over 2000ft (610m) in elevation.

What to spot...

From tiny ladybugs to enormous condors, a variety of wildlife thrives inside this isolated park. Birders will have a field day checking off various riparian, woodland and chaparral species, and even amateurs may be able to spot a raptor, such as a golden eagle or peregrine falcon flying around the park's high cliffs. Inside Balconies and Bear Gulch Caves you can spot Townsend's big-eared bats. Other bat species roost in rock cracks or under tree bark in the park. Dusk is a great time to see many species flying around.

CALIFORNIA CONDOR Pulled back from the brink of extinction, North America's largest land bird spreads its wings almost 10ft (3m) wide and can fly over 150 miles (241km) in search of food.

TOWNSEND'S BIG-EARED BAT Immediately recognizable by its extra-long ears, this brown bat roosts in the darkness of talus caves.

BLUE OAK Providing shelter and acorns for animals and shade for human campers, this woodland tree is just one of California's 20 majestic native oak species.

252

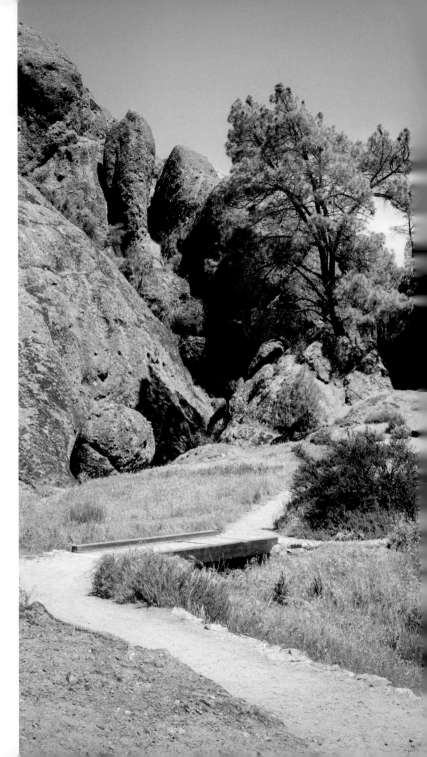

Itineraries

Hike the High Peaks loop, eyes peeled for California condors, hire a guide for a day of rock climbing, or admire the bats at Bear Gulch or Balconies caves.

◄ Pack plenty of water for a hike in this park.

➡ A Californian condor spreads its wings. Baby condors hatch in May.

01
An afternoon

On your drive between Southern California's desert parks and the redwoods of Northern California, take the slower, scenic route up Hwy 101 along California's Central Coast, instead of the I-5 Fwy – then you'll have time for a quick detour to this peaceful park. On the park's west side, roll into Bear Gulch just in time to set out a picnic lunch underneath shady oak trees.

After stopping into the visitor center for a trail map, set out on foot to make a circuit of the High Peaks. As the trail grows ever narrower, climbing up steps carved into the stone, stop to spot myriad birds and for panoramic photos of the rocky pinnacles set against the mountains of the Coast Ranges beyond. Look out for rare California condors, which have a white spot on the underside of each of their black wings. As you loop down and around back to Bear Gulch, swing out to Bear Gulch Caves, where bats roost among the talus rocks.

02
A day

You can see and do a lot in just one day at this surprisingly small park. Start by driving across the valley flatlands to the park's east entrance. Stock up on drinks and snacks at the campers' general store, just inside the park. Keep driving west to Bear Gulch, where rangers at the visitor center can give you a free map and talk over all of your hiking options. But if you've only got one day, you'll want to do the High Peaks loop, hiking more than 5 miles (8km) up to the very tip of rocky precipices, then loping back down to Bear Gulch.

After lazing in the shade to have lunch and take a quick rest, follow a much easier hiking loop that leads to and through Bear Gulch Cave. Straggly Grey Pines are the most abundant trees in the park and the only pine tree species found here. Look out for their head-sized pine cones! If you're able to extend your time, there are regular talks on condors, evening programs and star-gazing parties on most weekends during the year.

03
Three days

In three days you can explore places that most day-trippers miss. On day one, cruise from Hwy 101 over to the park's east side and pitch a tent at Pinnacles Campground, where you can swim in the pool. Head west to Bear Gulch and hike to its namesake cave, then hoof it up the High Peaks Trail for a sunset photo. Head back to your campsite for s'mores and storytelling. On some weekends, especially during spring and summer, you may be able to join a ranger for an after-dark astronomy session or a moonlight hike. Devote all of day two to climbing Chalone Peak, the park's highest point, where the views will make you forget the effort it took to get up there. Otherwise, hike the mostly flat trail to Balconies Cave and back on the Balconies Cliffs trail (5.3 miles round trip). On your final day, rope up (with expert help if required) on one of Pinnacles' famous climbing routes, pitting your agility against the sheer walls and oddly shaped rocks of this volcanic landscape. Full-day courses will give novices truly useful climbing skills.

49

CA

Redwood National & State Parks

In foggy forests among emerald fern groves, some of the world's tallest trees have been shooting skyward for 2000 years.

Redwood

Imagine how peaceful it is to walk among a forest of coast redwood trees, over 60 times taller and hundreds of years older than you are. The stillness of the eternal watch they keep from high in the green canopy will slow your heartbeat, relax your pace and clear your mind. Despite its name, it's not just redwoods that this partnership of national and state parks protects. It is also a safe haven for other threatened species, such as Chinook salmon that spawn in freshwater streams, Steller (northern) sea lions who haul out on coastal rocks, and California spotted owls, those great hunters who perch in the branches of mature conifers.

Tragically, less than 5% of California's old-growth redwood forests have never been logged. Almost half of what remains lies inside this web of federal and state parks, extending from the edge of the Pacific Ocean to inland forests and prairies where elk graze, and along wild rivers where Native American tribes traditionally hunted and fished.

In 1918, citizens united in the Save the Redwoods League to rescue these primeval forests from destruction by loggers. Their activism was rewarded first by the creation of the three California state parks – Prairie Creek Redwoods State Park in 1923, Del Norte Coast Redwoods State Park in 1925, and Jedediah Smith Redwoods State Park in 1929 – and then again in 1968 with the creation of Redwood National Park. In the 1980s Unesco declared this region a World Heritage site. Redwood National Park and its three partnership state parks together protect more than 200 sq miles (518 sq km), 133,000 acres of land and almost 40 miles (64km) of rugged, undeveloped Pacific coastline. Bathed in a temperate rainforest climate,

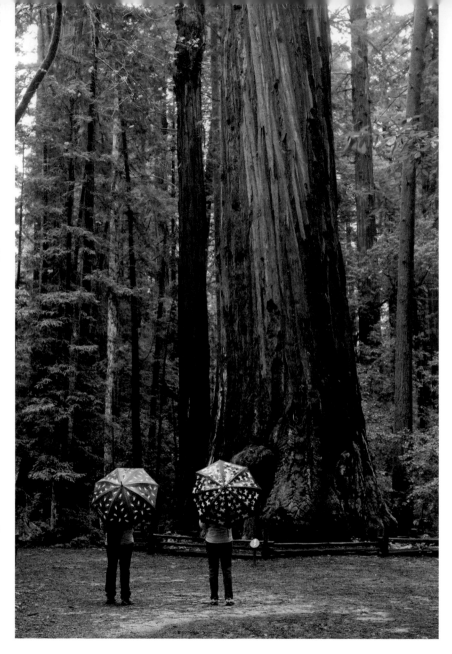

the parks receive up to 140in (356cm) of rain every year. This cool moisture, along with rich forest-floor soil and the trees'

ability to sprout new buds in burls, allows coast redwoods to reach lofty heights and venerable old age.

When to go
The parks are open year-round. The sunniest weather arrives from May through October, when most visitor facilities are open. Winter brings the cold and rain.

Getting there
From San Francisco it's a five-hour drive on Hwy 101 north to the national park's visitor center. Over the next 50 miles (80km), you'll pass the three state parks on the way north toward the Oregon border via Crescent City.

Events
In July the Tolowa Nation Honoring Dance is held in Jedediah Smith Redwoods State Park. December's Candlelight Walk is among the ancients of Prairie Creek Redwoods State Park.

Accessibility
All the visitor centers, campgrounds and cabins – and many trails in the parks – are accessible.

Park in numbers
217 Area in sq miles
379.1 Height of Hyperion (ft)
45% California's remaining old-growth redwoods protected here

Stay here...

 Gold Bluffs Beach Campground
Just over two dozen sites wait at the end of a dirt road in Prairie Creek Redwoods State Park. Solitude, ocean views and nearby hiking trails feature in this coastal preserve, with soft sand only a short walk away. Reserve campsites a long time in advance.

 Mill Creek Campground
Located in Del Norte Coast Redwoods State Park this gorgeous spot provides the most space between campsites and is quiet and serene – making it a favorite of families. Note that there are restrictions on the size of vehicle or RV that can be parked here.

 Historic Requa Inn
On the banks of the Klamath River, not far from the ocean, this 1914 hotel beckons with a welcoming ambience and wondrous meals . Old-fashioned rooms are tech-free (no TVs or phones) and have antique furnishings such as claw-foot tubs. Rent the cottage for a romantic weekend spent by the wood-burning fireplace

Do this!

Scenic driving
If you're impressed by the scenery along Hwy 101, just you wait until you motor down the paved Newton B Drury Scenic Parkway, bordered by awe-inspiring stands of tall trees – or take bumpy Davison Rd out to Gold Bluffs Beach and backcountry Howland Hill Rd to the Stout Grove of old-growth redwoods.

Cycling
Most national and state parks don't allow mountain biking, but these parks do, along a few old logging roads and specially designated trails. Cycle among the ancient trees, out to coastal bluffs or around gentle prairies. A mixed terrain of easy, level loops and steep climbs keep things interesting.

Kayaking
In summer, paddle a kayak down the placid Smith River, the largest free-flowing river in California. Rentals are available in Crescent City. For summertime ranger-guided kayak tours, sign up in person in advance at the Hiouchi Visitor Center, off Hwy 199 in the Jedediah Smith Redwoods State Park section.

◀ Jurassic giants in Henry Cowell State Park. Previous page: driving Newton B. Drury Scenic Parkway.

What to spot...

On the coast you'll find tidepools rich in marine life, such as the giant green anemone, and beaches where pinnipeds bark and bask. In misty forests, where the tallest trees grow, listen for varied thrushes, then quietly watch Roosevelt elk graze in nearby prairies. As you hike along trails, be careful not to step on the yellow-colored banana slug, which wriggles along the rich, dirt-covered forest floor in search of its next meal.

COAST REDWOOD Although *Sequoia sempervirens* isn't the largest or oldest tree in the world, it is indisputably the tallest. And redwood fossils have been found dating from the Jurassic period.

ROOSEVELT ELK North America's largest elk grazes on grasses, plants and berries. In autumn, the antlered males fight for mates.

MARBLED MURRELET Unusually, this North Pacific seabird with black-and-white plumage flies inland to lay its eggs, in nests high in the branches of old-growth conifers.

Hike this...

O1 Lady Bird Johnson Grove Trail
Younger kids will delight in this short, 1-mile (1.6km) nature walk with educational signs that teach about the tall trees' ecology.

O2 Fern Canyon Loop Trail
Birds serenade your 0.7-mile (1.1km) walk between mossy, fern-covered canyon walls, near Gold Bluffs Beach in Prairie Creek Redwoods State Park.

O3 Coastal Trail
The 70-mile (142km) Coastal Trail offers shorter jaunts and longer backpacks, along bluffs, past sea lions and out to secluded beaches.

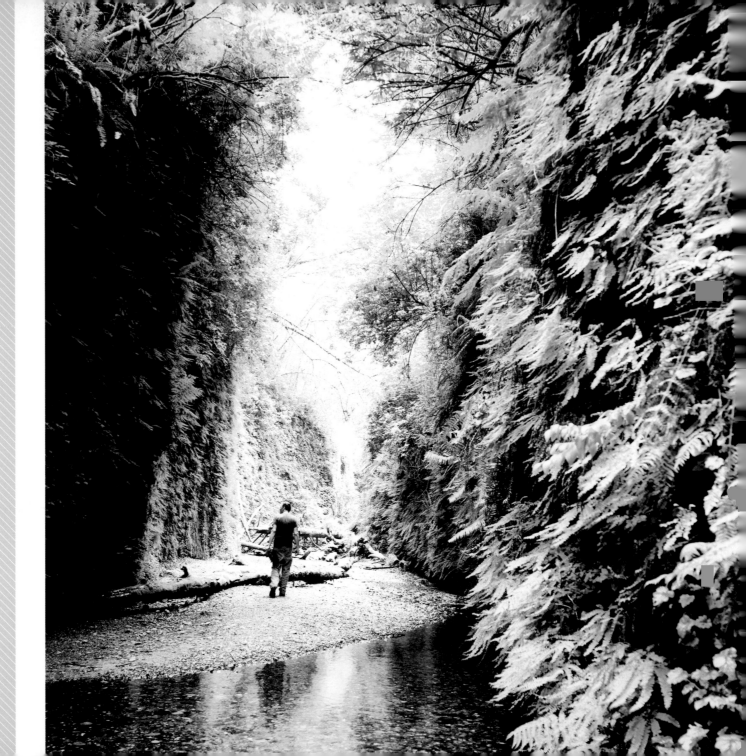

Itineraries

Marvel at the redwoods in the Tall Trees Grove, hike the Jurassic-ly green Fern Canyon or drive the Newton B Drury Scenic Parkway.

← Hiking Fern Canyon in Prairie Creek Redwoods State Park; sea lions live along the Redwood coast.
→ A Roosevelt elk.

01
A day

Driving north on Hwy 101 from the bayfront fishing town of Trinidad, the road curves toward the ocean and passes lagoons where birds flock and kayakers paddle. Stop at the national park's oceanfront Thomas H Kuchel Visitor Center to pick up information and to stroll along the wild beach. Just north of the town of Orick, take the signed turn-off for Lady Bird Johnson Grove, where a bewitching nature trail circles old-growth redwood trees as songbirds flit overhead. Drive further down the same side road and park by the trailhead for the hike to Tall Trees Grove, a memorable 5-mile (8km) round-trip that lets you gape in awe at some of earth's tallest trees, which grow almost as if in secret along Redwood Creek. You will need to reserve your Tall Trees permit at least 48 hours in advance online.

After your hike, drive back to Hwy 101 and head a few miles north to Prairie Creek Redwoods State Park. Watch giant Roosevelt elk gather at dusk in Elk Prairie before your drive up to the seaside village of Crescent City.

02
Two days

After a campfire breakfast by the meadow, walk over to the Prairie Creek Redwoods State Park visitor center to get hiking advice from the rangers – and to tarry by the crackling fireplace to dry out any dampness that crept into your bones overnight. Hiking trails start outside the front door, ranging from easy nature walks to hardy treks out to the coast. Don't miss driving the park's Newton B Drury Scenic Parkway, which winds for 10 miles (16km) between old-growth redwoods that rise like ancient gods on either side of a narrow ribbon of asphalt. Nearly all the campgrounds here require reservations months in advance, so plan ahead.

On the second day, leave the car behind for a leisurely bike ride on one of the park's many scenic roads, but bring lights as it's dark under the trees. Or head out to the coast to explore a different piece of the park as you trek along wind-swept ridges and down to forgotten beaches.

03
Three days

After sleeping soundly with the surf for your lullaby, pack up camp and drive back to Hwy 101 northbound. Cross over the Klamath River, a popular spot for fly-fishing, and pass ocean overlooks where you might be able to spot migratory gray whales in winter. Back in the car, keep driving north to Crescent City, with its mid-19th-century lighthouse and an endearing marine-mammal hospital you can visit. Outside town, turn onto backcountry Howland Hill Rd (which is dirt, but a 4WD isn't required), the route to some of the most impressive old-growth redwoods inside Redwood National and State Parks. Jedediah Smith Campground's wooded campsites alongside the Smith River are perfectly set up for family fun. Or enjoy the quiet peace and less crowded camping offered at the Mill Creek Campground, located just seven miles south of Crescent City. To finish your trip, take a whale-watching tour for the day and head out to sea, or extend your trip with a once-in-a-lifetime backpack along the Coastal Trail.

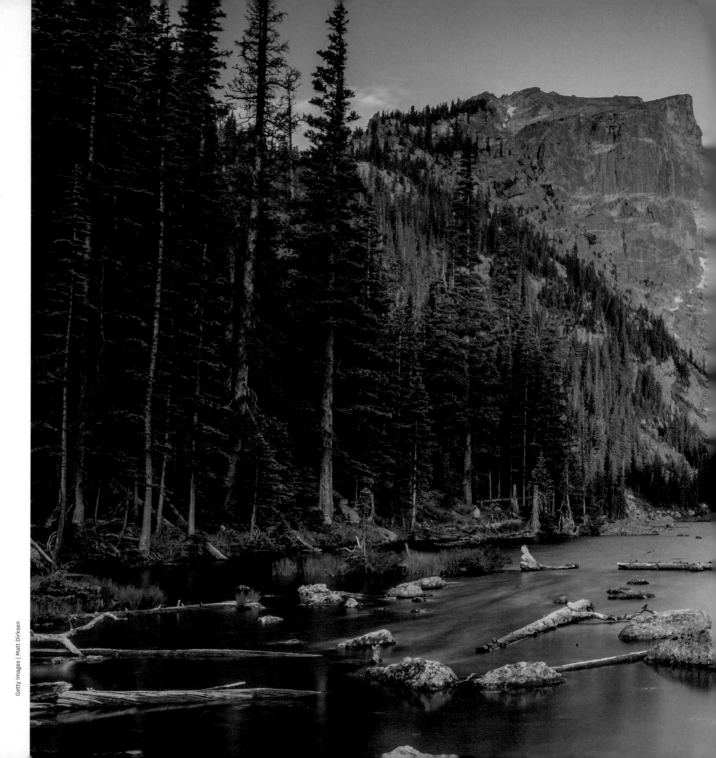

50

CO

Rocky Mountain National Park

Jagged peaks, eternally blanketed in glistening white snow, pierce the landscape of this alpine park, surrounded by thousands of acres of deep green virgin forest.

NATIONAL PARKS *of* AMERICA

Getty Images | Matt Dirksen

In winter, when the crowds have gone and the park lies hushed beneath feet of freshly fallen snow, you glide through open fields on cross-country skies, icy winds pinking your cheeks. In this high-altitude wonderland it's just you and the elk, encircled by cloud-piercing mountaintops. In the heart of America, this is a world unto its own.

The names of the mountains, lakes and regions within the park speak to its wildness. The Never Summer Mountains. The Mummy Range. Wild Basin. Loch Vale. Explore them by foot through day hikes or overnight backpacking trips; ride through them on horses; fish for mountain trout in their gin-clear waters. You'll be rewarded with sweeping vistas as far as Wyoming, quiet moments of peace deep within fir and spruce forests, and thrilling glimpses of moose and bighorn sheep roaming the tundra. Come in winter, when the park is blanketed in silver snow; in spring, when wildflowers spangle the meadows; in summer, when the animals frolic; or in fall, with its amber glow.

Paleo-Indians have been passing through the region for more than 12,000 years, while the Ute and Arapaho inhabited the area more recently. From the mid-1800s, homesteaders began claiming land in the area for farming and cattle-ranching, followed closely by tourists. Irish nobleman Lord Dunraven tried to claim much of the land for himself using the Homestead Acts, but angry settlers put an end to that idea. The national park was signed into existence by Woodrow Wilson in 1915.

Longs Peak, the park's tallest mountain, is so iconic it appears on Colorado's state quarter; the 14,259ft (4346m) peak is named after 19th-century explorer Stephen

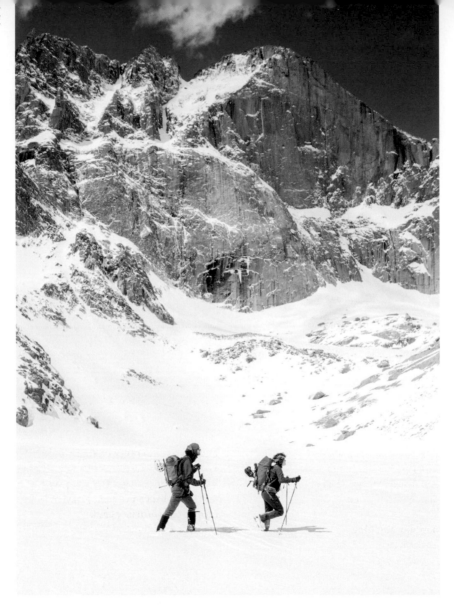

Harriman Long. A stone shelter on the popular Keyhole Route is a testament to the mountain's dangers: it's named after Agnes Vaille, a climber of the 1920s, who died (along with one of her rescuers) when she fell from the North Face.

⬆ A winter walk below Longs Peak, the park's highest mountain. Previous page: Hallett Peak is a popular Rocky Mountain hike.

Getty Images | Cavan Images

Toolbox

When to go
The park is most crowded in July and August, when wildflowers bloom and temperatures are comfortable. It's open year-round, but roads are often closed due to snow from mid-fall onwards.

Getting there
Denver is 90 minutes' drive away. The park's access towns are Grand Lake to the west and Estes Park to the east. A shuttle serves parts of the park from May through October.

Events
September means the Longs Peak Scottish-Irish Highland Festival in Estes Park. October is elk rutting season and the Elk Fest. January brings a popular winter festival to Estes Park.

Accessibility
Bear Lake Trail, Coyote Valley Trail, Lily Lake Trail and the Sprague Lake Trail are wheelchair-accessible, as are shuttlebuses and some campgrounds.

Park in numbers

415 Area in sq miles
72 Number of peaks higher than 12,000ft
355 Miles of hiking trails

Stay here...

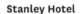 **Longs Peak Campground**
The park's accommodations are camping-only; if you want a roof, head to Estes Park or Grand Lake. This 26-site, tent-only campground is coveted by those making the early morning trek up Longs Peak. The scenery is stunning, but the air is thin – the campground is at 9400ft (2865m). Sites are all first-come, first-served.

Stanley Hotel
Stephen King spent a night at this grand Colonial Revival hotel, which inspired him to create the Overlook Hotel for *The Shining*. The Stanley embraces its creepy legacy, which includes a piano played by ghostly hands in the middle of the night, by offering daily ghost tours. Non-paranormal enthusiasts will be more interested in breakfasts served overlooking the Rockies and the cozy wood-and-bronze whiskey bar.

YMCA of the Rockies
This 860-acre complex is like an all-ages summer camp – calling it 'family-friendly' would hardly do it justice. With a games room, bikes, mini golf, archery, roller skating and more, you'll have to drag your kids to the park itself, just down the road. Book lodge rooms or cabins with kitchens and fireplaces.

Do this!

Scenic driving
The highest continuously paved road in America, the 48-mile (77km) Trail Ridge Rd passes through aspen and pine forests and crosses alpine meadows blanketed with fireweed and rosy paintbrush. Gaze across at peaks bluish-white with snow; the road's apex is above the tree line at 12,183ft (3713m). Look for elk, moose and bighorn sheep as you traverse between Estes Park and Grand Lake.

Snowshoeing
In winter, Rocky Mountain National Park becomes a wonderland of snow and ice, so strap on a clown-sized pair of snowshoes and float over feet of densely packed snow. The most popular snowshoe trails follow summer hiking paths with elk and mule deer easier to spot against the endless white than in summer.

Mountain-climbing
In hiking lingo, a '14er' is a mountain higher than 14,000ft (4267m). There are 53 in Colorado, but only one within this park: Longs Peak. 'Bagging' Longs is a bucket-list item for many hikers: the view from the summit is otherworldly. The hike doesn't need any specialized climbing equipment (in summer, at least) but its ledges, rocky scrambles and thin air make it a serious challenge.

What to spot...

Much of the park is covered in iconic aspen, as well as evergreens, such as ponderosa pine and Douglas fir. Mosses cushion the dark forest floor, while open meadows sway with pale green grass. Large mammals – black bears, elk and moose – lumber through the trees, while cartoon-cute marmots and pikas frolic on rocky slopes. The rivers' clear waters are famed for their wealth of trout. Birds of prey, such as eagles, hawks and kestrels circle the wide blue sky.

BIGHORN SHEEP Look for these handsome creatures, the park's official symbol, around Sheep Lake in spring and early summer, and on the park's eastern side in winter.

QUAKING ASPEN These slender, white-barked trees grow at altitudes as high as 11,000ft (3353m). In fall, their fluttering (hence the name) leaves turn an extraordinary gold.

COLORADO BLUE COLUMBINE Colorado's state flower, these delicate buds are classically pale blue and white, though they can sometimes be yellow or pink. They bloom from June to August.

Hike this...

01 Lily Mountain
Not remotely up for a '14er'? This modest 1.5-mile (2.4km) climb offers panoramic views over Longs Peak, Estes Park and the Mummy Range.

02 Cub Lake
A moderate, family-friendly 6-miler (10km) leads through open fields to a serene mountain pond full of lily pads and happily quacking ducks.

03 Twin Sisters Peak
Just a notch easier than Longs, this 11,428ft (3483m) summit can be reached by a quad-burning climb through rocky slopes and meadows of alpine flowers.

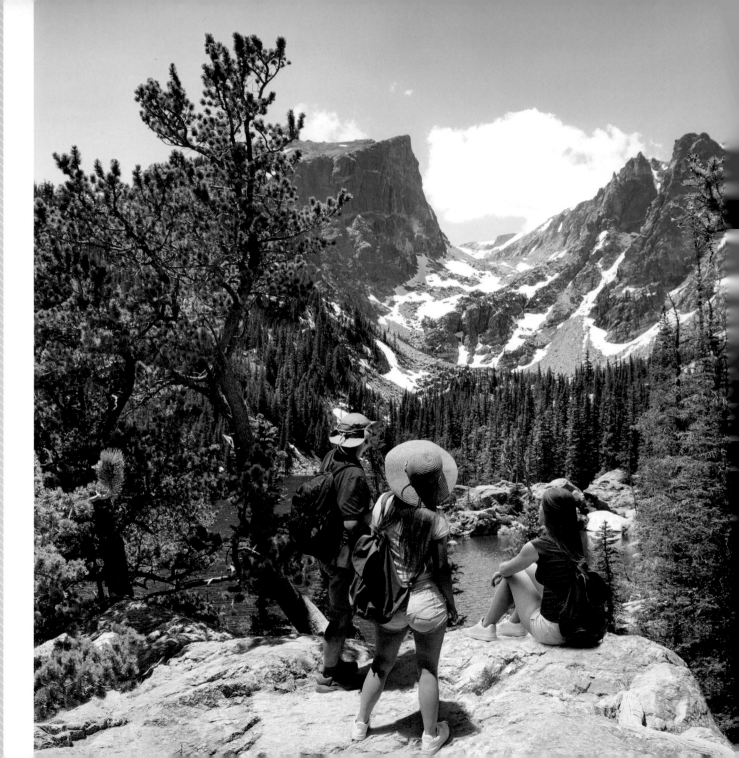

Itineraries

Hike the Wild Basin, overnight in Stephen King's The Shining *inspiration or mix with elk and moose at the Alpine Visitor Center.*

 It's a short hike to Dream Lake from Bear Lake trailhead.

 Look for tiger salamanders around Lily Lake.

01
A day

Get a quick mountain high by crossing Rocky Mountain National Park in one day via vertiginous Trail Ridge Rd. Fuel up for your day with breakfast at Big Horn Restaurant in Estes Park, where locals linger over sturdy plates of bacon and eggs. Once you hit the road, your first stopping point should be Rainbow Curve Overlook, with valley views from 10,829ft (3301m) up. Further along, you'll almost feel like you can touch the clouds at Rock Cut Overlook, 12,110ft (3691m) above sea level.

The barren brown-and-gray landscape feels alien – and cold! Don't miss the Alpine Visitor Center, where elk and moose graze the alpine meadows far above the tree line; stop here for lunch at the homey cafeteria. At Milner Pass the road crosses the continental divide. A quick hike will take you to Poudre Lake, with deep blue waters surrounded by Douglas fir. Check out the Holzwarth Historic Site, a restored 1920s ranch, before descending to Grand Lake to conk out in a soft bed at Shadowcliff Lodge.

02
Two days

Much of the park may close from mid-October, but for snow-lovers the fun is just starting. For a winter weekend getaway, begin with an amble on one of the lower-altitude eastern trails. The Pool, a flattish 2.5-mile (4km) route, winds past frozen waterfalls to the confluences of Spruce and Fern Creeks with the Big Thompson River. Go to the Hidden Valley area in the afternoon: the remains of a ski resort that closed in the 1990s have become a top spot for sledding and snow tubing (bring your own; no metal runners). At night unroll your warmest sleeping bag at Moraine Park Campground, open year-round. In the morning, strap on cross-country skis and go whooshing along Trail Ridge Rd, closed to cars but open to you! Outfitters in Estes Park and Grand Lake provide gear. Or reserve ahead to join a ranger-led snowshoe trip (January-March). The dazzling ice landscape of the Kawuneeche Valley is a top spot. Always check weather and avalanche conditions on the NPS site.

03
A week

Spend day one acclimatizing to the thin air in Estes Park, the park's major access town, which has plenty of cute shops and restaurants to keep you occupied. On day two, drive Trail Ridge Rd as far as the Alpine Visitor Center, stopping at viewpoints to gawk at the dazzling white peaks of the Mummy Range. On day three, hike Lily Mountain, a fairly short climb to a summit overlooking the eternal snows of Longs Peak, with Estes Park in the distance. Reward yourself with an overstuffed burrito and a margarita (or three) at Ed's Cantina and Grill. Book a fly-fishing trip with Kirks Flyshop for day four; the experienced guides will lead you to the most stunning of clear mountain streams. On day five, hit the trail with a half-day horse ride: icy pinnacles and barren slopes look better on horseback. On day six drive Trail Ridge Rd to where it crosses the continental divide at Milner Pass, with the green Colorado River flowing through the distant valley. On day seven, explore the waters around charming Grand Lake, on the park's west side.

51

AZ

Saguaro National Park

The saguaro thrives in its namesake park, where sun-baked trails meander through a desert wonderland of prickly cacti and savvy wildlife.

If you're pedaling the Cactus Forest Loop Drive in late spring, keep a lookout for the elusive saguaro blossom. Taking the stage atop the upper trunk and arms of the saguaro cactus, this striking white bloom will survive less than 24 hours, just long enough for pollination and a few lucky photographers.

Established in 1933, Saguaro National Monument was the first federal monument created to protect a specific plant. President Bill Clinton confirmed this mission in 1994 when he signed a congressional bill creating Saguaro National Park. What's so special about this cactus? For starters, its habitat is limited to the Sonoran Desert, which stretches across southern Arizona,

southeastern California and northern Mexico. Slow-growing saguaros take 50 to 80 years to reach a height of 10ft (3m), so they're not quickly replaced. Saguaros are also iconic symbols of the American West. You don't mess with legends like these.

Beyond stats and mythology, there's something engagingly human about this cactus. With sturdy trunks and thick arms, saguaros look like protective sentinels. Their charges? The prickly pear cactus, the barrel cactus and the deceptively fuzzy teddy-bear cholla cactus – don't give that show-off a hug. Wildlife includes roadrunners, gila monsters and javelinas. Rock art, rock shelters and milling sites are reminders of the Hohokam people,

who left the area 500 years ago. Other historic highlights include a 19th-century homestead and 1930s structures built by the Civilian Conservation Corps.

The park is divided into two distinct sections. Nature trails, petroglyphs and groves of saguaros grab the spotlight in the Tucson Mountain District, found on the western edge of Tucson. Thirty miles (48km) east, the Rincon Mountain District unfurls across six eco-zones, stretching from low-lying desert to the summits of mountains ranges. In the park, these mountain ranges are called 'sky islands.' Noted for their isolation and eco-system diversity, they rise starkly – and photogenically – from the desert floor.

Toolbox

When to go
The park is most inviting between October and April when temperatures hover in the 60s and 70s F (16 to 26°C). Spring wildflowers bloom from late February through early April; cactus blossoms appear in May and June. The temperature can be over 100°F (38°C) May through September.

Getting there
Both sections of the park border Tucson. Speedway Blvd is the most convenient connector between the western Tucson Mountain District and the eastern Rincon Mountain District. The I-10 is the nearest interstate. You'll need a car.

Events
The Labor Day 8-Miler & 5K Run/Walk has been held in September for 50 years.

Accessibility
The Desert Ecology Trail and a portion of the Mica View Trail are graded to ADA standards. The Desert Discovery Trail is paved.

Park in numbers

143 Area in sq miles
8666 Highest point (ft)
78 Percentage designated wilderness

Stay here...

Gilbert Ray Campground
You can snooze beside saguaros standing guard at this county-run park, which is set just a short bike ride away from the Tucson Mountain District, the Arizona-Sonora Desert Museum and Old Tucson Studios.

Hotel Congress
History, rock and roll and good cheer collide at the convivial Hotel Congress, which doubles as the soul of Tucson. A little bit retro, a little bit wild, this was outlaw John Dillinger's final hideout in the 1930s. Today, this downtown hotel welcomes all comers with three bars, a restaurant, live music and no in-room TVs.

Backcountry camping
Six lonely campgrounds dot the Saguaro Wilderness Area, which sprawls across the Rincon Mountain District. No motorized vehicles are allowed, and each campground is at least 6 miles (10km) from the trailhead. Your post-hike reward? Constellations and cacti without the crowds. A permit ($8 per night) is required.

Do this!

Horseback riding
As your horse clip-clops past the prickly pears, kicking up dust and pestering roadrunners, it feels like the Old West never disappeared – the only thing missing is Gene Autry and a cowboy song. Several outfitters and ranches lead trips in and around the Rincon Mountain District.

Cycling
Wind in your hair, buttery pavement beneath your wheels, sky islands in your sightline and a devil's array of cacti keeping you firmly on the road. For cyclists, the 8-mile (13km) Cactus Forest Loop Dr is an invigorating introduction to the park. Scenic overlooks line the ride. For off-road cycling, the Cactus Forest Trail divides the loop and rolls past historic lime kilns.

Petroglyph hunting
Prehistoric Native Americans carved more than 200 images into the rocks clustered in the Signal Hill Petroglyph Area in Saguaro West. Created 550 to 1550 years ago, the mesmerizing images – also known as rock art – can be found on a rocky hill a short walk from the Signal Hill Picnic Area.

◧ The slow-growing saguaro cactus can live up to 200 years.
▶ A flowering saguaro cactus.

Hike this...

01 King Canyon Trail
In the western district, this 7-mile (11km) hike kicks off across from the Arizona-Sonora Desert Museum and switchbacks to the 4687ft (1429m) summit of Wasson Peak.

02 Douglas Spring Trail
This 5.2-mile (8.4km) round-trip trail climbs from saguaros to desert grasslands in the Rincon Mountain foothills. Views include the Santa Catalina Mountains and a seasonal waterfall.

03 Tanque Verde Ridge Trail
Bring your hiking stick for this rugged and steep 18-mile (29km) round-trip in the eastern district. It climbs to Tucson Basin views and Tanque Verde Peak, which rises to 7040ft (2146m).

500px | Emitry Vinogradov; Carol Polich

What to spot...

The Tucson Mountain District supports desert scrub and desert grassland communities. This lower-lying district, noted for its thick groves of saguaros, is home to desert dwellers like the desert tortoise and Gambel's quail. The loftier Rincon Mountain District holds six distinct ecosystems: desert scrub, desert grasslands, oak woodland, pine-oak woodland, pine forest and mixed conifer forest. Large mammals, including black bears and white-tailed deer, roam the higher elevations of the sky islands within the district.

SAGUARO CACTUS Average lifespan? 150 to 175 years. Filled with water, a saguaro (sah-wah-row) can weigh 6 tons (5443kg) and grow to a height of 50ft (15m). It's illegal to harm or move one, not to mention dangerous – a shooter was killed in 1993 when he blasted off the arm of a saguaro and it fell on him.

WESTERN DIAMOND-BACKED RATTLESNAKE A diamond pattern runs the length of this venomous pit viper, one of six species of rattlesnake in the park. Black-and-white bands border its rattle.

JAVELINA If it looks like a pig and rolls in mud like a pig, it must be...a peccary. Yep, these herd-traveling desert dwellers are members of the hoofed peccary family – they're not wild pigs. Javelinas are dark-haired, with poor eyesight and a strong sense of smell.

268

Itineraries

Get up close to saguaros and wildlife at the Arizona–Sonora Desert Museum, hike King Canyon Trail to Wasson Peak then picnic at sunset at Gates Pass Overlook.

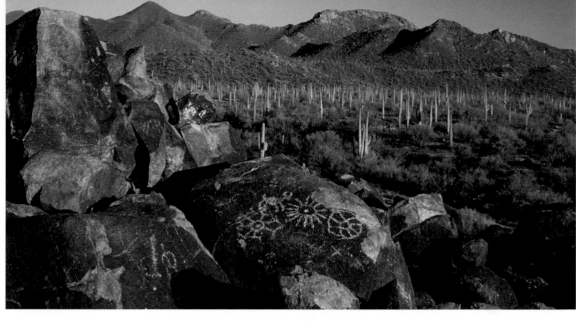

◄ A black-tailed jackrabbit.
► Petroglyphs by the Hohokam people represented animals, astrological symbols and people.

01
One day

For a Sonoran Desert primer, spend your morning exploring the excellent Arizona-Sonora Desert Museum. Listen for javelinas rustling in the underbrush, look for coyotes loping across the sand and take snapshots of the desert flora. For lunch, swing down to divey but family friendly Tiny's Saloon & Steakhouse for a burger.

With upraised arms, the saguaros at the Tucson Mountain District entrance look ready to welcome you with a high-five. Instead, examine the cacti on the well-labeled Cactus Garden Trail beside the Red Hills Visitor Center. This short trail passes chollas, saguaros and prickly pears. Roadrunners dart across your path as you motor to the Bajada Loop Drive, where saguaros bask in the sunlight. Enjoy a picnic at the Signal Hill Trailhead, then hike up the trail for ancient petroglyphs. For more desert exploring, follow King Canyon Trail to the top of Wasson Peak for 360° desert views.

End with sunset views of the Sonoran Desert from Gates Pass Overlook to the east. Spend the night at Gilbert Ray Campgound.

02
Two days

The next day, drive into Tucson, stopping by Pep & Pastry for breakfast. Think pork belly eggs benedict and sweet potato hash with goat cheese mousse. As you approach the Rincon Mountain District, modernity surrenders to the Old West. The mountains loom larger. A dusty horsetrailer clangs past. And the road into the park? The Old Spanish Trail – even its name sets an adventurous mood.

Interactive exhibits inside the Rincon Mountain Visitor Center explore the desert's charms, but it's hard to resist the call of the Cactus Forest Loop Drive outside. This 8-mile (13km) drive swoops through a cacti wonderland. For closer views, hike the Mica View Loop Trail, stopping for lunch at the picnic area. In the afternoon, catch the ranger program. Afterwards, for a taste of pioneer history, enjoy a ramble on Freeman Homestead Trail. For sunset desert views climb the Tanque Verde Ridge Trail.

Back in Tucson, stroll the indie shops and eateries on 4th Ave. Pass the night at the lively Hotel Congress.

03
Three days

On day three, delve into local history with a walk through the Barrio Histórico District. This compact neighborhood was an important business district in the late 19th century. Today it's home to funky shops and galleries in brightly painted adobe houses. From here, drive eight miles south of the city to the dazzling white towers of Mission San Xavier del Bac. Rising from the dusty desert floor, the mission is a mesmerizing structure that brings an otherworldly glow to the scrubby landscape. Nicknamed 'White Dove of the Desert,' the original mission was founded by Jesuit missionary Father Eusebio Kino in 1700, but was mostly destroyed in the Pima uprising of 1751.

In the afternoon, a two-hour guided horseback tour into the foothills of the Rincon Mountains in Saguaro East will sate your inner cowpoke. Return downtown for dinner at El Charro Cafe for delicious Mexican food and fabulous margaritas. The year of this rambling hacienda's centenary is 2022. It's known for its *carne seca* (sundried lean beef).

52

CA

Sequoia National Park

Lose yourself in the Giant Forest, explore an underground marble cave or power-climb stairs to the summit of a granite dome.

Shutterstock | Belikova Oksana

Serene in its magnificence, this southern Sierra Nevada park doesn't boast about its record-breaking natural attractions – though it should. The highest peak in the lower 48 states? Here Mt Whitney soars above the clouds on the eastern side of the range (though you can't reach the peak from the park). The world's biggest tree? Crane your neck up at the Giant Forest's General Sherman Tree, which measures more than 100ft (30m) around its trunk and 275ft (84m) tall. California's longest cave? You'll find it here, too – in addition to alpine lakes that sparkle like precious gems, cascading rivers that feed roaring waterfalls and wildflower meadows where yellow-bellied mountain marmots whistle at hikers passing by.

In 1890, the same year Yosemite was declared a national park, Sequoia National Park was created by the US Congress to protect rare giant sequoia trees from further logging. The largest living things on Earth, these trees grow only on the western slope of the Sierra Nevada mountains, where they can live for more than 2000 years. The first national park rangers sent to protect these giants were African American regiments of 'buffalo soldiers' from the US Army Cavalry. The first waves of visitors didn't start arriving until the 1927 opening of the scenic Generals Highway, which still slowly switchbacks up from the foothills to the Giant Forest.

When spring wildflowers cover the hillsides at lower elevations inside the park, you can hike to waterfalls that gush through river canyons. During summer, higher-elevation trails wind through the Giant Forest and to the top of Moro Rock, where you can soak up panoramic views of snaggle-toothed peaks along the Great

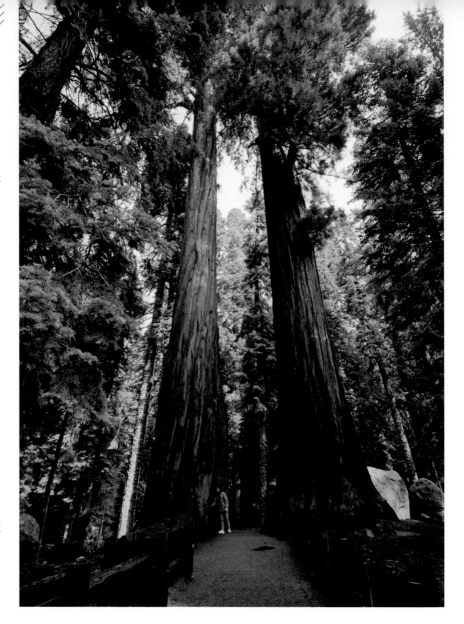

Western Divide. Ambitious backpackers leave on high country trips from the remote Mineral King Valley, which is reached via a twisting road with nearly 700 hairpin turns (quite a workout behind the wheel!).

⬆ The giant sequoia can grow to the height of a 26-storey building and live for 2000 years. ➡ Tunnel Log. Previous page: dawn breaks over the Sierra mountains.

Toolbox

When to go
Summer is the most popular time to visit. Spring brings wildflowers and waterfalls. Fall is less crowded, but still temperate. In winter, expect snow. Mineral King Valley is open only from late spring through early fall.

Getting there
The park is a 3½-hour drive north of Los Angeles. In summer only, buses to the Giant Forest depart from Visalia, in California's Central Valley. Seasonal, in-park shuttle buses are free.

Events
The three-day Dark Sky Festival in late summer features events across Sequoia and Kings Canyon.

Accessibility
Free wheelchair loans are available at the Giant Forest Museum and the Lodgepole Visitor Center on a first-come first-served basis. A paved wheelchair-accessible trail leads to the General Sherman Tree.

Park in numbers

631 Area in sq miles
52,500 Volume of General Sherman tree (cu ft)
14,505 Height of Mt Whitney (ft)

Stay here...

 Lodgepole Campground You'll need to reserve well ahead to stay in the park's most popular campground, especially if you want a prime campsite next to the river. The seasonal park shuttle bus stops here, making it easy to head over to the Giant Forest or to Crescent Meadow for hiking and wildlife-spotting.

Bearpaw High Sierra Camp
This is an unforgettable overnight trip: hike 11.5 miles (17.7km) into the wilderness along a gorgeous trail to reach these canvas tent cabins. Rates include a hot breakfast and dinner, and you can buy a boxed lunch to tote along with you on the trail the next day.

Wuksachi Lodge
The park's top-end lodging is not much more than a glorified, multi-story motel, but the woodsy setting near the Giant Forest is spectacular. The lodge's well-reviewed restaurant and a full calendar of activities for families are bonuses, as are steeply discounted room rates during the off-season.

Do this!

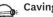 **Caving**
Carved by an underground river, 10,000-year-old Crystal Cave is full of stalactites, stalagmites, hanging curtains of milky-white marble and other bizarrely beautiful formations – all of which you can see on a family-friendly guided walking tour. Just watch out for bats and spiders! Diehard cavers can sign up for all-day spelunking adventures.

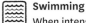 **Swimming**
When intense, mid-summer heat washes over the foothills, families flock to swimming holes near Potwisha and Hospital Rock. Later in summer, you can take a dip at Lodgepole Campground. Just make sure that the water levels in the park's rivers have dropped low enough to be safe; ask a park ranger to be sure.

Stair climbing
Huff and puff up more than 350 steps (over 300ft) to the top of Sequoia's granite dome for mind-boggling views of the Great Western Divide, running north-south through the middle of the park. Built in 1931 by the Civilian Conservation Corps (CCC), the granite-cut steps have study handrails for gripping.

🢀 Winter can bring snow and closed roads from November to April. Some low-level campgrounds remain open.

What to spot...

Possessing an incredible range of habitats, from the low-elevation foothills of the Sierra Nevada to the rising peak of Mt Whitney, this park has a cornucopia of flora and fauna that will keep you busy with binoculars for days, weeks or years. Recently, Sierra Nevada bighorn sheep have been returned to their historic range here after being driven almost to extinction. The grizzly bear wasn't as lucky: it was eradicated from the park in the 1920s.

BLACK BEAR Male black bears weigh an average of 300lb (136kg) to 350lb (159kg) and eat voraciously whenever they're not hibernating during the colder, snowier months.

GIANT SEQUOIA These towering trees have bark stained deep red by tannin, which helps protect them from wildfires. Surprisingly, they also depend on fire for their seeds to sprout.

YELLOW-BELLIED MARMOT In high mountain meadows, this furry rodent perches atop rocky outcroppings, where it can quickly hide from predators.

Hike this...

O1 General Sherman Tree & Congress Trail
This 2.1-mile (3.4km) paved loop through the Giant Forest passes the largest living thing on Earth – the General Sherman Tree – and numerous impressive contenders.

O2 Tokopah Falls Trail
Bring the kids on this pleasant, 3.5-mile (5.6km) riverside walk through a glacier-carved canyon, ending at a 1200ft-high (366m) waterfall, best viewed in spring.

O3 High Sierra Trail
This epic trail climbs from 6700ft to an altitude of 10,700ft, crossing ridges, rivers, lakes and waterfalls and offering jaw-dropping mountain and valley views. It stretches 72.2-miles (116.2km) one-way.

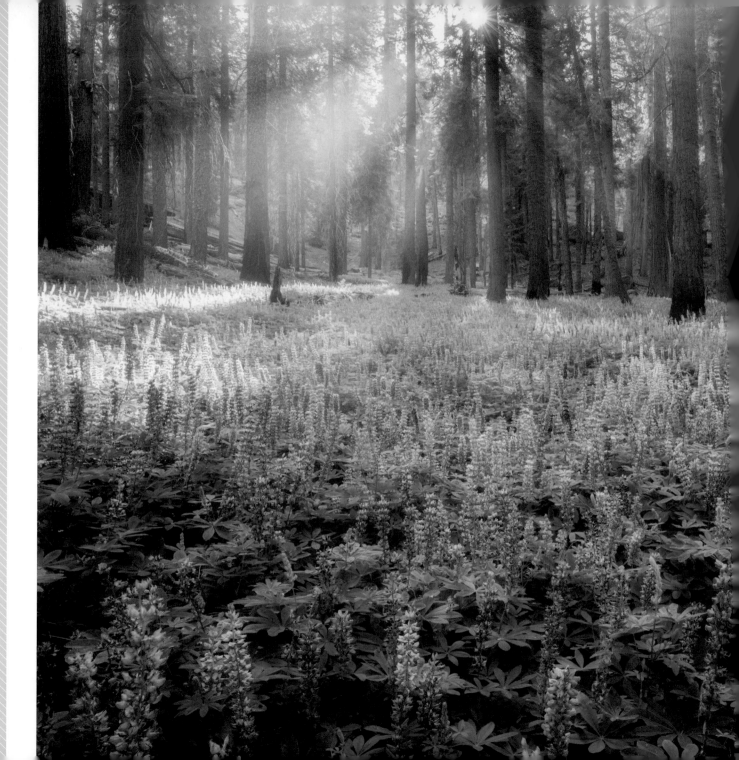

Itineraries

See the world's biggest tree at General Sherman Tree trailhead, tour Crystal Cave or take the hair-raising drive to Mineral King Valley.

◀ The General Sherman tree.
Lupines in Sequoia National Park.
➡ The Sawtooth trailhead in Mineral King Valley.

01

A day

Head straight to the heart of the park to the enchanting Giant Forest. To get there on the historic Generals Hwy, it's a steep, narrow and twisty 16-mile (26km) drive uphill. The park's Foothills Visitor Center and the Giant Forest Museum are the best places to get oriented. Outside the museum, catch the free seasonal shuttle bus north to the General Sherman Tree trailhead. Inspect the world's biggest tree then lose the crowds on the adjoining Congress Trail, which passes several huge trees, including the Chief Sequoyah Tree and the President Tree. Return to the museum; from there catch another shuttle to Moro Rock, where you can climb to the summit for panoramic views. Further along the same shuttle route is Crescent Meadow, where wildflowers bloom in early summer and black bears often ramble. Around sunset, drive north to the Wuksachi Lodge for a nice dinner, or just beer and pizza on the deck. Sated, backtrack to Lodgepole Village and your forest campsite next to the Kaweah River.

02

Two days

Follow the day one itinerary then catch the shuttle bus or walk over to the Lodgepole Cafe for a quick breakfast, then stop inside the visitor center to buy tickets for an afternoon tour of Crystal Cave. Return to Lodgepole Campground, then head out on the Tokopah Falls Trail, which rises gently through the forest to a cascade that runs down granite cliffs. Stare up at the enormous Watchtower rock formation, which looms high above the canyon floor. Have a picnic by the falls, then hike back to the campground. Pick up your car and take a winding drive down to Crystal Cave, where tour guides will take you behind the historic Spider Gate to wander among magical-looking stalactites, stalagmites and other abstract geological shapes.

Afterwards, drive down the Generals Hwy to the Foothills area of the park, where you can cool off with a dip in the Kaweah River in summer. Head outside the park to the town of Three Rivers to find lodging and a filling dinner.

03

Three days

Follow the two-day itinerary then stock up on food, drinks and gas for a scenic drive to Mineral King Valley. It can take two hours to drive just 25 miles (40km) from Three Rivers town to the valley, since the road makes almost 700 hair-raising turns and gains 7500ft (2286m) in elevation. The road passes by small waterfalls, picnic areas and old-fashioned cabins before finally petering out in a glacier-carved valley where miners once staked silver claims. All around you are skyscraping mountains, such as the 12,343ft-high (3762m) Sawtooth Peak. Wrap your car in a plastic tarp secured with rope to protect it from being chewed on by hungry marmots, then hit one of the steep hiking trails that lead up from the valley to alpine lakes. When you return to your car after such a hike, you might feel like staying the night at Cold Springs Campground. At least linger long enough in the valley to see the setting sun cast an alpenglow on the peaks.

53

VA

Shenandoah National Park

There are scenic drives, and then there's Skyline Dr, the 105-mile (169km) road riding the spine of Shenandoah's ancient Blue Ridge Mountains.

Shutterstock | Zack Frank

To the west of Skyline Dr, the silver Shenandoah River glides through the lush valley far below. To the east, the green hills of the Virginia Piedmont roll gently towards the horizon. The slopes are frilled pink with rhododendron and mountain laurel, the roadside carpeted with blue-purple columbine and sweet ox-eye daisies. Watch closely (if you're not driving!) and you might just see a falcon circling overhead.

The origin of the name 'Shenandoah' is a bit of a mystery. It's almost certainly of Native American origin – some say it means 'river of high mountains,' 'silver waters,' or even the rather romantic 'daughter of the stars.' According to one legend, George Washington named the river and its valley after an Oneida chief who led native warriors in support of the colonists in the Revolutionary War. Whatever the truth is, this area looms large in Virginia's imagination.

Inhabited seasonally by native tribes, Shenandoah was permanently settled by Europeans in the 18th century. These settlers built farmsteads and mills and planted apple orchards along the slopes, and began logging the ancient forests. To create the park in the 1930s, the government had to resettle nearly 500 families; they then allowed the farmland and logged forests to regrow naturally – a novel idea at the time. Today, a few crumbling foundations and moss-choked cemeteries are all that remain of these early mountain communities.

Shenandoah runs north–south along a narrow stretch of the Blue Ridge Mountains. The peaks are mostly gentle, but a few will satisfy hardcore hikers. The former farmland has transformed into sylvan hollows where white-tailed deer graze and dark, ferny

↑ A pair of black bear cubs means mama must be somewhere near. Previous page: sunrise in Shenandoah National Park.

forests shot through with silvery mountain creeks and waterfalls. Only two hours or so from Washington, DC, Shenandoah is a favorite getaway of harried bureaucrats and other city-dwellers.

Toolbox

When to go
The park's open year-round, but some facilities close in winter. The magical red-and-gold fall is the most popular season, with summer close behind.

Getting there
The park straddles the Blue Ridge Mountains. Its north access town, Front Royal, is a two-hour drive from the airports of Washington, DC; its south entrance, Rockfish Gap, is about an hour from the college town of Charlottesville.

Events
There are night sky talks at Big Meadows every month or so in good weather. July means the delectable Blackberry Delight berry festival. The Thanksgiving buffet at Skyland is very popular; book ahead.

Accessibility
All campgrounds have accessible sites. The 1.3-mile (2.1km) Limberlost Trail is wheelchair accessible.

Park in numbers

311 Area in sq miles
15 Park's width at its widest (miles)
1 Park's width at its narrowest (miles)

Stay here...

Big Meadows Lodge
A classic National Parks charmer, this rambling stone-and-brown-wood lodge has a homey Great Room lined with couches and rocking chairs. On chilly nights guests pack in to play board games by the stone fireplace. Rooms are spartan but comfy; private cabins are worth the extra money, especially the ones with fireplaces. The grounds are home to hundreds of deer.

Lewis Mountain Cabins
These rustic cabins are several steps up from a tent but still offer a back-to-nature vibe. Humble one- or two-bedroom units have private bathrooms. Roast your hotdogs in the fire pits outside – don't forget the marshmallows – or dine nearby at Big Meadows. A good choice for families, and those traveling with pets.

Big Meadows Campground
In wildlife-rich Big Meadows, this campground plays host to deer, wild turkeys and the odd bear. The 221 sites are tree-shaded and close to some of the park's finest hikes, including three waterfall trails. Some sites have views over the meadows, fringed with blackberry bushes; if you're lucky, you can pick some before the bears do. Its central location off Skyline Dr makes it a top choice.

Do this!

Scenic driving
The only road through the park, Skyline Dr skirts the peaks of the Blue Ridge for 105 miles (169km), passing enough scenic views for a lifetime (well, technically 75). To the west is the patchworked Shenandoah Valley; to the east are the green hills of the Virginia Piedmont. In spring, trillium, violets and bloodroot carpet the slopes, while in summer azaleas and mountain laurel are at their best.

Wildlife-watching
In the middle of the park, the tree-lined ridges open up to reveal a wide silver-green meadow. White-tailed deer munch away like warm-blooded lawnmowers; black bears forage for berries around the edge; chipmunks and squirrels run frantically up and down. Spread out a picnic and watch Mother Nature's show (but don't feed the bears!).

Climbing
Experienced climbers flock to Shenandoah's crags, but even a newbie can appreciate the thrills with a guided trip. Instructors with Shenandoah Mountain Guides will meet you in the park and show you the ropes (literally) at spots like Little Stony Man Cliff. Adrenaline plus mountain air make a very heady combo.

What to spot...

As a forested oasis on the crest of the Blue Ridge Mountains, Shenandoah provides an important landing spot for migrating birds. It's also a year-round home to such bird species as red-tailed hawks, Carolina chickadees and barred owls. Some 50 types of mammal roam the pine, oak, hickory and poplar forests, notably black bear and white-tailed deer. Exposed rocky outcrops, protected valleys and deep woods are home to more than 1400 types of plants, from wildflowers to ferns to mosses.

CAROLINA CHICKADEE With gray bodies, black caps and big black eyes, these tiny birds are cartoon-cute. Listen for their call of chicka-dee-dee-dee, or look for them nesting in tree holes.

WHITE-TAILED DEER You'll have no trouble spotting these increasingly un-shy mammals, who graze in meadows, stroll through campgrounds and dart in front of cars.

MOUNTAIN LAUREL In summer, these glossy green shrubs gush forth with foamy white-and-pink flowers. They often grow on steep, rocky slopes, and can be seen from Skyline Dr.

Hike this...

O1 Dark Hollow Falls
Deceptively difficult for a short hike, the payoff from this 1.4-mile (2.3km) round-trip is the sight of 70ft (21m) of water flowing over ancient lava rock.

O2 Snead Farm Loop
This 3.7-mile (6km) loop passes wildflower-spangled meadows on the way to an old homesteader barn; it's relatively flat.

O3 Old Rag Mountain
The park's most challenging hike, this 9-mile (14.5km) circuit involves several hairy scrambles on bare rock. Your reward? Stunning panoramic views for dozens of miles.

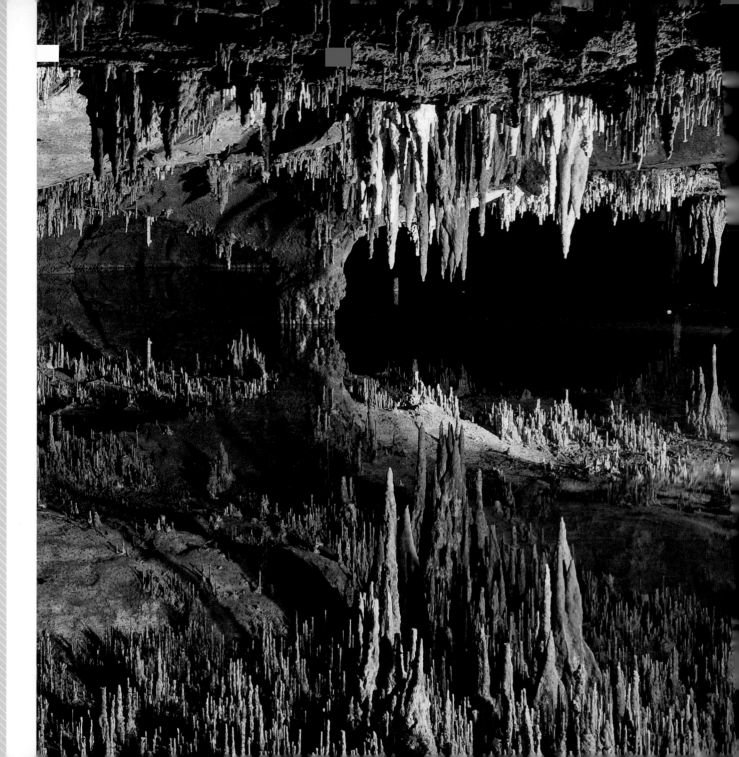

Itineraries

Get the binoculars ready for wildlife-watching at Big Meadows or Hawksbill Mountain, particularly for peregrine falcons. Horseback ride at Skyline Dr's highest point for wonderful views.

◄ A Carolina chickadee. Dream Lake in Luray Caverns, just west of the park boundary.
► Autumn in Shenandoah.

01
A day

Center yourself in the middle of the action at Big Meadows, where morning is prime wildlife-watching time. Park at the visitor center and set yourself up with your camera for an hour or two; it's like being on a mini safari in the middle of the American South. Take the short-but-steep trail to Dark Hollow Falls, where water cascades over mossy black volcanic rock into a clear pool; take the time to walk a little further to see some of the smaller falls of Hog Camp Branch. Refuel with lunch at Big Meadows Lodge – an overflowing sandwich or plate of fried chicken will hit the spot. Admire the classic 'parkitecture' of the Great Room, with massive windows overlooking the valley. Next, make your way up the Hawksbill Mountain summit, binoculars in tow for spotting the rare peregrine falcons that nest in the area. Drive north, stopping for stunning Shenandoah Valley views at the Crescent Rock and Pinnacle Peak overlooks before exiting the park via Thornton Gap.

02
Two days

'Do' Skyline Dr in its entirety, entering from the north at Front Royal on day one. Hit the Dickey Ridge Visitor Center for maps and exhibits before heading south. The first big overlook you'll get to is Gooney Run, named after the rapids that course through the valley. Forge onward to Range View Overlook, with views over craggy Stony Man Mountain, all the way to the bluish peaks of the Alleghenies. At Elkwallow Wayside, stock up on fruit and jerky and have a picnic lunch a few miles south at Pinnacle Peak's panoramic overlook. Finish the day at Big Meadows Lodge, challenging fellow travelers to board games in the Great Room as the night sky turns from blue to black outside. On day two, get up early for some wildlife-watching in the meadow, then head south as far as the trailhead to Blackrock Summit. Do the entire trail, including the spur, which leads to an enormous boulder field at the summit. Exit at Rockfish Gap for some hawk-spotting before heading onward to your final destination.

03
Five days

Spend day one in the cute access town of Front Royal, with some of the best (and cheapest) antiquing we've seen. On day two, enter the park from the north, taking in the luscious overlooks of the chartreuse-and-yellow Shenandoah Valley and the rolling hills of the Virginia Piedmont. Book an afternoon horseback ride at Skyland Lodge, a classic stone-and-wood national parks lodge at Skyline Dr's highest point.

Rise early on day three for the full-day climb up Old Rag Mountain. Give your legs a rest the following day with a visit to Luray Caverns just west of the park, a vast, dripping cave best known for its 'Great Stalacpipe Organ,' which taps stalactites with rubber mallets to play a melody. Head back into the park and spend the night at Big Meadows, then show up on time for your guided climbing and rappelling adventure – the park's a mecca for climbers. There's nothing like hanging 100 feet over the valley floor to make you forget the annoyances of daily life.

54

ND

Theodore Roosevelt National Park

For Roosevelt, this was 'a land of vast, silent spaces, of lonely rivers, and of plains where the wild game stared at the passing horsemen.' Little has changed.

Populated by thousands of animals – and very few people – Theodore Roosevelt National Park is spread across three sites in the unforgiving wilderness of North Dakota's Badlands. The South Unit, North Unit and Elkhorn Lodge are delicately laced together by three threads: the Little Missouri River, Maah Daah Hey Trail and the memory of a man who helped shape the entire national parks system.

In 1883, seven years after Custer passed through en route to his infamous engagement with Sitting Bull's Sioux warriors, a young Theodore Roosevelt came to North Dakota's Badlands to hunt.

While here, he discovered a powerful love for the land. This passion informed his attitude towards conservation when he became president, and during his time in the White House he would go on to protect 230 million acres (930,777 sq km) of American wilderness. Under Roosevelt, five new national parks were created and the Antiquities Act was passed, enabling presidents to protect national monuments – many of which would later become parks.

The Oval Office was where he did his best work, but Roosevelt was most at home in the Badlands backcountry, where he operated two ranches. The region turned from hunting ground to healing

ground when his wife and his mother died within hours of each other on Valentine's Day, 1884, and he sought sanctuary in the wilderness.

After Roosevelt himself died in 1919, three years after the National Park Service was established, the region was explored as a possible park site. By 1935 the Roosevelt Recreation Demonstration Area had been established; 11 years later it became the Theodore Roosevelt National Wildlife Refuge. President Truman created the Theodore Roosevelt National Memorial Park in 1947 – the only National Memorial Park ever established – and in 1978 it was reclassified as Theodore Roosevelt National Park.

Toolbox

When to go
The park is open year-round, but most visitors aim for the long summer days. Winter commonly sees road closures. Wildflowers bloom in late spring and early fall.

Getting there
The park is spread across three separate units in western North Dakota. The South Unit entrance is near Medora, reached via I-94. The North Unit is 70 miles away (113km), up I-85, en route to Watford City. Elkhorn Ranch is midway between them; it's best accessed via the South Unit.

Events
The Dakota Nights Astronomy Festival is on the last weekend in August.

Accessibility
All three visitor centers, plus picnic areas, are accessible. Accessible trails include Skyline Vista Overlook, Boicourt Overlook and the Little Mo Nature Trail.

Park in numbers

110 Area in sq miles
2855 Height of Buck Hill, the highest point (ft)
70 Optimum size of the wild horse population

Stay here...

 Cottonwood & Juniper Campgrounds
Picture this: you wake to a Badlands' birdlife ballad – and then, upon looking through the tent door, discover you're sharing a campground with a couple of bison. It's enough to make you feel like Teddy Roosevelt himself...and this scenario is a distinct possibility in the park's established campgrounds: Cottonwood in the South Unit and Juniper in the North Unit. Both sites occupy spots alongside the Little Missouri River, and both offer grills and picnic tables. Juniper is more serene, partly because the North Unit is less visited, but also because there's no traffic noise.

Backcountry camping
It's possible to camp in the backcountry for free with a Backcountry Permit. Horseback riders can camp in the backcountry, or stay at Roundup Group Horse Campground in the South Unit.

Rough Riders Hotel
In a great location near the South Unit Visitor Center, this place has ample charm in its modern, elegantly furnished rooms set in a historic 19th-century building.

Do this!

Wildlife-viewing
Following in Roosevelt's footsteps, people still come here to hunt animals – although cameras have now replaced rifles. The park boasts many mammals, including bison, feral horses, coyotes, elk, bighorn sheep, white-tailed and mule deer, and prairie dogs.

Canoeing & kayaking
An adventurous way of linking the park's three sections in summer is by taking a float trip down the Little Missouri River. It's 107.5 miles (173km) from Medora (near the South Unit) to Long X Bridge on US Hwy 85 (near the North Unit). A gentle paddle will take around five days (unless the water is low, when portages may be required).

Maah Daah Hey Trail
This spectacular trail, 144 miles (232km) in its entirety, links all three units of the park. It draws hikers, horseback riders and mountain bikers. The latter rate it as one of the country's toughest off-road cycle trails. There are nine developed campgrounds along the trail.

◀ Burly grazers in Theodore Roosevelt National Park.
▶ Watchful prairie dogs are a common sight in the park.

Hike this...

01 Wind Canyon Trail
A quick, 0.4-mile (0.6km) stroll along a wind-sculpted canyon in the South Unit rewards a half-hour's effort with fantastic views over the Little Missouri River – a great sunset-watching spot.

02 Caprock Coulee Loop
One of the best hikes in the park, this 4.4-mile (7.1km) North Unit trail takes you past forest, grasslands, and dramatic rock formations with panoramic views and wildlife watching en route (especially if you go early in the morning).

03 Jones/Talkington/ Paddock Loop
For a real overnight badlands backcountry adventure, try this 23.4-mile (37.7km) South Unit epic on for size. It combines the upper and lower Talkington and Paddock trails.

What to spot...

The diversity of its ecosystem is one of the park's biggest drawcards. Besides big-ticket, crowd-pleasing mammals, such as mountain lion and bison, the park has 186 species of bird, including golden eagles, ruby-throated hummingbirds, sharp-tailed grouse, wild turkeys, belted kingfishers and several species of owl. Some are permanent, others migratory. Remember that bison and feral horses can be dangerous – take care during backcountry encounters. The venomous prairie rattlesnake is particularly active during warmer months.

PORCUPINE Charismatic Badlands residents, porcupines can often be seen alongside the park's roads at nighttime, and during daylight hours in trees and bushes feeding on twigs.

FERAL HORSE Found only in the South Unit (and often seen by people exploring the Scenic Loop Dr), the park's feral horses are descendants of domestic stock.

PASQUEFLOWER In April, this is typically the first flower to burst into bloom: its appearance is seen as an announcement that spring has arrived in the Badlands.

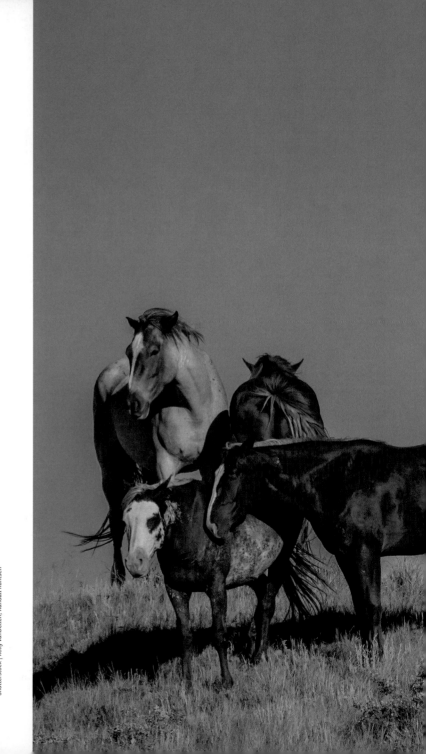

Itineraries

Explore the Scenic Loop Dr, watch bison, longhorn steers and prairie dogs on Little Missouri National Grassland or hike through junipers into Painted Canyon.

← The feral horses of the park are carefully managed.
➡ The cabin at Theodore Roosevelt's Maltese Cross Ranch.

01

A day

Stopping in at the South Unit's Medora Visitor Center, learn about the park's history, and the life and legacy of the man it's named for, before exploring the preserved Maltese Cross Cabin – Roosevelt's first residence here and a building that's survived a series of remarkable journeys. Then it's time to experience the wilderness and wildlife that so inspired the president-to-be with a counter-clockwise spin around the 36-mile (58km) Scenic Loop Dr, keeping your eyes peeled for prairie dogs and bison as you go.

Punctuate the drive with short hikes to get a proper taste of the park, starting with a stroll along the Ridgeline Walk, armed with a brochure about the region's ecology. A little further around is the short, steep climb to the park's highest accessible point, Buck Hill.

With the sun sinking fast, pick a place to watch it set – from the highpoint at the end of the Boicourt Overlook Trail, with its vista across the Badlands, or from the Wind Canyon Trail, where views extend over the Little Missouri River.

02

Two days

After a day exploring the South Unit, watch the setting sun turn the Badlands crimson, then head to Cottonwood Campground. Above your tent the Milky Way spills across the sky. Wake early and drive 70 miles (113km) to the park's North Unit. Greet the first rays of light at the Oxbow Overlook, where the Little Missouri takes a dramatic turn to the east

Behemoth bison feed on the lawns of the expansive grassland, and there's a small herd of longhorn steers, a living history exhibit maintained in memory of the days when these magnificent animals were driven along the Long X Trail by cowboys – a lifestyle that captivated Roosevelt. To continue the wildlife theme, hike a short section of the Buckhorn Trail to a prairie dog town to observe a community of these photogenic rodents. Return to the car: the River Bend Overlook awaits, and it's a fitting finale, delivering fine views of the colorful river.

03

Four or more days

With more time, explore the park's North Unit first, spending a night at the Juniper Campground and doing a day-hike along the whole Buckhorn Trail.

En route to the South Unit, stop to explore Painted Canyon, where a nature walk takes you through rock layers and junipers into the canyon itself – the perfect place for a picnic lunch. To investigate some of the park's less trodden trails, dedicate a day to doing the Petrified Forest Loop. This stunning hike loops around the northwest corner of the South Unit, threading through ancient petrified forests and raw Badlands wilderness before returning along a section of the Maah Daah Hey Trail.

Round your trip off with an adventure to the undeveloped site of Roosevelt's Elkhorn Ranch, found in a remote area of the park 35 miles (56km) north of Medora. This refuge, the third unit of the park, was the conservationist president's true Badlands home – and it's not hard to see why he fell in love with it.

55

VI

Virgin Islands National Park

These 15,000 acres of jade-green mountains, sugar-white sands and reef-studded turquoise seas make for one of America's most breathtaking parks.

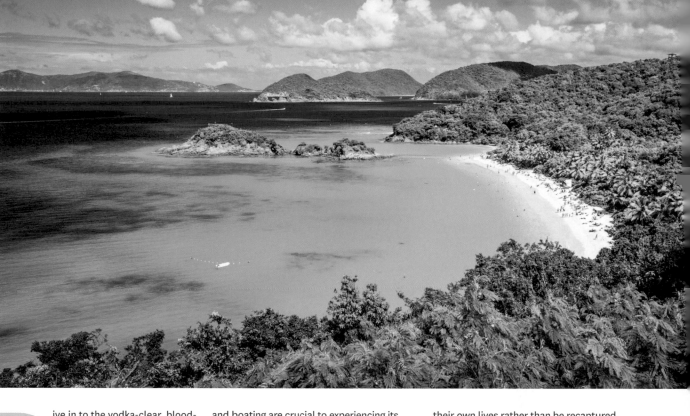

Dive in to the vodka-clear, blood-warm waters of the Caribbean Sea, gently kicking your flippers as you glide over reefs, rocks and gardens of swaying seagrass. Gaze down at healthy sea fans and plate coral, all increasingly rare in the world today, due to warming oceans. To your right, a spotted eagle ray with a wingspan longer than you flies through the ocean like a strange bird. To your left, a green sea turtle – born when the US was still fighting WWI – nibbles experimentally on a rock. Everywhere around you, fish in all the colors of a Crayola box flit hither and thither.

Some 40% of Virgin Islands National Park is underwater, so snorkeling, diving, swimming and boating are crucial to experiencing its beauty. The above-water parts of the park ain't bad either, with mountains tumbling towards the sea, and miles of pale-sand beaches and hidden coves.

Native Carib and Arawak people lived on these islands before the arrival of Columbus, leaving behind petroglyphs and other artifacts. Danish settlers arrived here in the 1600s, planting sugar and cotton with the labor of enslaved Africans. In 1733, 150 enslaved people on St John revolted against their enslavers, one of the first such rebellions in the Americas. Danish officials begged for help from the French in nearby Martinique, who sent a militia to put down the rebellion; many enslaved people took

their own lives rather than be recaptured. Slavery would not be abolished in the Danish West Indies for more than a century.

Denmark sold the Danish West Indies to the United States in 1917. On a Caribbean cruise, Standard Oil heir (and UFO fan) Laurance Rockefeller fell in love with the area. He acquired 5000 acres (20 sq km) of land, which he donated to the federal government. The park was established in 1956. In 2017, Hurricanes Irma and Maria ravaged the islands, eroding beaches, destroying infrastructure, and damaging reefs.

⬆ St John's Trunk Bay is the islands' most popular beach.
➡ Sea stars at Leinster Bay.

Toolbox

When to go
The weather is generally lovely year-round, but June through November is hurricane season. Accommodations are most expensive December through April.

Getting there
The park covers 60% of the island of St John and nearly all of nearby Hassel Island. To get to St John, fly into St Thomas, cross the island via car or taxi, and take the ferry. You'll want a car to explore. Cruz Bay, on the west side, is the main settlement.

Events
Late June and early July's St John Festival, commemorating the end of slavery, makes Cruz Bay hop.

Accessibility
Trunk Bay has beach wheelchairs and accessible parking and services. Francis Bay has a wheelchair accessible boardwalk trail, and Annaberg Plantation has an accessible path.

Park in numbers

23 Area in sq miles
133,000 Annual visitors
302 Species of fish here

Stay here...

Cinnamon Bay Campground
The hurricanes that swept through the Caribbean in 2017 destroyed the only campground within the park's boundaries. At the time of writing, operators hoped it would reopen for the 2021 season, but check the concessionaire's website (www.cinnamonbayresort.com) for the latest updates.

Estate Lindholm
Set amid 18th-century Danish plantation ruins, this upscale 17-room B&B is a quick walk from the park boundary. It's family-run and earns high marks for friendliness. The hillside location, on the east side of Cruz Bay, makes for its scrumptious ocean views.

Concordia Eco Resort
South of Coral Bay on the island's east coast, this sustainability-minded spot is continuing to rebuild from Hurricane Irma. Sleep in sunny studios amid tangled vegetation on the hillside overlooking Salt Pond Bay, each with its own deck for lazy evenings. The beach is a 15-minute hike away.

Do this!

Snorkeling
Put on fins and a mask and dive into a psychedelic wonderland. The sea floors of Honeymoon Bay and Hawksnest Bay sprout delicate elkhorn coral and dance with iridescent fish. At Trunk Bay, an 'underwater trail' has plaques explaining the wildlife. It's crowded, but good for beginners. Maho Bay's seagrass makes for prime sea-turtle spotting. Soft corals have recovered from the 2017 hurricanes; hard corals, such as elkhorn, will take longer.

Fishing
For many, a day spent casting into the park's teeming waters is the best part of the trip. Depending on the time of year, the quarry includes yellowfin, tiger grouper, blue runner and bonito. Tarpon and bonefish are catch-and-release only; check the NPS website for other restrictions.

Beach-going
The best thing about Virgin Islands National Park is that you don't have to do anything more than snooze on a beach and get up occasionally to cool down in the sparkling surf. Popular Trunk Bay has lifeguards, showers and a snack bar. Honeymoon Beach, a bone-white paradise straight out of a brochure, is best reached by a 30-minute hike.

See this...

01 Yawzi Point
Poke around Dutch colonial stone house ruins and hidden rocky beaches around this 0.3-mile (0.5 km) stretch of forest.

02 Francis Bay Boardwalk
This family-friendly elevated 0.5-mile (0.8km) walkway follows the edge of a salt pond and passes through bird-filled mangrove forests, ending in a lovely crescent-shaped beach.

03 Cinnamon Bay Trail
Follow the old Danish plantation road for 1 mile (1.6km) through the jungle, passing old sugar factory ruins and stopping at an overlook for dazzling ocean views.

What to spot...

With emerald mountains plunging towards the shoreline, Virgin Islands have a dramatic variety of ecosystems. Subtropical forests, salt ponds, cactus scrubland and mangroves are alive with birds like smooth-billed ani, bright warblers and tiny hummingbirds. In the park's vast underwater precincts, living reefs teem with tropical fish and dolphins, and sea turtles stop by for a bite. At twilight, bats – the island's only native mammals – swoop and dive in the purple sky.

MANGROVES These tangle-branched shoreline trees live in brackish water, their underwater roots serving as nurseries for all manner of fish, sharks and algae.

BANANAQUIT These small, yellow-bellied birds are ubiquitous throughout the Virgin Islands (they even show up on the state seal), flitting from flowers to branches to shrubs.

GREEN SEA TURTLE The largest of the hard-shelled turtles, these mammoths can grow to 500lb (227kg). Maho Bay is known as a good turtle-spotting location.

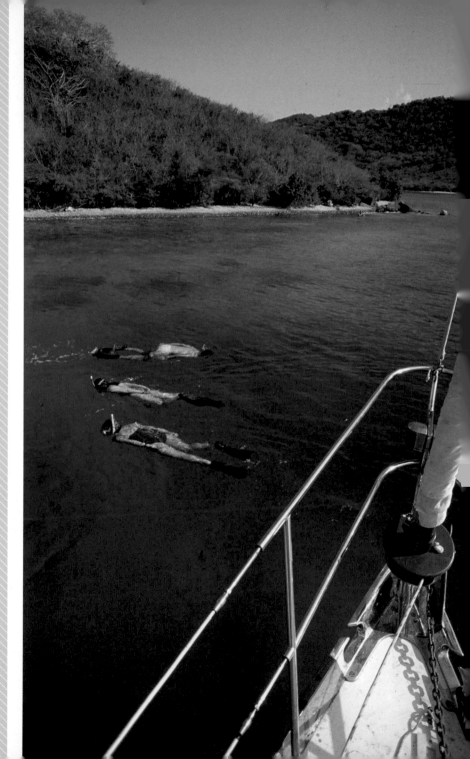

Itineraries

Snorkelers will love Trunk Bay's Underwater Trail, Maho Bay or Coral Bay. On land, hike the Reef Bay Trail or bird-watch at Francis Bay.

◄ Snorkelers in Leinster Bay.
➡ A sugar mill at the Annaberg Plantation ruins. Lucky snorkelers may spot a green sea turtle.

01

Two days

Base yourself in Cruz Bay, still lively despite the post-hurricane decline in visitors. It's the easiest jumping-off point to explore your surroundings: hike through the deep, wet forest to the spooky ruins of the Annaberg sugar plantation, swim to the tiny island in the middle of the bay's azure waters and lounge in the powdery sand. If you're feeling ambitious in the afternoon, head west to Trunk Bay, where the Underwater Trail is a top choice for newbie snorkelers. For dinner, it's back to Cruz Bay to sample pan-Caribbean specialties like grilled mahi mahi with rum and mango sauce at Morgan's Mango. The next day, wake for an early swim before setting off on a day cruise. Look out for dolphins and sea turtles as you sail the clear water, anchoring in quiet coves for splashing and snorkeling. Watch the sun set a furious orange as you head back to port. That night, treat yourself to a Frozen Painkiller (rum, coconut cream, pineapple, orange, and nutmeg) and a poke bowl at the Longboard, a popular casual spot.

02

Five days

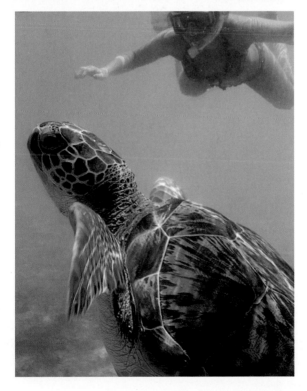

On day one, take a scenic drive along North Shore Rd, stopping for a dip at Hawksnest Bay and Trunk Bay, two of the best-recovered and most popular beaches. Day two, snorkel Maho Bay, keeping your eyes open for sea turtles, octopuses and angel fish. Walk the short trail around nearby Francis Bay, a top bird-watching area. On day three, explore Annaberg Plantation, the atmospheric stone ruins of a plantation where enslaved people once harvested sugar cane. Afterwards hike down to Leinster Bay and swim across to tiny Waterlemon Cay for some of the park's best snorkeling. Have dinner in Cruz Bay; its west-facing location offers superb sunsets. Take a yacht tour on day four or do a scuba trip, scouring the depths for rays and nurse sharks. On your last day, book a guided kayak tour along the island's coastline, where rainbow-colored fish swim under your boat as you paddle.

56

MN

Voyageurs National Park

Once a thoroughfare for French fur traders, who traveled thousands of miles each summer, this national park near the border with Canada is now a watery playland for boaters in search of big fish.

If only these rocks could talk. That thought inevitably crosses one's mind while standing on exposed two-billion-year-old granite – that's half the age of planet Earth – looking out over the yawning expanse of 24,000-acre (97 sq km) Lake Kabetogama. In total, Voyageurs National Park encompasses four massive, linked lakes that stretch 56 miles (90km) long. The Ojibwe Indians have lived in this region for centuries and were crucial trading partners with the French Voyageurs traveling from Montreal in search of 'soft gold' – the beaver pelts that kept all of Europe in hats until the mid-1800s. Prospectors found actual gold on Little America Island in 1893, and in the early 1900s timber barons logged the entire region. A few of the old-growth white pines remain, reminding visitors just how majestic the forest here once was.

Established in 1975, Voyageurs National Park is 39% water. Below its surface swim trophy walleye, northern pike and smallmouth bass. Above water, bald eagles stalk prey from the top of stately pines and loons trill haunting cries from one lake to the next. Unlike Minnesota's Boundary Waters Canoe Area Wilderness, which is directly east, motorized boats are allowed in Voyageurs, which makes the park more accessible to families, and folks who may not want to heft a canoe from lake to lake. While the four big lakes – Rainy, Kabetogama, Namakan, and Sand Point – are the main draw, the 75,000-acre (304 sq km) Kabetogama Peninsula wilderness is dotted with chains of smaller lakes.

The park is a different world in the winter. Ski, snowshoe or snowmobile the vast white expanse, or try the – underrated! – sport of ice fishing. Northern Minnesota often records the lowest temperatures in the Lower 48, but the payoff is the sight of a solitary wolf running across a frozen lake, the dancing emerald pulse of the Northern Lights or a fresh walleye dinner in January.

⬆ All the park's campsites are only accessible by watercraft but canoes and rowboats can be rented.

Stay here...

 Kettle Falls Hotel
This historic hotel at the junction of Rainy and Namakan lakes, built by a timber baron in 1910, was the epicenter of bootlegging during Prohibition. A short hop from the Canadian border and 15 miles (24km) from the closest road, the only way in is by float plane or boat (the hotel offers waterside transfers). Choose from an antique-filled hotel room or a villa that sleeps up to eight people.

 Woodenfrog State Forest Campground
Carved out of the boreal forest on Lake Kabetogama's shore, each of the 60 sites at this primitive campground

feel luxuriously private. There's a beautiful strip of beach for all and easy access to the lake, which makes this a budget-friendly jumping off point for adventures in the park. You can rent canoes and kayaks, or have a meal at the nearby Arrowhead Lodge

Northern Lights Resort
Sitting pretty overlooking Lake Kabetogama, this longstanding favorite offers well-equipped all-wood cabins with one to five bedrooms; the best have fireplaces and decks with sweeping lake views. You can hire canoes, kayaks and motorboats and get loads of tips on park exploring.

Do this!

 Fishing
A Minnesota rite of passage, walleye are exciting to catch because they are so unpredictable. They swim deeper in the hottest months and feed right before sunrise or after sunset, but they also show up in unusual places (and are delicious to eat).

Canoeing
There's nothing as peaceful as paddling through a lake, listening to the wind whistle through the white pines. Paddle quietly enough and you'll become part of the scene, in which a mama duck may be shepherding her ducklings, a loon is trilling its cross-lake call to a wayward

mate, or a moose is crashing through the underbrush on the shoreline. Voyageurs Outfitters offers canoe hire from all park visitor centers, and runs a range of guided trips. They'll also ferry you out to remote campsites.

Cross-country skiing & snowshoeing
Most years from late November to April, the park is a silent expanse of white. It may seem frozen and lifeless, but the park is magical at this time of year – packs of timber wolves sprint across the lakes, 20lb northern pike lurk under the ice, and snowy owls take flight. Hire skis and snowshoes from the Rainy Lake Visitor Center.

What to spot...

Dense with birch, aspen, spruce, and pine, this northern boreal forest is alive with wild critters, including moose, bear, wolves, fox, white-tailed deer and beaver. Most don't announce their presence, but the more time you spend in these woods, the more signs of wildlife you'll see everywhere – domed beaver dams rise out of swampy lakes, eagles' nests balance atop dead trees, and pine needles from the lowest branches of balsam fir trees have mysteriously disappeared, the handiwork of hungry moose.

LOON This iconic black-and-white symbol of the north has exotic red eyes and a speckled body that disappears into the mottled shimmer of the lake. Unlike most birds, the loon has solid bones, which make it a powerful diver. Its most enduring feature is its eerie, unmistakable call.

BEAVER Hunted almost to extinction by the mid-1800s for the fur that supplied most of the fashionable hats in Europe, the beaver has bounced back. These fascinating herbivores spend the winter under the ice, feeding on tree branches they stored up over the winter.

BALD EAGLE This once-endangered symbol of the USA has flourished under its protective status. It's still a thrill to see this massive, white-and-gray raptor perched at the top of a white pine, silently stalking its prey.

Hike this...

01 Cruiser Lake Trail
This 9.5-mile (15.3km) hike, accessible via boat from Rainy or Kabetogama lakes, allows you to get deep into the interior wetlands – where you may see moose.

02 Anderson Bay Trail
Off Rainy Lake, this 1.75-mile (2.8km) loop ascends a white granite cliff where you'll have staggering views over tiny islets and the North Woods abutting the water's edge.

03 Blind Ash Bay
The 3-mile (4.8km) trail starts at the Ash River Visitor Center and traverses a steep grade to an overlook of Kabetogama Lake before plunging back into the pines.

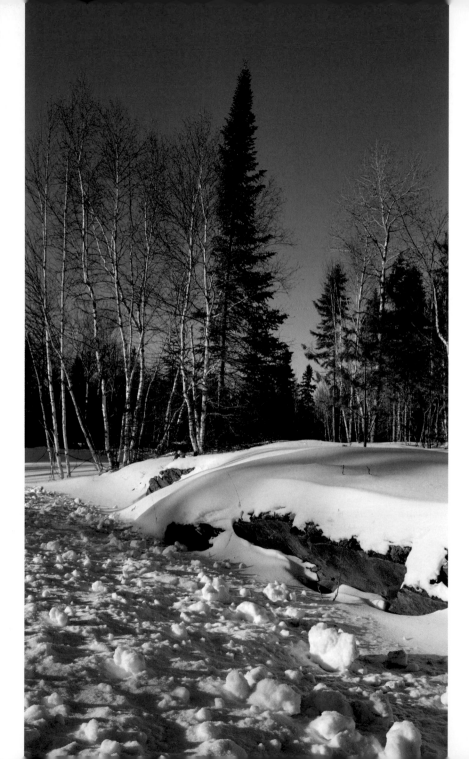

Toolbox

When to go
The park is officially open year-round, but only one of three visitor centers, Rainy Lake, is open in the winter. To beat the heat, the mosquitoes and the crowds, visit in September. For the best walleye fishing visit in the spring or fall.

Getting there
Just south of the Canadian border, Voyageurs is 275 miles (443km) directly north of state capital Minneapolis, roughly a five-hour drive. All three visitor centers are easily accessible off US Hwy 53.

Events
In late July, the Crane Lake community features canoe rides, music, food and family activities. In August, Ranier hosts a summer festival.

Accessibility
All three visitor centers are accessible, as are all NPS boats. The Kabetogama Lake Overlook (a 0.2 mile trail) and the first quarter mile of the Oberholtzer Trail are accessible.

Park in numbers

341 Area in sq miles
550 Length of shoreline (miles)
500 Number of islands

Itineraries

Canoe your way down War Club, Quill and Loiten lakes; hike the Cruiser Lake Trail or rent a houseboat for an extended trip.

← Lost Lake campground; a wintery scene. → Canoeing is a calming way to get around.

01
Two days

Far from the interstate and fast-food America, Voyageurs is a destination park that requires a few days and a good boat to fully explore. Start off by paddling in a 26ft (8m) 'North Canoe,' a replica of the massive boats the Voyageurs paddled in the 1700s; book ahead for this tour departing from the Kabetogama Visitor Center. Later that day learn about the park's history and its watery expanse, by visiting the historic Ash River Visitor Center, housed in a log cabin built in 1935. Nearby, you can experience the park's beauty on the Blind Ash Bay Trail. The walk through boreal forest culminates with a panoramic view over Kabetogama Lake. On day two hire a boat or arrange a water taxi (Border Guide Service is one reliable outfitter) and head over to Lost Bay where you can take some fabulous hikes into the misty forests. Highlights include Jorgens Lake, Elk Lake and Cruiser Lake. Keep an eye out for moose, beavers and bald eagles. End the evening stargazing in the pollution-free skies (star charts are available at the visitor centers).

02
Four days

Experience the best of both worlds – the big water of Lake Kabetogama and the smaller inland lakes on Kabetogama Peninsula. Camp at Woodenfrog State Forest Campground and get an early start the next morning before the waves get big. Paddle your own boat or a rental northeast to the trailhead of Locator Lake Trail; stash the boat and portage the gear 1.9 miles (3km) into Locator Lake, where you'll find more of the park's canoes (be sure to pick up a key from any of the three visitor centers to access a boat from the park's supply of inland-lake canoes). Paddle across the lake to the campsite and spend the next two days exploring the daisy chain of War Club, Quill and Loiten lakes (all of which have their own park canoes, so no portaging is necessary). The thrill of canoeing here is that the weather can change quickly, forcing even skilled campers to stay on their toes. Whether paddling on a mirror-calm lake, surfing 3ft (1m) swells or emergency bivvying through a storm, every day is unique.

03
Six days

Since almost half of the park is water, skip land-based accommodations and opt for a houseboat, especially if your priority is fishing, sunning and finding secluded swimming holes. The freedom of going in any direction at any time of day is addictive. But the quality of rental houseboats varies greatly across the four lakes, so do some homework before paying a deposit. (The fleet at Voyagaire Lodge & Houseboats is one of the best.) Starting at the southern end of Crane Lake, there's 56 miles (90km) of park to explore. Putter through Sand Point Lake to the Kettle Falls Historic District on the north end of Namakan, or stop off to hike the beautiful 1.75 mile (2.8km) Anderson Bay Trail off Rainy Lake. Park rules require that the boat be moored at night, but maritime maps mark all of the well-spaced and secluded overnight camping sites. Hiring a fishing boat with a motor is required (per Coast Guard rules) for every houseboat, so anyone onboard can check the lunar tables and sneak away during peak fishing hours.

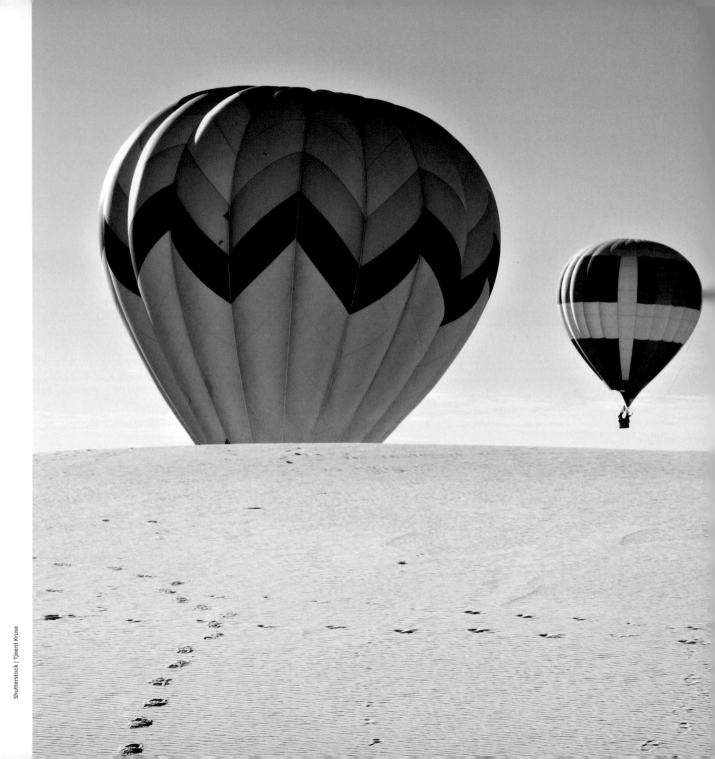

57

NM

White Sands National Park

The scenic drive plunges visitors into a photogenic land of shifting white sands where animals adapt, plants hold tight and plastic saucers swoop down sand dunes.

Shutterstock | Tjeerd Kruse

Trains of white gypsum sand dance and skitter across Dunes Drive in America's newest national park, drawing you forward with a hypnotic pull. And when the pavement ends, the hard-packed road merges into an otherworldly sea of white. As you squint at the horizon from your car, it's hard to decide if this is a futuristic landscape straight from your favorite sci-fi novel or a dip into Alice's Wonderland. The metallic Interdune Boardwalk and the park's silver picnic pods look like they dropped in from the future, and missile tests launched at the nearby White Sands Missile Range occasionally force the closure of park grounds. As for Alice's Wonderland, the animals and plants that call this striking place home have adapted to the landscape and its dangers with cartoonish yet ingenious efficiency: pale blue lizards have disposable "breakaway" tails and tiny white pocket mice sport fur pouches on their snouts, primed to efficiently store seeds. A few hardscrabble plants poke up though the sands, their complex root systems holding tight against the impetuous grains.

How did this unusual place come to be? Hundreds of millions of years ago a vast sea covered the Southwest. As its waters rose and fell, it shed layers of minerals, including gypsum. Over the millennia, tectonic plates beneath the region collided and retracted, forming today's mountain ranges. The plates then pulled further apart, forming basins. The Tularosa Basin filled with sediments carried down from the mountains by the Rio Grande. These sediments eventually blocked the outlets that once carried the water to the sea. Today, rain and

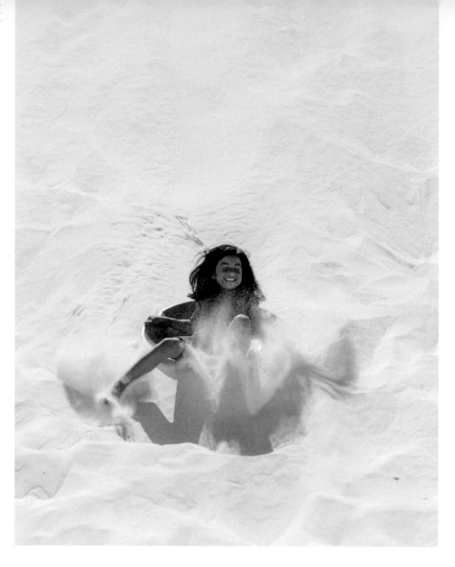

snowmelt form temporary lakes. The water evaporates, leaving small grains of white gypsum to blow and gather into dunes. This shimmering white backdrop is a photographer's dream. Colors pop against the bright white sand during the day while the sky glows in luminous lavenders and pinks above the dunes as the sun goes down.

⬆ Beg, borrow or buy a sled for some sandy, sliding fun. Previous page: the annual White Sands Balloon Fiesta at Alamogordo.

President Herbert Hoover established White Sands National Monument in 1933, with the purpose of preserving its unique features. It became the country's 62nd national park in December 2019.

Toolbox

When to go
Conditions vary throughout the year. Your best bet is fall, when days are sunny and daytime temperatures average 80° F (27° C). Spring can get windy. Temperatures from June through August average 95°F (35°C).

Getting there
The park is 225 miles (362km) south of Albuquerque via I-25, about a 3½ hour drive. The closest airport is in El Paso, TX, which is 85 miles (137km) south of the park. There is no public transportation to the park or within the park.

Events
On the six Full Moon Nights (Apr–Oct) the park stays open late and hosts programs. Held in July, Mothapalooza celebrates the park's endemic moths.

Accessibility
The 0.4-mile (650m) round-trip Interdune Boardwalk is an elevated and wheelchair-accessible trail with exhibits about wildlife and geology.

Park in numbers
225 Area in sq miles
60 Highest dunes (ft)
4.5 Mass of gypsum sand in dunefield (billion tons)

Stay here...

Backcountry camping

With star-studded skies and rolling dunes as your backdrop, an overnight in one of ten backcountry campsites feels like an exotic adventure. No water or toilets are available, and you should pack a map and compass. But camping isn't too treacherous – you're only required to hike one-mile from the scenic drive. Permits ($3 per person) available at the Entrance Booth on Dunes Dr.

Cloudcroft Mountain Park Hostel

On the western outskirts of high-elevation Cloudcroft, this lurid-blue hostel on 28 woodsy acres is the best lodging deal around. Entire families can fit in the large rooms, which are simple but tidy. Shared bathrooms are clean, and there's a fully equipped kitchen with coffee and tea. The hostel is 30 miles from the park.

Aguirre Spring Campground

This appealing campground wins you over with its breathtaking setting. Perched beneath the spires of the Organ Mountains on a lofty wooded slope, campsites have a sweeping view of White Sands National Park and the vast Tularosa Basin.

Do this!

Scenic Driving

Dunes Drive, an easy 16-mile (25km) scenic road, swoops into the heart of the world's largest gypsum dune field, which covers 275 sq miles. Along the way, get out of the car to romp in the sand, enjoy a picnic in a silver pod or escape the crowds on a hike into a dune field. Don't forget your sunglasses – the sand is as bright as snow.

Sledding

Those hankering for a thrilling downhill plunge can hop onto a waxed plastic saucer then hold on tight as they swoosh down a dune. Spring for a saucer at the visitor center gift shop (new/used $19/$10); you can sell it back at day's end (new/used $5/3).

Outdoor Learning

White Sands may be a small park, but it offers a super-sized schedule of tours that spotlight its unique characteristics. Nightly sunset strolls focus on plants, wildlife and geology. Rangers share unique stories about the park under a lunar-lit sky on the monthly full-moon hikes (Apr-Oct). Visitors learn how the rare and valuable dunes were created on the monthly Lake Lucero tour (Nov-Mar).

What to spot...

The dunes may look devoid of life, but this ethereal landscape hosts more than 800 animal species. A variety of plant life grows here too, from cacti to desert grasses to a handful of hardy trees. One common trait across species? Adaptability. Mammals are often nocturnal, scavenging and hunting at night when temperatures are cooler. Animals lower on the food chain use camouflage, speed and disposable appendages to evade their predators. Plants are equally hardy, growing tall or toughening up their root systems to withstand the ever-shifting sands.

APACHE POCKET MOUSE These impossibly cute foragers store seeds in fur-lined pouches growing on the side of their cheeks. They carry the seeds back to their burrows. Efficient kidneys allow the tiny rodents to live for weeks without water.

LITTLE WHITE WHIPTAIL Found only in White Sands National Park, these long-bodied lizards can shake free of their tails to escape predators. Speed and their pale-blue and white coloring are additional survival tools. They sniff out prey with their forked tongue.

PROTOGYGIA WHITESANDSENSIS Discovered in 2007, this white moth was the first moth species new to science ever found in the park. More than 60 new species of moth have subsequently been discovered here. The Protogygia Whitesandsensis lives nowhere else on Earth, making it endemic to White Sands.

➡ The park protects the largest gypsum dunefield in the world. Look also for huge selenite crystals, the crystalline form of gypsum, around Lake Lucero.

Hike this...

01 Interdune Boardwalk
Lined with informative exhibits, this pet-friendly elevated boardwalk unfurls above the sand and rolls into a dune field. The trail is .4 miles (650m) round-trip.

02 Dunes Life Nature Trail
Scan for animal tracks on this one-mile (1.6km) family friendly loop where you might see paw prints from badgers, kit foxes and rodents. Follow the blue markers labeled with a playing-card club sign.

03 Alkali Flat Trail
Ready to ditch the crowds? The Alkali Flat Trail – a five-mile (8km) out-and-back – will oblige. This sandy path climbs up and down dunes before ending beside a dry lakebed. The trail is considered strenuous.

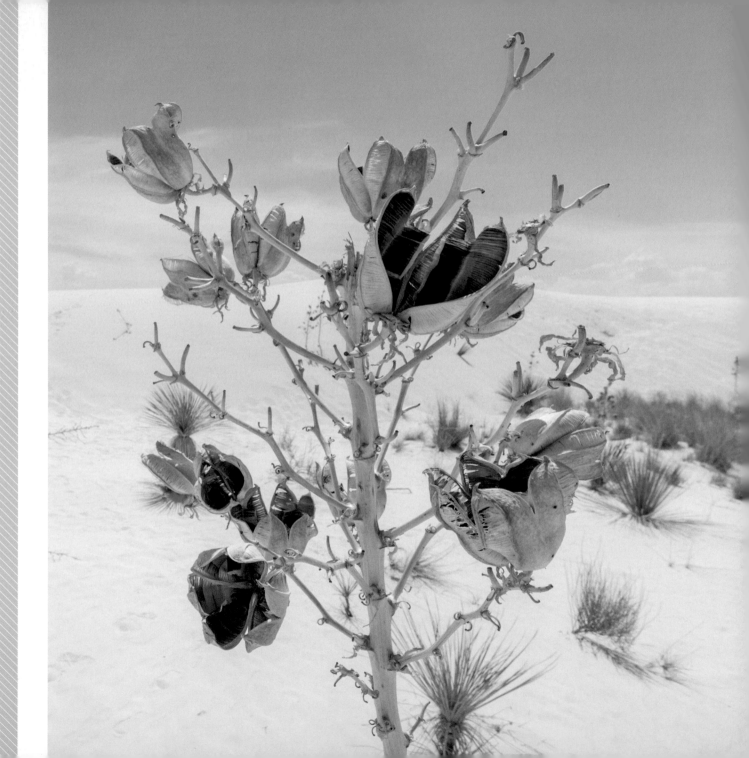

Itineraries

Otherworldly adventures include a stroll on an elevated metal boardwalk, a picnic in a space-age silver pod, a hike into the shimmering sands and a final swoosh down a dune on a plastic saucer.

 Some plants survive in the sand, such as this yucca.
 The New Mexico Museum of Space history has quite a collection of missiles.

01
One day

Stop by the visitor center to peruse the ranger talk schedule, stroll the desert nature garden and view the film *Land in Motion*. And pop into the gift shop to buy a plastic saucer – sledding is in your future! If you haven't packed a picnic, sandwiches and cold drinks are for sale.

Just beyond the entrance station, the 16-mile (26km) round-trip Dunes Drive lures you forward with the promise of the Interdune Boardwalk. Here, a short trail heads into the dunes on an elevated boardwalk, where exhibits introduce you to the many wonders of the landscape.

Back in your car, the dunes become more pronounced at mile four when the pavement ends. At six miles, look for just the right dune area to picnic and play. You'll have several choices as you circle the loop at the end of the drive. Spend the next hour or two sledding the dunes, tossing a Frisbee and enjoying lunch. The Alkali Flat Trail starts at the end of the scenic drive. This five-mile trail is strenuous, so just go as far as you like to get a feel for the landscape. End your day with a ranger-led sunset stroll.

02
Two days

Follow the one-day itinerary but skip the ranger-led sunset walk and begin your own backcountry hike. At your campsite you'll be hugged by the dunes and dazzled by the stars. Sites are first-come, first served and require a one-mile hike from Dunes Drive. Get a permit ($3 per person) at the entrance booth. On your drive out of the park in the morning, explore the short trails you skipped the prior day: the Dune Life Trail showcases animal life in the park while the new Ice Age Trail, a loop trail scheduled to open in 2021 or so, will spotlight the fossilized footprints of mammoths, giant ground sloths and dire wolves as well as thousands of human footprints. One Saturday per month from November through March, rangers lead morning tours of Lake Lucero. These hikes discuss the creation of the distinctive dunes.

With its sprawling deserts and sunny skies, southern New Mexico has long been a test ground for missiles, rockets, bombs and spacecraft. To learn about the region's space-age history, leave the park and drive 20 miles northeast to Alamogordo. Spend an hour perusing exhibits about space exploration at the New Mexico Museum of Space History, a four-story cube surrounded by historic missiles. Grab lunch then drive 40 minutes north to the Three Rivers Petroglyph Site, where six centuries ago the Jornada Mogollon people incised more than 21,000 petroglyphs onto boulders atop a low ridge.

Your adventure ends two miles above the desert in Cloudcroft, home to an early-19th-century downtown surrounded by hiking and biking trails in Lincoln National Forest. Sip a craft beer at Cloudcroft Brewing Co then dig into a fine steak dinner at Rebecca's inside the Lodge Resort & Spa. Bed down amongst Victorian trappings at the Lodge or in the more casual Cloudcroft Mountain Park Hostel.

White Sands

58

SD

Wind Cave National Park

In the Black Hills of South Dakota, beneath prairie-roaming bison and backpackers, an apparently endless cave mysteriously breathes, whispering secrets from a hidden world.

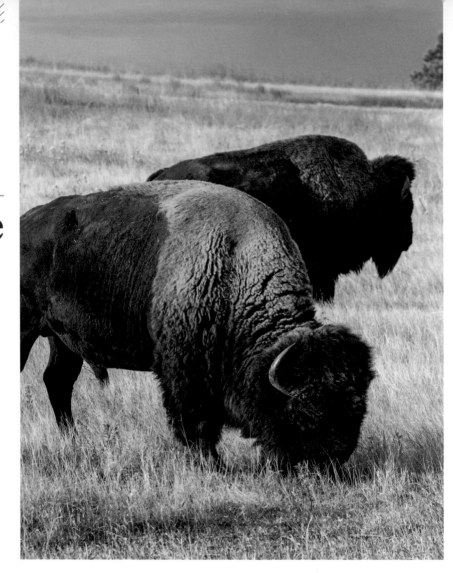

and out of the cave – but the effect is spellbinding.

The site has been sacred to the Sioux Nation Lakota for centuries, but in 1881 it caught the attention of two wandering white men, Tom and Jesse Bingham – apparently by knocking Tom's hat off with a dramatic exhalation. In 1890, the South Dakota Mining Company paid Jesse D McDonald to search the caves for potential bounty. He discovered no tangible treasure – but McDonald sensed he'd found something almost as lucrative as minerals.

With his family – notably his son, Alvin, who methodically mapped the caves – and a partner, McDonald began running candlelit tours of the cave. Within a few years, however, Alvin had died and the partnership with 'Honest John' Stabler turned sour, resulting in a court case about who owned the rights to the site. It was decided that neither party did, and in 1903 the region joined a clutch of unique wilderness areas to be protected by President Theodore Roosevelt, becoming one of the world's earliest national parks, and the first one focused on a cave.

But what few visitors expect from Wind Cave National Park, even now, is how much there is to see and do beyond the cave. Animals range across the park, including hundreds of bison, and there are 30 miles (48km) of hiking trails.

The subterranean universe of Wind Cave is an otherworldly place, where around 150 miles (240km) – and counting – of explored passages eventually give way to black holes that disappear still further into the shadows, leading to as-yet-unknown depths. The seemingly infinite caverns feature impossibly intricate 'boxwork' formations, 60- to 100-million-year-old honeycomb-like calcite formations that are seen almost nowhere else on the planet.

And yes, it's true. The cave does breathe. In and out, like a slumbering dragon. The scientific explanation is prosaic – it's the barometric pressure equalizing inside

⬆ The Wind Cave bison herd, one of the nation's most important in terms of genes, was restored more than 100 years ago.

➡ A resident great horned owl.

Toolbox

When to go
The cave and visitor center are open year-round, and the underground temperature remains a steady 53°F (12°C). Hiking is best enjoyed May to September, while wildflowers are a colorful attraction in spring.

Getting there
Wind Cave is between Hot Springs and Rapid City, less than an hour's drive from Mt Rushmore. From Rapid City, the scenic route is via Needles Highway, through Custer State Park to the park's north entrance. Large RVs and trailers go via Hot Springs. Driving through the park is free, but there's no public transportation.

Events
In the fall, bugling elk are a big draw to the Black Hills.

Accessibility
Short tours of the cave are available by advance booking. The entrance to Wind Cave, the visitor center, a picnic area and two campsites are accessible.

Park in numbers

53 Area in sq miles
149 Miles of known caves
400-450 Bison

Stay here...

Camping
Pitch your tent on a proper prairie, on the flanks of the Black Hills and at the edge of the forest, and let the wildlife come to you. Tent and RV sites are available at the park's mystifyingly quiet Elk Mountain Campground, which is open year-round and features fire pits, plus drinking water and flush restrooms from late spring to early fall. Deer are common visitors, there's an informative evening ranger program and the night sky here is spectacular.

Backcountry camping
In the northwest part of the park hikers can strike out along routes, including the Centennial Trail, and spend a night under the stars on the prairie. Primitive camping is free, but a Backcountry Permit form must be completed in the visitor center.

Blue Bell Lodge
In Custer State Park, a short drive north of Wind Cave, the Blue Bell has a mix of good-value accommodation, including four-person log cabins with stone fireplaces and vaulted ceilings. There's a decent restaurant and loads of activities in the nearby park (hiking, horse riding, kayaking, wildlife encounters).

Do this!

Caving

Naturally, it's the Wind Cave that pulls people in, and myriad tours allow visitors to explore many of the passages that have been mapped thus far. An interesting option is the Natural Entrance Cave Tour, where you can see the small hole that led to the original discovery of the cave. Beyond the standard Garden of Eden and slightly longer Fairgrounds tours, it's also possible to do some more-involved candlelit and crawling tours.

Wildlife-spotting
Beyond the cave, the park's impressive wildlife is a major attraction. Hundreds of bison roam freely across the small park – alongside pronghorn, mule deer, and prairie dogs – and visitors very commonly encounter these animals. Elk, which occupy the forests, can be heard bugling during fall.

Horseback riding
With 33,851 acres (137 sq km) of open prairie and forest, Wind Cave is ideal for exploring on horseback. Riders need to get a (free) permit, and avoid maintained trails and campgrounds. Guided trail rides are also available in adjoining Custer State Park.

Hike this...

01 Rankin Ridge Nature Trail
At the end of a scenic drive, this easy, 1-mile (1.6km) loop features 14 interpretive stops. You can't climb the tower, but the trail boasts good views of the Black Hills.

02 Boland Ridge Trail
One of the best walks for spotting wildlife this 5.2-mile (8.4km) roundtrip walk offers fine views of the Black Hills and Red Valley, with the possibility of seeing bison, elk and pronghorn.

03 Centennial Trail
A 6-mile (10km) section of this epic, 111-mile (179km) Black Hills trail takes hikers across prairies, through forests and along Beaver Creek. For a full-day outing, loop back along the Lookout Highland Creek Trail.

Getty Images | StefaniePayne; Shutterstock | Agnieszka Bacal

What to spot...

The park sits on a riparian seam where the mixed-grass prairie of the Great Plains runs into the ponderosa pine forest of the Black Hills, and this wonderful mix of terrain accommodates an eclectic range of wildlife. Several mammalian species hunted to near-extinction in the 19th century, including bison, have been successfully reintroduced. Bird species range from prairie falcons and meadowlarks to forest-dwelling nuthatches, owls, woodpeckers and wild turkeys.

BLACK-FOOTED FERRET Reintroduced to Wind Cave in 2007, these beautiful and rare animals help control the park's population of prairie dogs in the absence of apex predators, such as wolves.

PRAIRIE DOG Possibly the park's most popular characters, these sociable, rabbit-sized rodents build 'towns,' with dedicated sleeping quarters and toilets. They earned their 'dog' tag thanks to their canine-like bark.

PURPLE CONEFLOWER Each spring, wildflowers set the park's mixed-grass prairies ablaze. Besides looking pretty, the purple coneflower has been used by Native Americans here for centuries for its painkilling and curative properties.

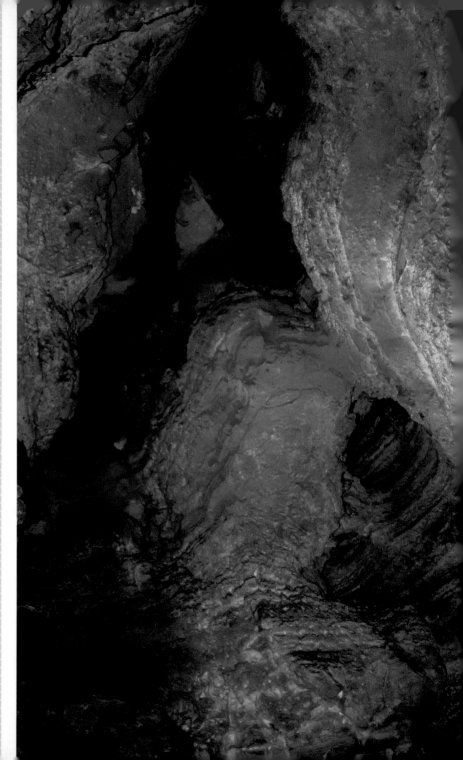

Itineraries

Hike Lookout Point Trail to Beaver Creek for wildlife watching, then choose between the Garden of Eden Tour or, for spelunkers, the Wind Cave Crawling Tour.

 Natural rock formations in one of the park's caverns. ➡ The park's pronghorn antelope feed on grasses and sagebrush.

01

One day

The visitor center's staff, exhibits and video displays do an admirable job of explaining the park's attractions – from its ultra-intriguing underworld to the richness of the prairie life on the surface. After getting an overview of Wind Cave's allure, visit the cave on a guided tour. The 90-minute Fairgrounds Tour takes you on a 0.6-mile (1km) subterranean stroll where you'll see some of the exquisite cave formations that Wind Cave is famous for, including boxwork, cave popcorn and flowstone.

Back above ground, you have time to explore the 1.2-mile (1.9km) Elk Mountain nature trail before taking a spin along the scenic drive, enjoying views of the Black Hills and spotting bison as you go. In Lakota tradition the first bison came from Wind Cave. From 1830, 40 million animals were killed in a 55-year period.

Reach Rankin Ridge with enough daylight left to check out the 1-mile (1.6km) nature trail before heading north on Highway 87, leaving the park behind.

02

Two days

After doing the one-day itinerary, get an early start on your second day. Set off on a 4.5-mile (7.2km) loop along Lookout Point Trail, returning on Centennial Trail. Beginning in the morning means you avoid the worst of the heat, and it also gives you a slightly better chance of seeing wildlife. The trail takes you across the undulations of the prairie and over Lookout Point to finish at Beaver Creek. Head back to the crossroad with Centennial Trail and follow that back to the trailhead. Explore the rest of the scenic drive, but keep one eye on your watch, because this afternoon you've booked a cave tour with a difference. The Candlelight Tour promises to take you back in time, to the end of the 19th century, when young Alvin McDonald was painstakingly making notes as he wandered around the unmapped underground wilderness into utterly unknown subterranean territory. It's a two-hour adventure that takes place in one of the less-trodden corners of the cave, and you can't wait.

03

Three or more days

The only way to really slip into Alvin McDonald's shoes is to sign up for the most extreme and exciting of the excursions into the park's caverns: the Wind Cave Crawling Tour. As the name implies, this will see you do some proper spelunking (under supervision of experts, of course). The tour takes place well away from the busier areas of the cave, and takes four hours in total. When you emerge, blinking, back into the sunlight, have a picnic in the area by the visitor center.

After exploring the nature walks around the center, it's time to go and bag a good pitch at the first-come-first-serve Elk Mountain Campground. Once you've seen the sun go down, lie on your sleeping mat and watch the sky come alive with a billion and one stars.

On the second day, break camp and begin another adventure, taking on a section of the Highland Creek Trail, spending a night out in the backcountry and then returning south on day three along the Centennial Trail.

59

AK

Wrangell-St Elias National Park

America's largest national park offers uncharted adventures among the peaks, rivers and glaciers of one of the world's last great frontiers.

Getty Images | Fotosearch

Kicking off expeditions into this nearly impenetrable wilderness is a challenge. But with the right skills, a healthy budget and a good helping of courage, a journey through this vast, 13.2-million-acre park – that's an area six times the size of Yellowstone – can deliver unprecedented solitude, adventure and chart-topping views.

This park is so big, so grand, so wild that you'll find hyperbole and superlatives on every corner. Not only is it the largest national park in the US, but if you combine its area with neighboring parks (Glacier Bay National Park and Preserve; Kluane National Park and Reserve; and the Tatshenshini-Alsek Provincial Wilderness Park in Canada), you have the world's largest international protected wilderness. Nine of the 16 highest peaks in the US are found here, including Mt St Elias, the second highest in the US. Take it from another perspective: the park starts at sea level and rises all the way to 18,008 ft (5488m). It's also home to a number of awe-inspiring glaciers. The Nabesna Glacier is 80 miles (129km) long, making it the longest non-polar valley glacier in the world, while the Malaspina Glacier is larger than the state of Rhode Island. You can top it all off with turn-of-the-20th-century mining towns; the sinuous Copper River, which is chock-full of salmon; an active volcano; and roaming herds of caribou.

Mostly covered in glaciers, ice and rocky mountaintops, the park has a fascinating geological past from its location at the corner of four major mountain ranges – the Wrangells to the north; the Chugach, on the southwest coast; the coastal St Elias Mountains, which rise from the Gulf of Alaska; and the eastern edge of the Alaska

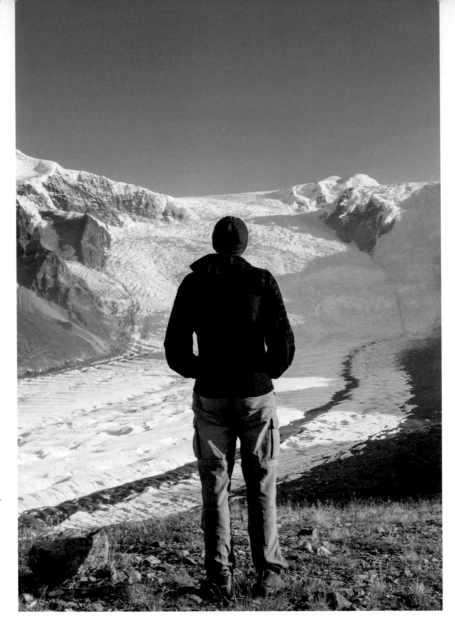

Range, which defines the park's northern border. All of this geological grandeur hides treasure beneath: between 1911 and 1938, mines in this region extracted huge amounts of gold and copper.

⬆ Glaciers cover a quarter of the park. ➡ The aurora borealis. Previous page: bush airplanes, like this Super Cub Piper, are the fastest way to explore the park.

Shutterstock | Galyna Andrushko; David_Pastyka

Toolbox

When to go
You can visit the park year round, but most people go from June to August. Visit at the edges of this high season and you may not find anybody staffing the visitor center or hotels.

Getting there
The McCarthy and Nabesna Rds take you to the edge of the wilderness and the park's two visitor centers, where you'll find a few old mining towns, lodges and short hikes. If you have the budget, hire a bush plane to drop you for remote hiking, climbing and paddling.

Events
McCarthy's eccentric underside roars wild on the Fourth of July with parades, hula-hoop contests, and music until the sun sets.

Accessibility
The main visitor center has a paved nature trail and accessible ramps. The historic Kennecott site has made some improvements in recent years to its accessibility.

Park in numbers
20,625 Area in sq miles
18,008 Height of Mt Elias (ft)
12 Volcanoes in the park

Stay here...

 Ultima Thule Lodge
This remote lodge on the Chitina River offers unexpected luxury in the middle of the bush. Rest up in the wood-hewn cabins before heading out on wild adventures. Room rates include a guide, bush plane service, equipment and al fresco lunch.

Ma Johnson's Hotel
Back in the mining heyday, McCarthy was the party and brothel district for wrung-out miners looking for some release after months working the Kennecott Mines. Ma Johnson's preserves the relics from this era, with small rooms featuring antiques and other rustic touches. The real treat here is sitting on the front porch as you plan your next day's adventure.

Public Use Cabins
This is the Alaskan experience at its finest. Fly in, or hike for a million miles, to stay in one of the park's 14 designated public-use cabins. Most were old prospector, trapping or hunting cabins. None are fancy but the public-use cabin at Peavine on the Chitistone River has been renovated to meet accessibility standards.

Do this!

Flightseeing
The scale and grandeur of this park only makes sense from the air. Head out for a once-in-a-lifetime flightseeing tour to see the mountaintops, glacier valleys, snowfields, rivers and untrammeled wilderness that make this one of the most iconic and dramatic mountain landscapes on earth. Add a stop in the bush for some unbelievable backwoods hikes

Rafting
Take a full-day float on the Kennicott, Nizina and Chitina rivers, with a return flight to McCarthy on a bush plane. The run through the steep-walled Nizina Canyon is a real highlight. Not far from here, the Copper River Delta offers spectacular birding and some easy canoeing.

Glacier hiking
Traveling on a glacier is an otherworldly experience that's both transformative and just a bit scary – these moving frozen flows are masterworks of nature. Head out with crampons and axes for nearby day hikes on the Root Glacier, or find some vertical ice on an afternoon ice-climbing adventure.

← September sees rich fall colors arrive on the alpine tundra of Wrangell-St Elias National Park.

What to spot...

Given the park's unique range – from snowcapped peaks and glaciers to spruce forests and bogs – there's an interesting combination of plant and animal life to be seen here. Stop for a while to scan the horizon and you might just spot Dall sheep, or look near willow bogs for moose. Along the salmon streams you'll find plenty of birds, and even a few large mammals, such as grizzly and black bear, mountain goats and caribou. The park also has two herds of transplanted bison.

BALD EAGLE These birds of prey love being by the riversides, with plenty of other avian species. Fact: bald eagles' heads don't turn fully white until their fourth or fifth year.

CARIBOU These stately ungulates reach up to 400lb (180kg). The park hosts 3 of the 32 herds in the state of Alaska, with 950,000 animals. Unlike other deer, both sexes grow antlers.

SALMON A critical food source for Alaska Natives, bears and hungry fishers, salmon run these rivers. In a few remote villages, you might even find fish wheels used to catch them.

Getty Images | Cappan

Hike this...

O1 Root Glacier Trail
Head out from Kennicott on this classic 8-mile (13km) round-trip that takes you to the glimmering blue-and-white wonderworld of the Root Glacier.

O2 Bonanza Mine Trail
From Kennicott, this steep trail ascends 3800ft (1158m) in a 9-mile (14.5km) round-trip that takes you to an amazing viewpoint – where you can see the confluence of the Root and Kennicott glaciers.

O3 Nugget Creek Trail
You can backpack pretty much anywhere in the park. This rugged route takes two or three days, with stops at a rustic cabin, mine and glaciers.

Itineraries

Hike Root Glacier and Bonanza Mine trails, paddle the rivers, ice-climb the glaciers or have a bush plane drop you into remote escapism.

← Ice hiking on Root Glacier, for the experienced only.
→ The characterful frontier town of McCarthy; Kennicott mill.

01

Three days

There are only two rough roads that lead into the park. The McCarthy Rd is the most popular and takes you through excellent hiking territory, past the Kuskulana River, with its towering bridge, and on to the Kennicott River, where you cross a footbridge to access wild-haired McCarthy; stop here for the night or take a shuttle on to Kennicott, where you'll find the majority of park services.

Spend your second day getting acquainted with the park, taking day hikes on the Root Glacier and Bonanza Mine trails, and a fun history tour of the town. If you're not tuckered out, check out an evening park ranger program at the Copper River Princess Wilderness Lodge or head to McCarthy for some bluegrass stomp sessions.

On day three, take on a little more adventure with a paddle down nearby rivers or an ice-climbing glacier adventure. On your return, stop in the small village of Chitina for salmon fishing and bird-watching, before heading back to daily life.

02

Seven days

If time and money aren't an issue, here's a dream itinerary. Start with a drive along the Nabesna Rd. Stop in at the Slana Ranger Station for some tips on local hikes, then continue to Kendesnii Campground for a night or two of chilled-out camping, with day trips along the nearby Skookum Volcano Trail, a 2.5-mile (4km) trail that explores an eroded volcanic system. End the hike on an alpine pass where Dall sheep are often sighted. Return to the main road and head to the southern entrance at

McCarthy. From here, you may consider three nights in the remote Ultima Thule Lodge, or spring for a bush plane to take you to one of the far corners of the park. There are 14 backcountry log-cabins in the park, left over from the mining and trapping days; some sit idyllically on lakes and are easily accessed by bush plane. If you have time, consider a skiing or climbing expedition on one of the peaks found here. End your trip with a paddle on nearby rivers or a flight down to Cordova for sea-kayaking.

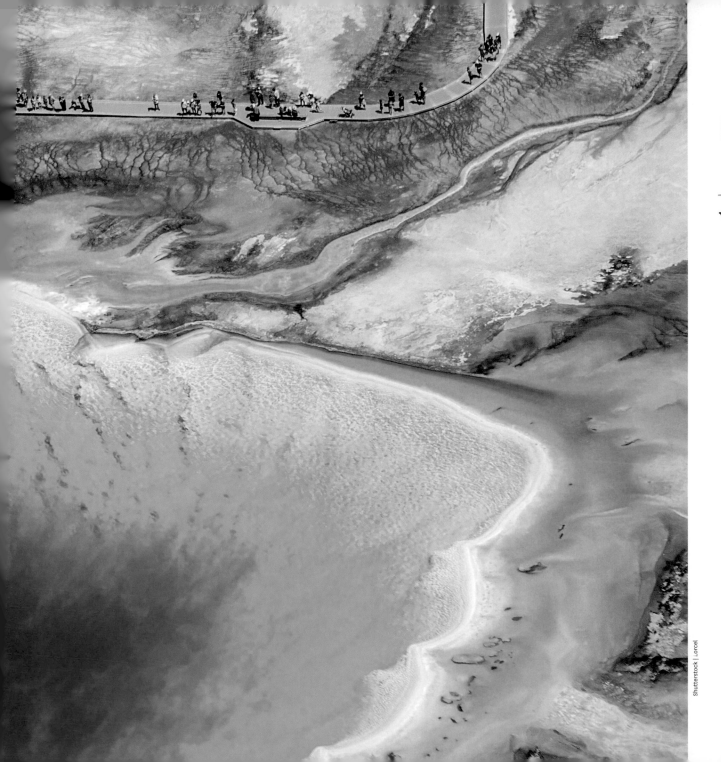

60
WY
Yellowstone National Park

Yellowstone looms large in the public's imagination, the name people are most likely to associate with 'national park' – the very symbol of the American West.

Few who haven't visited Yellowstone know how weird it is. Weird in a good way – a fantastic way – but weird nonetheless. This isn't all scenic mountains and wildflower meadows. This is fields of bubbling mud like something out of *Curse of the Swamp Creature*. This is cracks in the earth that belch steam and howl like the mouth of hell. This is pastel-blue hot springs that will boil an adult alive in three seconds flat. This is geysers that erupt without warning, sending sulfurous water hundreds of feet in the air. And sure, there are also scenic mountains and wildflower meadows – and a pretty darn photogenic canyon, some grand glacial lakes and magnificent old park lodges, all raw logs and antlers and three-story stone fireplaces. But first and foremost, Yellowstone is about its geothermal features, in all their bizarre glory.

Yellowstone sits atop an active caldera, the remains of a supervolcano that last erupted 650,000 years ago. Volcanic activity beneath the caldera gives rise to more than 10,000 geothermal features within the park, from geysers to pools of bubbling mud to fumeroles (cracks in the ground that release steam) to hot springs. Wandering through Geyser Country, the area of the park with the most impressive geothermal features, is like visiting another planet. Time things right, and you can see half a dozen geysers erupt within a few hours.

Yellowstone was inhabited by Native Americans for some 11,000 years before trapper John Colter, the first European-American to see it, reported it in 1807 as a place of 'fire and brimstone.' President Ulysses S Grant signed Yellowstone into existence in 1872, making it the world's first national park. Most visitors arrived here by

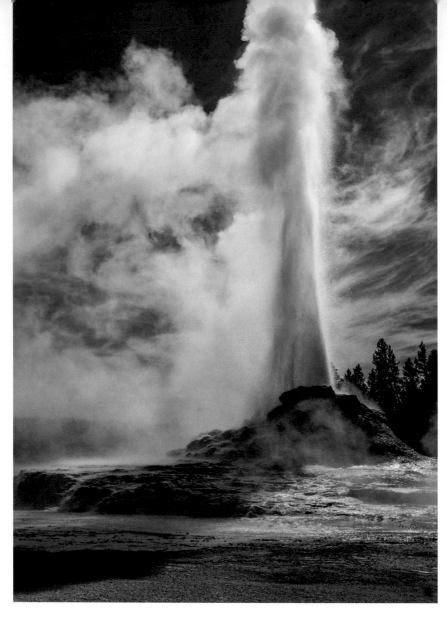

rail until the mid-1900s, when it became a magnet for a new breed of car tourists. Today, more than 3 million visitors hit the park each year. To visit Yellowstone is to cross a major item off many people's bucket list.

⬆ Castle Geyser in the Old Faithful area, named for its buttresses.
➡ Chilling at Mammoth Hot Springs. Previous page: Grand Prismatic Spring in the Midway Geyser Basin.

Toolbox

When to go
As Yellowstone's roads can become very busy in July and August, the most pleasant times to visit are early spring to early summer and late summer to early fall. You'll still have warm enough weather.

Getting there
There are small airports at Jackson Hole, Cody and West Yellowstone, but Salt Lake City and Denver, both about a day's drive away, are the nearest major facilities.

Events
Early April and early November are when roads are open to bicycles but not most cars. Summer is rodeo season in Cody.

Accessibility
All campgrounds have at least one accessible site except Fishing Bridge RV Park. Manual wheelchairs are on loan at most visitor centers. There are many accessible walkways and trails throughout the park.

Park in numbers
3468 Area in sq miles
300 Height of highest geyser, Steamboat (ft)
728 Number of grizzly bears

Stay here...

Slough Creek Campground
You'll likely hear howling wolves from your tent at this stunningly located campsite, off a dirt track in wildlife mecca Lamar Valley. It's one of 12 NPS campsites in the park; only Mammoth is open year-round.

Old Faithful Inn
An example of 'parkitecture,' this 327-room lodge is a log palace. The open three-story lobby is all glossy wood and candelabras; day-trippers sit around the stone fireplace. It's been a popular choice since it was built in 1903 – fortunately, rooms have been updated since then, with simple, plaid furnishings and wooden desks.

Canyon Lodge and Cabins
The park's biggest facility was recently updated to more eco-friendly standards; its five new lodges are all LEED certified. Bathroom counters are made of recycled glass, while furniture was hewn from trees killed by pine beetles. The mix of cabins and traditional hotel rooms make this a good choice for families and larger groups.

Do this!

Geyser-watching
Old Faithful is not Yellowstone's biggest geyser. It's simply faithful. Erupting every 90 minutes, it's one of six that park officials offer eruption time predictions for. Get there early and you can catch Old Faithful exhale 3700 to 8400 gallons (14,000 to 31,800L), then hit the boardwalk path to watch neighbors, such as Riverside and Daisy, in action.

Boating & floating
Vast, blue and very deep, Yellowstone Lake is the biggest lake in America above 7000ft (2134m). Skip across its waters in a rented sailboat or explore its bays and channels in a canoe. For a grand adventure, paddle the Lewis River Channel between Lewis Lake and Shoshone Lake. Or take the relaxed route by floating down the Yellowstone River in a raft.

Wildlife photography
People pilgrimage from every corner of the earth to shoot pictures of the bison, wolves, mountain goats, birds, butterflies and more that roam and flutter across Yellowstone. In winter, capture the contrast of a gray wolf's fur against the snowy Lamar Valley. In spring, mule deer gambol across meadows spangled with wildflowers. In summer, osprey can be caught nesting. In fall, snap the drama of elks rutting along the Madison River.

What to spot...

The sheer number and variety of large mammals have given Yellowstone the reputation as a sort of safari park; you'll see what we mean when you wind up in a 50-car jam behind a grizzly. But almost every part of the park is unbelievably rich in flora and fauna, from the songbird-filled lodgepole pines and slopes of fiery-tipped Wyoming paintbrush to mountain goats scrambling up rocky outcrops. There are some 1300 species of native plants, including dozens of rainbow-hued wildflowers.

GRIZZLY BEAR In summer, the iconic bears can be most easily spotted in the meadows between Tower-Roosevelt and Canyon, and in the Hayden and Lamar valleys. Lock up your food!

BISON Yellowstone has nearly 5000 bison, who have lived here since prehistoric times. Look for them in the Hayden and Lamar valleys.

GRAY WOLF Killed off by ranchers in the early 1900s, wolves were reintroduced in 1995; there are now about 100 in the park. Lamar Valley is your best bet to see them.

Hike this...

O1 Fairy Falls trail
For a bird's-eye view of psychedelic Grand Prismatic Spring, hike this popular trail for 1 mile (1.6km), then cut left up a faint track leading up the slope.

O2 Mt Washburn
Peak-baggers can't miss this 10,243ft (3122m) summit, with 360-degree views over Yellowstone Lake and the Hayden Valley – all the way to the Beartooth Range. Leave early to beat crowds. A hard 5 miles (8km).

O3 Black Canyon of the Yellowstone
Descend into the depths of this 2,000-ft (610m) canyon, crossing raging waters via suspension bridge, for some of the park's wildest hiking. The 14 miles (22.5 km) make for a perfect 2-day trek (backcountry permits necessary).

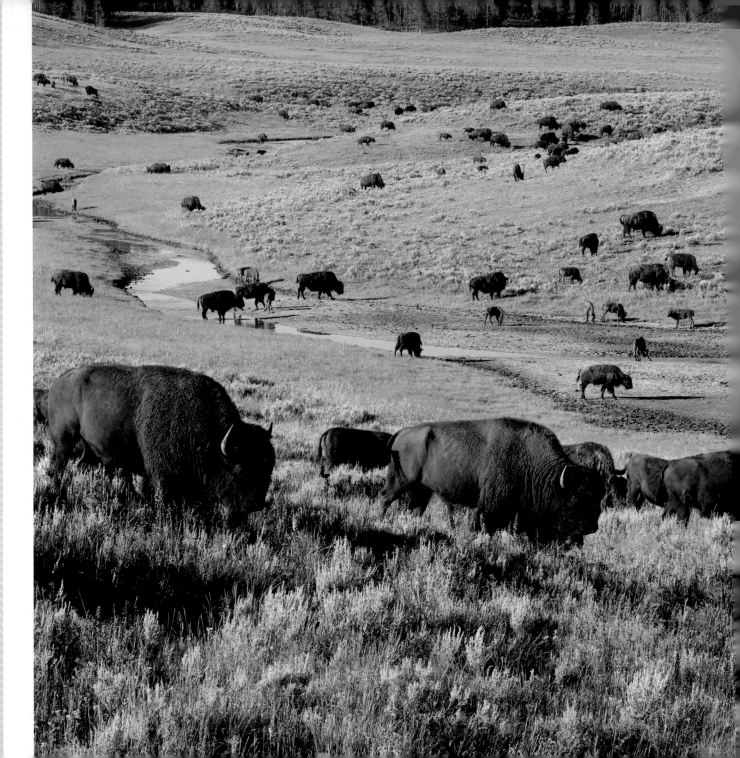

Itineraries

Follow the geyser trail from Old Faithful to Norris Geyser Basin for eruption suspense; hike Yellowstone's Grand Canyon; or kayak, swim or fish in Yellowstone Lake.

◄ Yellowstone is the only place in the US where bison have lived continuously since prehistoric times. ► Lone Star Geyser. Previous page: Yellowstone River.

01

Two days

You can drive the entirety of the figure-eight shaped Grand Loop Rd in two very packed days, seeing most of the park's most iconic sights. Start off early at West Thumb, hitting Old Faithful and the rest of the geyser trail at the first daylight eruption times. Proceed to Grand Prismatic Spring to gawp at the neon blues and reds, then head north towards Norris, where the Norris Geyser Basin is home to some of the coolest, loudest, most colorful thermal features in the park. Nearby are the Artist Paintpots, so called for their colorful hues of mud. Grab some fortification at Canyon Village, then end the day watching osprey fly over Yellowstone Lake. The next morning, drive straight to Grand Canyon of the Yellowstone and watch the early sun play across the pastel rockface. Continuing northwest, take in the falls around Tower Junction, than hit the sulfur-smelling terraces at Mammoth. Dine on bison steaks at the classy Mammoth Hot Springs Dining Room while elk graze on the hotel lawn outside.

02

Four days

Do everything in the two-day itinerary, but take your time with it. Plan on saving the Grand Canyon of the Yellowstone for the third day, so you can spend several hours hiking around the rim or down Uncle Tom's Trail. Spend the afternoon of the third day around Yellowstone Lake, which is a fly fisher's paradise, with endless edges to explore by kayak or canoe. Dine at Lake Yellowstone Hotel Dining Room (reservations necessary), a grand old establishment where duck risotto and local steelhead trout are served on white tablecloths.

Pick at least one full day-hike for the fourth day – Mt Washburn is always popular or, for fewer crowds, try the 16-mile (26km) loop through Pelican Valley, where the rolling hills are carpeted with wildflowers, and grizzlies amble through the meadows looking for berries. If you don't have to leave early on the fifth morning, do some dawn wildlife-watching before heading home – staying near the Lamar or Hayden valleys will make this easier.

03

A week

Follow the two-day itinerary to pack in the classic sights on the Grand Loop Rd. Then spend the rest of your trip exploring the park's wilder side. Even in summer's busy season it's easy to escape crowds in the backcountry. Plan a two-day backpacking trip for days three and four: Black Canyon of the Yellowstone or Shoshone Lake, the largest backcountry lake in the continental US. There are some 300 backcountry campgrounds (permits required), so you'll have plenty of space – but take bear precautions seriously. On day five, try wildlife photography in Lamar Valley. Depending on the season you can spot wolves, elk, pronghorn, bald eagles and more. For dinner, tuck into barbecued ribs at the cowboy-chic Roosevelt Lodge. On the sixth day, join a kayak tour with a local outfitter, paddling past active geysers under an endless sky. On your last day, take in Mammoth's terraces then exit the park for an afternoon of R&R at Chico Hot Springs in Pray, Montana.

61

CA

Yosemite National Park

Celebrate a glacier-carved landscape of granite peaks, wildflower meadows and alpine lakes in one of the USA's oldest national parks.

Yosemite

Entering Yosemite Valley, the panoramas from roadside Tunnel View make everyone gasp. Standing above the lush green valley floor, carpeted with meadows and a meandering river, you'll view a scene that's been 10 million years in the making. On the right, Bridalveil Fall gushes over cliffs, while above it hang the pointed Cathedral Rocks. On the left, El Capitan towers more than 3000ft (914.4m) above the valley floor – it's the largest granite monolith in the world, issuing a siren's call to rock climbers. Far off in the distance is the curved tooth of the polished granite Half Dome, the park's most famous landmark. Yet all this is only the beginning of Yosemite's natural wonders.

The Sierra Nevada mountains – what naturalist John Muir anointed as 'the Range of Light' – are California's backbone. As recently as 10,000 years ago, during the last ice age, glaciers were still hard at work shaping these mountain peaks, alpine lakes, granite domes and river canyons and valleys. Yosemite's showstopping landscapes are matched by its wealth of wildlife. Spot a black bear sauntering beside the trail below Glacier Point. Capture a portrait of summer wildflowers at Tuolumne Meadows. Ogle giant sequoia trees that have been growing in Mariposa Grove for almost two millennia.

Yosemite is a park for all seasons. When snowmelt in the Sierra Nevada high country makes rivers swell, waterfalls in the valley spring to life. When summer warms the grassy meadows, lakes and high-mountain passes, hikers and backpackers set out on overnight trips while families swim and cycle around the valley. In fall, rock climbers can still be spotted hanging off granite walls

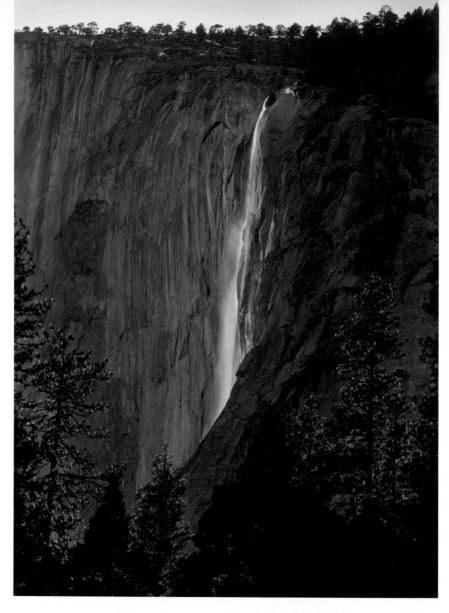

and boulders. Even winter is a beautiful time to visit, especially after a snowstorm – when you can snowshoe or cross-country ski through fresh powder to icy waterfalls or hushed groves of giant sequoia trees.

⬆ Horsetail Fall catching the sun.
➡ Glacier Point. Previous page: Yosemite Valley from Tunnel View, with Bridalveil Falls, El Capitan and Half Dome in the distance.

Toolbox

When to go
Yosemite Valley is open year-round. High-elevation Tioga Rd to Tuolumne Meadows and Glacier Point Rd both close after the first major snowfall in fall; they reopen the following year in late spring or early summer.

Getting there
Yosemite is a four-hour drive from San Francisco. Amtrak trains stop in Merced. From Merced, YARTS buses connect to the park. Free shuttle buses circle Yosemite Valley year-round.

Events
Horsetail Fall enthralls visitors during the naturally occurring firefall phenomenon in February. The park recognizes Earth Day in mid-April with events.

Accessibility
There are a limited number of manual wheelchairs for rent. Most sections of the paved one-mile Lower Yosemite Fall Trail are wheelchair accessible.

Park in numbers

1190 Area in sq miles
1890 Year the park was established
2425 Height of Yosemite Falls (ft)

Stay here...

Ahwahnee Hotel
Designed by famed park architect Gilbert Stanley Underwood in the 1920s, this elegant stone and wood hotel in Yosemite Valley has hosted everyone from Queen Elizabeth II to Steve Jobs. If you're there in winter, curl up with a hot toddy by the roaring fireplace in the Great Lounge.

High Sierra Camps
Five dormitory-style tent cabins dot the backcountry surrounding Tuolumne Meadows. An appealing option for day hikers who are not fans of backpacking, these popular lodgings come with beds, wool blankets and showers. A lottery system doles out reservations for the short opening season, which runs June through September.

Wawona Hotel
Step back into Victorian times at this national historic landmark, located in the southern area of the park not far from the Mariposa Grove of giant sequoias. Built in 1876, the white, multi-story hotel has wraparound verandas, cocktails and evening entertainment. Civilized vacation resort activities include golf and tennis.

Do this!

Rock climbing
Yosemite Valley is a wellspring of modern rock climbing in the US. Yvon Chouinard (founder of the Patagonia brand) and Royal Robbins were among the first to tackle these granite slabs. Today you'll find big-wall climbers hanging out at Camp 4 near El Capitan in Yosemite Valley from spring through fall, and at high-elevation Tuolumne Meadows, with its many granite domes and bouldering opportunities. Look for a new interactive climbing exhibit in the Yosemite Valley Visitor Center.

Swimming
Splash in the Merced River on a hot summer's day, or brave the icier waters of alpine lakes, such as Tenaya Lake (off Tioga Rd near Tuolumne Meadows), which has a sandy, crescent-shaped beach.

Skiing & snoeshowing
Yosemite Ski and Snowboard Area is California's oldest ski resort. Beginners can learn to swoosh downhill on skis or a snowboard here, while cross-country enthusiasts can ski along Glacier Point Rd to a hut overlooking the valley. For snowshoeing, go tramping around the valley or to groves of giant sequoias.

There are dozens of hiking routes around Yosemite Valley.

What to spot...

Yosemite was designated a World Heritage site in 1984, partly because of its rich natural resources. An astonishing variety of wildlife ranges across more than 1000 sq miles (2590 sq km) of wilderness and along two nationally recognized 'Wild and Scenic Rivers,' the Tuolumne and the Merced. Over a thousand plant species thrive here, as do more than 400 vertebrate animals in varied life zones, from chaparral-covered foothills to stream-fed alpine meadows to glaciers high above the tree line.

SIERRA NEVADA BIGHORN SHEEP This endangered horned animal with a white rump-patch grazes craggy peaks and alpine meadows, where it is rarely seen by humans.

BLACK BEAR Faster and usually bigger than you are, black bears can eat up to 20,000 calories a day while preparing for their winter hibernation.

WESTERN TANAGER The male of this forest bird species is easily spotted – look for its bright-red head, yellow breast and black wings.

Hike this...

O1 Mist Trail
It's a thrilling, 1.6- to 5.4-mile (2.6 to 8.7km) climb up slippery stone steps from Yosemite Valley to the top of Vernal and Nevada falls.

O2 Cathedral Lakes
Take a moderate forest climb to two alpine lakes tucked beneath the white granite flanks of the Cathedral Range. The hike is 7.6 miles round trip (12.2km).

O3 Half Dome
This is an epic, all-day 14-mile (22.5km) hike and climb to the top of the park's most famous granite dome; advance permits required (by lottery).

Itineraries

See Yosemite Falls, the tallest waterfall in North America, watch the sun set from Glacier Point or laze by Tenaya Lake.

← Half Dome. The fastest time to climb El Capitan is less than two hours. → Plan road trips carefully around the park, with summer crowds and closed roads in winter.

01

A day

The road into Yosemite Valley winds beneath trees beside the Merced River, where early morning fog may linger. Stop the car and get out for the short stroll to Bridalveil Fall, a monumental cliffside cascade. Further east, leave your car behind in a day-use parking lot and hop on the free shuttle bus to Yosemite Village for a trail lunch from Degnan's Deli or to Yosemite Valley Lodge for a sandwich from Base Camp Eatery. Ride the shuttle bus to the Happy Isles stop. Beeline to the Mist Trail where you'll climb the steep stone staircase to

the top of not one, but two waterfalls where rainbows shimmer in the spray.

After hiking back to the trailhead, catch the shuttle bus to Yosemite Village to peruse fine-art prints at the Ansel Adams Gallery and the free history, ecology, art and rock climbing exhibits inside the visitor center and museum. Walk to Yosemite Falls, a triple-tiered beauty that's the tallest waterfall in North America. As the sun sets, cross the road to the Mountain Room restaurant for dinner and drinks.

02

Two days

After waking up at your campsite underneath pine trees in Yosemite Valley, rent a bike to explore the meadows and lakes on designated trails or join a guided hike-and-bike tour. El Capitan Meadow is a grand spot to enjoy a picnic lunch while watching rock climbers scaling the granite monolith. In the afternoon, drive up Glacier Point Rd, stopping to scramble up Sentinel Dome and ogle the one-mile drop at Taft Point before arriving at the famous viewpoint. From Glacier Point, you can look

straight out at Half Dome and down over Nevada and Vernal Fall. Watch the sun set, then head back down to the valley.

Reserve a table for dinner in the grand dining room of the Ahwahnee Hotel, or else content yourself with drinks and small bites in the hotel's convivial lounge, where the piano tinkles with old-fashioned melodies from the early 20th century. Before going back to camp, take a stroll in the moonlight by the Merced River, crossing over the historic Stoneman Bridge.

03

Three days

Follow the two-day itinerary then, on day three, drive up scenic Tioga Rd, which follows an old pioneer wagon trail and an even earlier Native American footpath. Your final destination is Tuolumne Meadows, fed by streams and blushing with wildflowers in early summer. En route, pull over at high-elevation Olmsted Point for a different perspective on Yosemite Valley – you'll recognize Half Dome in the distance. From the vista point, free seasonal shuttle buses head east to Tuolumne Meadows, where

you can hike up granite domes and picnic by the river. After lunch, return to Tenaya Lake and laze by the beach all afternoon or take a chilly swim. If you'd rather stretch your legs, tackle the short hike to Dog Lake then climb a spur trail to the summit of Lembert Dome for impressive 360° views of Tuolumne Meadows and the Cathedral Range.

In late afternoon, if you're reluctant to leave all this High Sierra beauty, pitch a tent or rent a canvas tent cabin at Tuolumne Meadows on your last night.

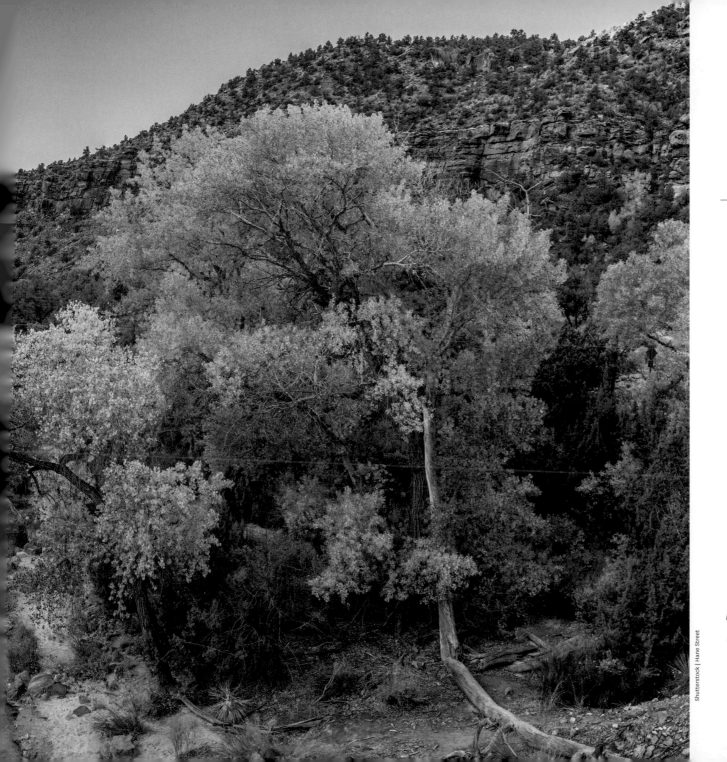

Shutterstock | Hane Street

UT

Zion National Park

This is the most grandiose of Utah's national parks. With its castle-like walls, weeping rocks and shadowy narrows, Zion Canyon beckons like a valley of enchantment in an epic storybook.

Your adventure begins on the Zion–Mt Carmel Hwy as it twists through groves of golden sandstone. Gripping the wheel, you wonder about the 1.1-mile (1.8km) tunnel ahead, a Depression era marvel that jackhammers through a sandstone wall. And suddenly you're inside its darkness. Arched galleries flash past, offering a glimpse of the red-rock grandeur to come.

The heart of the park is Zion Canyon, a verdant valley flanked by walls of Navajo Sandstone. These cliffs, soaring more than 1000ft (305m) feet overhead, began as sand dunes close to 200 million years ago. After a turbulent period of geological uplift, the Virgin River and its tributaries began carving the canyon and its narrows. Today, the riparian landscape attracts wildlife galore – as well as beauty-seeking tourists. To reduce congestion, the park prohibits cars on the canyon floor from mid-March through November and on weekends in February; park shuttles stop at nine sights and trailheads. The most popular locations and activities often require reservations and permits, so plan your trip well in advance.

The Kolob Canyons section of the park, home to a high-elevation scenic drive, is 40 miles (64km) northwest. Southern Paiute Indians roamed these lands before the arrival of Mormon settlers in the mid-1800s. Mukuntuweap National Monument, which was named after the Southern Paiute word for 'straight canyon,' was created in 1909. The name was changed to Zion National Monument in 1918 – 'Zion' being a biblical term for a place of refuge or sanctuary – and the national park was established the following year. Today, with its skinny slot canyons and vertigo-inducing cliffs, the park is a prime spot for

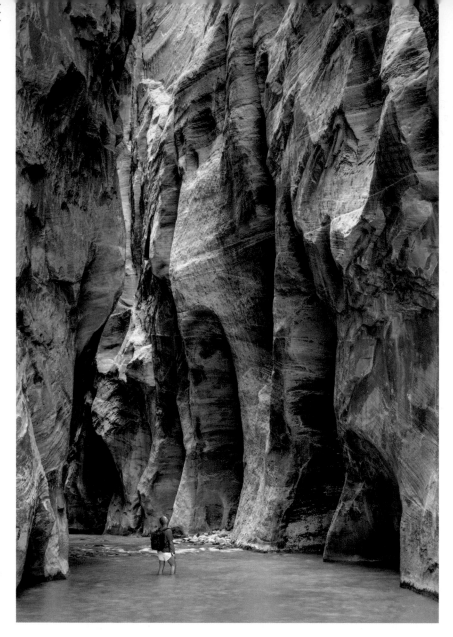

Getty Images | Michele Falzone

outdoor adventures, from canyoneering and rock climbing to multi-day backpacking wading through the Narrows or tackling some of the 90 miles (145km) of park trails. But the allure of the park is also writ small. The low-key spots – a weeping rock, hanging gardens, hidden ponds – may impress you as much as the red rock.

Toolbox

When to go
High season is May through September, but temperatures commonly soar to 100°F (38°C) while visitors clog the canyon floor. May brings both wildflowers and bugs. Fall is cooler and ideal for hiking.

Getting there
Zion Canyon borders the town of Springdale in southwestern Utah. The park can be reached from the west or east on Hwy 9. Las Vegas is 160 miles (257.5km) southwest via Hwy 9 and I-15. Kolob Canyons is 30 miles (48km) northeast of St George, Utah, off the I-15.

Events
The Dixie Round Up takes place in St George each year in September and includes a rodeo. The Zion Half Marathon in February has amazing views at every turn.

Accessibility
All park shuttles are wheel-chair accessible. The Pa'rus Trail is paved and Riverside Walk may be navigable too.

Park in numbers

229 Area in sq miles
6521 Height of Observation Point (ft)
79 Species of mammal

Stay here...

Zion Lodge

The wide and grassy front lawn here is a gorgeous place to daydream. Crisp blue skies, crimson cliffs and a homespun brown lodge frame this inspiring spot. Rooms in the lodge and its cabins channel the Old West with a bit of style – and no TVs. Overnight guests are permitted to drive into the canyon to park at the lodge.

South Campground & Watchman Campground

A dip in the adjacent Virgin River is a pleasant way to cool off before settling into your camp chair. Once settled, cottonwoods provide the shade while sandstone cliffs offer the view. Both campgrounds are within walking distance of the Zion Canyon Visitor Center. Book ahead.

Zion Mountain Ranch

Just three minutes from the park's east entrance, this bucolic ranch offers gorgeous log-cabin accommodations, big fireplaces and even bigger views. Kids will love horseback rides, while adults will like the privacy (and private sauna) of the multi-room cabins.

Do this!

Canyoneering

Rappelling into a narrow slot canyon is just one part of a canyoneering adventure in Zion – expect to do some wading, scrambling, swimming, hiking and problem-solving ('Just how do we escape this diabolical maze?'). The names of Zion's most famous slot canyons evoke their individual charms: the Narrows and the Subway. Check ahead as many canyoneering trips require permits.

Cycling

Fill up your water bottles for a morning pedal on the Zion Canyon Scenic Drive. This 7-mile (11km) strip of easy pavement runs alongside the Virgin River as it unfurls beneath iconic big rocks, from the Court of the Patriarchs to Angels Landing. No cars are allowed in high season.

Bird-watching

As you scan the skies from your perch atop Angels Landing, keep watch for California condors soaring gracefully between the sandstone monoliths – their 9½-ft (3m) wingspan is something amazing to behold. But California condors are just the start: the bird list at Zion includes 261 species.

◪ Hiking the Narrows inside Zion Canyon. Previous page: the Virgin River flows through the park.

What to spot...

Elevation at Zion stretches from 3666ft (1117m) at Coal Pits Wash to 8726ft (2660m) at Horse Ranch Mountain. Four ecosystems exist between these extremes: desert, riparian, piñon-juniper and conifer woodland. Within these pockets of life are more than 1000 species of plants. Among the mammals you might spot are mule deer, bighorn sheep and rock squirrels. A further 28 reptile species and over 250 bird species seek food and shelter here too.

CALIFORNIA CONDOR These enormous scavengers, which date from prehistoric times, have a massive wingspan. They almost became extinct in the 1980s, but a successful breeding-and-release program has boosted their numbers.

ARIZONA TOAD This plump brownish toad looks for love in shaded, high-elevation tributaries of the Virgin River. The male mating call is a 6-second, high-pitched trill.

PIÑON PINE Famous for their crooked trunks and nutritious edible seeds called 'pine nuts', piñons grow on dry and rocky sites at high elevations, often near juniper trees. Slow growers, they can take 80 years to reach 10ft (3m). ·

Hike this...

01 The Narrows
Iconic and challenging, this 9.4 mi (15km) round trip hike squeezes through wet and skinny canyons along the Virgin River's North Fork.

02 Angels Landing
Possibly America's best day hike, this 5.4-mile (8.6km) round-trip trail hugs a cliff, climbs tight switchbacks and crosses a thin ridge flanked by sheer drops. The reward? An epic view of Zion Canyon.

03 Canyon Overlook
The easy 1-mile (1.6km) round-trip hike takes you to awe-inspiring views of the canyon. Perfect for families or an inspiring sunrise jaunt.

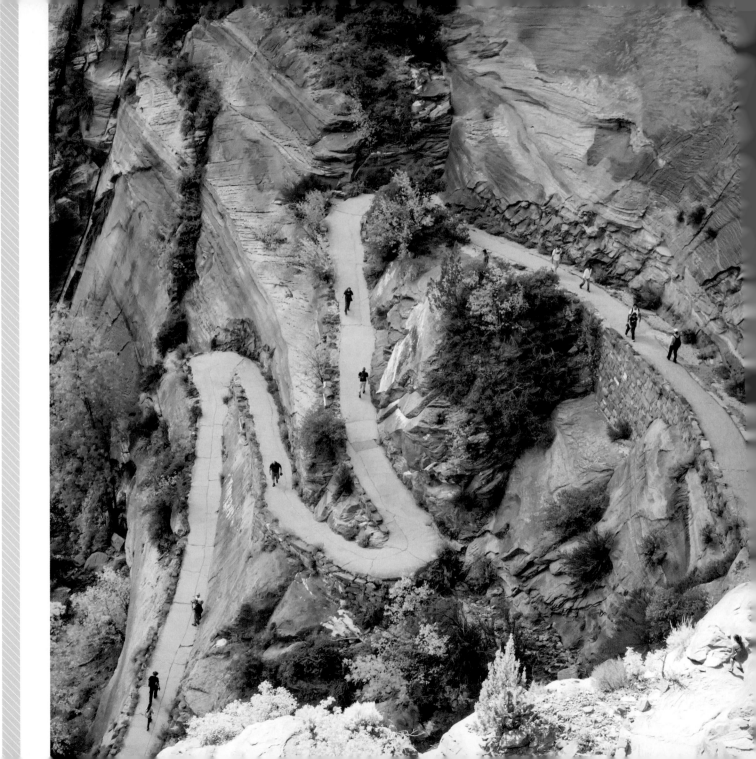

Itineraries

Summit Angels Landing for sheer canyon views; hike the Narrows; go canyoneering; or admire red rock grandeur on Kolob Canyons Rd.

 Inside the Narrows; walking up Walter's Wiggles to Angels Landing. The view over the canyon from Angels Landing.

01

A day

Baby, it's a busy day. Hop the Springdale shuttle to the Zion Canyon Visitor Center. From here, the visitor shuttle rolls into the canyon, where splashes of riparian greenery soften the majestic red walls. Your stop? The Grotto, the starting point for the Angels Landing Trail. Cross the Virgin River and look up...up...up. Hmm, just where have those angels got to? Now it's choice time. If you continue all the way to the top, it's a full day strenuous hike, rewarded by amazing views and just a bit of sore legs.

Alternately, you can get in a series of quick hikes to the Lower Emerald Pool and the Canyon Overlook. For a taste of the Narrows, ride the shuttle to the Temple of Sinawava stop at the end of the route. From here, follow the Riverside Walk 1 mile (1.6km) upstream, then splash into the mouth of the dragon, otherwise known as the Narrows. End this wild day with a hearty meal in Springdale, and perhaps some moonlight walking amongst the glimmering Utah stars.

02

Two days

Swoop into the park on the exhilarating Zion–Mt Carmel Hwy and stop by the Zion Canyon Visitor Center during summer for the 'Ride Along with a Ranger' tour, a 90-minute introduction to the park. Enjoy lunch at the Zion Canyon Lodge, then explore the canyon by bike or by horseback. Dig into *carne asada* tacos at the Whiptail Grill in Springdale for dinner, then return to the park for an evening ranger talk about wildlife, history or the starry skies. The next morning, fuel up with coffee and crepes at MeMe's Café in Springdale, then tick more adventures off your life list. Test your endurance on the Angels Landing Trail; if you have a fear of heights, rather than Angels Landing, huff and puff up to vast views on the Observation Point Trail, which tops out at 6521ft (1988m); or rappel into a slot canyon (you'll need a permit and canyoneering outfitters in Springdale can kit you out). Post-adventure, celebrate with a rib-eye and a Utah-brewed Polygamy Porter at Bit & Spur Restaurant & Saloon.

03

Four days

Begin the morning with green-chile and-chorizo omelet at Oscar's Cafe. You'll burn off this meal on tomorrow's adventure: the 16-mile (26km) trek from Chamberlin Ranch known as the Top Down Narrows. After breakfast, stop by the Zion Canyon Visitor Center for questions about weather and campsites. You'll need to reserve your permits in advance. Loosen your muscles with an easy afternoon hike to the Emerald Pools, followed by an afternoon ranger talk or a scenic drive on the Zion–Mt Carmel Hwy. Day two begins the real adventure: the trail from Chamberlin Ranch to the Narrows leads to a wonderland of canyon walls, tight passages and hanging gardens, not to mention splashing and wading aplenty. Find your reserved riverside campsite and enjoy your night in the wild. On day three, emerge just north of the terminus of the Riverside Walk and explore more of the canyon (if your legs allow). Spend your last day driving Kolob Canyons Rd, with views of cliffs, mountains and finger canyons.

Second Edition
Published in May 2021
by Lonely Planet Global Limited
ABN 36 005 607 983
www.lonelyplanet.com
ISBN 978 1 8386 9449 4
© Lonely Planet 2021
Printed in China
10 9 8 7 6 5 4 3 2 1

Managing Director, Publishing Piers Pickard
Associate Publisher & Commissioning Editor Robin Barton
Art Direction Daniel Di Paolo
Layout Kerry Rubenstein
Editors Cliff Wilkinson
Index Christina Webb
Wildlife illustrations Holly Exley
Cartographer Wayne Murphy
Print Production Nigel Longuet

Written by: Amy Balfour, Becky Ohlsen, Carolyn McCarthy, Emily Matchar, Greg Benchwich, Regis St Louis
Cover images ©: IMB / AWL Images; Justin Foulkes; Checubus / Shutterstock; Matt Munro; Mark Read

LONELY PLANET OFFICES

USA
230 Franklin Road, Building 2B,
Franklin, TN 37064
T: 615-988-9713

IRELAND
Digital Depot, Roe Lane (off Thomas St),
Digital Hub, Dublin 8,
D08 TCV4

STAY IN TOUCH
lonelyplanet.com/contact

Paper in this book is certified against the Forest Stewardship Council™ standards. FSC™ promotes environmentally responsible, socially beneficial and economically viable management of the world's forests.